AF305112

Robert Frank

**Books and Films
Published by Steidl**

Front and back cover:

Robert Frank checking wetproof printing for *The Americans*
on Steidl's Manroland press, Göttingen, 2007

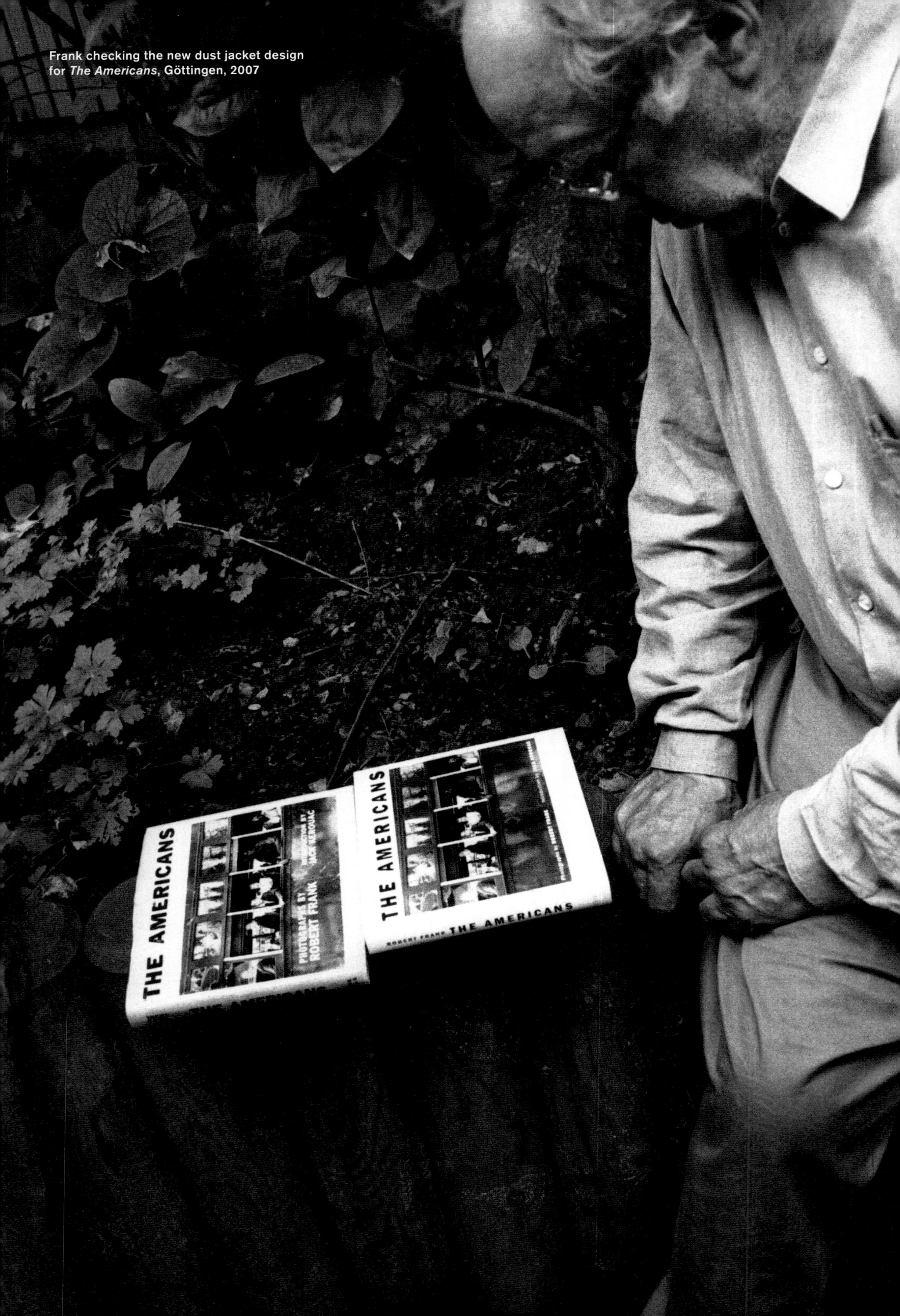

Frank checking the new dust jacket design for *The Americans*, Göttingen, 2007

Introduction

Peter Pfrunder, Director of Fotostiftung Schweiz

Photographs can be shown printed in books, or in exhibitions as objects hanging on a wall—these two forms of presentation have prevailed above all others throughout the history of photography. Even the emergence of digital screens has not replaced them: fleeting pixel images (despite their own distinct qualities) have not really been able to overcome the meaningful power and sustainability of the book and exhibition. These two media are the major forms of expression between which most photographers make their personal choice: some like nothing more than to see their work in a museum, others have a book in mind even before completing their photographs.

Robert Frank belongs, without a doubt, to the second category. Already in the 1940s, when he had earnestly begun to search for an appropriate form for his pictures, did he greatly prefer the book to the exhibition. He has always made physical book dummies with scissors and glue, conceiving double pages and sequences, and carefully arranging his pictures into strong rhythms—until they formed a coherent whole, like the words and sentences of a story. For Frank, the book was always more than a vessel for his photos. Again and again he created a unique space for mood or sound that is only understood through the interplay of its individual parts; an object whose format, materiality, printing quality and content form a unity; an associative flux of pictures that enables manifold and multilayered ways of reading.

Robert Frank's books are artist's books, creations that reveal their author's handwriting not only through the individual photographs but by their overall flow and workmanship. They are exhibitions on paper which he largely self-curated—up until the point at which every author needs a critical counterpart, someone to hold up a mirror during the realization of their ideas. In Gerhard Steidl Robert Frank found such a counterpart:

the ideal printing and publishing personality, one who listened and looked, one who projected himself both into Frank's world of pictures and thoughts, as well as into his silence—all to better express the essence of the work in book form.

Between 2004 and 2019 Steidl produced 32 publications together with Frank, most as first editions, a few as revised new editions. This editorial achievement cannot be praised highly enough—without it, many of Frank's works would no doubt not have found their way to publication. A deep and fruitful collaboration developed over the years, through which Frank, for whom control over his work was extremely important, wholly trusted Steidl's creative companionship. In a certain sense Frank's books are comparable with literary works, whose quality is likewise owed to the interactions with their publisher, discussions with their editor, and the attentions of their translator. For Frank, Steidl was all of these in one: publisher, editor, translator—and of course printer.

Comparisons between literature and Robert Frank's work are actually not so far-fetched. Among the fixed stars of his literary firmament Frank counted, for example, Robert Walser: for Frank, Walser's sweeping vision gathered diverse aspects, and through the atmospheric combined them into a heterogeneous whole. Walser's secret is the particular voice and inflection of his texts. The unfulfilled desire for closeness in his poems allows for sadness to emerge, yet not despair. Instead, Walser liberates through small paradoxical inflections. What remains, is yearning. Frank and Walser: two kindred spirits.

For Robert Walser's introverted work there is no better medium than the book. In the same way, Robert Frank's photographs are inseparable from his books: they are the backbone and the pearl necklace of his œuvre.

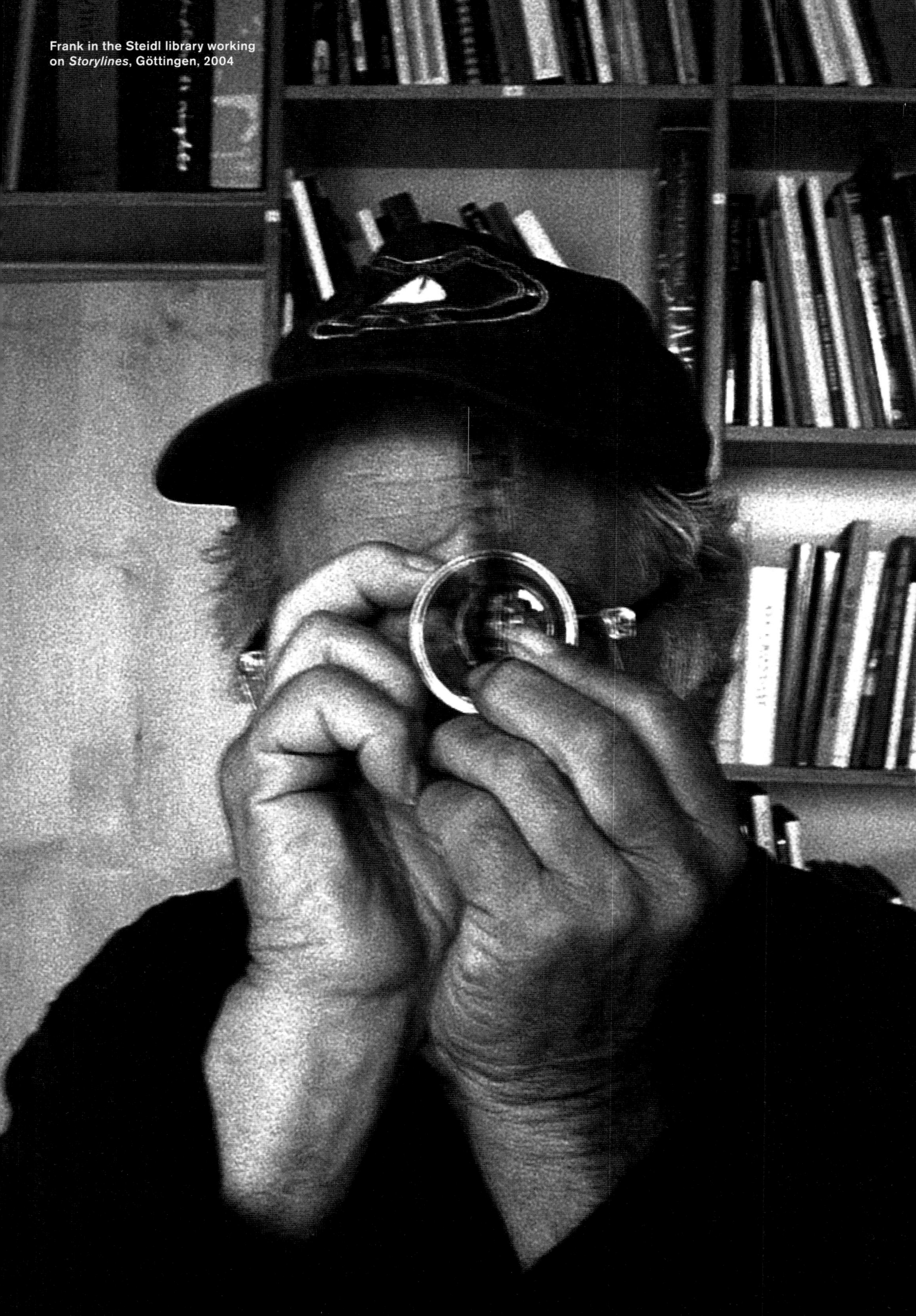

Frank in the Steidl library working
on *Storylines*, Göttingen, 2004

Contents

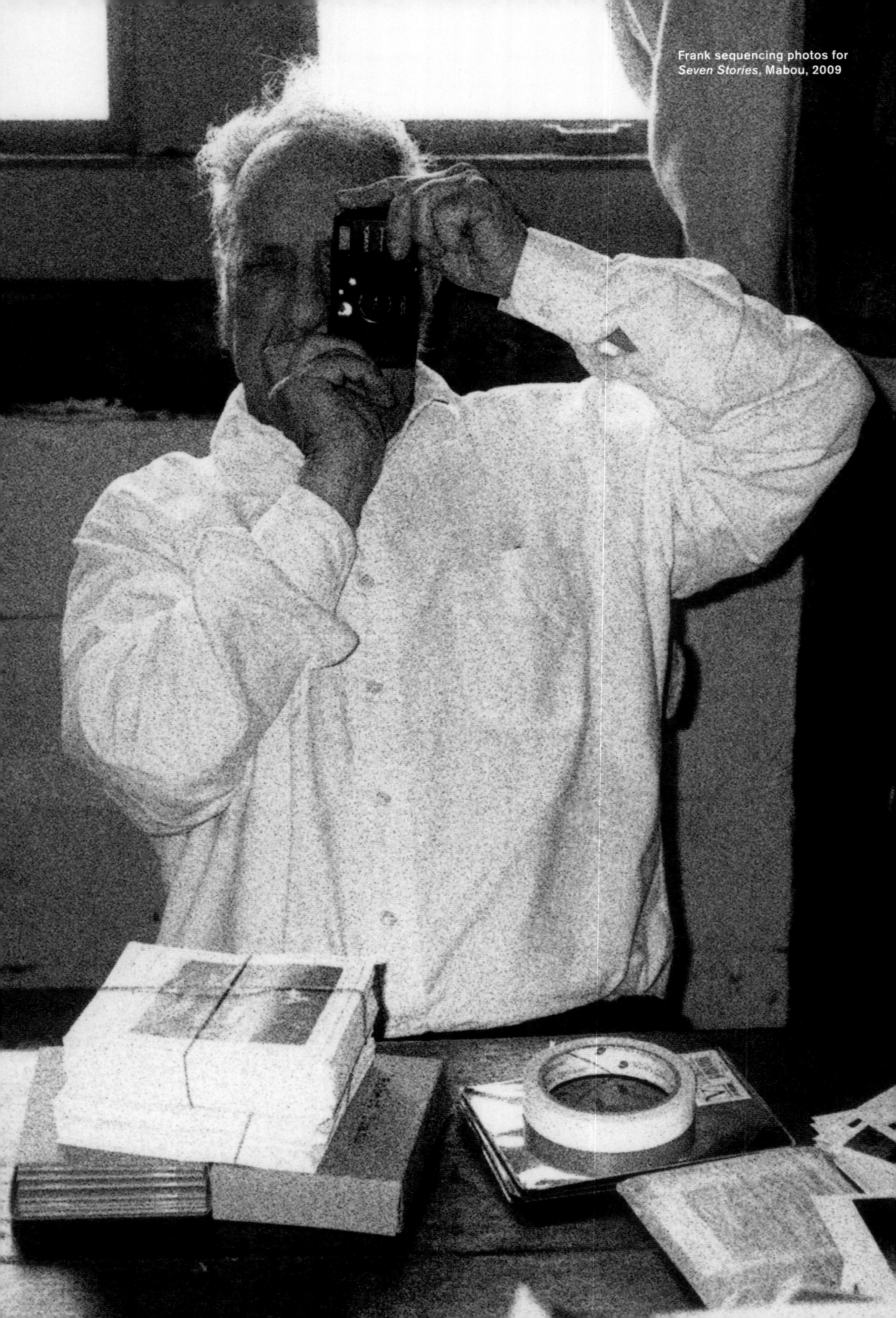

Frank sequencing photos for
Seven Stories, Mabou, 2009

The Robert Frank Project

Gerhard Steidl

I began working with Robert Frank in 1989 when Swiss publisher Walter Keller asked me to print Robert's *The Lines of My Hand* for his imprint Scalo. Walter thought it'd be easiest if I just printed the book together with Robert: "You'll both get along well on press," he said. I was touched by the trust Walter placed in me, and this marked the first time Robert travelled to Steidl at Düstere Strasse 4 in Göttingen. Up until 2003 I printed many of Robert's books for Scalo and he always came to Göttingen to sign off every printed sheet. Indeed the idea that an artist personally visits us at Steidl to participate in all aspects of the bookmaking process was pioneered with Robert, and has been crucial to our book culture since.

In 2004 Scalo closed its doors and Robert and I decided to continue working together. I engaged Ute Eskildsen as editorial advisor and with Robert we made a plan for all his books—past, present and future—that we called *The Robert Frank Project*. Its aim was to publish and preserve all aspects of Robert's creativity, and to ensure his bookmaking legacy: to print his new books as he created them, to reprint classic titles like *The Americans* along with some lesser-known rarities and previously unseen works, and to restore and release his film œuvre on DVD. Over the years, this plan blossomed into the 32 publications that are explored in the book you are now reading.

Books and Films Published by Steidl has been conceived as a detailed workshop report about crafting books with Robert, a look behind closed doors—and so each book is documented with its cover, double-page spreads, an explanatory text and bibliographic details; alongside interviews, essays and behind-the-scenes photos.

Throughout the decades Robert and I developed an unusual and productive bookmaking rhythm I feel very lucky to have been part of. First Robert would contact me (by letter or phone) with the idea for a new book. In early winter I'd visit him at Bleecker Street to pick up his handmade book dummy as well as original prints for scanning. In the winter and spring we'd work on the book at Steidl, and in summer I'd travel to Robert at his weather-beaten wooden house in Mabou, Nova Scotia, to show him the first test-prints. The final book would be printed in fall, at the latest ready as a Christmas gift for Robert, which I'd personally deliver.

I hope *Books and Films* conveys a sense of this wonderful rhythm and of Robert's genius; and that they inspire you on your own bookmaking adventures.

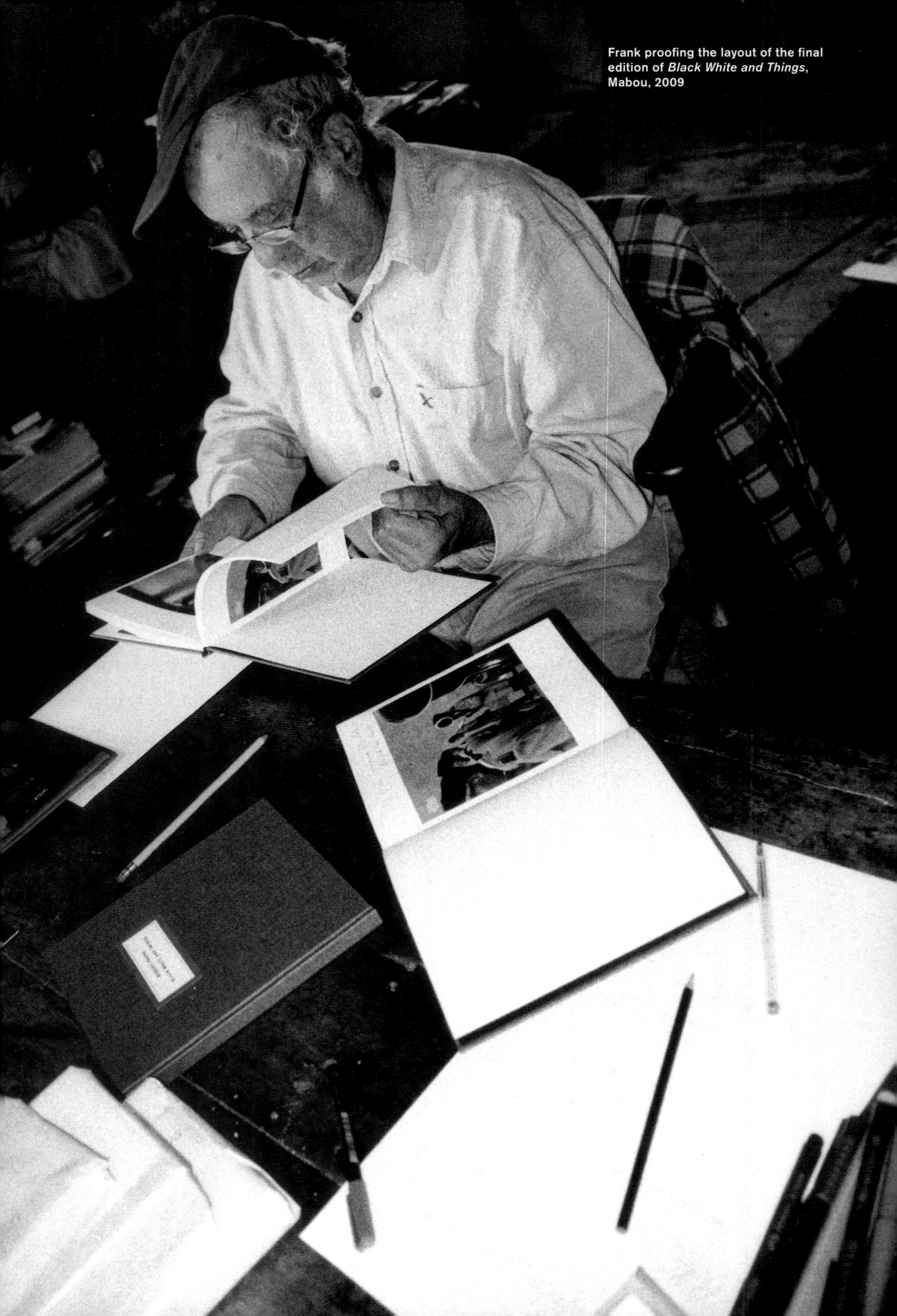

Frank proofing the layout of the final edition of *Black White and Things*, Mabou, 2009

Possibly, Everything:
An Interview with Robert Frank

Introduction by Meeka Walsh
Interview by Robert Enright and Meeka Walsh

Originally published in *Border Crossings*
Issue 125, January 2013

Robert Frank has always produced books of photographs. He made his first one, *40 Fotos*, in 1946, a spiral-bound, single edition of 40 images he'd taken between 1941 and 1945 and assembled as a portfolio he would use in seeking employment. It accompanied him on his trip to New York in 1947 and helped him secure work with Alexey Brodovitch at *Harper's Bazaar*. In 1948 he travelled to South America and from the photographs he made there produced two handmade copies of a book he called *Peru*; one he kept and the other he gave to his mother for her birthday. In 1949 he made a small book of Paris photos— *Mary's Book*—a courtship gift to his first wife, Mary Lockspeiser, whom he married in 1950. And in 1953 he produced *Black White and Things*, an edition of three. That book mapped the course Robert Frank would follow in all the work he did. Everything is there: the place of memory, the use of sequencing, a reliance on intuition, the rigour and emotional courage of poetry— and trusting and leaving space for the viewer.

The poetry is important—it's all important, but like Kerouac wrote in his introduction to *The Americans*, published in 1959, "Anybody doesn't like these pitchers don't like poetry, see? Anybody don't like poetry go home see television shots of big-hatted cowboys being tolerated by kind horses." In the interview that follows we talked with Robert Frank about the form of narratives—in his books and in his photographs assembled from multiple images—being more poetic than literal and linear. His response was the elliptical poetry you recognize from the few lines he writes in his books, from the words inscribed on the photographs themselves. "It's just the friends I have, people I know… It's just the people I know and it's where I live."

The recent books, *Pangnirtung*, *Paris*, *You Would*, *Park/Sleep*, *Valencia 1952* and *Tal Uf Tal Ab*, were the provocation for this conversation because, as Robert wrote to us when we'd completed our first conversation for *Border Crossings* in 1997, "in Mabou interview about intuition and memory for Meeka and Robert and continue…" From the outset of his career, and maintained into the present, he has followed the instructions he printed on the photograph, *Mabou in the Winter*, 1989—a grey image, soft, the sea in the distance and in the foreground covering a stump, a blaze of snow, white and frothed like steamed milk spilling over onto the ground beside it. The image is mounted on the lower portion of a grey sheet. At the top of the photograph he has written, "Hold Still, Keep Going." The place between hold still and keep going is the unachievable state in which we live if we interrogate our lives. It is like the very point of the fulcrum on which Frank's work teeters, seeking only the briefest sustainable balance. It is the existential conundrum— hold still, keep going—life's joke, that shimmer of equivocation that he has always pursued in his work, and risking the balance, he has urged, "keep going." In our conversation in 1997 he told us that it was important to continue. "You have to continue and you have to set yourself a real high level."

Unswerving consistency in the way a life is lived and the work produced, and to be resolute from the very outset, is truly remarkable. But this is so with Robert Frank. The pull against assertions has always been his manner of responding. In January 2013 he told us, "I always knew what I didn't want. That was the rule in my life. I absolutely knew what I didn't want; that gave me the idea and the rest was intuition…" Reflecting, and also gentler now in his consideration than he was able to be as a young man leaving Switzerland, he acknowledged, "It's sad when you know the only thing you want to do is to get away from what someone is offering you. Sad for them. But I knew right away there was no compromise." And since our conversation at this point had returned to those early decisions to leave, Robert Frank mused on the lives of his Swiss contemporaries, cousins who had visited America for a period, then returned, settled down in family businesses and are well off. "I'm well off too, but my way," he added, thoroughly Frankian. "Everything not to do I learned from Switzerland." No need to consider if even the smallest sliver of sentimentality had cleaved a narrow wedge in the rigour of his thinking or his work.

But room for poetry and beauty and friends, always. In the opening pages of *You Would* there is a joyful photograph of Allen Ginsberg, Peter Orlovsky and Julius Orlovsky. Peter and Julius stand in profile behind Ginsberg, so engaged they appear to be chanting, almost devotional. Ginsberg faces his friend's camera, his intelligent face animated—full bushy beard and lively mass of dark hair capped by a white straw boater with a striped band. They must have stopped on a roadside and are standing in a summer field. The book opens with them because "these are my old friends. They were just walking around on a trip to Kansas and that is how I like to remember them, with Ginsberg wearing his hat. The light was wonderful. There is a certain beauty of a photograph when it is spontaneous."

In Paris he'd always found beauty too, and light and romance. There were flowers everywhere on the streets, and in his photographs. In *Tulip, Paris*, 1950, a man in a heavy wool coat fills most of the frame.

This is post-war Paris, but he is young and the sure future is ahead, and in his present moment is a young woman, almost not visible, whose eyes, behind her dark glasses, must be seeking this young man who is just beyond her immediate gaze. She doesn't see him, but he sees her and he holds behind his back the gift of a single tulip. Immanence, romance and hope. New York and America weren't romantic but they were the place of possibility and Robert says readily, "New York made me. It was my luck to come to America." It was the place where he could develop his own style, make the work that was distinctly and uniquely his.

But home is another matter. The photograph *Mabou*, printed in *Tal Uf Tal Ab*, shows three open doors, one to the other leading from the camera and the nearest door, through the others, to the window and its vertical rectangle of light. The open door, the homely comfort of worn paint and the unguarded access of openings speak of home. When asked about this photograph Robert Frank replied, "I have a good feeling about living in that house in Mabou." Bleecker Street is a good house too, where he and his wife, the artist June Leaf, have lived for a long time, but the attachment is to the house in the photograph. "It's a place I have more feeling about. I have much more attachment to the place in Canada. [Bleecker Street] happens to be a nice house but it is still temporary."

That wonderful contingency, the gently goading and impelling restlessness. Always making work, always questioning, always moving on.

—

The following interview was conducted at Bleecker Street in New York on January 18, 2013.

BORDER CROSSINGS: How are the decisions made about what gets published in The Robert Frank Project? In the last four years six books have come out, and there is already another book in 2013. Do you make those decisions?
ROBERT FRANK: No, it is mostly Steidl who asks me if I have work. I mean, I keep the photographs. I have A-chan who makes my enlargements and I just choose 30 or 40 photographs and send them to Steidl and he makes the book. I trust what they do at Steidl. He's a good printer and he does it right and, anyway, I think little mistakes are sometimes the right thing.

BC: Have you been going back through your archive? The time span of the photographs in the books is intriguing. An image of Kerouac from the '50s will be linked with an image from Pangnirtung taken some 40 years later.
RF: Sometimes, if there is a personality that I want to have in the book, I'll go back to get a photograph—of Kerouac or somebody else, but otherwise the books are pretty much limited to two or three years. I know it looks like a lot of books but I don't make that many; Steidl is very productive and he makes the scans and sends me the idea of the book and the layout. I agree and say it's okay. Most often I want less photographs than he suggests.

BC: But are the image-to-image arrangements in the book decisions that you make? Is the sequencing essentially your determination?

RF: Yes, I do the sequencing. Sometimes I have a text or an idea and I put it in. It can be something I've saved from a conversation with a guy, mostly about Switzerland—I think it's quite amazing the ideas they have.

BC: Is your memory so good that when you are doing one of these books you can remember the image you need? Do you remember everything you took?
RF: If I have an idea of making a book from the last five or ten years I go back to the contact sheets because most often I have made the prints before. Whenever I see something good on the contact sheets I choose the good print or I have Ayumi make another print that is better and that is how the books are made.

BC: You have always constructed narratives more out of a poetic sense than a literal one. So what was the idea behind You Would?
RF: Let me look at it. I don't think there's a big idea behind it. It's just the friends I have, people I know. That's the book, really. In this one I liked the hand of Nixon, which was part of a job I did in 1960. Very seldom did I put something in from an assignment.

BC: Next to Nixon's right hand is one of only four color photographs in the book—the clouds, the line from a Rolling Stones song and then a Polaroid of Gerhard Steidl beside another Polaroid of Kafka here on Bleecker Street. What were you thinking about in pairing those two images?
RF: It's just the people I know and it's where I live. A lot of the pictures are in Canada, where I like to photograph because it is beautiful, and then I go back to old pictures. This picture is from Mississippi and it is one of the first pictures I took in America. Next to it is a photograph of Truman in the car.

BC: His open car is speeding down Park Avenue in New York City in 1948, and there is a large flag attached to the front bumper. Do you know that in The Americans there are six photographs in which the American flag appears?
RF: First of all, it is a good-looking flag and you can't go wrong with it. But there aren't that many flag pictures in *You Would*. These are friends. Like the guy who sells guitars in his shop in New Glasgow; or my lawyer from Los Angeles and his boyfriend; or my friend from Portugal, who is quite an amazing guy. He collects cactuses. This is taken by Paolo Roversi, an Italian photographer, who came to visit. This was my best friend in Switzerland, he's a geologist and he was an important guy, but he must have disappeared because I haven't heard from him anymore.

BC: June turns up in a number of the photographs and when she appears, it's almost as if she's an actor in the theatre going on around her.
RF: Well, she's a very social person and she is interested in people and people are interested in her.

BC: Is Alberto Aspesi the clothing designer whose clothes you put on people from Cape Breton for a fashion shoot?
RF: Yes, he told me he didn't care who I put the coats on. He's a very special guy. He said do whatever you want, so I photographed some old men in his clothes.

When you have somebody like that you can work for them and you can do good work. It is the only way. When people tell you how to do it or what to do, then it doesn't work.

BC: *Here is an interesting pair: a series of erotic shunga images opposite an innocuous restaurant wall menu on the facing page. That's clearly a choice you made?*
RF: Well, it's the same idea. This is very nice. It's French. I think it was a scroll that was rolled up. It's sitting on a very old, heavy, large tool that I have around here somewhere.

BC: *Early in* You Would *there is a picture of Ginsberg, Orlovsky and Julius. Why was that the opening foray for this book?*
RF: Because these are my old friends. They were just walking around on a trip to Kansas and that is how I like to remember them, with Ginsberg wearing his hat. The light was wonderful. There is a certain beauty of a photograph when it is spontaneous.

BC: *In* Tal Uf Tal Ab *I particularly like the Mabou photograph looking through three doors towards a window. Did you know that was going to be a good image?*
RF: Well, I just do it because I saw the shape of the window and I think I can add something to the mystery. I'm lying on my bed and I see the doors. It was how they made these houses. These old houses had a beauty that new houses don't have. They're cold. I have a good feeling about living in that house in Mabou. I like this house on Bleecker because I've lived in it for a long time but I'm not attached to it like I am to the house in Mabou. It's a place I have more feeling about. I have much more attachment to the place in Canada. This is just temporary. It happens to be a nice house but it is still temporary.

BC: *Do you think of New York as temporary as well?*
RF: Well, I am conservative. We could have sold this house many times. But I don't want to change it; I like the place for what it is. It's not my idea to make it bigger or paint it. Now you couldn't even paint it because this side of the street is protected. They are making an attempt to save what's here and this is a fairly nice row of houses.

BC: *The landscape seen through the window of an open car door in Mabou puts me in mind of the photograph you took with the girl framed inside the hearse door in London.*
RF: The photograph in London with the child running away from the hearse was taken when I photographed every day, looking for pictures. This is different. I am in a peaceful place, nothing happens and nobody is around.

BC: *One of your most moving photographs, called* Sick of Goodbyes (1978), *is a recognition of loss. I have a sense that the images in these books are much happier.*
RF: Well, it's my life and it's happy because these are my friends and they are people who I feel good to be around.

BC: *Who is Reginald Rankin and how did you end up going to Pangnirtung with him?*

RF: He's a really good Canadian friend from Mabou. He's now in Halifax and he has political aspirations. His father had the co-op in Mabou and was very important in Cape Breton, so Reginald walks a little bit in his footsteps. Back in the '90s he had a job in the north. I went there because of him and that's how the Pangnirtung images came about.

BC: *If I hadn't known that you took these photographs, I still would have recognized them as Robert Frank photographs. You managed somehow to make even the remote Arctic settlement of Pangnirtung your own.*
RF: But this was a place where there were only stones. There were just stones in that place, round stones, which you can see on the cover photograph. The houses are these boxes that are brought in and people live in them; they give them oil to make sure nothing freezes. You know, I am attracted by extremes and the life there is extreme. It was difficult with the people. I don't like to just photograph people because it is kind of an intrusion. If I had lived there for a few months, then it would have been possible to take photographs of the people.

BC: *You are right about the extremes, but the opening photograph of Pangnirtung Harbour is romantic and moody.*
RF: It is idyllic but it is also tough there. When you go out in a boat they take you to a place that may not be the best place to make a photograph. And I am always attracted maybe a little bit more to it because it makes a stronger photograph.

BC: *You use a photograph of one of the houses in Pangnirtung as the last image in* Tal Uf Tal Ab *and on the left-hand page is a photograph of Kerouac. Why that combination?*
RF: I have very few photographs of him. I put it there because I wanted to close the book with him, and then there would be nothing else. That was in Florida and it was after the Guggenheim trip.

BC: *So why is the last image in the book from Pangnirtung?*
RF: Well, Kerouac's got a suitcase, so he's going somewhere.

BC: *What does "Tal uf Tal ab" mean in Swiss German?*
RF: It's a Swiss saying that is often used. Up is basically the direction you go in Switzerland and sometimes it's a long trip. Mountain climbing was one of my base experiences. It was the way you travelled, starting at four or five o'clock, early in the morning. You would go slow and every 15 minutes you would stop. That was a better education than I got from all my schooling as a child. Life outside in nature. When I went mountain climbing and skiing, those were the best times I had in Switzerland. That was the best school.

BC: *Was your father an outdoorsman?*
RF: Only in a car. He never walked a block. He wanted a good life. I always knew what I didn't want. That was the rule in my life. I absolutely knew what I didn't want; that gave me the idea and the rest was intuition. Then coming to America I didn't want to fit in to the way photographers did commerce. I could see I had choices.

BC: I was surprised to learn that before you came to America you had only seen one black person—a woman—and you didn't know what a homosexual was. How sheltered was your upbringing in Switzerland?
RF: Well, at the time I grew up there were no black people in Switzerland. There was one black woman living in Zurich. It was a very isolated life. I don't complain about it but it was cut off, especially when there was war all around the country because of the Germans.

BC: When you say you always knew what you didn't want, did you also know what you did want, and was it America?
RF: It was the obvious place to come. In Europe the Jewish middle class learned English and so you would go somewhere where it was spoken. And most people of that class who were my age, my cousins, would come to America and stay for six months and then go back, each one of them. I'm the only one that stayed. Because for them life was good; there were no surprises. You knew what you would get staying in Switzerland. They had their families and they took over the businesses and they all were well off. I'm well off too, but my way. Everything not to do I learned from Switzerland.

BC: The only American you met was this man who came to your father's house for dinner and he proceeds to fall asleep after eating?
RF: That was Mr. Callaher, a guy from Chicago. We were just so happy to have an American come to our house. My father imported radios from Sweden and from America and the guy came to do some business with my father. It was the only time that someone had come for dinner that I had any interest in.

BC: And then he falls asleep?
RF: Well, my father also slept, every day on the couch. He would smoke a cigar and then he would fall asleep. Then he went to a café. In a way, he was a bon vivant but he had a business. All the conversation at the dinner table was about money. My mother was a sad woman who had bad eyes and she became blind by the time she was 40. She had a hard life but she was a brave woman. Her father was a Russian immigrant who started a factory for bicycles in Basel and did very well. He was a very smart guy but my father didn't get along with him. He didn't talk much and he was different. I think he died when I was about 12.

BC: What was the reason for doing Henry Frank, Father Photographer, the book of your father's photographs?
RF: That was really because of François-Marie Banier, the French guy. I showed him some of the photographs. But my father wasn't serious; he just liked to take photographs. He had glass plates and quite a good camera. It was funny, I remember coming back from America, and I already had a job and a book published, and my father said, "I'm a photographer, too, so now you can enter the business." He had absolutely no sense of it. But he liked me better than my older brother. He knew he would have trouble with my brother, so he wanted to persuade me to enter his business, but I knew I would never do it.

BC: Did he know it, too?
RF: I think so. But he tried. I knew I would never want to live the way he did.

BC: When did you start taking photographs?
RF: I think I got a Rolleiflex for my birthday before I left. I apprenticed with a very nice older man who lived on the top floor of our apartment building. He was a retoucher and I said, I want to learn from him. My father said okay, he liked the man and he could see that he was somebody good, so there was no point in arguing. It's sad when you know the only thing you want to do is to get away from what someone is offering you. Sad for them. But I knew right away there was no compromise. I had to get away.

BC: Compromise hasn't been one of your major characteristics has it?
RF: Well, maybe it is a kind of egotism; you wish to be successful or be better than someone else. I had that in me to compete and to come out on top. Coming to New York and becoming a photographer was tough business in a way, with all these fashion photographers.

BC: Did you also know what it was you didn't want to do when it came to photography?
RF: Well, I had to find out. I knew I didn't want to be a fashion photographer, but that was where the money was. Alexey Brodovitch, who was art director at Harper's Bazaar, was nice to me and he said, "Well, you can make these little pictures for the shopping section in the back of the book." So I made five or ten pictures and for each picture I think I got paid $30 or $35, which was a lot of money at that time. I was lucky, but then I went to Peru right away.

BC: Why did you choose Peru?
RF: I saw books and it was a far away country. It was adventure. It's a very beautiful country to travel in. It was romantic; just the opposite of working in America. There are no romantic places here.

BC: But when you first came were you astonished by America?
RF: Yeah, and I knew I wouldn't go back. An old German guy took me to Times Square for two or three days and when I saw that I said I would never go back to Switzerland. It was very strong, all the people and the traffic and everything. It was simple. You had the feeling that this was where it was happening.

BC: When you began to take photographs did you also know who you didn't want to look like? When you go to Paris you shoot at night, and you must have known Brassaï's Paris by Night. Were you already looking for a way to do Robert Frank night photographs?
RF: Intuitively you know as a photographer that you have to find your own style, something where people can say this is a photograph by Robert Frank. This was the dream I wanted to achieve. So I worked for that. Intuitively it felt right to do that and I didn't want to be like the other photographers who I got to know here, mostly guys who came from the army after the war and who became quite well known fashion photographers.

BC: In your night photographs in the Paris book there are no theatrical images, like Brassaï's Bijou in Montmartre. His images are shot in-close, whereas

yours are more middle range and they are not demi-monde pictures. Was that a deliberate way of not doing an image that had already been done?
RF: I don't know how conscious I was not to at that time. I had it in me not to copy and not to be too much influenced by somebody else. But I liked his photos and I went to see him.

BC: Did you have to avoid Kertész as well?
RF: No. I thought he was a very good photographer. There was a difference in how he photographed; there was more sensitivity. He had a book called *Day of Paris* that was a very good book.

BC: There is one photograph in your Paris book of a woman lying on the ground, foreshortened and with a bouquet of flowers next to her, that reminds me of Kertész.
RF: Well, he certainly influenced me. I knew his photos and I knew him, too.

BC: Was it natural for you to call on other photographers? Was there a kind of brotherhood?
RF: In Paris it was easy because they all lived close by. And I was the youngest.

BC: Did your experience in America change how you photographed Paris when you went back after a couple of years?
RF: I wanted to find a place in Paris. I knew people but I couldn't find a place and I also knew I wouldn't get paid. I couldn't make a living there as a photographer but here I could. It's simple. Here everything was possible. I didn't know that and I would not say that but I thought it was possible here. And I still think that. I still do think that. New York made me. It was my luck to come to America. And then I went to Canada. The smallness of Switzerland had had an effect on me. I realized what a small, threatened country it was, especially for a Jew. You were near disaster, so you wanted to get away.

BC: In the Paris book there are a number of lovely photographs of couples—the young man with the tulip, the older couple in the Tuileries. There's a real sense of romance in the images you take there.
RF: Yeah, it was my age and my love for Paris. You couldn't love New York, but I really loved it there.

BC: The photographs are atmospheric, even lyric.
RF: It was the city that made that. Wherever you looked there was beauty, in the buildings, the parks, in a lion monument in the 14th arrondissement. Wherever you looked, it was easy to see the qualities of Paris, the light.

BC: You choose six of the Paris photographs to put in Black White and Things *when you put together that book in 1952.*
RF: But there were probably even more photographs from London. I thought they were stronger and I felt that was a period I wanted to get away from. I went to Spain, too.

BC: What drove you to change so much? The blacks in the London and Wales photographs are dense and rich

and you immediately leave it behind. Were you restless by instinct and didn't want to repeat yourself? You never settled for very long.
RF: I think it was the influence of America once I tasted it. I came here and went back to Paris but I think my intuition told me that the real thing was America and not Europe. I was clear about that.

BC: You said that you knew what Walker Evans's images looked like and you knew what you didn't want. But interestingly, you took a copy of American Photographs *with you in the car on your road trip across the country. Was it a tribute or a reminder of what you didn't want to do?*
RF: Well, his photographs had a big influence on me and I did go to some of the places he suggested. He was the photographer who influenced me more than anybody else.

BC: More than Bill Brandt with his miners?
RF: Yeah. I helped Evans doing his jobs. The way he photographed influenced me because he looked at it straight. That was his lesson; he photographed it just straight. It was very strong to learn that from somebody who did it without compromise. We got along very well. He liked me and so he would tolerate me. But he was not a nice man. He believed in breeding, in good schools. But when somebody was good, he would stand up for them. I went to see him later on when he was not so well and he would lie on his bed and say, "Don't bring any of those Ginsberg guys. I don't want to see any of those types. Don't do that."

BC: Walker Evans's introduction to The Americans *was pretty tight ass.*
RF: I couldn't use it and he got very upset when I went to Kerouac. There was no choice. But we stayed in contact and he came up to Mabou. He had a hard life when he got older. He liked big cars. He would say, "Okay now, I'm going to photograph, so take the car away. Don't come near me." He didn't want anybody to watch him photograph. I could understand. I would be the same. I don't want anyone carrying my camera around.

BC: The Paris book includes a photograph of a palm reader's station and it shows a poster with "Les Lignes de la Main" written above a drawn hand, and underneath are written the words "sciences et mystères." Did that image become the title and the icon for the cover of The Lines of My Hand, *the book you would do some 15 years later?*
RF: It probably came from that. June drew the hand for me. I also like the cover photograph of the Paris book. It's a movie poster decorating the outside of a pissoir.

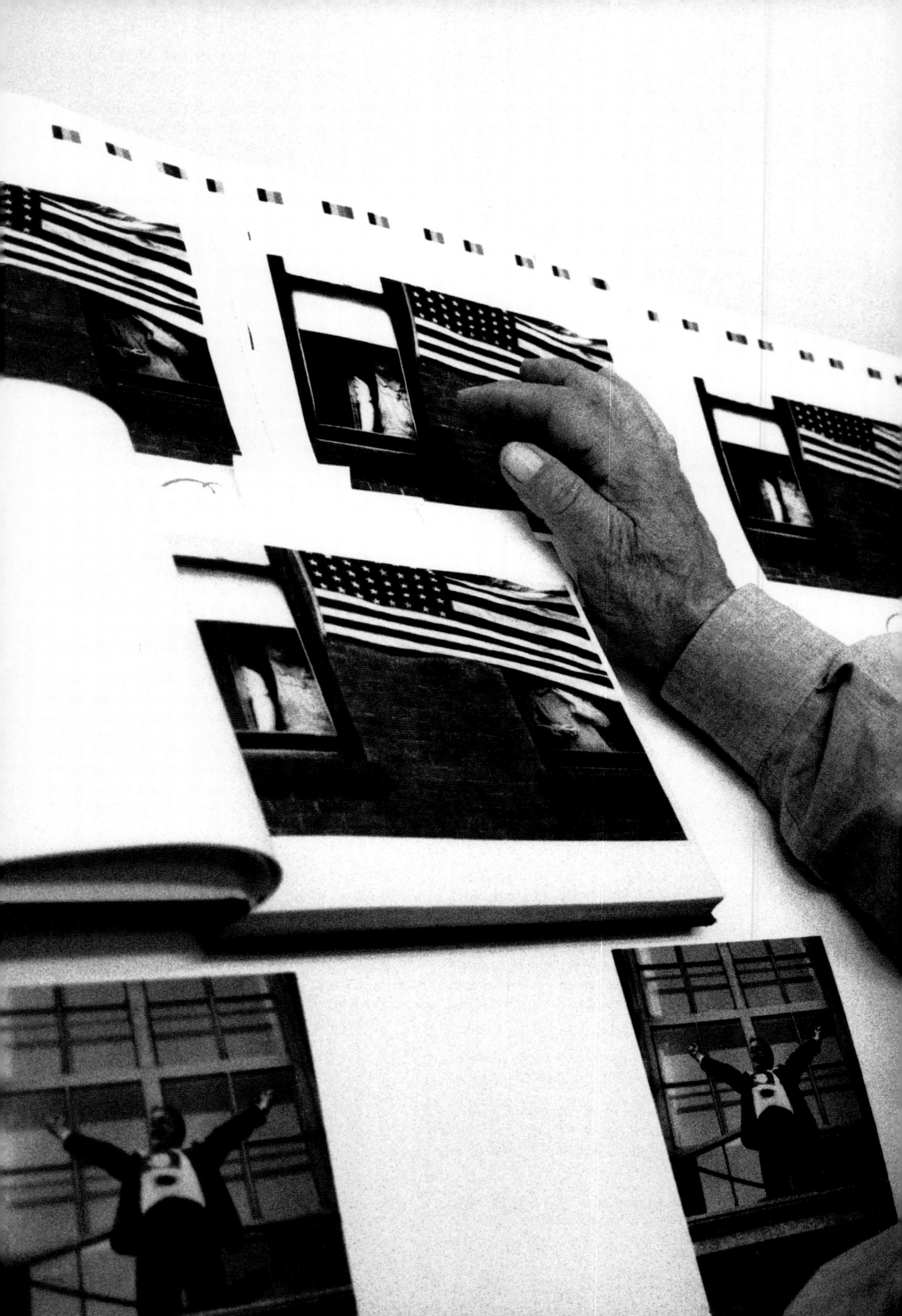

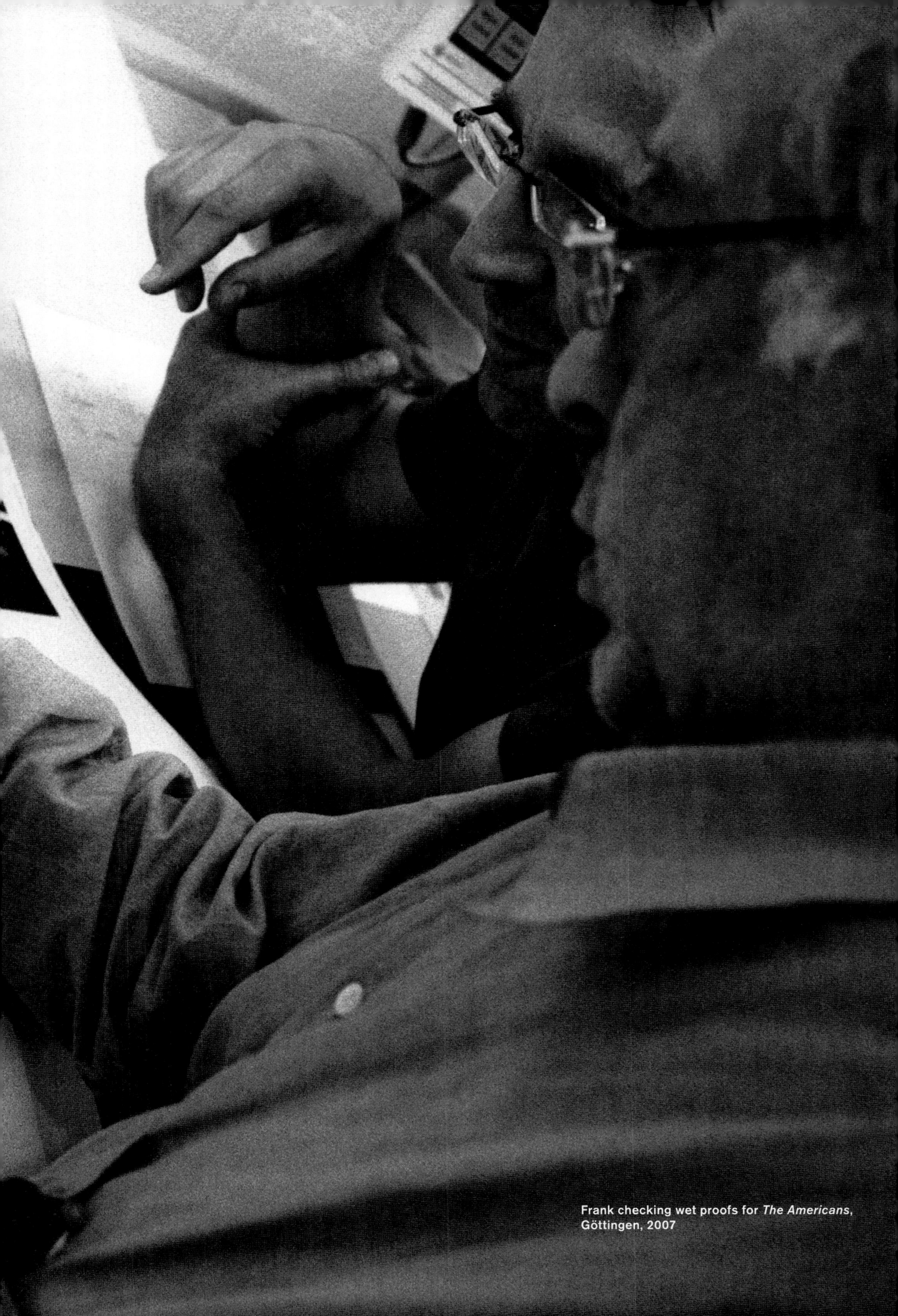

Frank checking wet proofs for *The Americans*, Göttingen, 2007

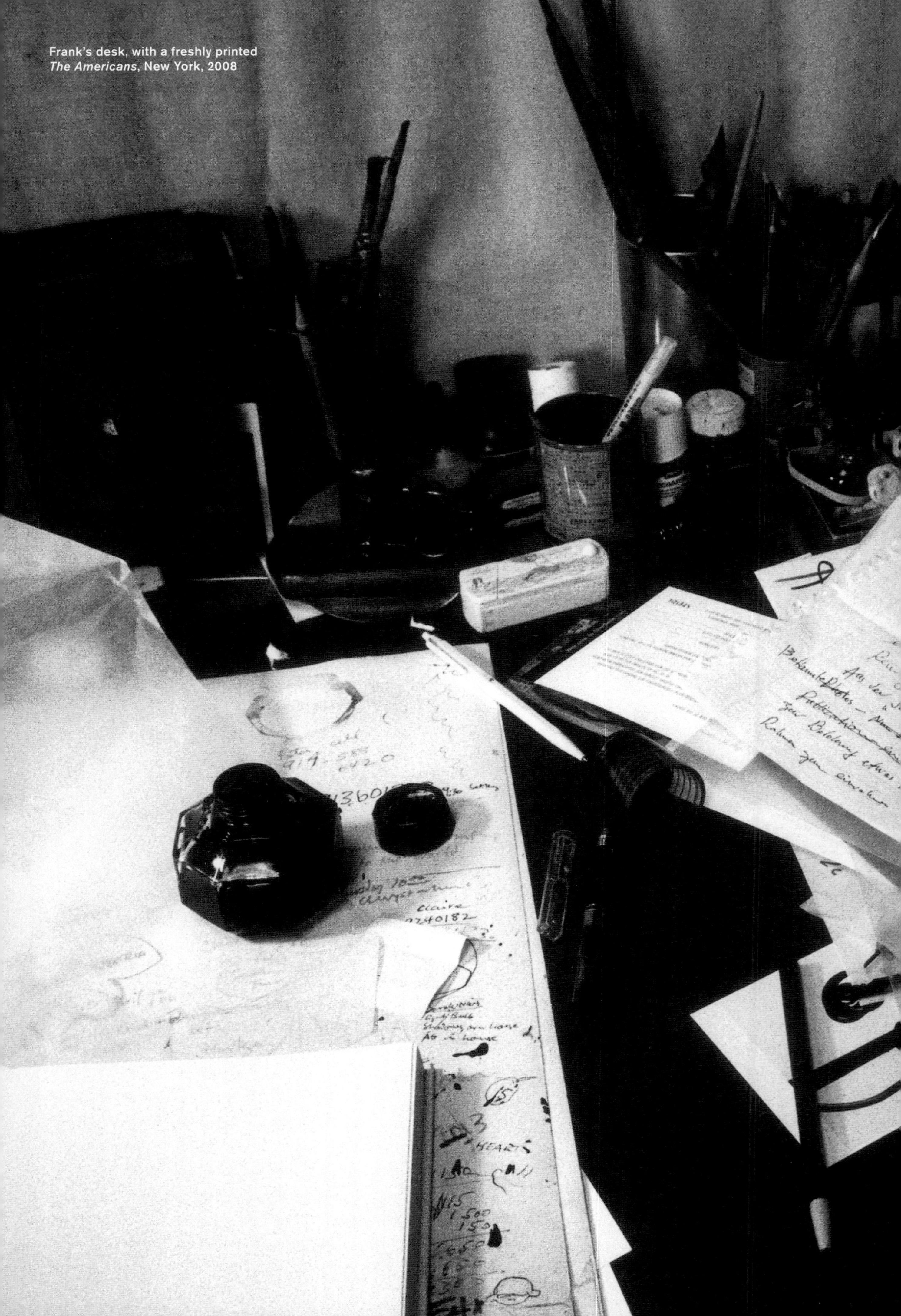

Frank's desk, with a freshly printed
The Americans, New York, 2008

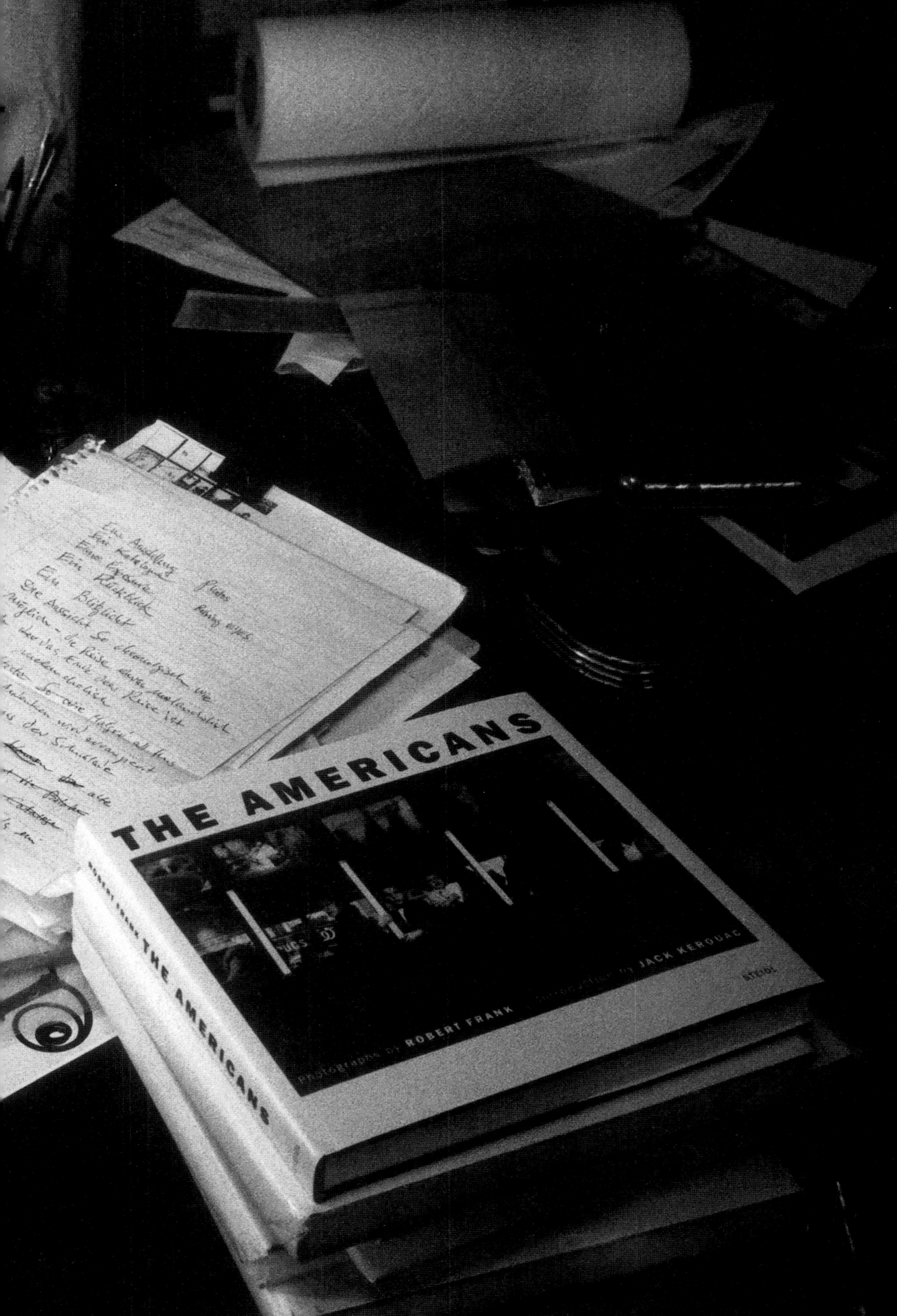

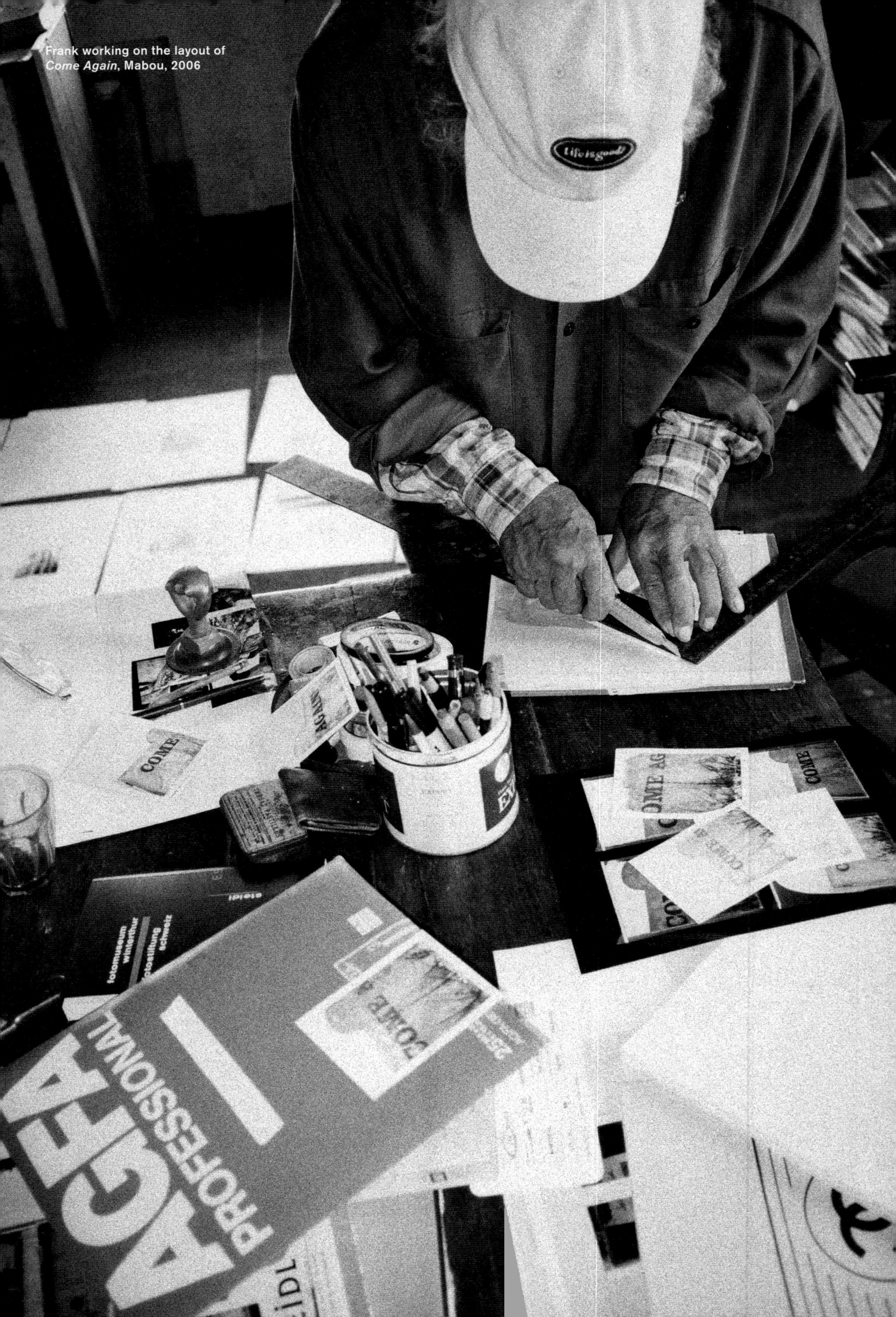

Frank working on the layout of
Come Again, Mabou, 2006

Books Published by Steidl
2004–2019

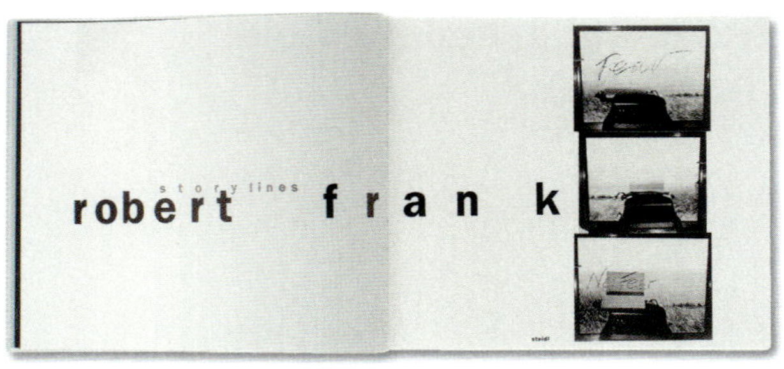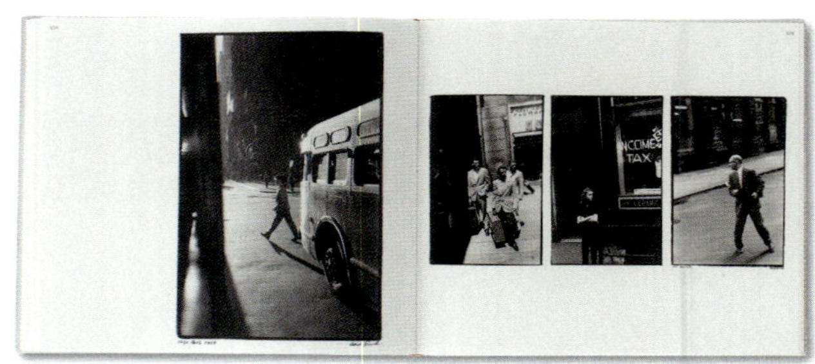

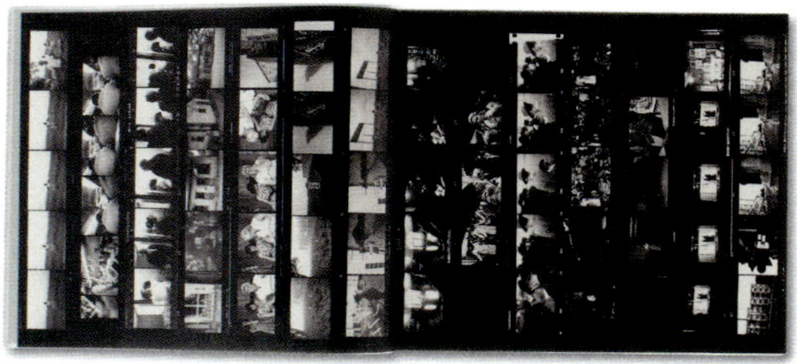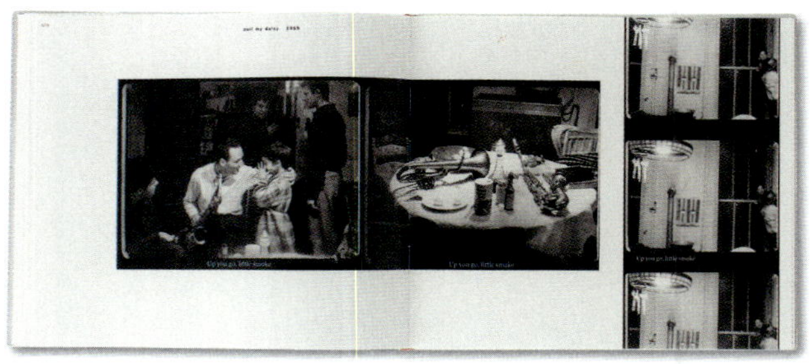

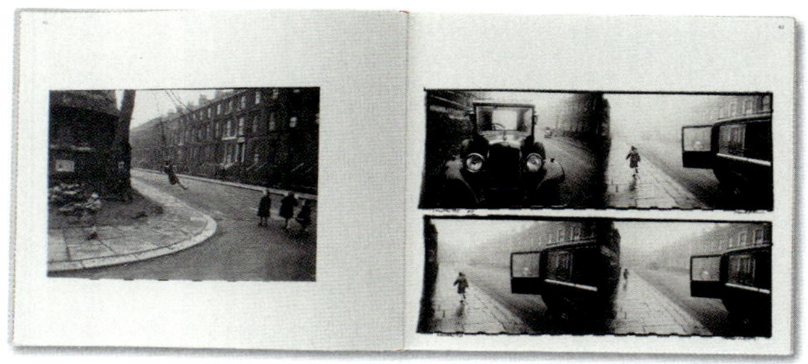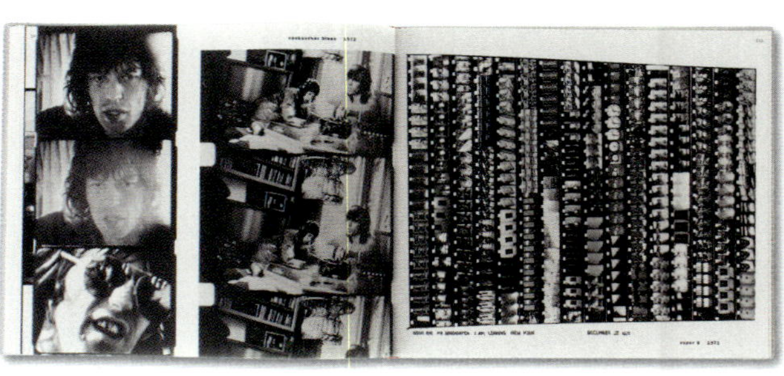

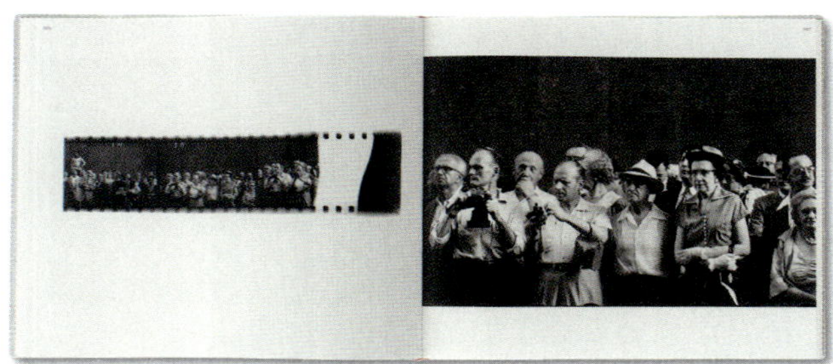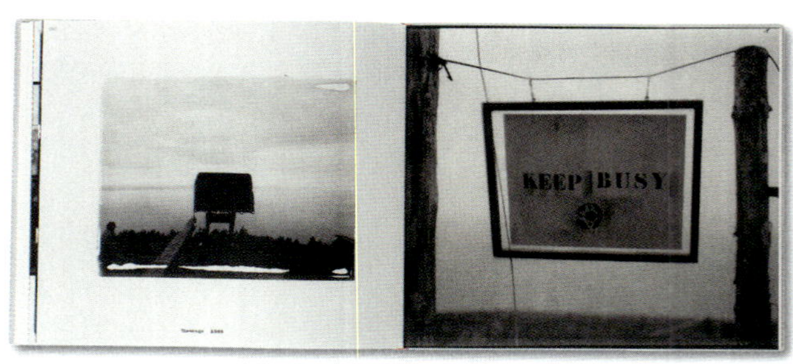

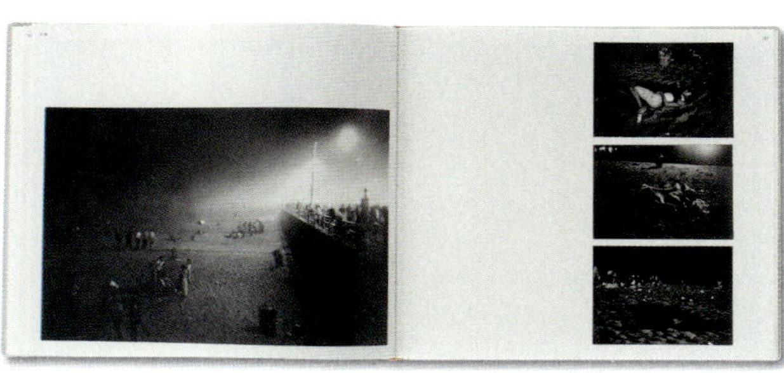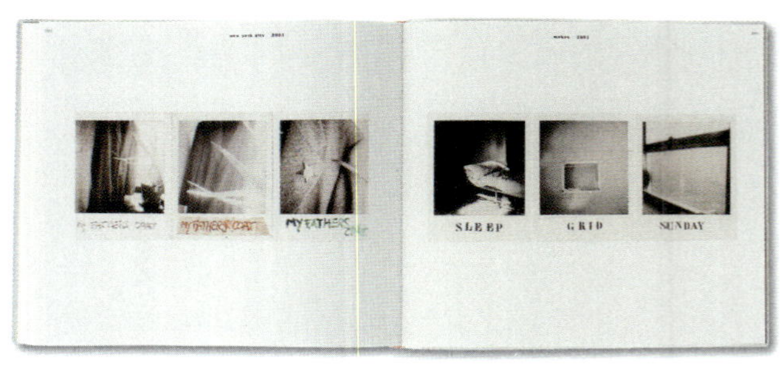

Storylines

Published by Steidl, 2004

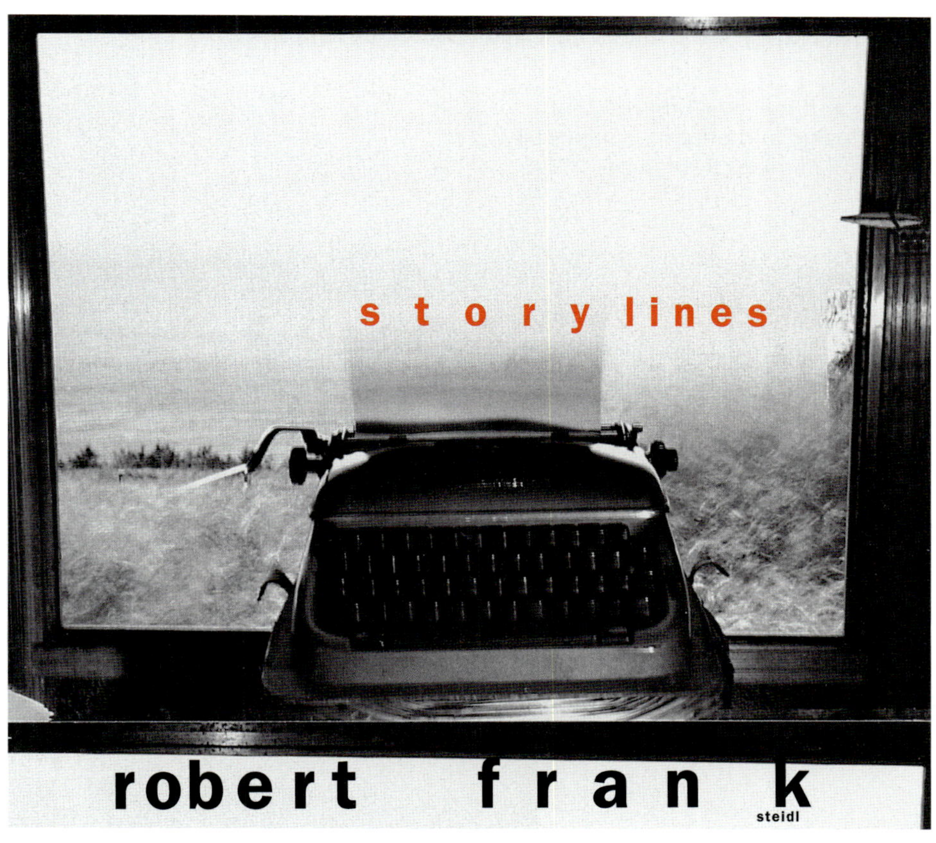

Texts by Ian Penman
and Vicente Todoli
Book design by Robert Frank,
Gerhard Steidl and Claas Möller
208 pages
11 × 9.4 in. / 28 × 24 cm
228 black-and-white
and 19 color photographs
Tritone and four-color-process
Plastic softcover

ISBN: 978-3-86521-041-8

Storylines accompanied an exhibition at Tate Modern, London, in 2004 highlighting Frank's experimental use of narrative in photography and film. The exhibition included work from films and photographs (including Polaroids, contact sheets and recent digital stills) and several artist's books. The photographs are from locations as distant as Peru, London, Wales, Coney Island and Chicago.

The Making of Robert Frank's Storylines (2004)

Photos and text by Gerhard Steidl
Book design and printing completed
between 8 and 20 September 2004

I love the fact that artists travel to us in Göttingen, with their photographs in their bag and ideas in their mind.

Our publishing house and press are in a couple of small converted houses in the center of this medieval city. It's all on a small scale, and a long way from the industrial zones that most people associate with printers.

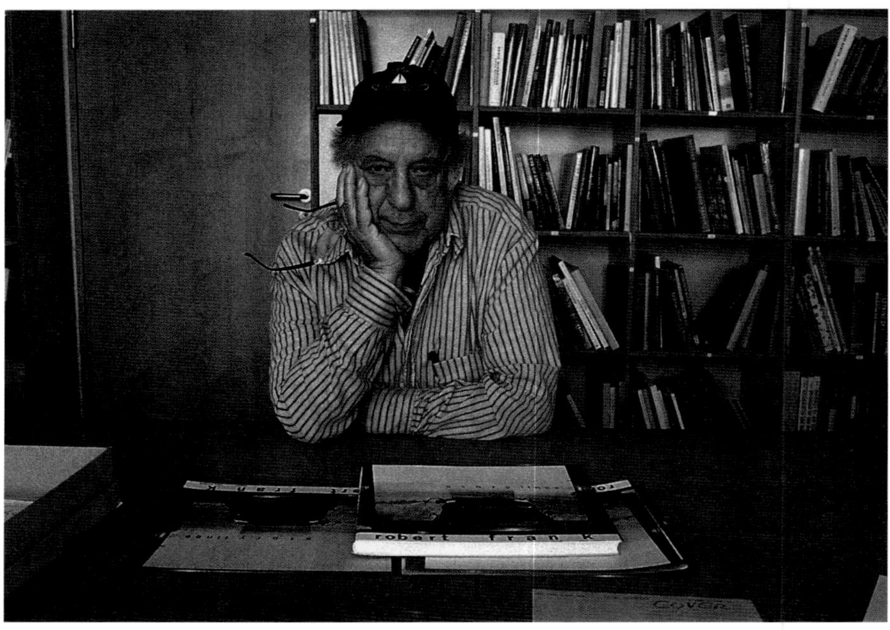

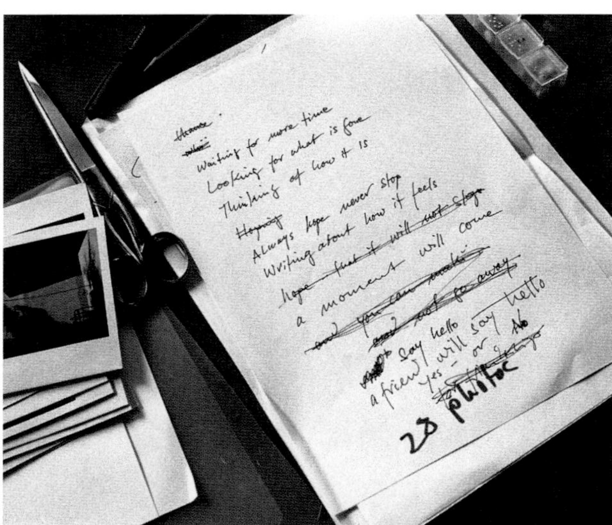

On the top floor of the main house is our library. It's where work begins on most of our books and it will be Robert Frank's work place for the next few days.

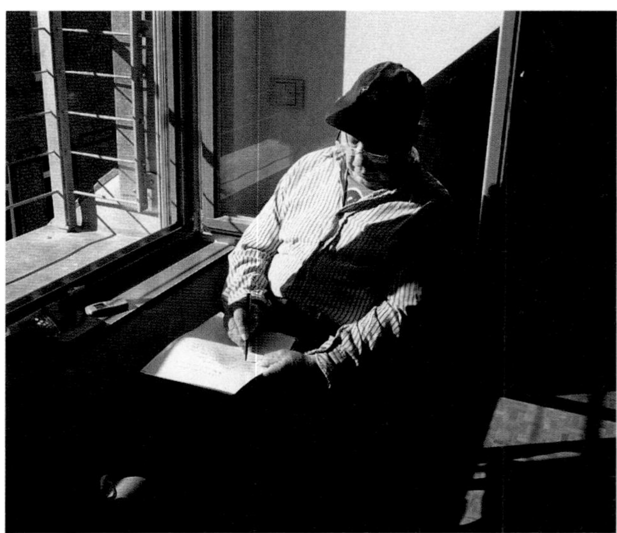

"

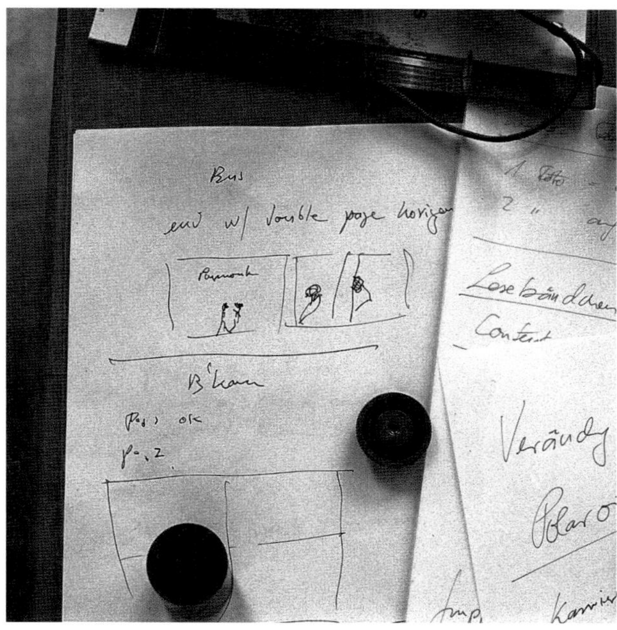

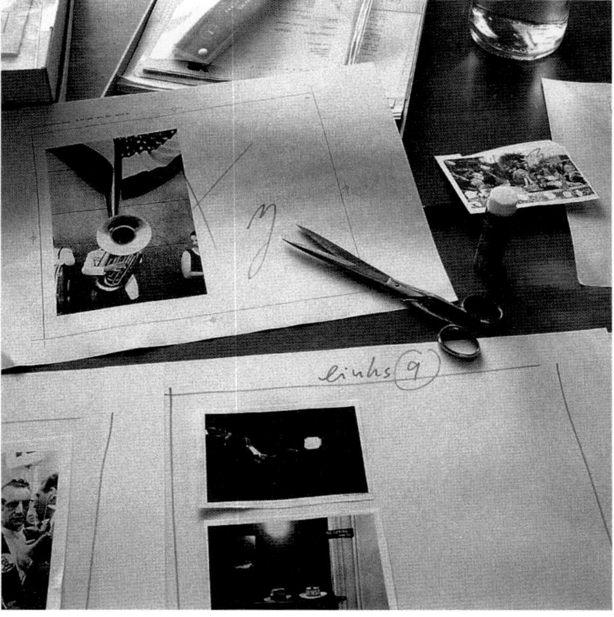

I like to do the structural work with an artist on the large wooden table. We cut out photographs and think about sequences; we discuss the format and start to lay-out the chapters. This handicraft approach allows you to move back-and-forth and it is usually a slow process, but this time is necessary because it lays the foundations for the book.

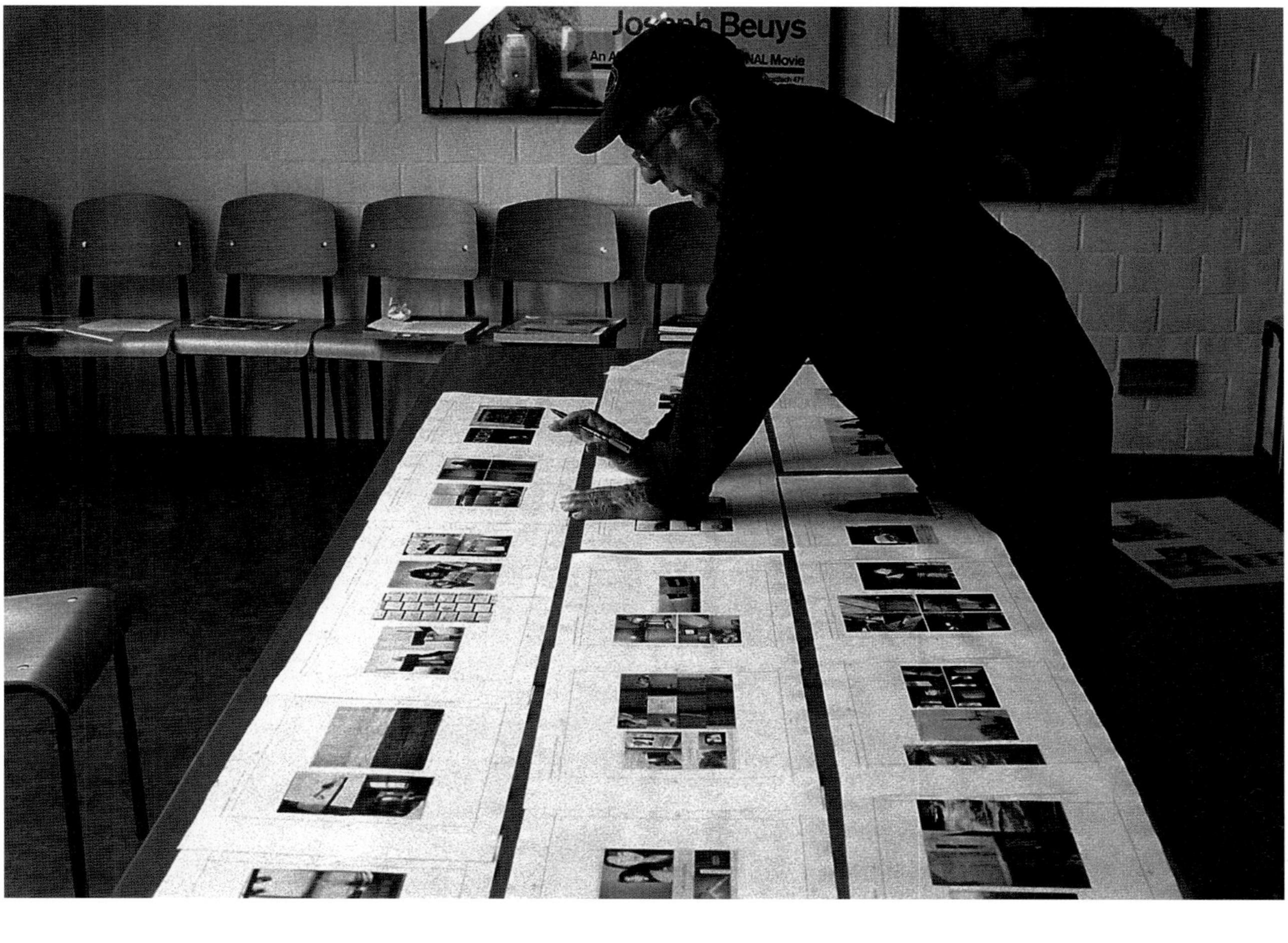

As soon as possible we make a full-size dummy. The first proper maquette conveys a real sense of the subsequent printed and bound book—an intimate object that you can hold in your hands; a sequence of pages that you can leaf through. At this stage I usually have a sense of whether the idea will work or if there are any conceptual flaws in our approach. It may be easier to scroll through a file on a computer screen but you don't get the impression you have with printed pages. Our set-up is of course entirely digital but I treat myself to the luxury of switching between digital and analogue.

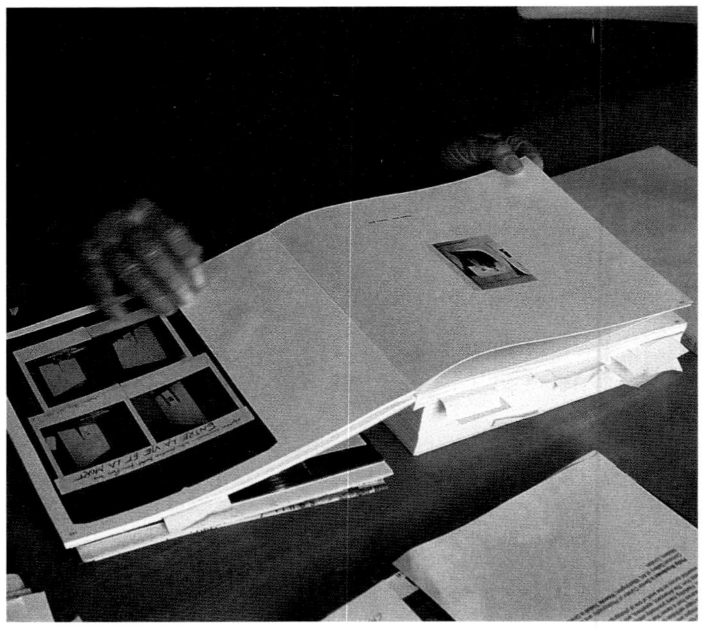

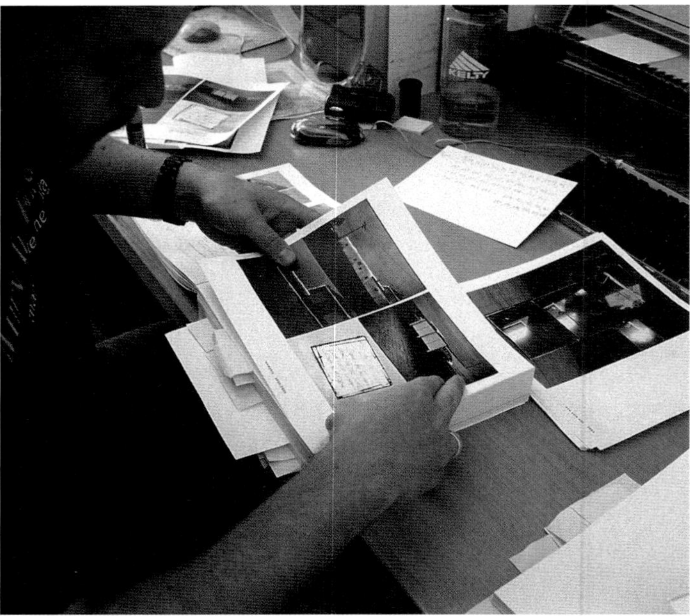

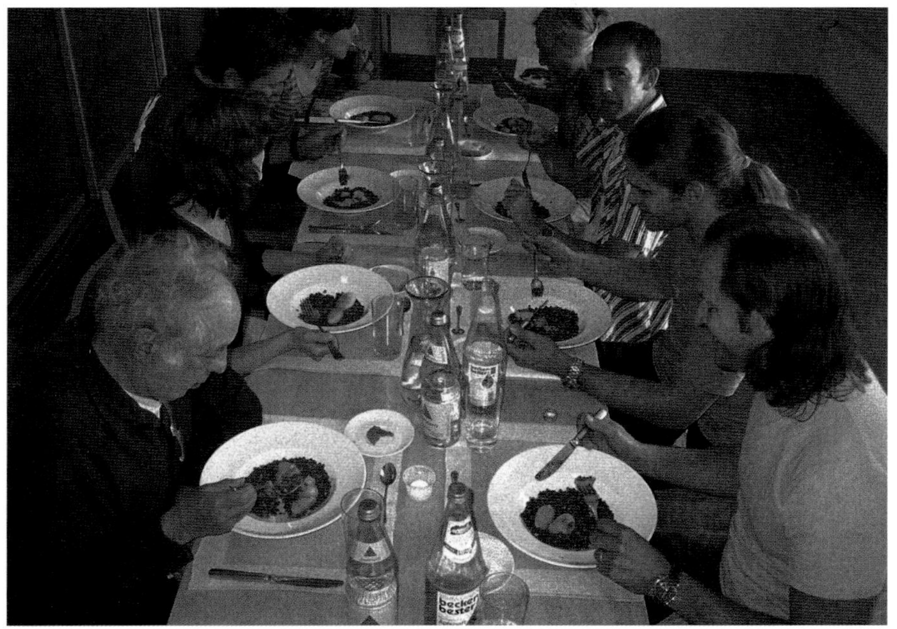

In former times the artists always left the building for lunch and we would have to track some of them down in the pubs a few hours later. Now nobody is allowed to leave—and lunch is cooked by our chef Rüdiger Schellong in our dining room across from the library on the third floor. I often think that our building is a submarine—as soon as everyone is on board, we dive underground, and there's no fresh air or daylight before the end of the journey.

We continue to develop and improve the hand-glued maquette in parallel to the completion of high-res-data on the computers in the floor below the library. When a sequence is finished we put in the captions and deal with all the textual elements. Michael Mack managed the requirements of Tate Modern's exhibition list and Robert Frank's spontaneous ideas. In the end Robert wanted to use very few of the 150 captions, just sufficient to structure the stories in the book. Michael, Robert and I then checked through the final sequence.

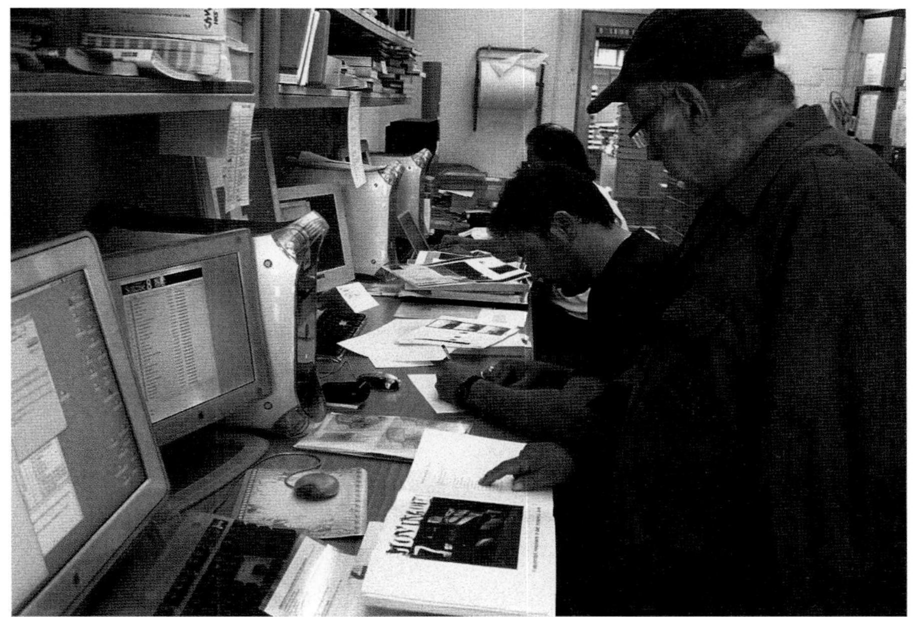

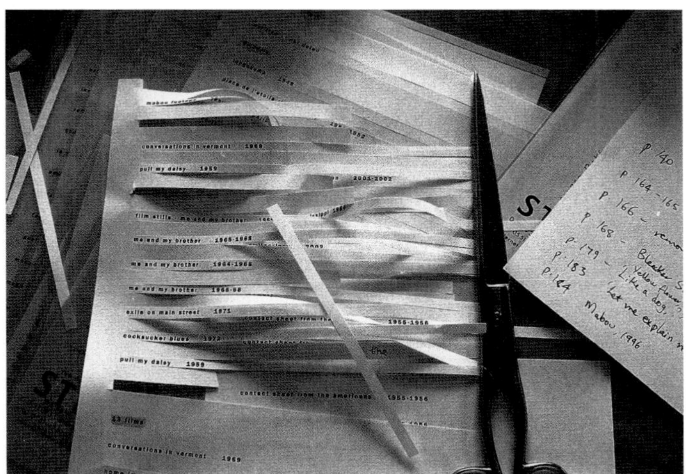

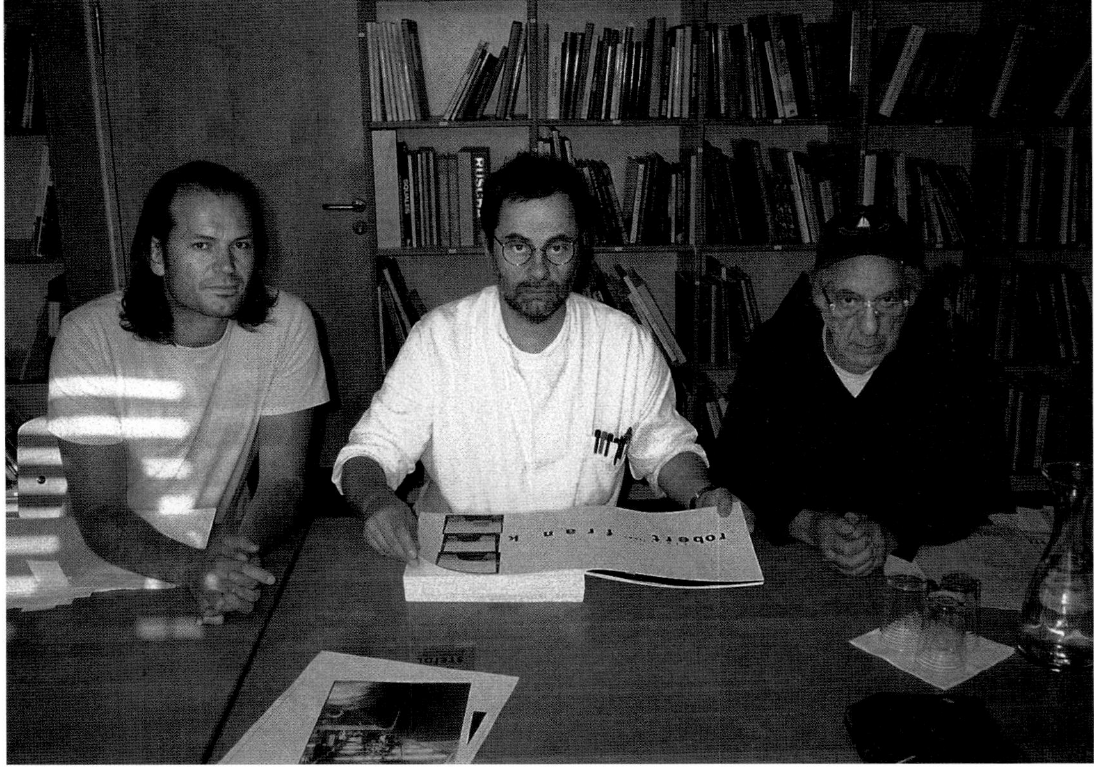

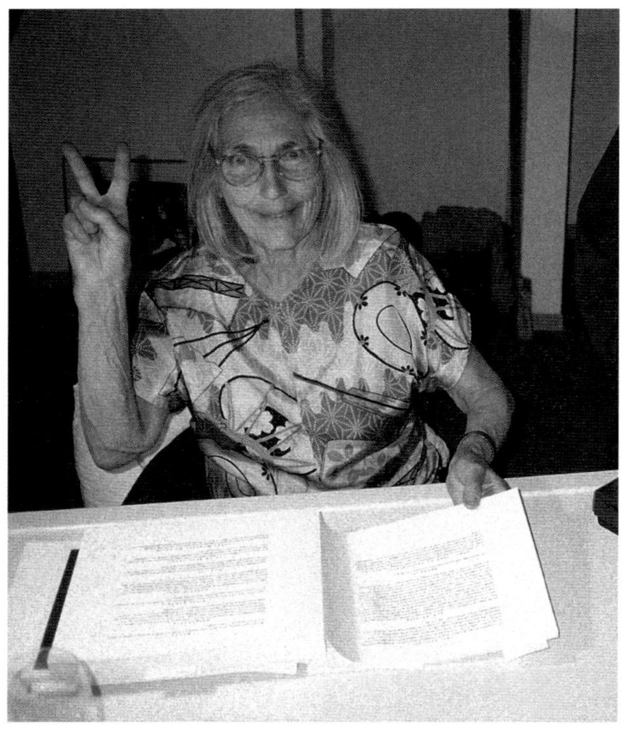

Our guests stay in the Halftone Hotel, our apartments right next door to the publishing house. It means that we can easily knock on June's door deep in the night and drag Robert out of bed when we have to talk about the very last detail.

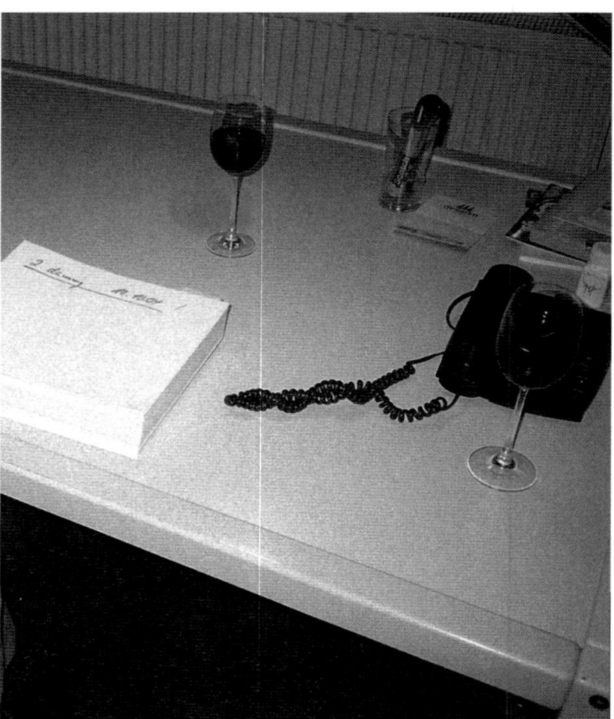

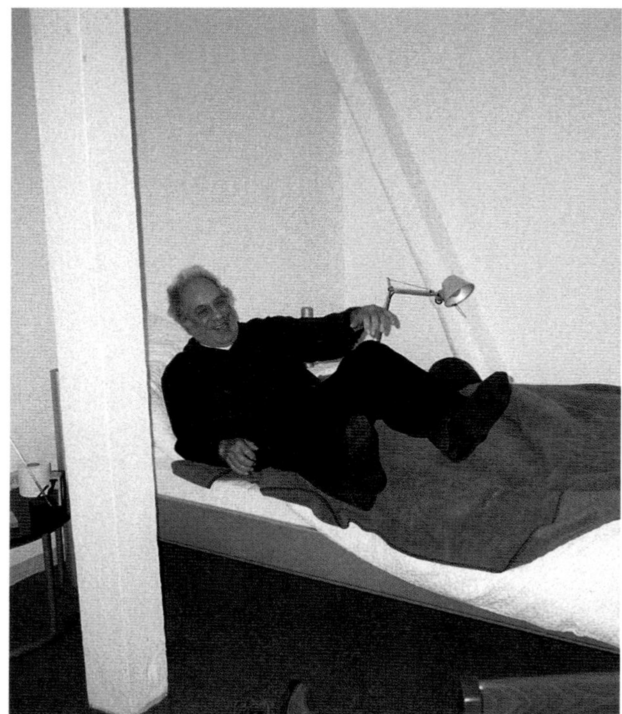

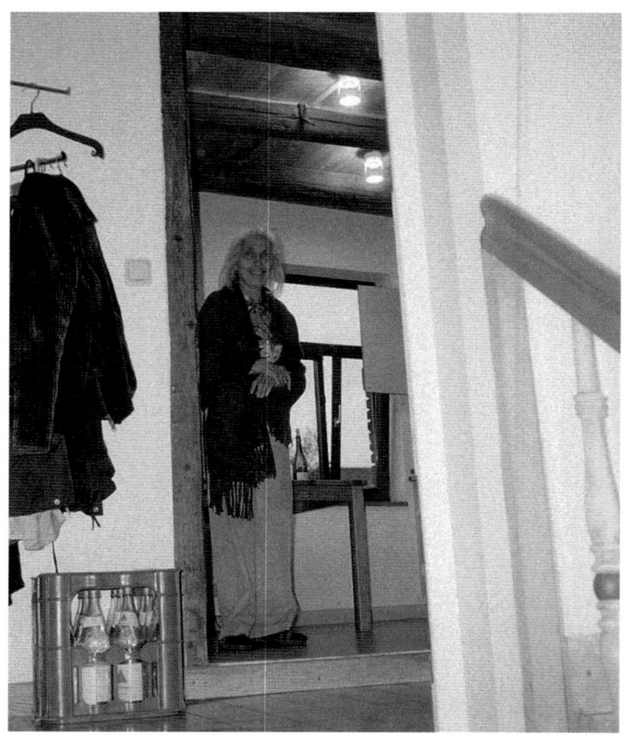

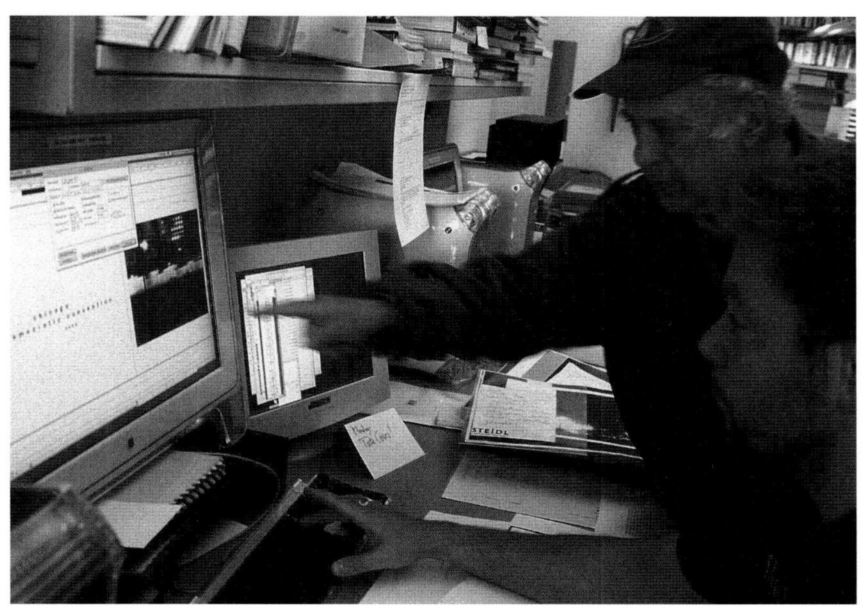

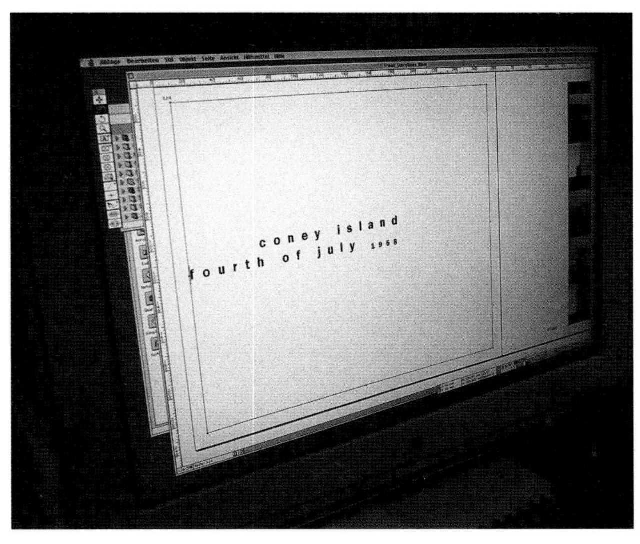
coney island
fourth of july 1958

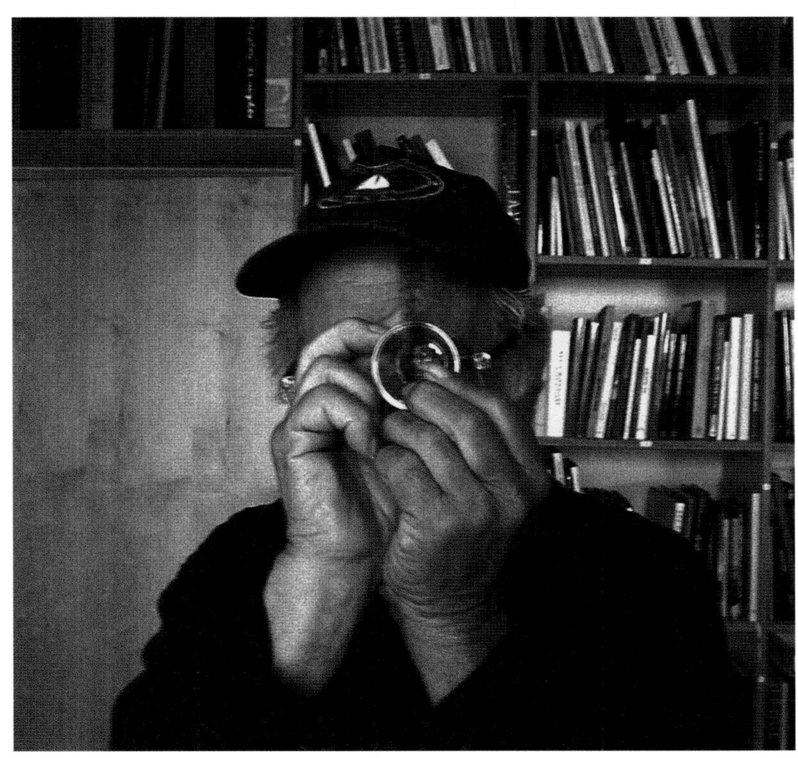

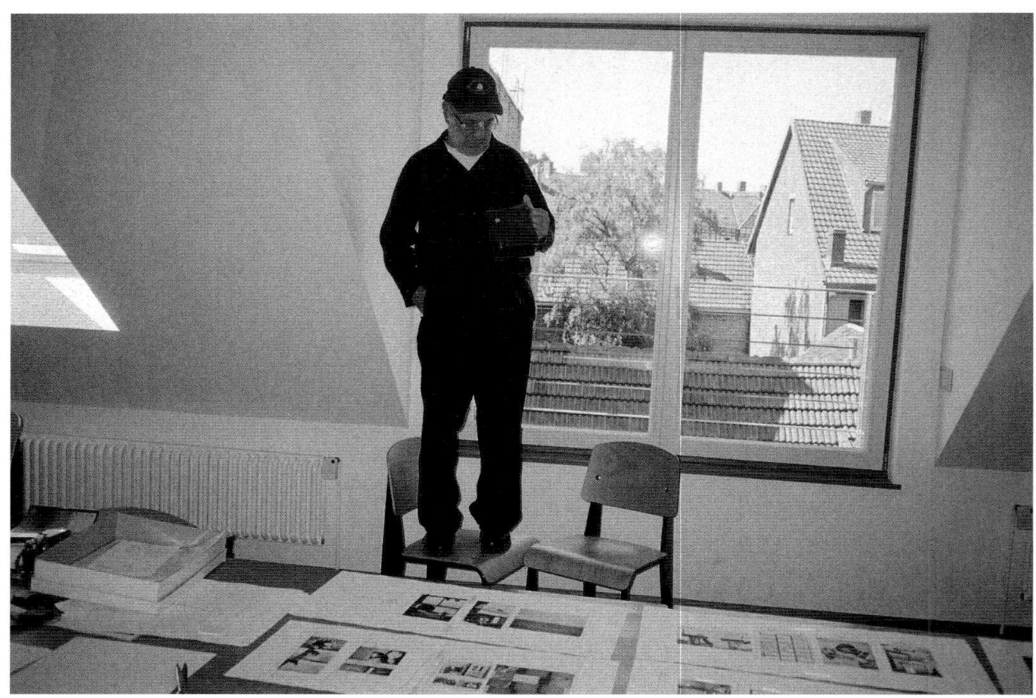

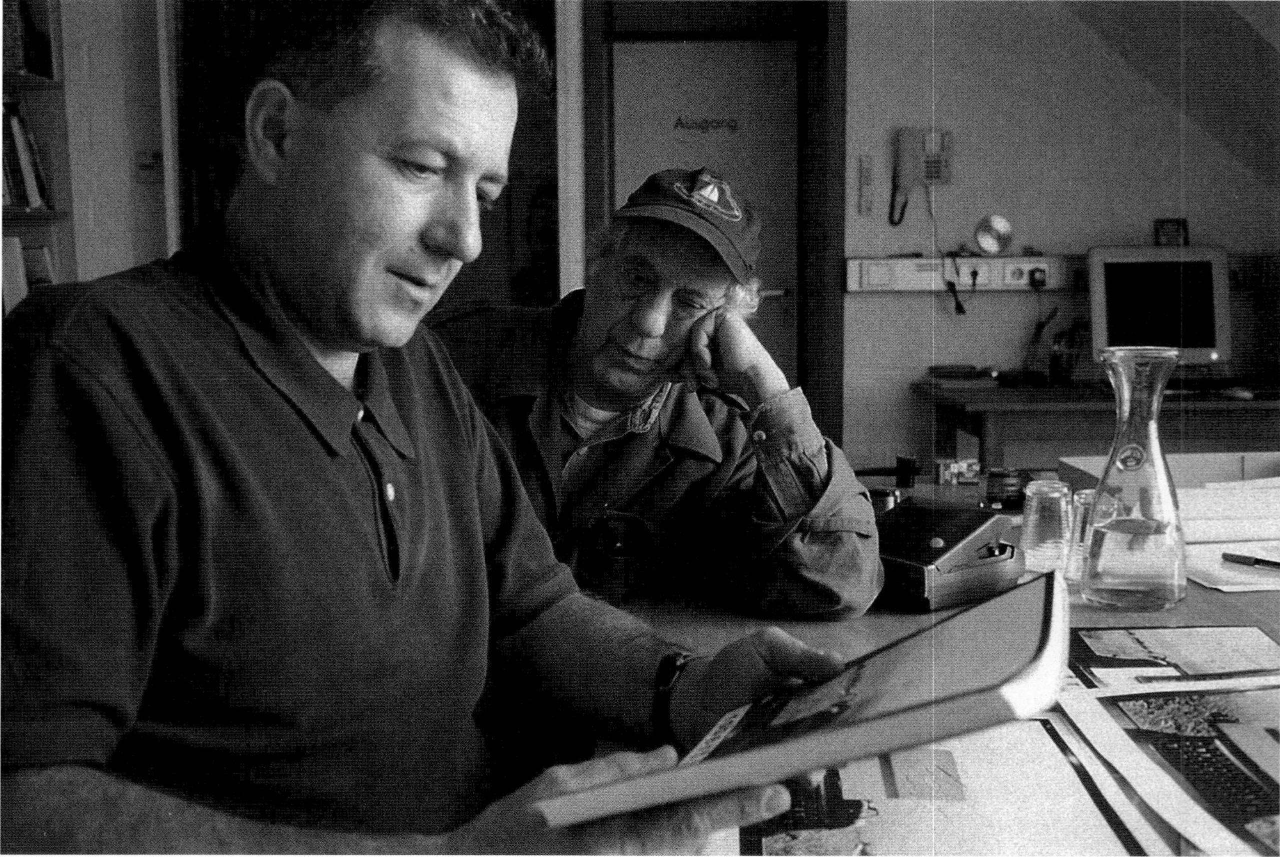

Of course you never produce a book just for yourself. The first reader of Robert's book is Vicente Todolí, director of Tate Modern. When we had our first meetings in Bleecker Street, New York, he told Robert and me about his clear vision for the exhibition. This became the basis of the book and in discussion Robert said that he wanted a "disrespectful photobook," not a monograph or retrospective in the classical sense. We agreed on a light-weight book, bound in a flexible material like a pocket calendar. Vicente likes what we have done and has some good ideas for final improvements. We're now ready to print.

On the ground floor we run films from the digital files in our film-plotter and then printing plates have to be made from those films.

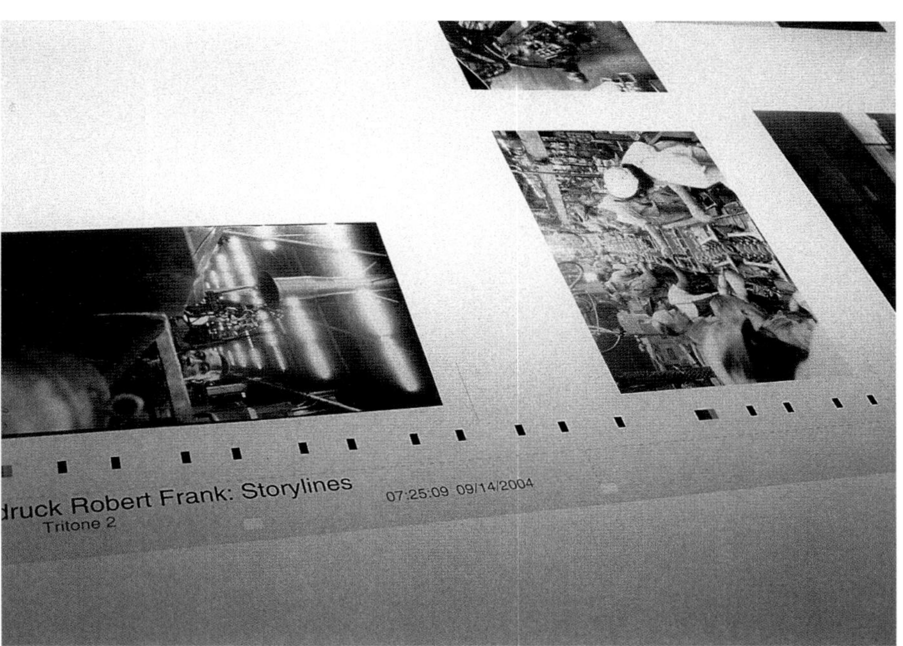

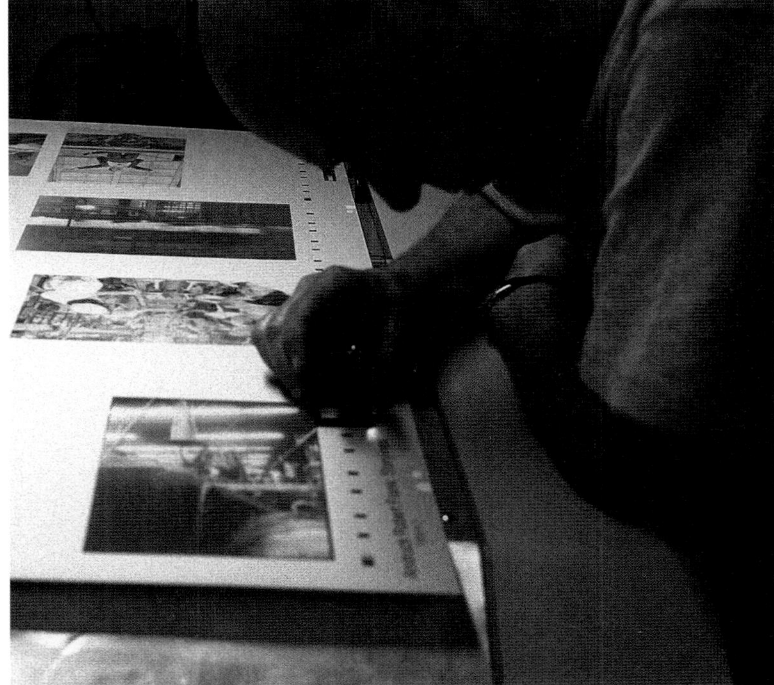

The technologies in the printing industry are constantly advancing but we always keep at hand a combination of the new and old, traditional techniques and modern technologies. Because in the end we need to have as many tools as necessary to produce the very best result in each particular case. It is not simply about machines—we maintain a high level of craftsmanship in our printing.

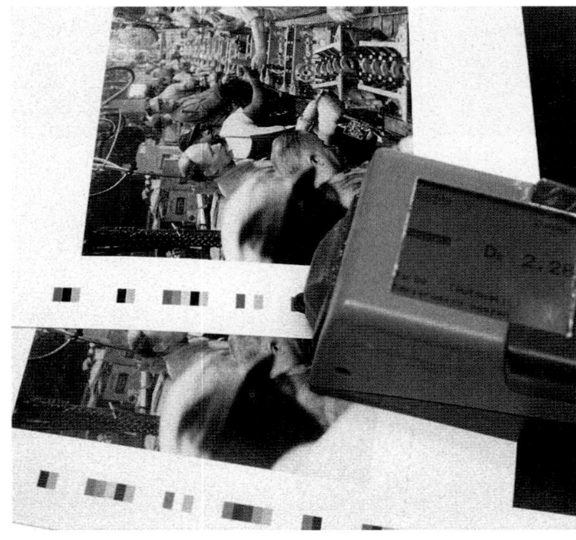

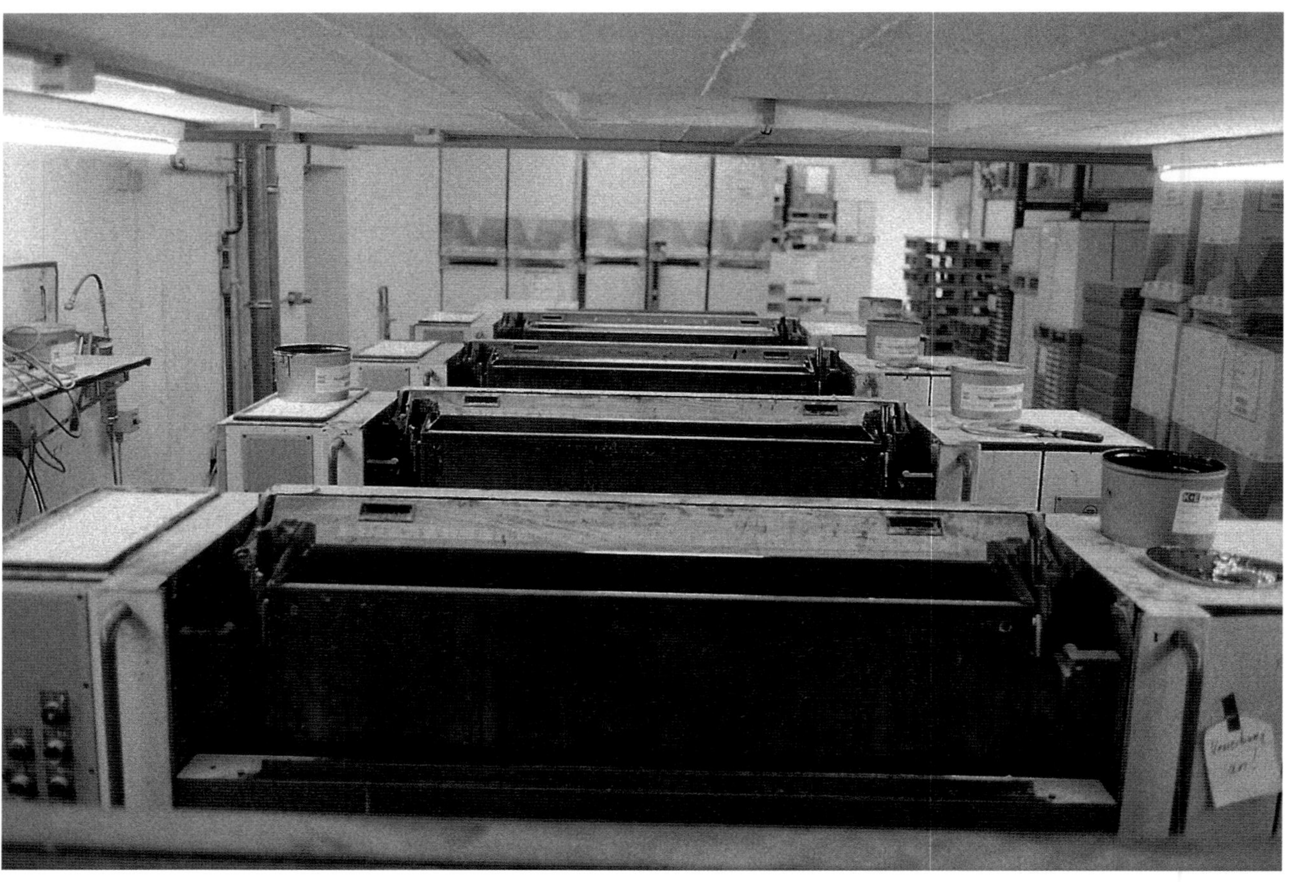

The start of the print run is very exciting. We work with a large-scale Manroland press which is on the ground floor of the building.

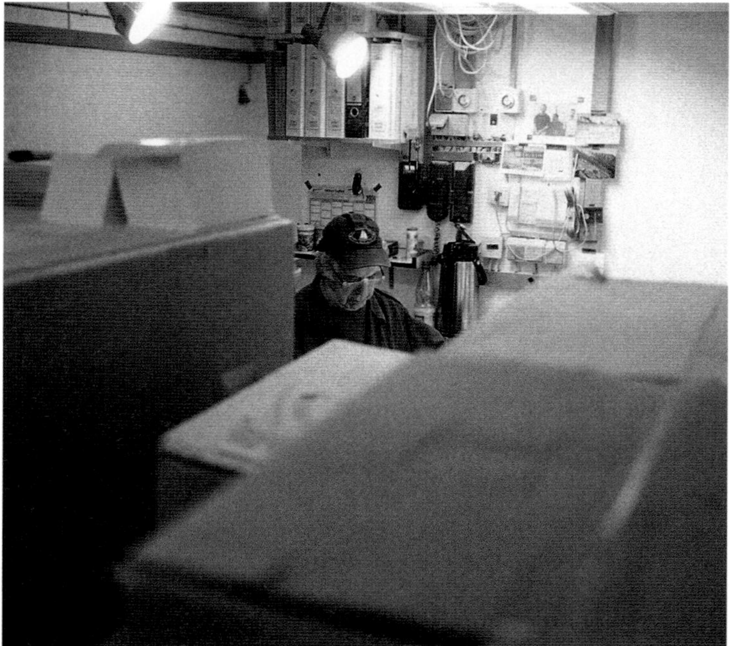

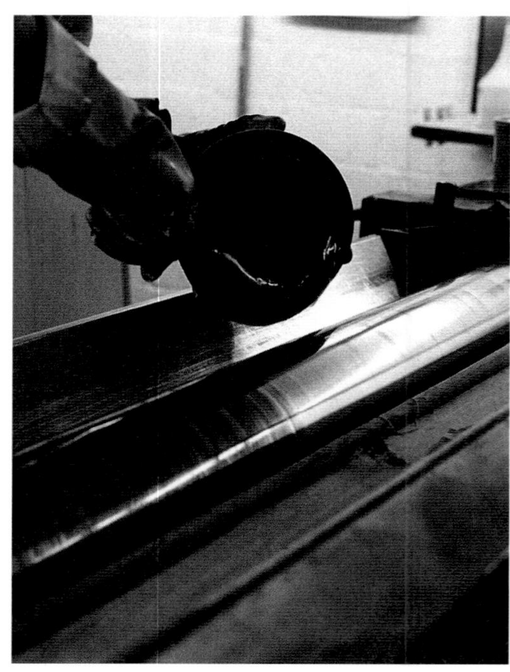

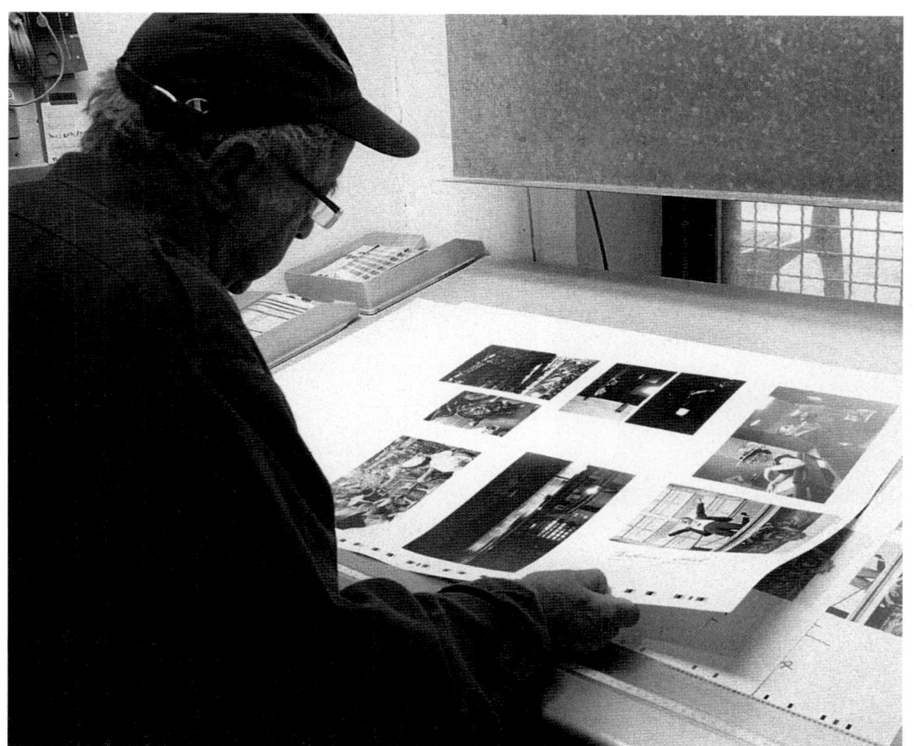

Each printing sheet has to be checked and approved by the artist. *Storylines* was printed in tritone for the black-and-white images and four-color process for the color. The whole procedure is the same as in the darkroom: you have to decide on the best grey and color tones by both looking and trusting your instincts.

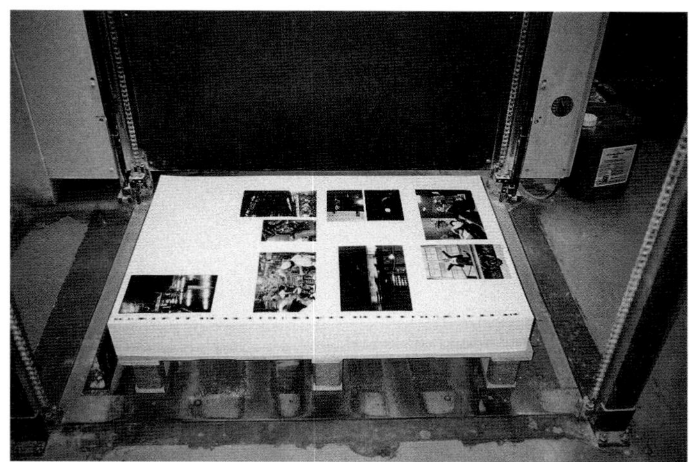

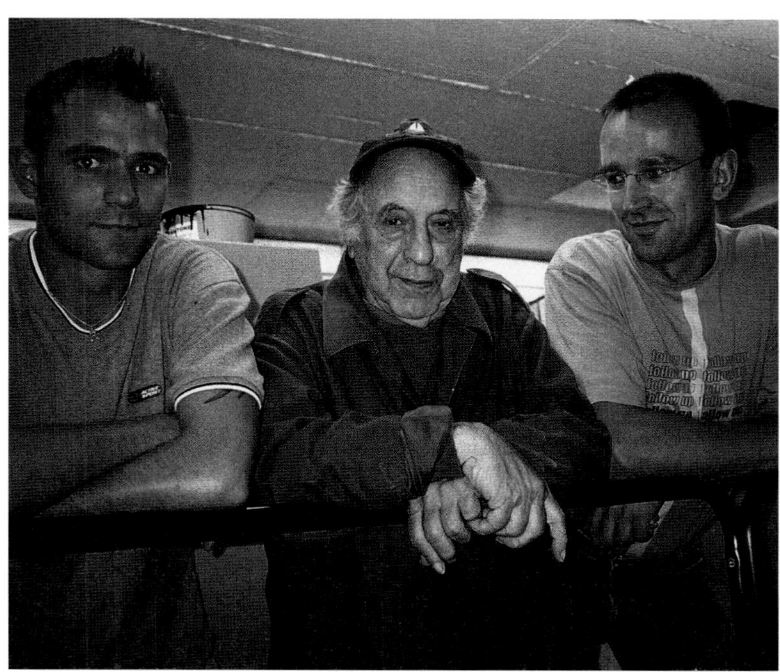

Printers and artists, standing together at the machine, are a sort of family. They can't keep any secrets.

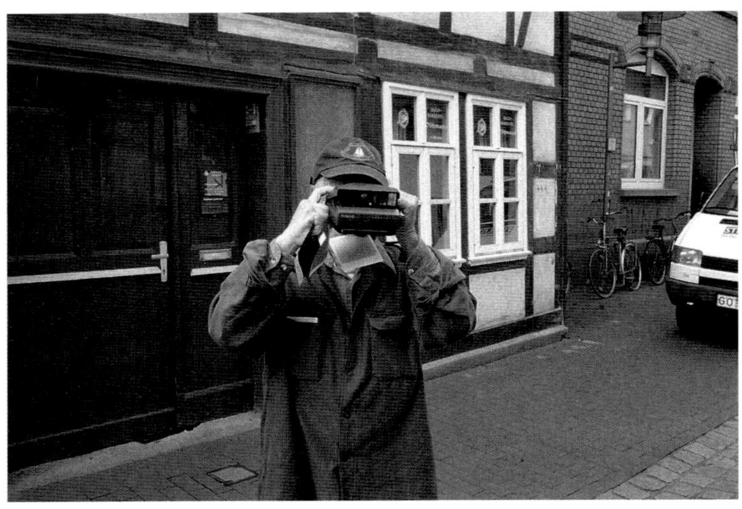

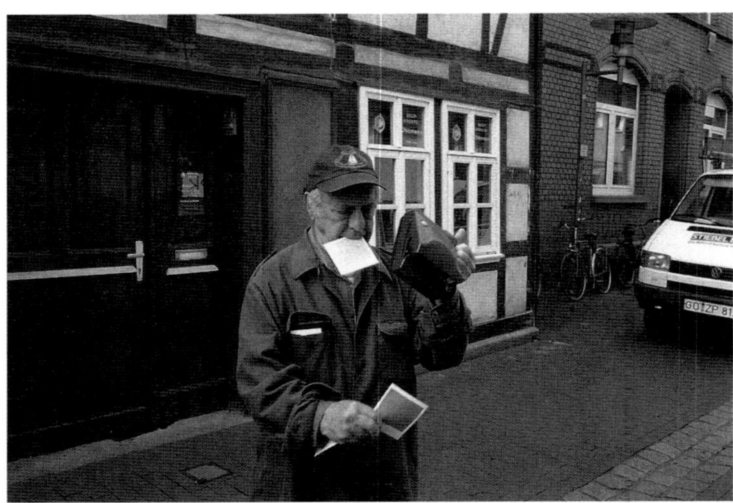

The work is almost finished. The whole staff comes together for a group portrait in front of Steidlville.

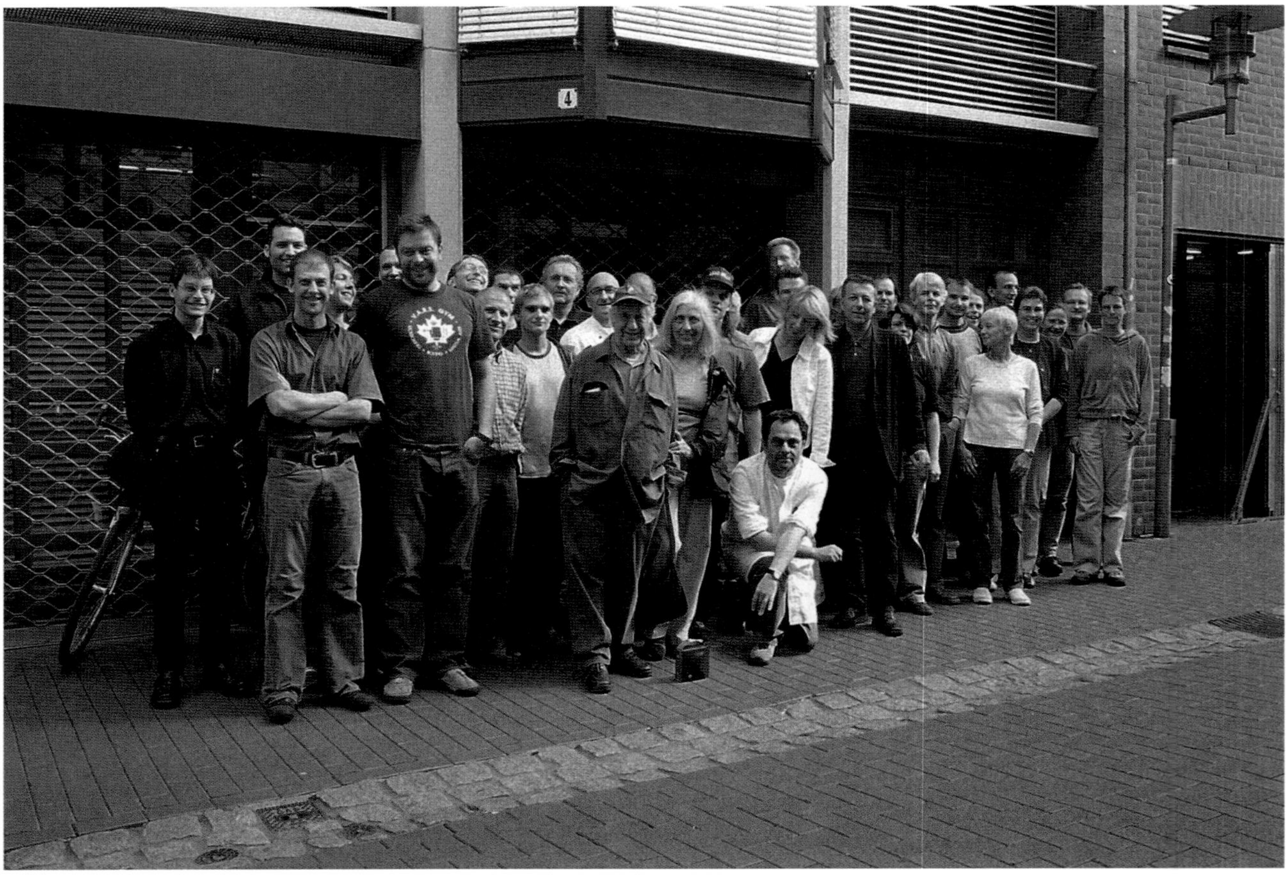

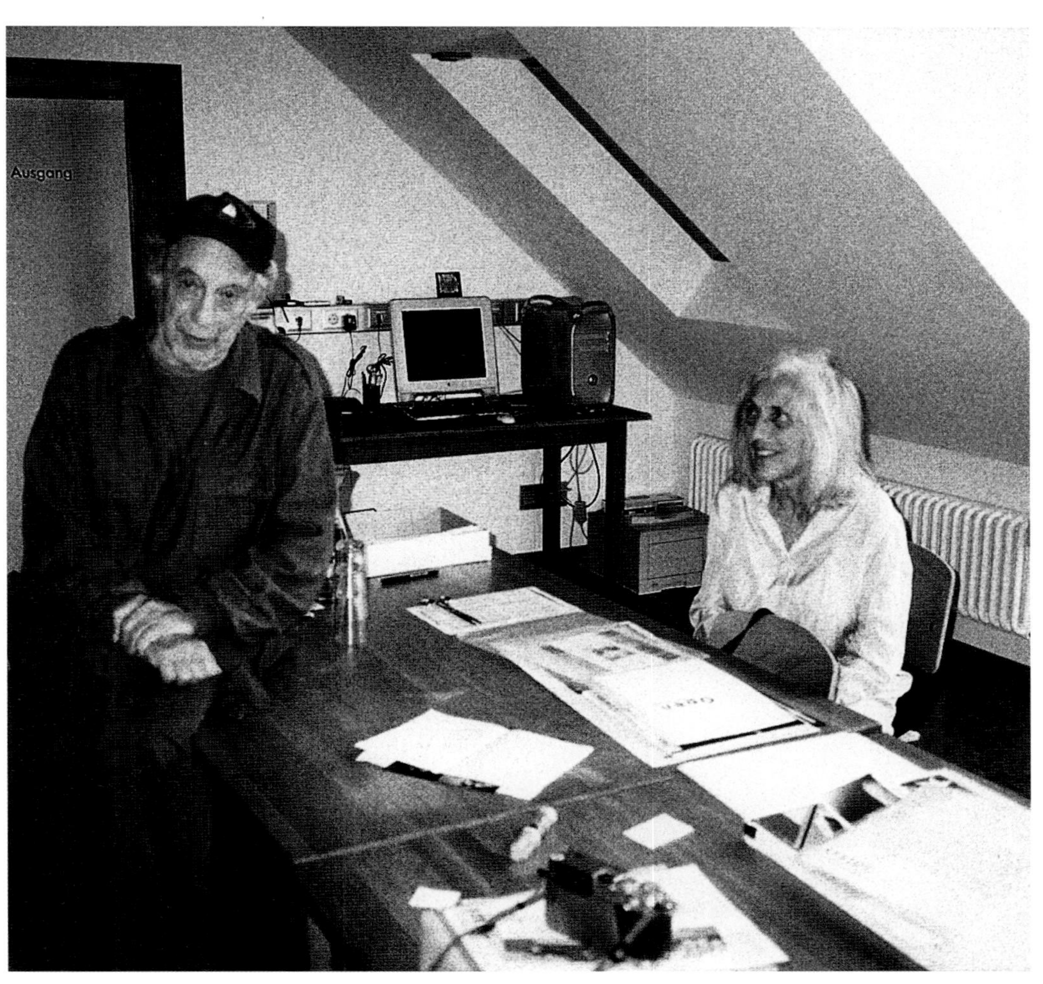

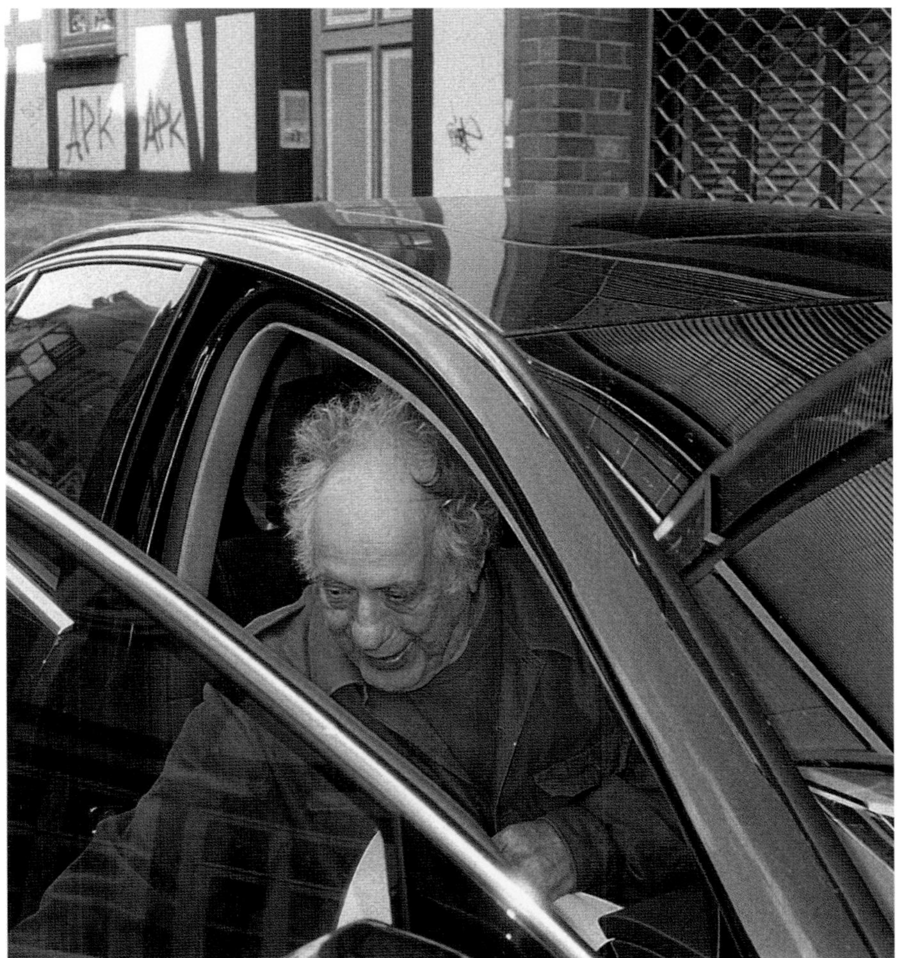

I always dreamt of having a small book factory. At the top, you throw in an idea and after a few days a finished book tumbles out below.

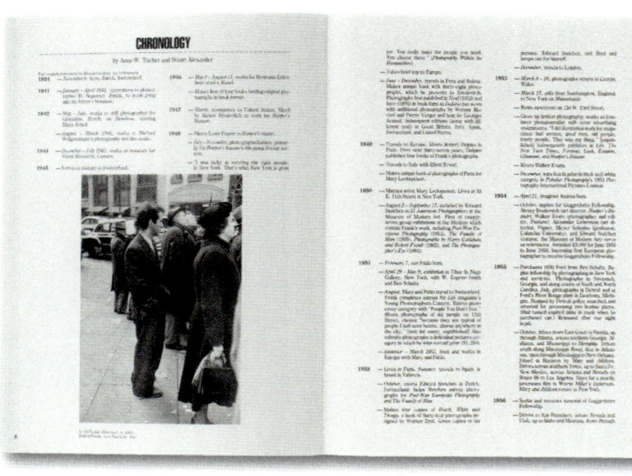
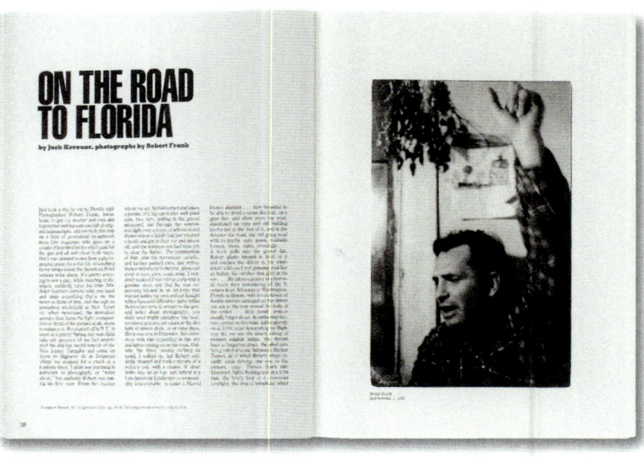
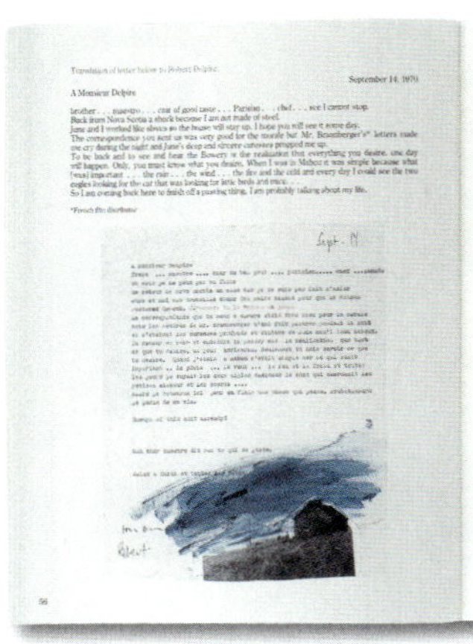
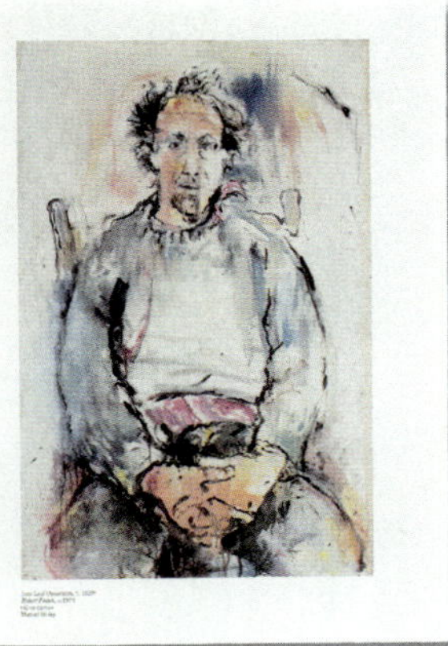
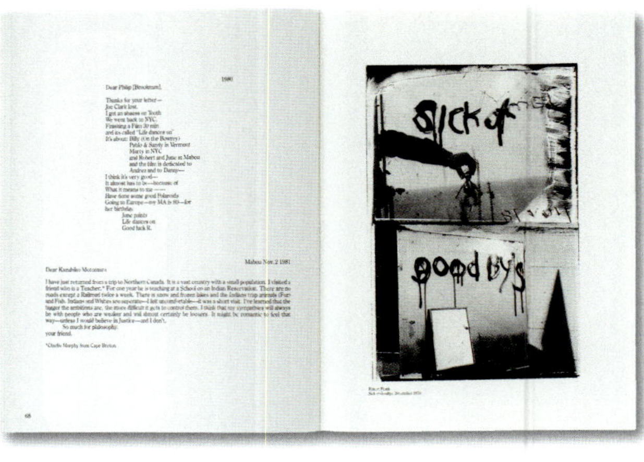
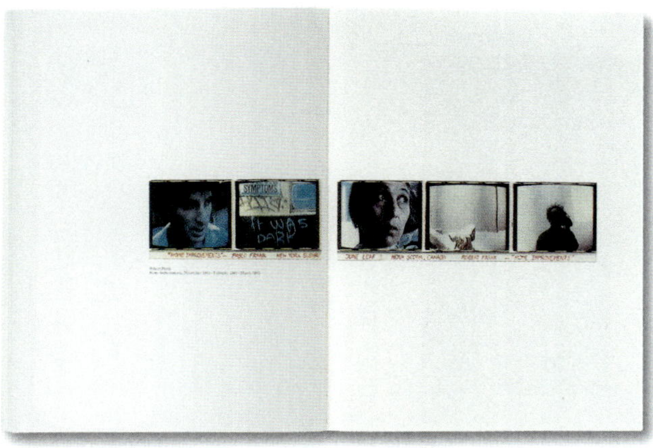
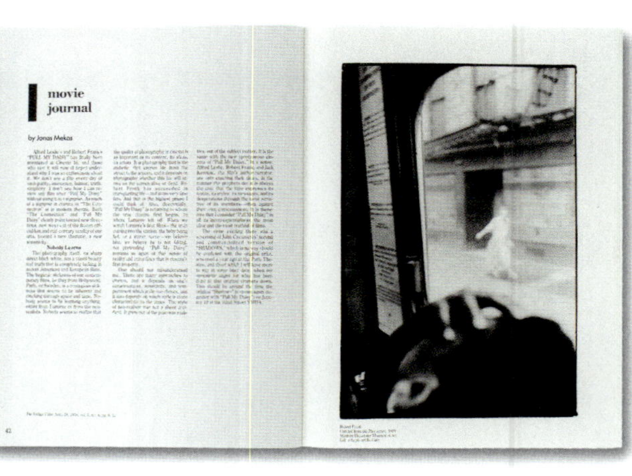
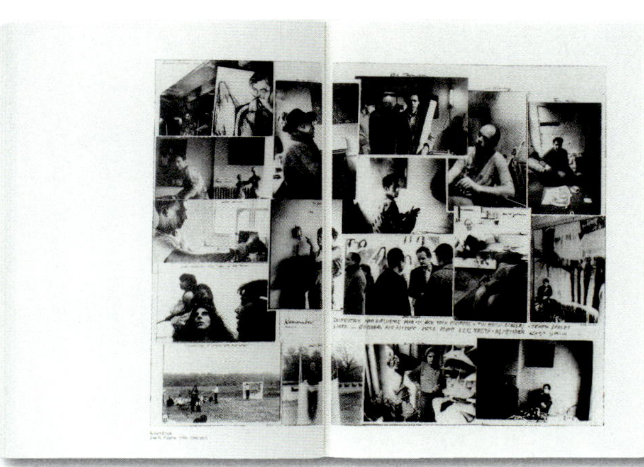
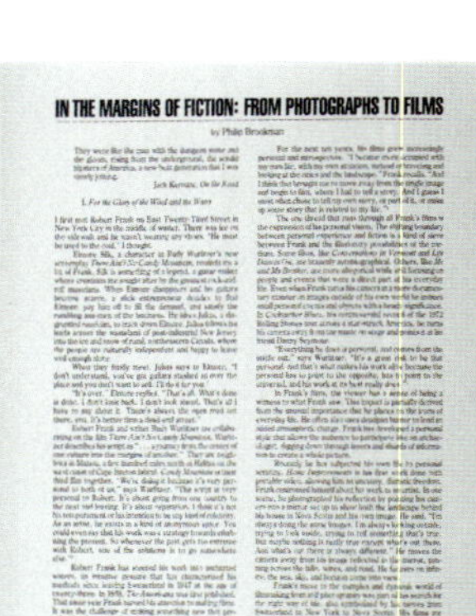
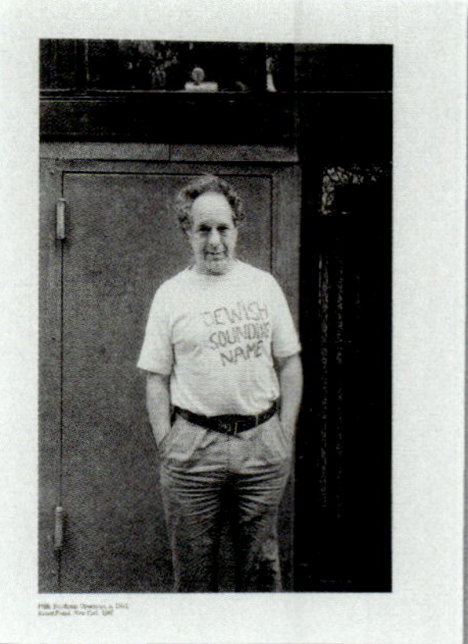

New York to
Nova Scotia

First edition published by the
Museum of Fine Arts, Houston, 1986
First Steidl edition, 2005

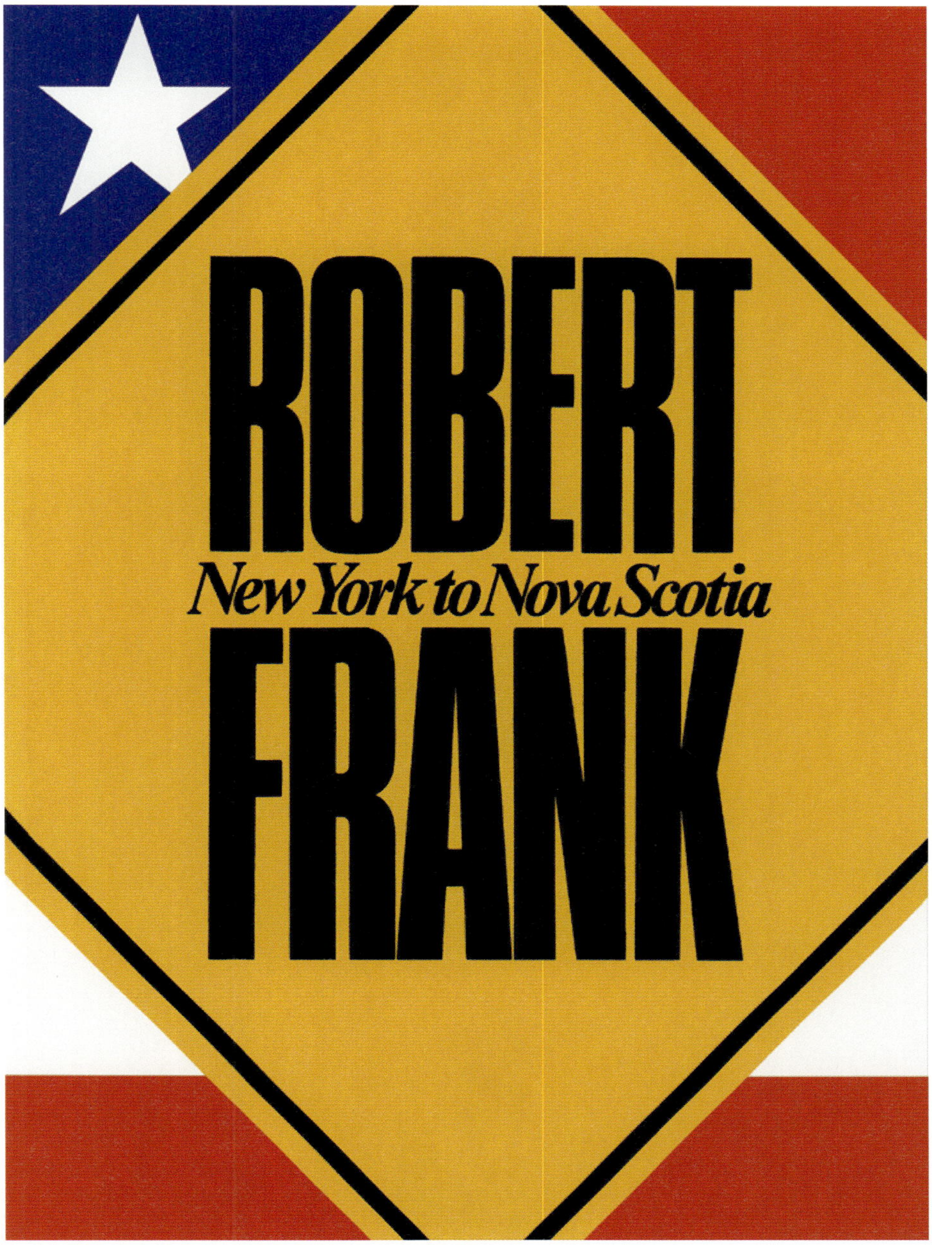

Edited by Anne Wilkes Tucker and
Philip Brookman
Book design by Arthur L. White
Texts by Philip Brookman, Robert
Coles, Hugh Edwards, Walker Evans,
Robert Frank, Allen Ginsberg, John
Hanhardt, Ian Jeffrey, Jack Kerouac,
Peter C. Marzio, Jonas Mekas,
Gotthard Schuh and Anne Wilkes
Tucker
112 pages
8.9 × 11.9 in. / 22.7 × 30.4 cm
1 color and 24 black-and-white
photographs and 8 illustrations
Tritone and four-color-process
Softcover

ISBN 978-3-86521-013-5

New York to Nova Scotia was originally published in 1986 to accompany
a retrospective exhibition of the same
name organized by the Museum of
Fine Arts, Houston, and has long been
out of print. The chronology and personal spirit of Frank's complex career
as a photographer and filmmaker are
evoked with previously unpublished letters, pictures, reviews and essays,
as well as photographs by Frank. Some
of the letters are by Frank; others were
written by photographers and contemporaries, such as W. Eugene Smith,
Louis Faurer, Keith Smith and Gotthard
Schuh, as well as by legendary cura-
tor Hugh Edwards and publisher
Robert Delpire.

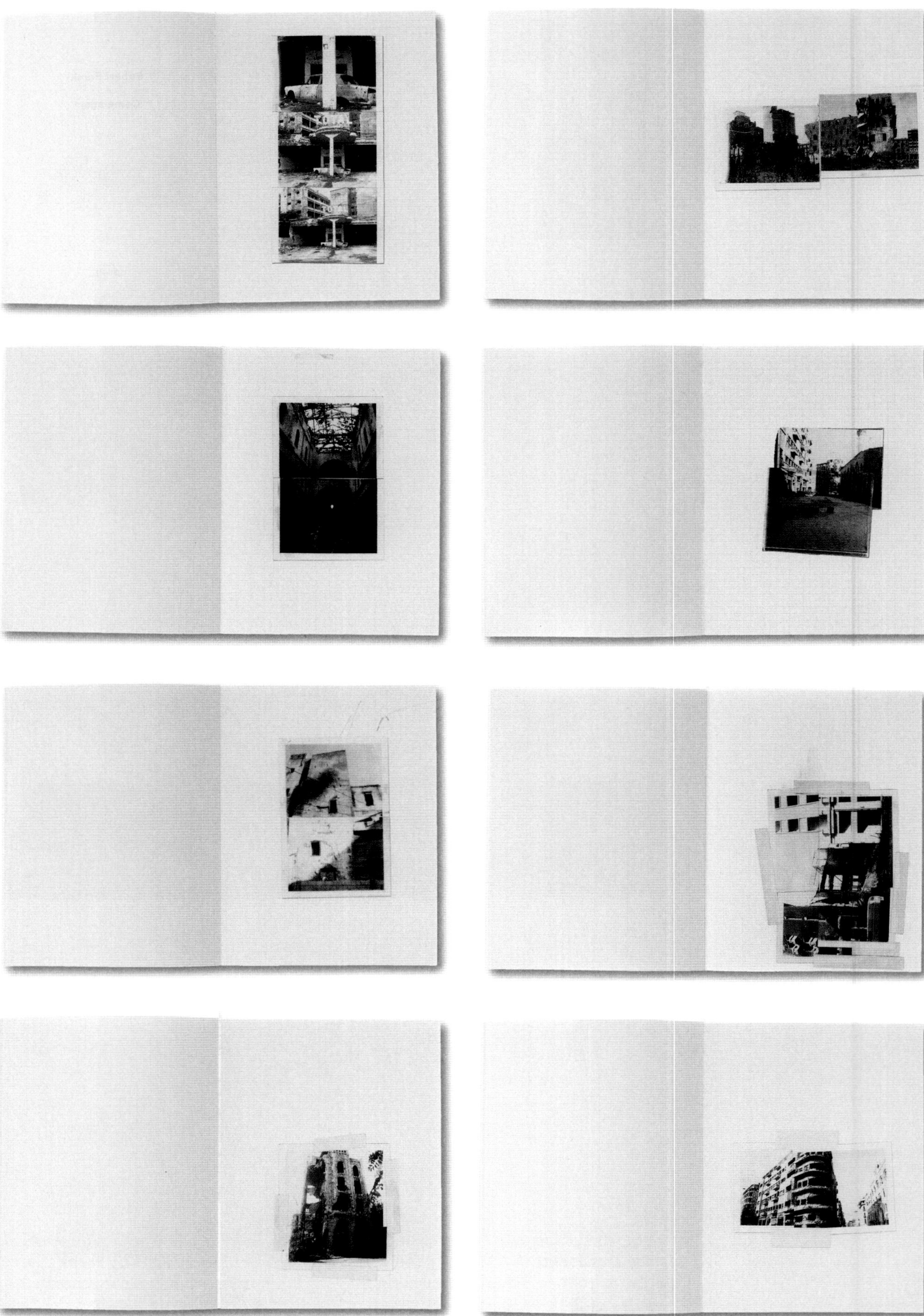

Come Again

Published by Steidl, 2006

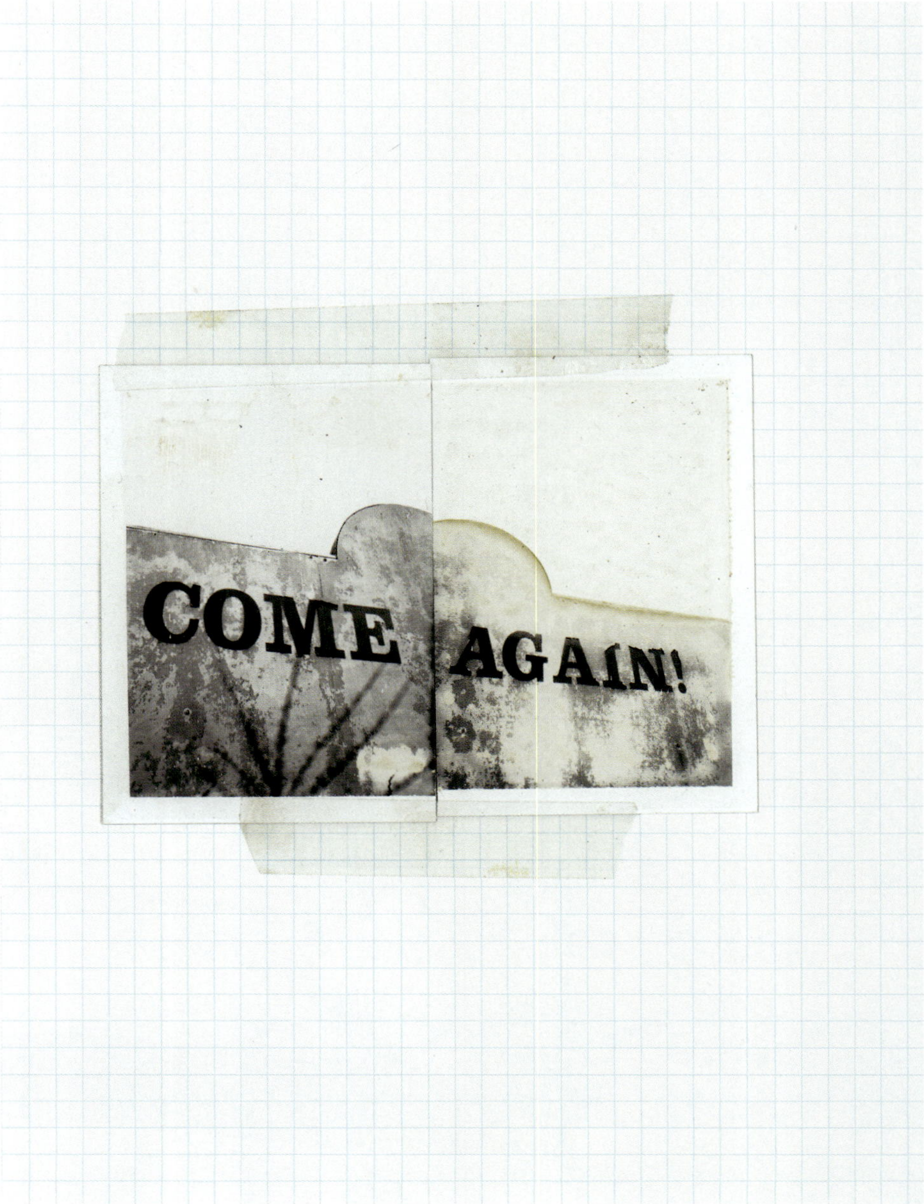

Book design by Robert Frank
and Gerhard Steidl
48 pages
8.4 × 11 in. / 21.5 × 28 cm
24 black-and-white photographs
Four-color-process with a glossy
UV varnish
Open-spine softcover in a sleeve

ISBN 978-3-86521-261-0

In November 1991 Robert Frank was invited to Beirut on a commission to photograph the devastated downtown of the city following the end of the Lebanese civil war (1975–1990). Together with the work of five other photographers, his images were included in the book *Beirut City Centre* (1992). Alongside his work for the commission he made many Polaroids of the city which he stored in his studio on his return home. Many years later Frank reconsidered the images and decided to title the work *Come Again*, but left the sketchbook as he had originally made it in Beirut. *Come Again* is a facsimile reprint of that object.

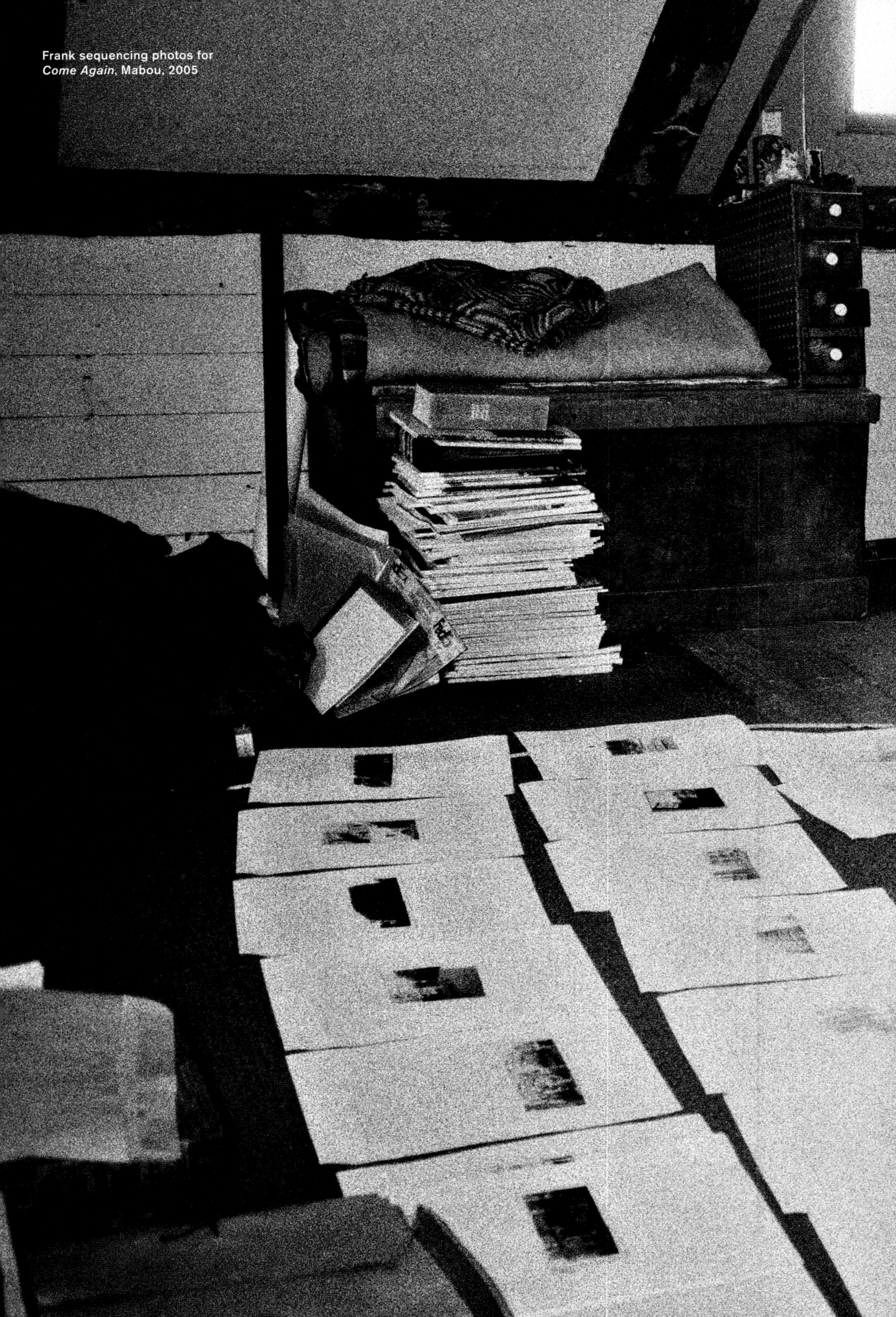

Frank sequencing photos for
Come Again, Mabou, 2005

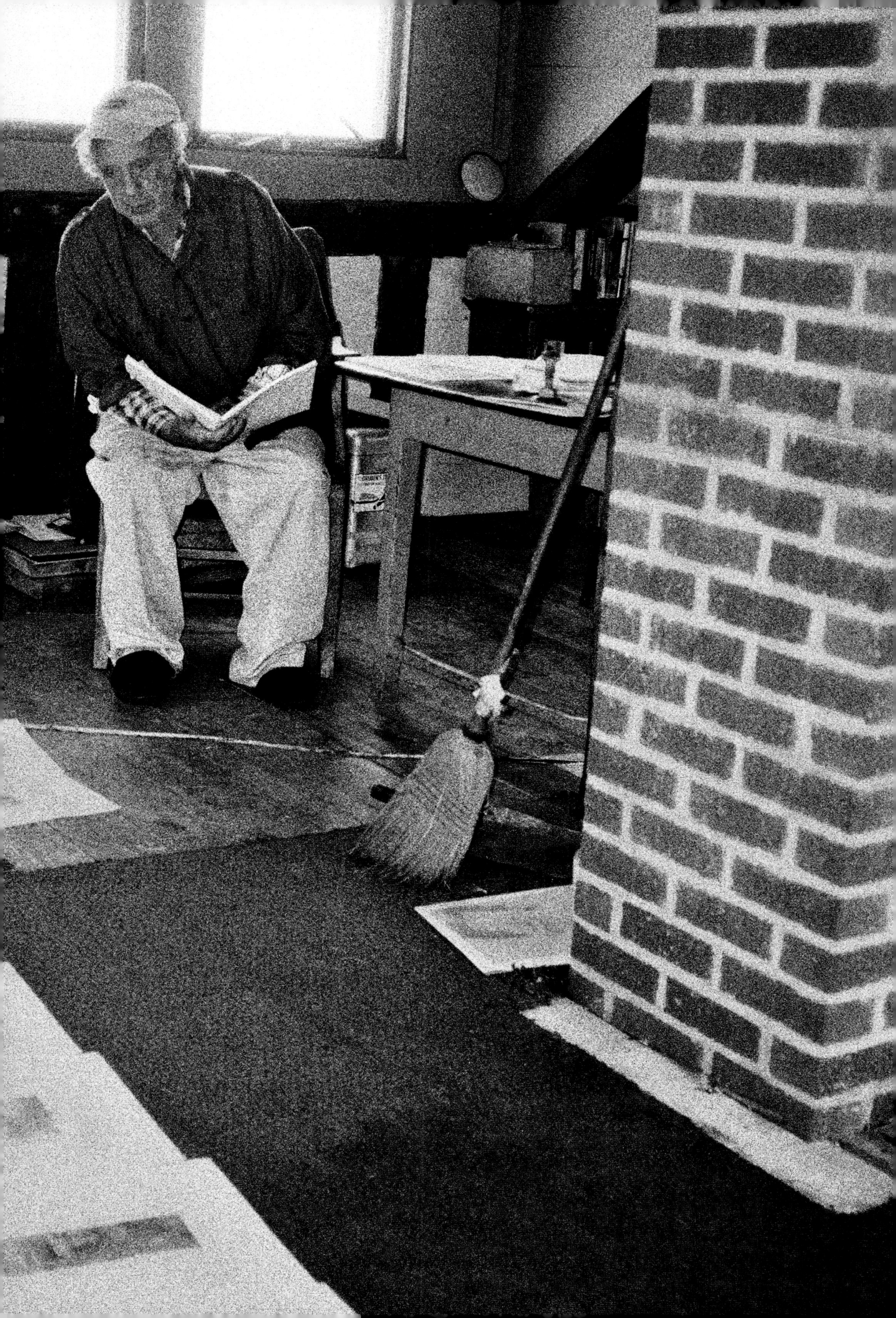

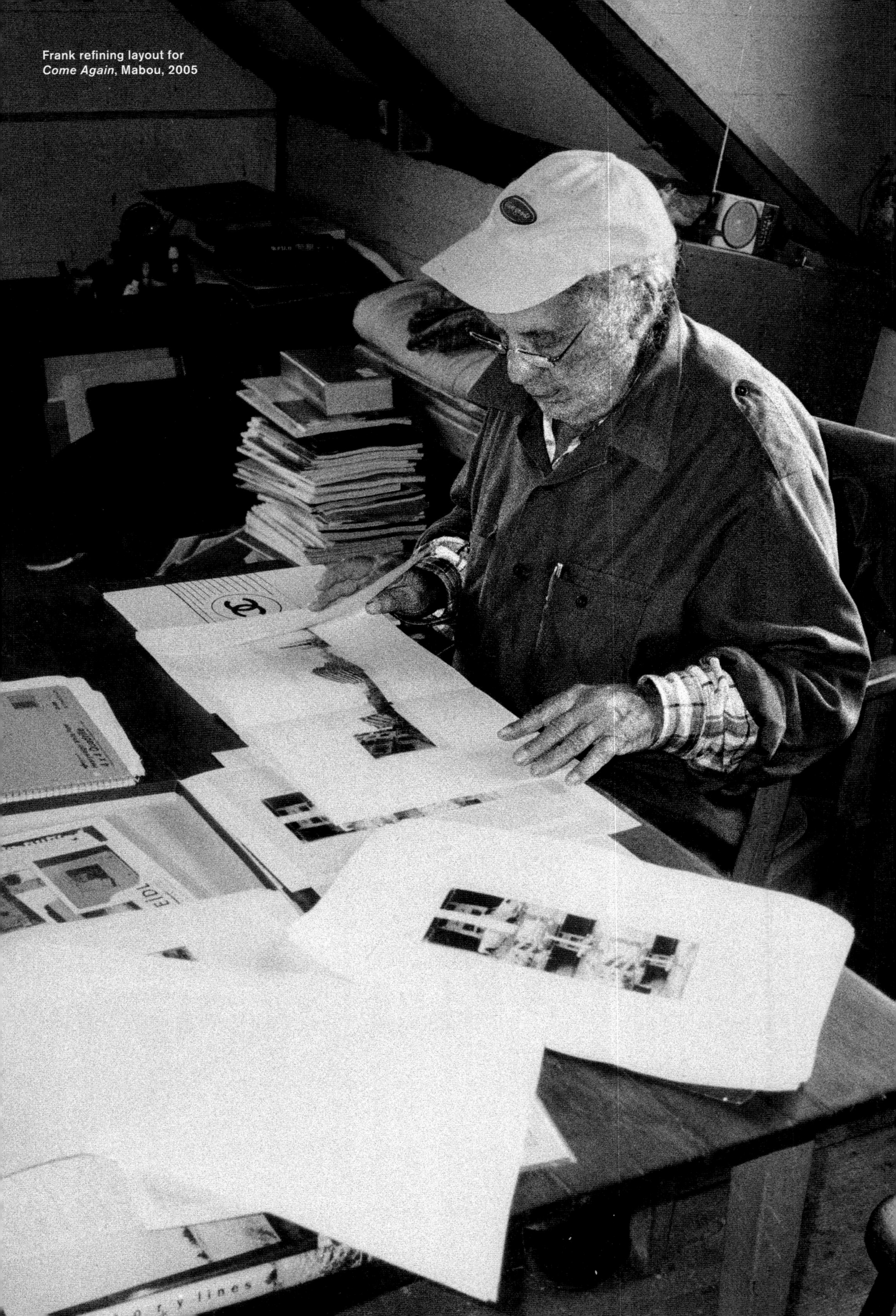

Frank refining layout for
Come Again, Mabou, 2005

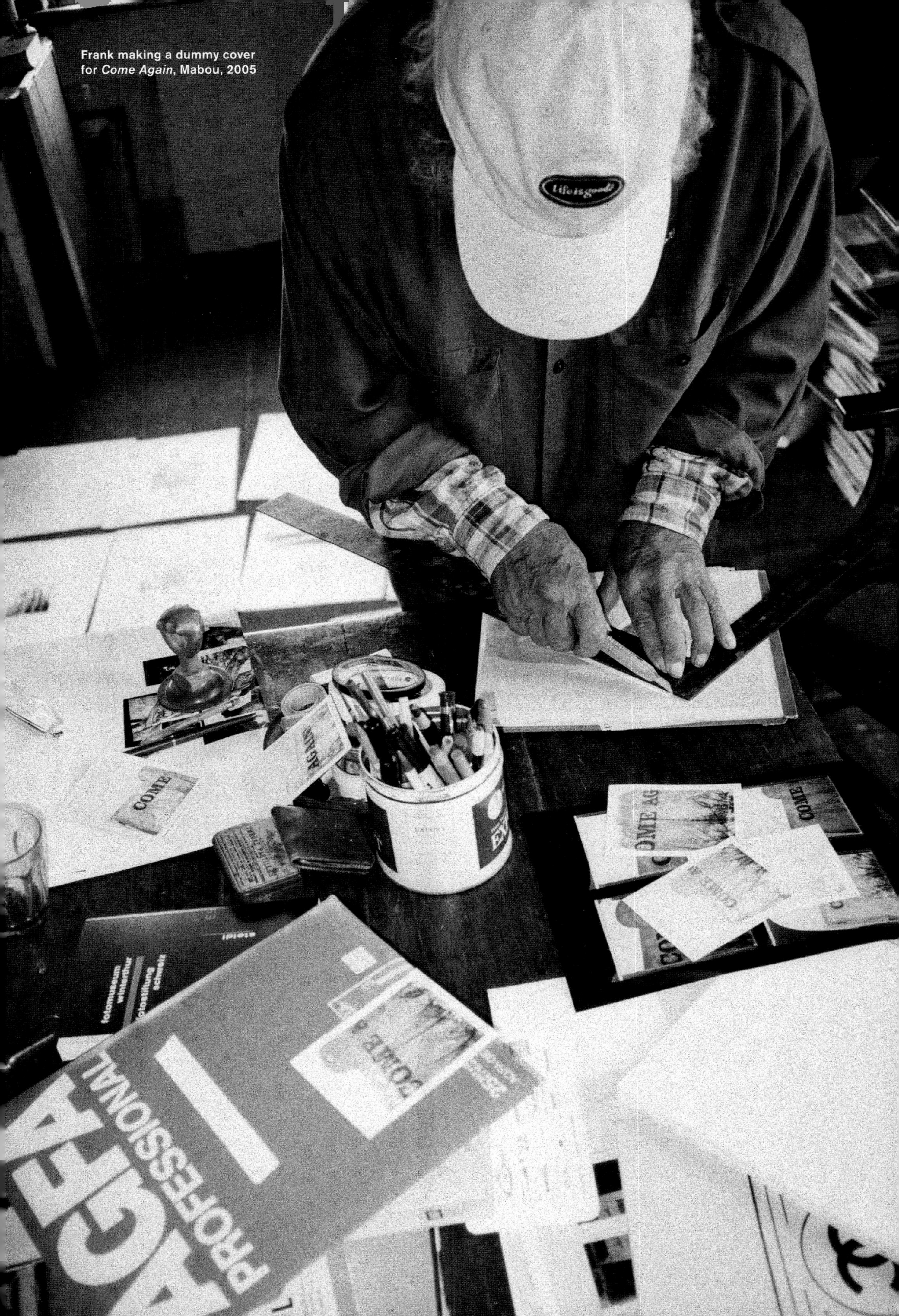

Frank making a dummy cover
for *Come Again*, Mabou, 2005

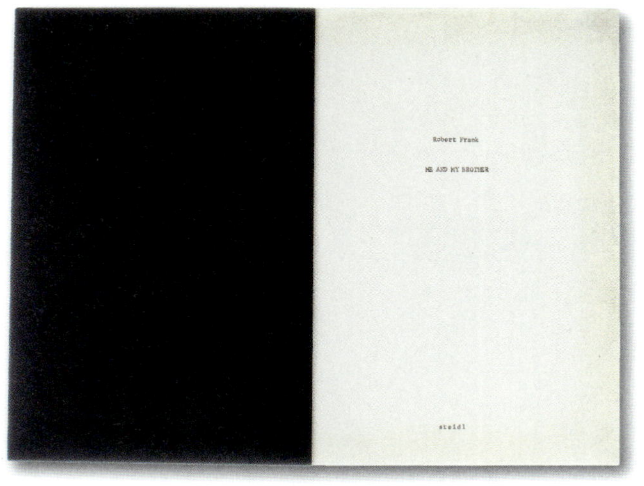
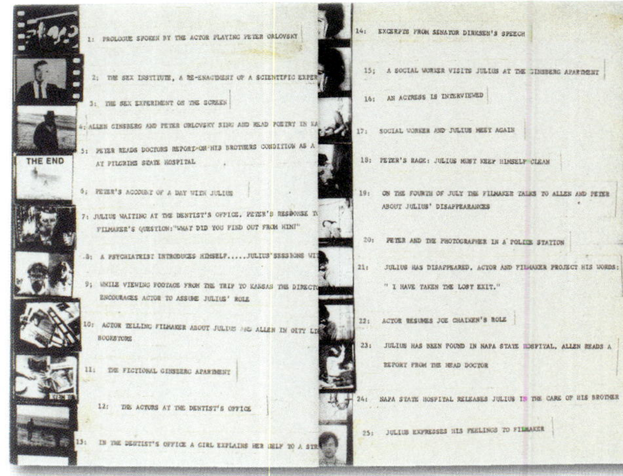

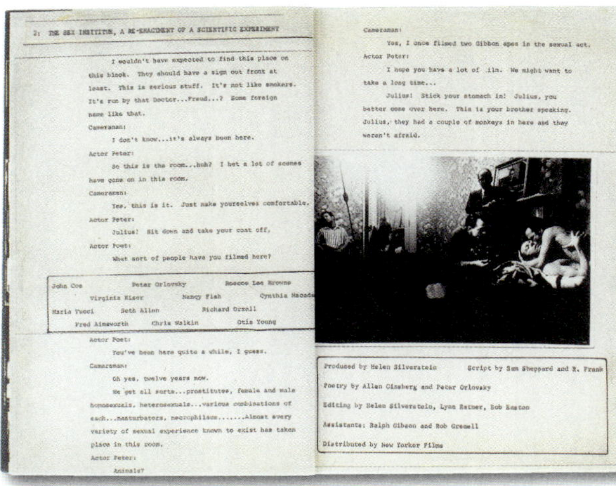
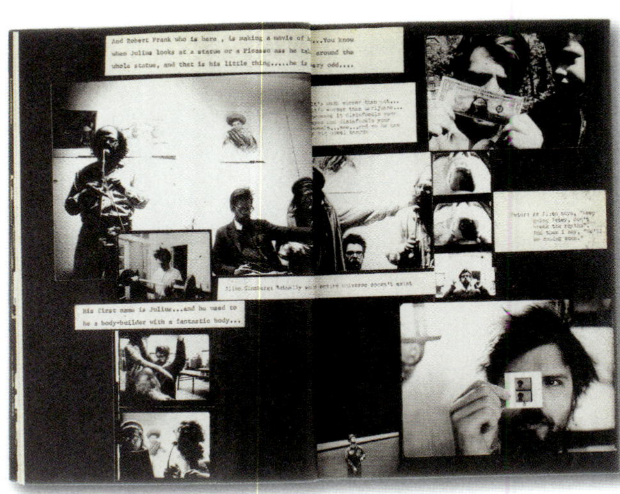

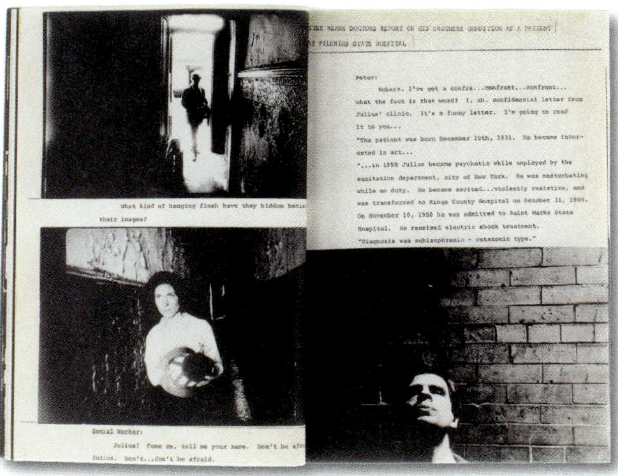
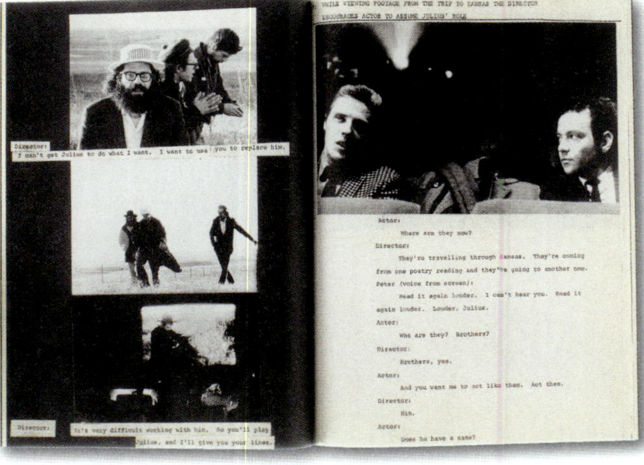

Me and My
Brother

Published by Steidl, 2007

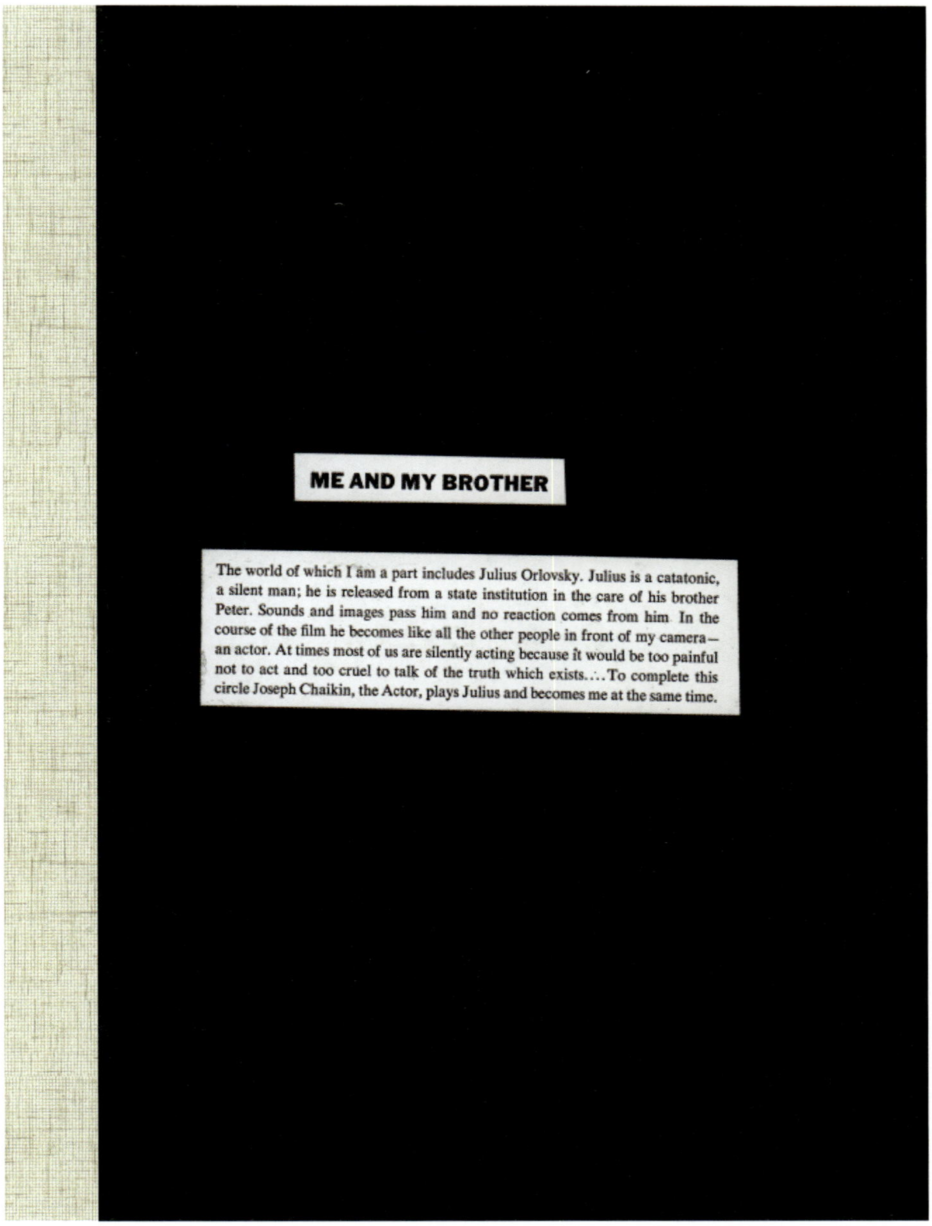

The facsimile reproduction on this page reads:

ME AND MY BROTHER

The world of which I am a part includes Julius Orlovsky. Julius is a catatonic, a silent man; he is released from a state institution in the care of his brother Peter. Sounds and images pass him and no reaction comes from him. In the course of the film he becomes like all the other people in front of my camera— an actor. At times most of us are silently acting because it would be too painful not to act and too cruel to talk of the truth which exists…. To complete this circle Joseph Chaikin, the Actor, plays Julius and becomes me at the same time.

Text by Robert Frank
Book design by Robert Frank
and Gerhard Steidl
72 pages
8.9 × 12 in. / 22.5 × 30.4 cm
37 black-and-white photographs
Four-color process
Half-linen softcover with a DVD

ISBN 978-3-86521-363-1

Me and My Brother was Robert Frank's first feature-length film, completed and first shown in 1968 at the Venice Film Festival. Everything which had defined Frank's art up to that point turns up in this film—the look at America "from the outside," the poetic libertinage of the Beats, the marginal in a central role. It celebrates the return of the poetic essay as assemblage, the affirmation of the underground as a wild cinematic analysis in the form of a collage, and skillfully weaves together opposites, plays counterfeits against the authentic, pornography against poetry, acting against being, Beat cynicism against hippie romanticism, monochrome against colored. The story contains bizarre twists and turns, and appears to be a rather artless film-within-a-film being shown at a rundown movie theatre.

The book is a facsimile of Frank's handmade maquette, combining the film script (typed by him on his mechanical typewriter) and set photographs.

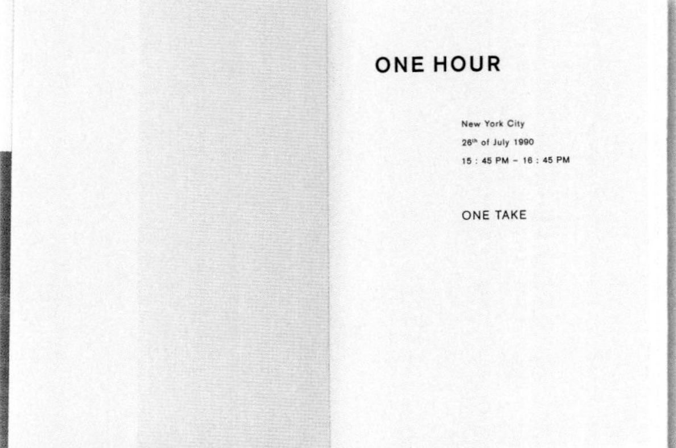

ONE HOUR

New York City
26th of July 1990
15 : 45 PM – 16 : 45 PM

ONE TAKE

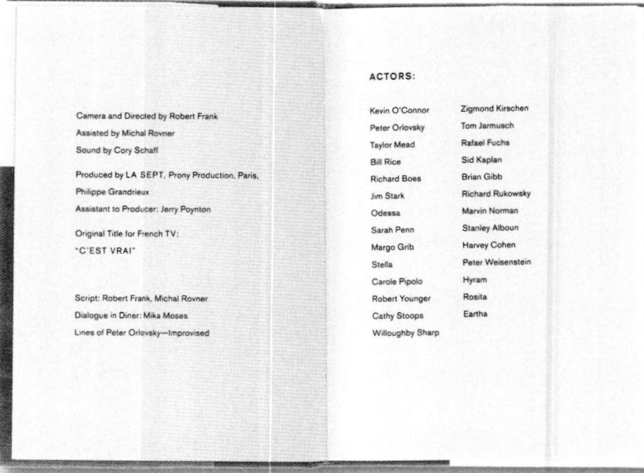

Camera and Directed by Robert Frank
Assisted by Michal Rovner
Sound by Cory Schaff

Produced by LA SEPT, Prony Production, Paris,
Philippe Grandrieux
Assistant to Producer: Jerry Poynton

Original Title for French TV:
"C'EST VRAI"

Script: Robert Frank, Michal Rovner
Dialogue in Diner: Mika Moses
Lines of Peter Orlovsky—Improvised

ACTORS:

Kevin O'Connor	Zigmond Kirschen
Peter Orlovsky	Tom Jarmusch
Taylor Mead	Rafael Fuchs
Bill Rice	Sid Kaplan
Richard Boes	Brian Gibb
Jim Stark	Richard Rukowsky
Odessa	Marvin Norman
Sarah Penn	Stanley Alboun
Margo Grib	Harvey Cohen
Stella	Peter Weisenstein
Carole Pipolo	Hyram
Robert Younger	Rosita
Cathy Stoops	Eartha
Willoughby Sharp	

Huh ? Yeah, maybe.

We've got plenty of time, don't worry about it.

After that I've got to go to Brooklyn.

Got to finish up a job there.

Where in Brooklyn ?

Park Slope.

It's last minute stuff. Giving me all this shit about it.

A couple of months.

But you know, it's winding down. It's almost done.

Is it still raining ?

No it stopped.

Oh, thank God.

Hey, you call Ian yet ?

No, I haven't. I suppose I should call him. I hope he's out of town.

My brother's like that too, you know. Poor guy.

Can't deal with anything. Nothing. He hands all his crap over to me.

Well, that's how it is sometimes.

I don't know.

16 / 17

Dressler and him are in the car crash and his, and they finally end up with him sticking his head out of the fuckin' roof.

Let her walk by Jerry. She's got another three months to live.

Zodiac.

Oh look at this.

Zodiac ? Is he the zodiac ? It should be what, what is his zodiac ? He's a scorpio.

Scorpio.

Look at this.

We must find the Zodiac Killer.

We're all good detectives, right ?

Oh.

Ah.

What are you guys doing ? Hey man !

We got time.

We've got all day Jerry.

That line. On The Waterfront.

Marlon Brando. I could have been somebody, I could have been a contender instead of a bum, which is what you are. A bum !

I see you tomorrow.

20 / 21

And Larry and I, we really talk about you often.

Yeah, and about Mary too, of course. Well you know. I really understand. You know, she is very ambitious.

I understand now, I see you and I'm talking to you. You know artists, they are ambitious. You too !

Well, I guess you try to forget. Oh, it's all so sad. You know, she only knows herself.

Well, why should I say that ? Right ?

You know, I guess, you can't live in the present. Right ?

Vicious hindsight. Don't try to correct what you can't change. One day at a time. One day at a time.

Well. Oh, you know what. I heard that Regina moved to Florence. You know, my older daughter Laura, she lives in Florence now too. She loves it.

Am I right ? Huh ? Yeah ! OK. Well.

Listen, say hi to June for me, OK. Are you still together ?

Oh, thats's good.

It was really nice to see you. Alright. You always did love corners.

24 / 25

Because that's fine with me. That's not why I'm here. I see things differently. I don't.

Let's go. Where's Peter. You want to call Peter ?

I'll call Peter.

PETER !

Peter. Peter.

Let him come for the ride.

Whatever you want.

Yeah !

I think, you know…

I've got a car, I've got a car with the door open.

Me and him will go in there and make like…

No, no.

I've got a car with the…

No, no. No room.

No. No. Fine. OK, OK. No problem

Take care Willoughby.

I've got a fuckin' car right there with the door open. Let's play a little scene with it.

Hold it.

38 / 39

Really ?

Yeah.

Fuck this.

They're gems, very controlled.

I didn't mean to interrupt your sixty minutes.

Well you know what…do sweetheart, you're handsome. You have to start looking at the girls. How old are you ?

Oh, I'm old enough.

That's right, you're sixteen. You like girls or boys ? You've got a lot of choices in New York City.

Do you think, do you think it's bad for a boy to say no on his first date ?

Give 'em a haircut. Got to get some dimples here on your chin. You'll be in the business.

You want to go see…We'll go see something.

Sure.

Look in the paper.

Just drop us off, Jerry.

Let's go to that fuckin' car. Do you know how to do the wires ?

Yeah.

74 / 75

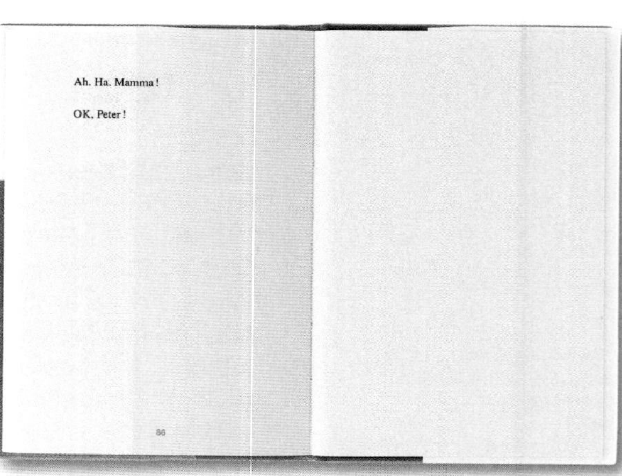

Ah. Ha. Mamma !

OK, Peter !

86

First published by Hanuman
Books, 1992
First Steidl edition, 2007

ONE HOUR

Robert Frank

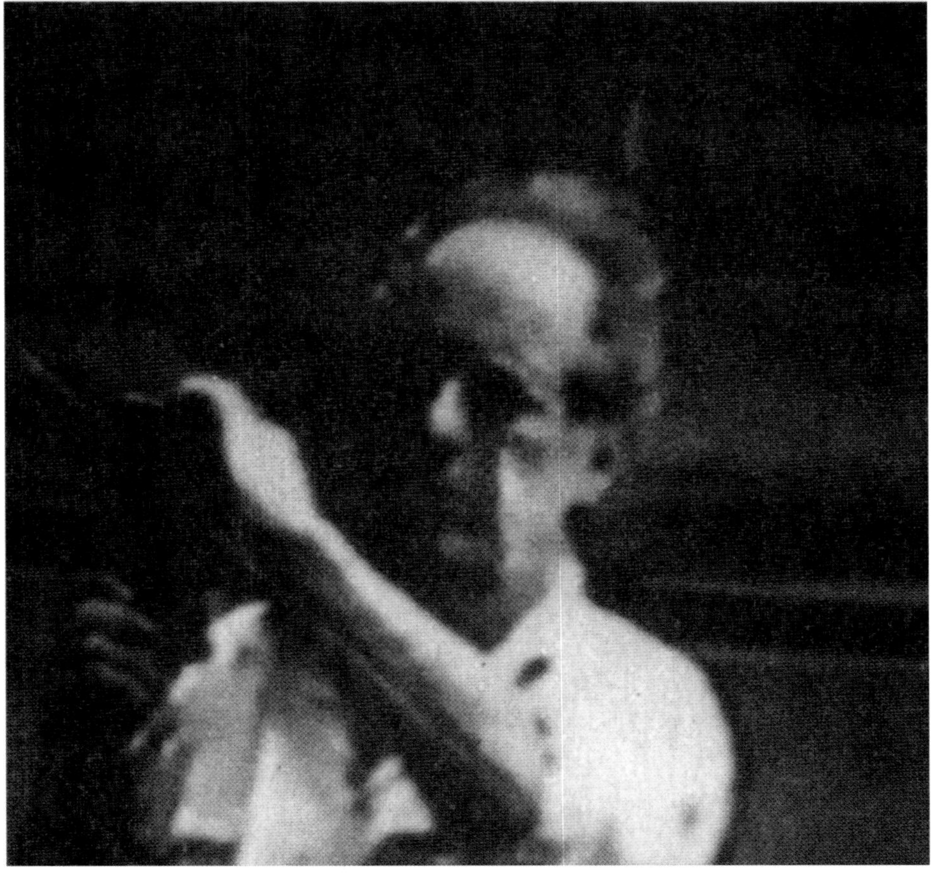

Robert Frank's *One Hour* is a single take of Frank and actor Kevin O'Connor either walking or riding in the back of a mini-van through a few blocks on Manhattan's Lower East Side. Shot between 3:45 and 4:45 pm on 26 July 1990, the film presents the curious experience of eavesdropping involuntarily on strangers. It appears to be a document of a journey but is also a kind of stream of consciousness retracing the same patterns and spaces.

This book is a reprint of a little-known Frank publication first issued by Hanuman Books in 1992, a tiny book comprising mainly a transcription of the dialogue heard but also two pages of credits: half a dozen production or crew workers and 27 actors. Unravelling the apparent documentary nature of the film, there is also an acknowledgement that the film has a script (by Frank and his assistant Michal Rovner), that a conversation heard in a diner is written by Mika Moses, and that Peter Orlovsky's lines (intercepted by Frank roughly halfway through the hour, in front of the Angelika Cinema on Houston Street) are "total improvisation."

Text by Robert Frank
and Michal Rovner
Book design by Robert Frank
and Gerhard Steidl
88 pages
4.1 × 5.9 in. / 10.5 × 15 cm
12 black-and-white film stills
Duotone
Clothbound hardcover with
dust jacket

ISBN 978-3-86521-364-8

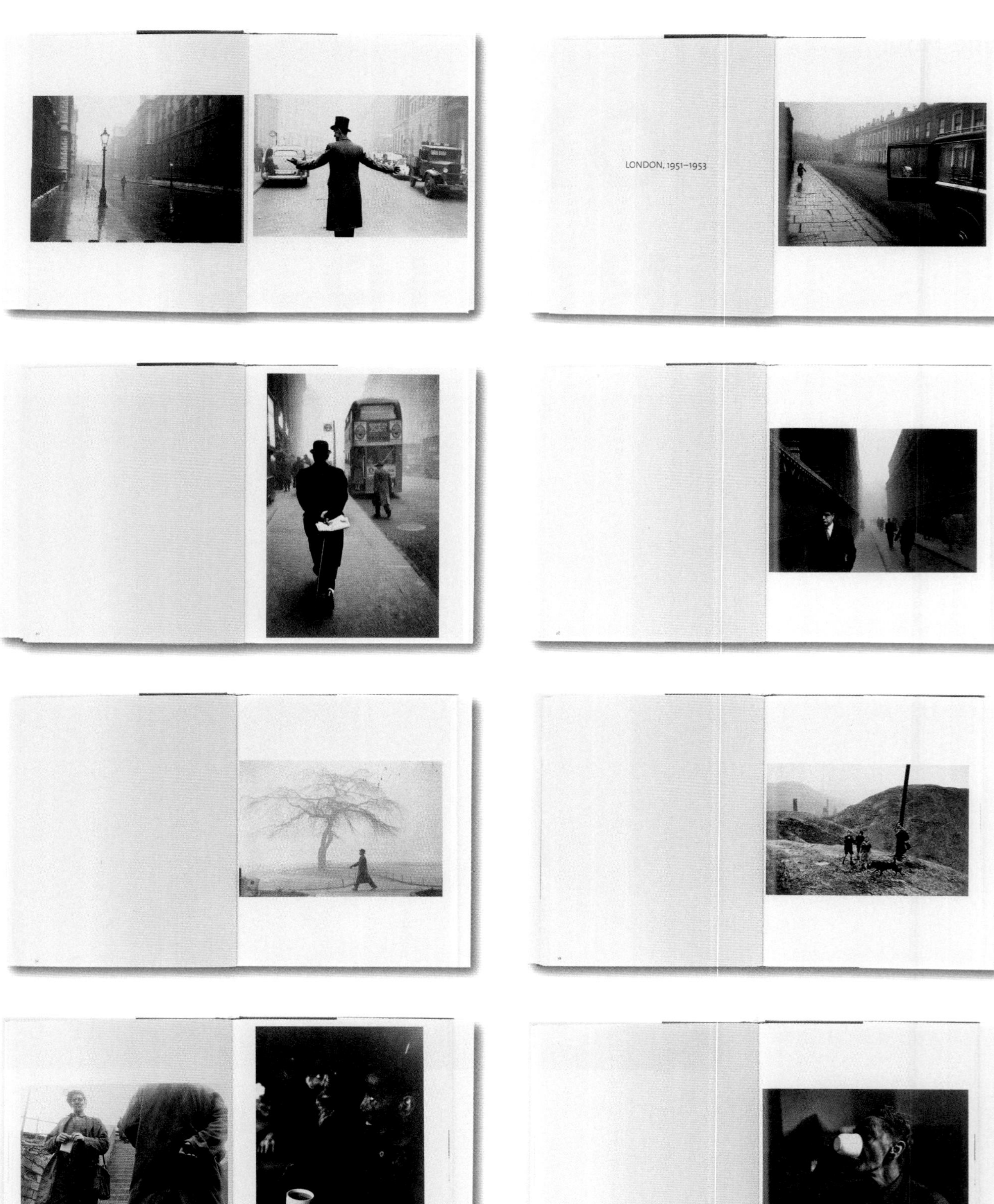

LONDON, 1951–1953

First edition published by
Scalo, 2003
First Steidl edition, 2007

LONDON/WALES

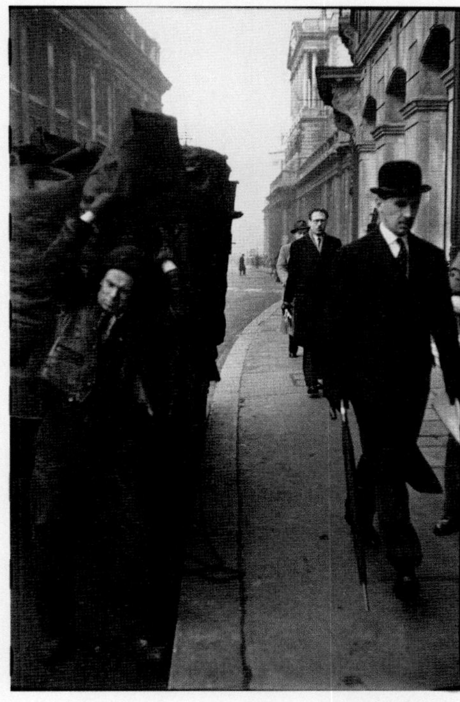

ROBERT FRANK

STEIDL

Edited by Philip Brookman
Text by Richard Llewellyn
Book design by Robert Frank,
Wyndham Boulter and
Gerhard Steidl
128 pages
7.6 × 9.4 in. / 19.3 × 24 cm
67 black-and-white photographs
Tritone
Clothbound hardcover with
dust jacket

ISBN: 978-3-86521-362-4

London/Wales brings together two distinct bodies of work to reveal a new understanding of Robert Frank's contribution to the history of photography. Juxtaposing the world of money and the world of work in post-war England, Frank photographed London bankers, workers and children, and Welsh coal miners and their families. These images poetically evoke relationships between the classes during a time of change in Britain. Setting a significant documentary precedent for Frank's best-known work, *The Americans*, *London/Wales* demonstrates the artist's early interest in social commentary, the narrative potential of photographic sequencing and his innovative use of the expressionistic qualities of the medium.

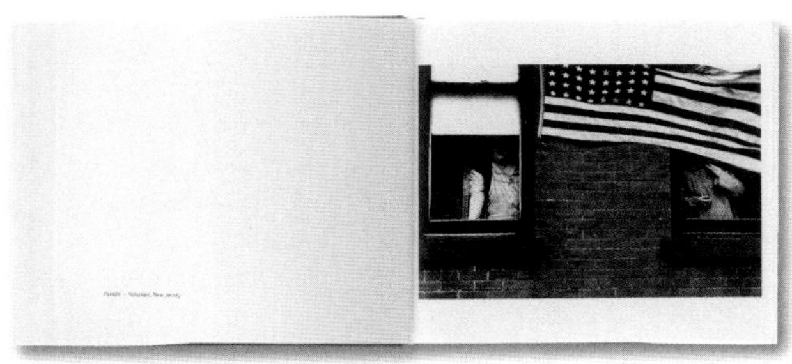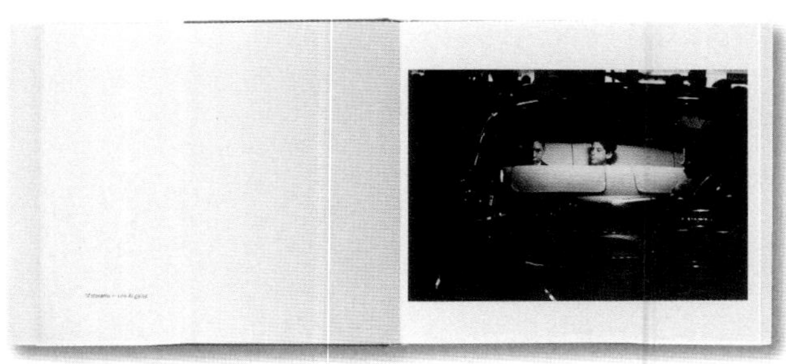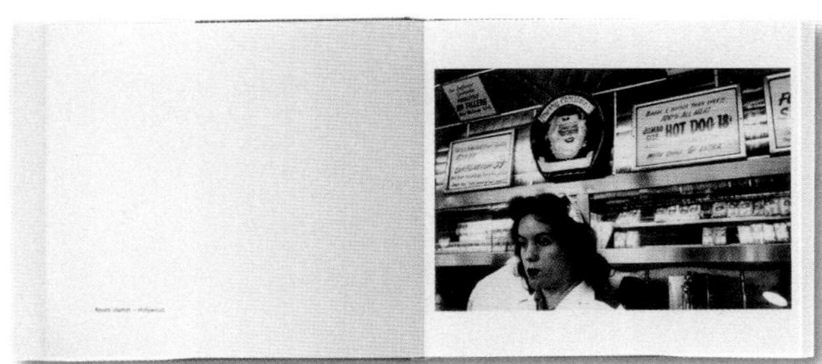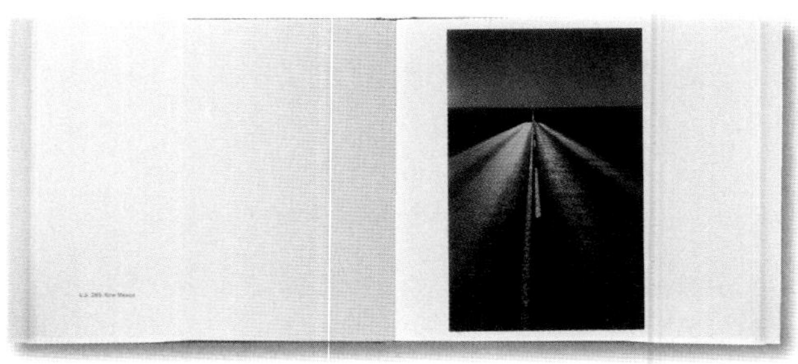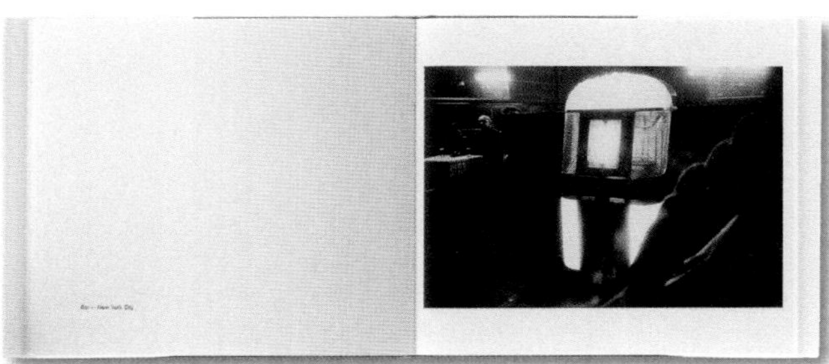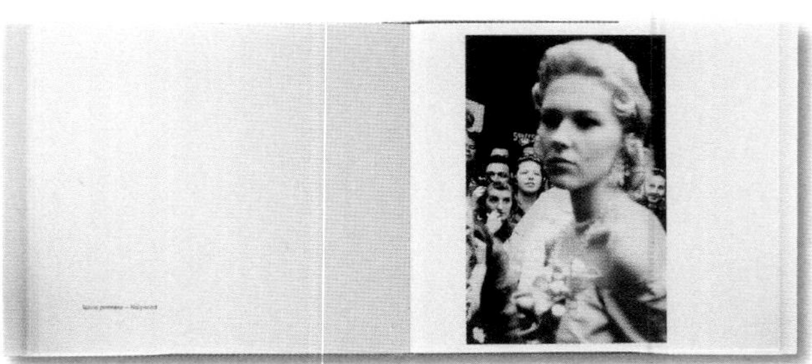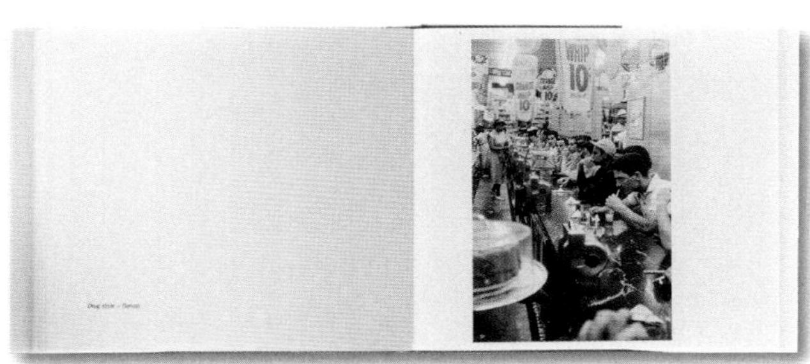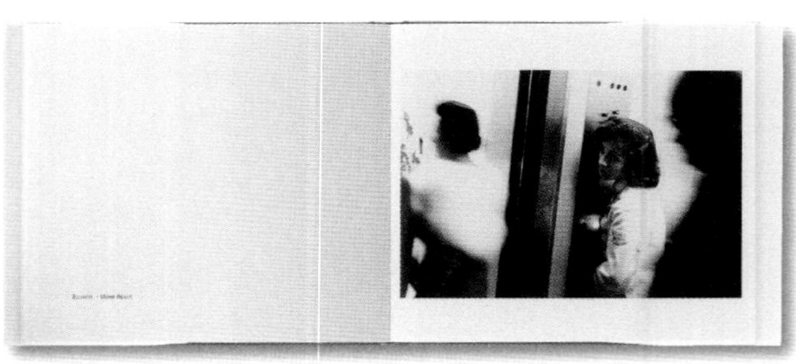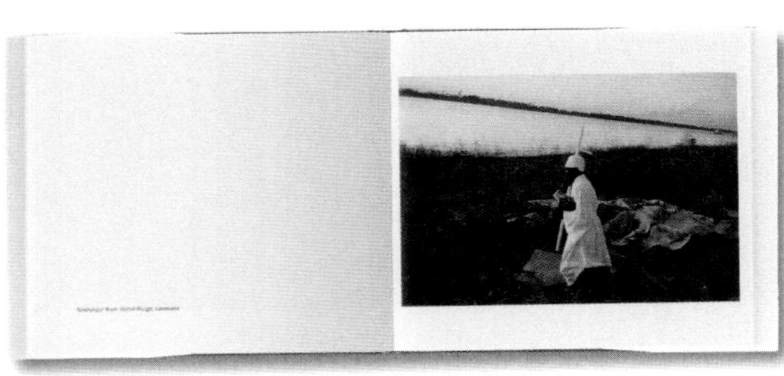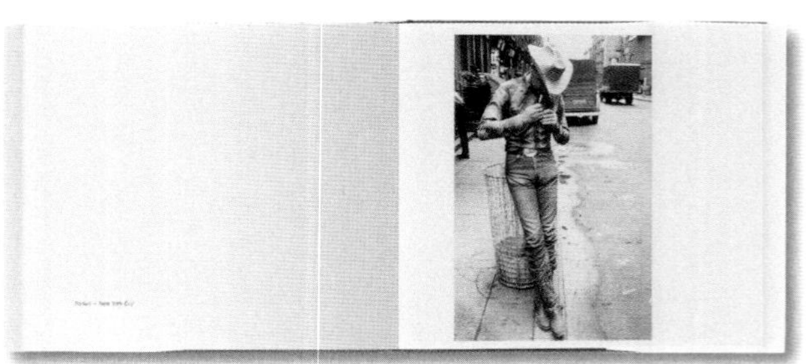

The Americans

First edition published by
Robert Delpire, 1958
First Steidl edition, 2008

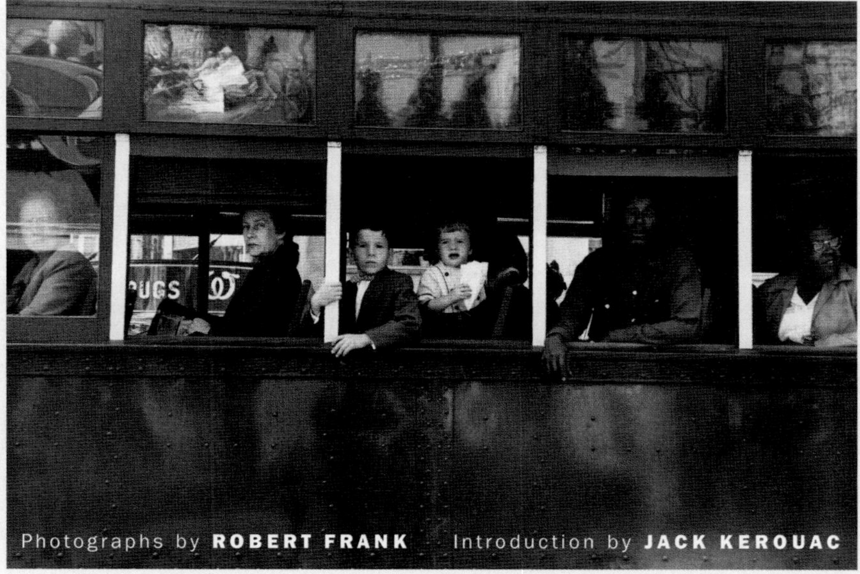

First edition published on 15 May 1958 by Robert Delpire
First Steidl edition published on 15 May 2008

Designed and printed with Robert Frank in Göttingen, July 2007
Book launch with Robert Frank at the Walter Reade Theater, Lincoln Center,
New York City, 15 May 2008

Introduction by Jack Kerouac
Book design by Robert Frank,
Gerhard Steidl and Claas Möller
180 pages
8.2 × 7.2 in. / 20.9 × 18.4 cm
83 black-and-white photographs
Tritone
Clothbound hardcover with
dust jacket

ISBN 978-3-86521-584-0

First published in France in 1958, then in the United States in 1959, Robert Frank's *The Americans* changed the course of twentieth-century photography. In 83 photographs, Frank looked beneath the surface of American life to reveal a people plagued by racism, ill-served by their politicians, and rendered numb by a rapidly expanding culture of consumption. Yet he also found novel areas of beauty in simple, overlooked corners of American life. And it was not just Frank's subject matter—cars, jukeboxes and even the road itself—that redefined the icons of America; it was also his seemingly intuitive, immediate, off-kilter style, as well as his method of brilliantly linking his photographs together thematically, conceptually, formally and linguistically, that made *The Americans* so innovative. More of an ode or a poem than a literal document, the book is as powerful and provocative today as it was more than 60 years ago.

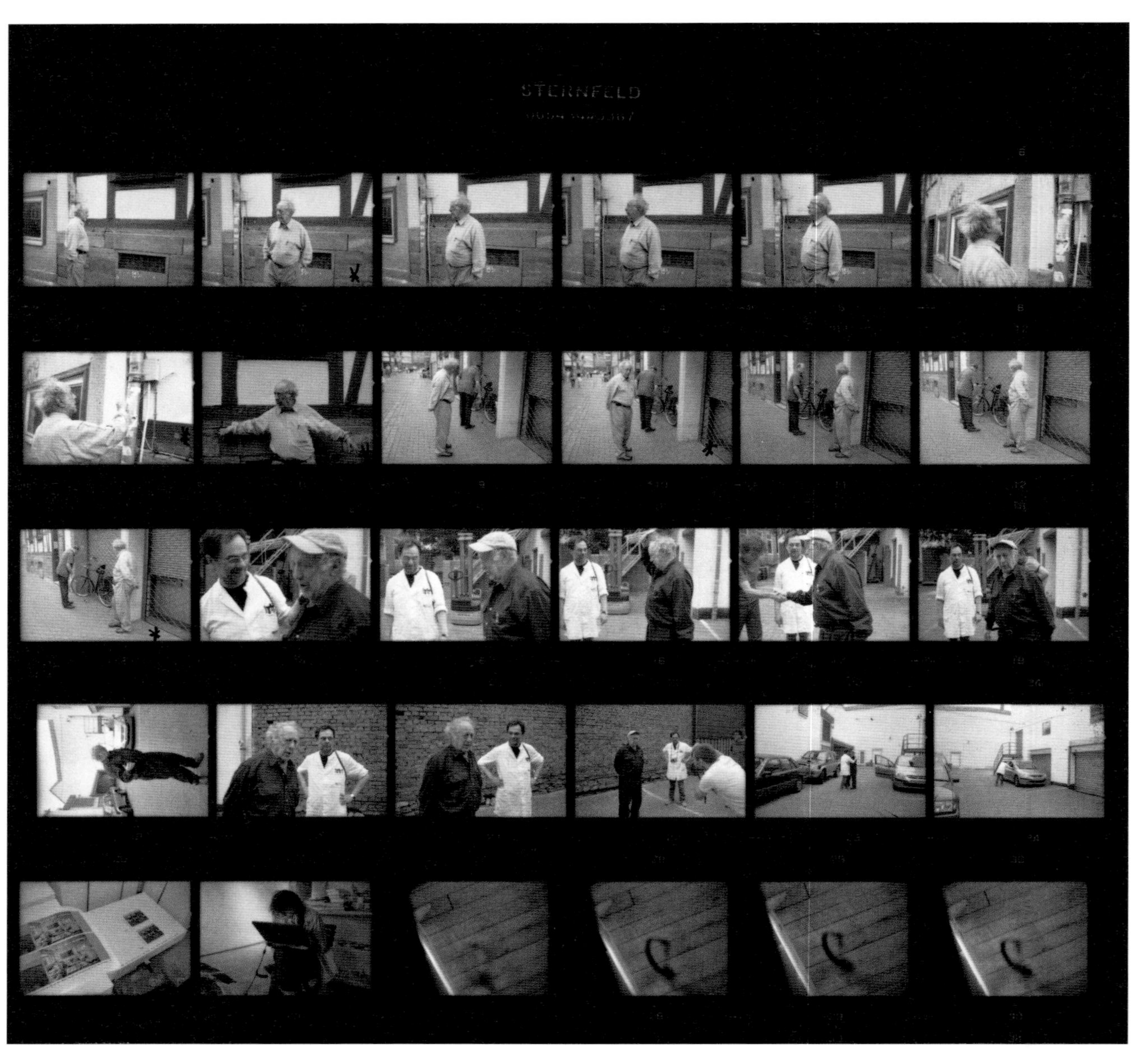

Photos by Joel Sternfeld

Robert Frank in Göttingen

Joel Sternfeld

Robert Frank and I must have made an interesting sight that warm July afternoon on Düstere Strasse. We resemble each other but he is older than I so no matter what we were up to we could have made sense as father/son.

And in one important sense we were: when I was becoming a photographer in the late 1960s, his book *The Americans* was already a landmark—that's much too weak a word but what other word for a body of work that changed the course of the river of photography in a way that it could never take the old course again.

I would look at it before I went to sleep and in the morning I would reach for it like a smoker reaches for a cigarette. I needed to see it again. The country was so bleak in those sooty pages, each one an artifact ripped from the landscape and brought straight to the bindery. Frank had found a way to give form to the formless lives that went unmilled in America.

Two years before I encountered his book I had taken my first cross-country trip—three of us in an immense gold drive-away car that needed to be delivered to its owner in Los Angeles. We sailed from the East Coast to the West in less than three days—one of us sleeping across the back seat, one up front trying to stay awake with the driver.

It was December. We angled into New Mexico as the sun was going down and pulled into an A&W Root Beer stand. The dirt parking lot seemlessly joined the desert and the desert night. A cold wind came up as the sky turned black—the same cold wind every traveller without a room feels as the sun goes down.

A wrapper from someone's fries blew into the desert in a moment of Americanized infinity. Frank's book reminded me of that moment. And now here he was on Düstere Strasse in Göttingen and here I was beside him. Inside at Steidl *The Americans* was being printed—the reproductions were to be as close a match as possible to the Delpire edition that had set photography on its fat ear when it first come out in 1958.

A very tired, 83-year-old Robert had come to Germany from Switzerland to supervise the printing— presumably the final edition of the book. I thought about the apocryphal tale of the young Robert Frank kicking in the swinging doors of a cowboy bar in Nevada, hollering in "You mother fuckers," before taking the picture and then running like hell. No running now but the mischief was still in his smile.

He had come to Europe to receivie a prize in Spain but the real agenda was to try out the Switzerland of his childhood as a place to come for his final days. Surprisingly, it had failed in that regard. Robert wanted to go home—to America.

"You can't go home again. Home hasn't changed, you have." How many others in a borderless world would face this dilemma?

The printing had been going on for two days and it was going well. Steidl was utterly himself—unshaved and getting things done. Robert was being especially sweet to everyone despite his exhaustion. I noted the care he took when he autographed books for Steidl staffers who timidly came up the stairs to the library. He took sincere interest in the work of other artists who waited in the library like it was a pitcher's bull pen—we were ready for the nod that would allow us to go downstairs to press.

He especially remarked a postcard that was being printed for Tacita Dean. It was of an olive tree in Spain that she had designated to be the one beneath which García Lorca and Salvador Dalí had conducted their suspected tryst. Robert pronounced it beautiful and asked her to sign one for him—for his postcard collection.

Earlier in the afternoon I had gone downstairs to watch as Robert corrected his sheets. I was taken aback by the precision of his memory of the Delpire edition. From the comments Robert was making I could see it wasn't just the first edition he was remembering—it was the moments out there, in 1950s America and how they had looked. The realization gave me a chill.

Here we were in the garden outside the press—I don't know if it was for the flat light, or for the pleasure of a summer day but Gerhard had placed an easel out the doors. Robert was trying to "open up" a person you can barely see behind the passengers in the windows of the streetcar in New Orleans. A bird came up and pulled my eye on as I tried to think about the provenance of the moment.

Every few minutes he would speak of his exhaustion and of his desire to go back to his hotel room but when a sheet came out his comments were acute—a lion always sleeps with one eye open. Later in the afternoon I went down to the carless street—none of the streets in Göttingen permit automobile traffic— and saw Robert wandering in the middle of the bricked roadway. He was ambling. I went up and asked him where he was going. He said he was going to hail a taxi and go to his hotel. One of us made a joke about escaping—Gerhard likes to picture himself as sheriff.

I told Robert I didn't think there were any taxis to be hailed but if he would just come back inside and

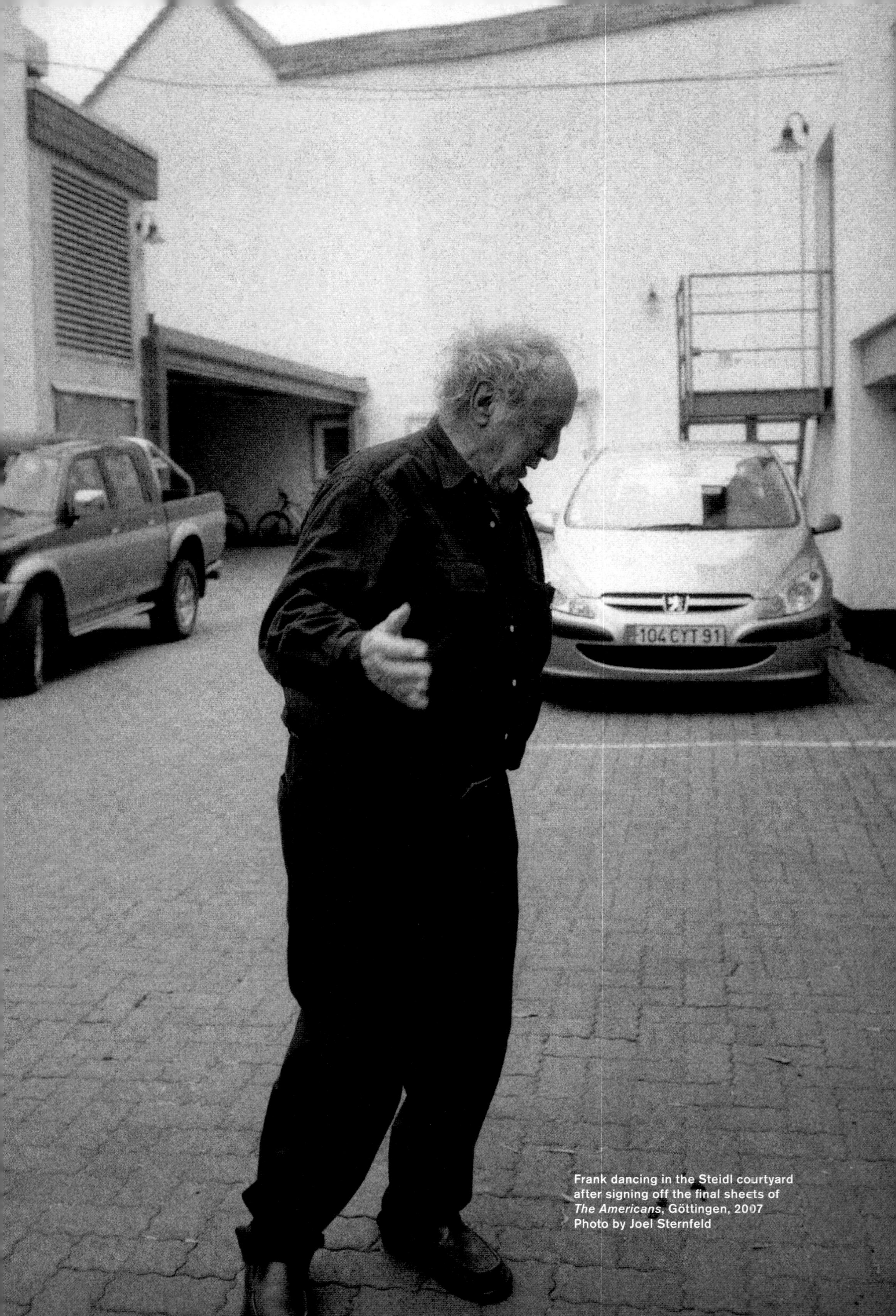

Frank dancing in the Steidl courtyard after signing off the final sheets of *The Americans*, Göttingen, 2007
Photo by Joel Sternfeld

finish the last form a taxi could be called. Robert made no direct response but he seemed glad of my company and he suggested that we go into the antique store across the street so he could look for postcards. (For a guy thinking about the end of things he was certainly keen about keeping his postcard collection up. Perhaps this was in the daytime: in the middle of the night there are no postcards to be collected.)

I went into *Kitsch & Kunst* with him—now I was AWOL too. There weren't really any postcards but there were some albums of family trips—journeys long ago cornered into sheets and now for sale.

As Robert leafed through them I went back to Gerhard to appraise him of the situation. He asked me to bring Robert back to press: the men were waiting, the press was idle.

What followed next is difficult to describe. Robert came out into the street and for the next hour he did a sort of performance. It was a dance of remembrance and reluctance with commentary by the performer interspersed.

In the grey July afternoon he appeared to be weightless—a trained bear doing slow-motion pirouettes. He butohed toward the door to Steidl but the closer he got to it, the more interesting everything outside it became. He would turn in the street, float up to a rain gutter and tap it. "I just wanted to see if it's made out of lead," he explained as his eyes followed it up to the roof. He went back into the street, pirouetted again and came back to the wall as his arms floated up a ledge which was at shoulder height. Did he know that he looked like Christ on the cross as he spoke of his desire to return to America? Of what a good country it was—it had given him his chance.

I thought about "home" and its power; and about an idea I have that many of the great practitioners photograph their "home" landscapes. I had excluded Frank from my thesis because America was not his home—but now it was. A phrase, "I did not choose this place but now I am of it," came to mind.

The moment was broken by a man with a sort of flame thrower. It was a blow torch with a three-foot extension tube off the nozzle so that a small flame could be used to burn weeds coming up through cracks in the sidewalk. Robert feigned fascination and he began questioning the operator of the device— soon others joined the conversation and there was a general discussion of the topic of weed killing with Robert a full discussant.

Eventually, after various other petite excursions Robert went in and finished the form. The next day he was in the library in a dark blue shirt and a baseball cap—shaved and with his hair combed he looked 25 years younger. His body had solidity—he was flying home from Frankfurt that afternoon.

Seeing him so transformed helped me to understand what I had witnessed the day before. Of course he was avoiding—why would he want to come in and say goodbye to the work of his youth? Didn't he tell us he was "sick of goodbyes"? Of course it was exhausting—putting a closure on the work that had defined a life must be. Which one of us would willingly approve a "final edition"?

I remembered these words, "There is no strange behavior, it's just that some behavior requires more understanding than other behavior."

Faced with no good choices Robert Frank did a dance.

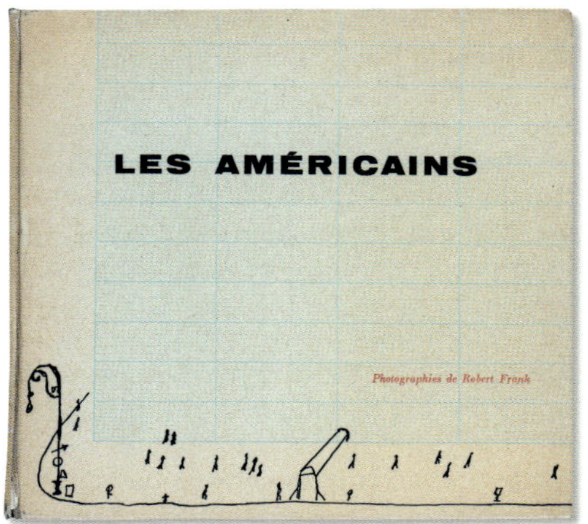

Delpire, 1958

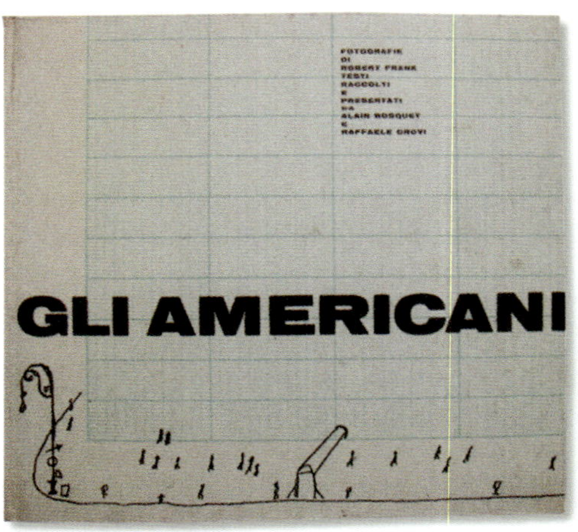

Il Saggiatore, 1959

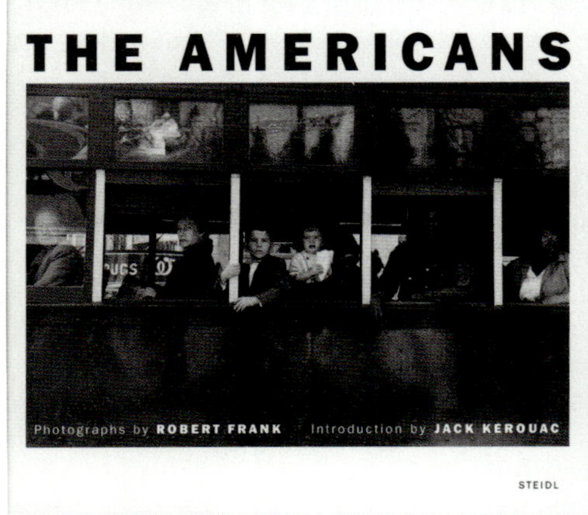

Grove Press, 1959

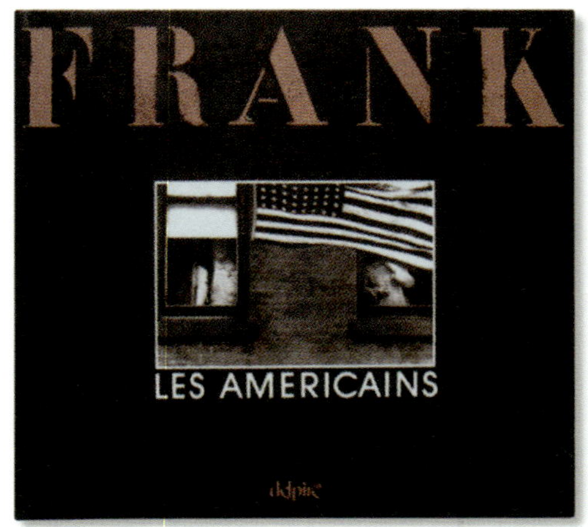

Delpire, 1993

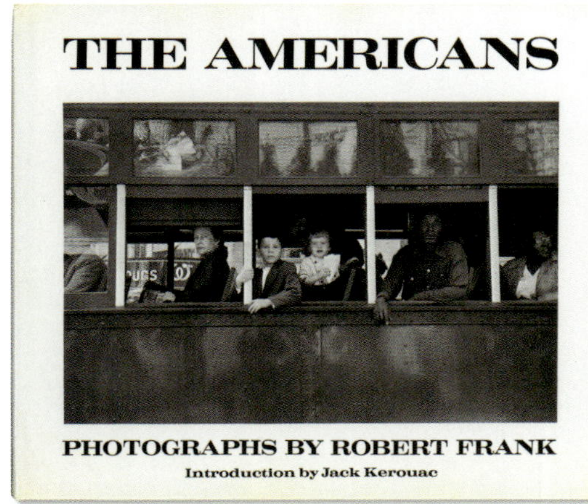

Aperture, 1969

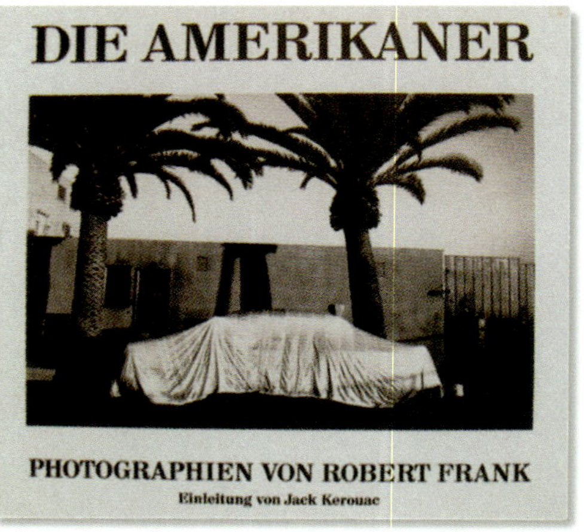

Christian, 1986

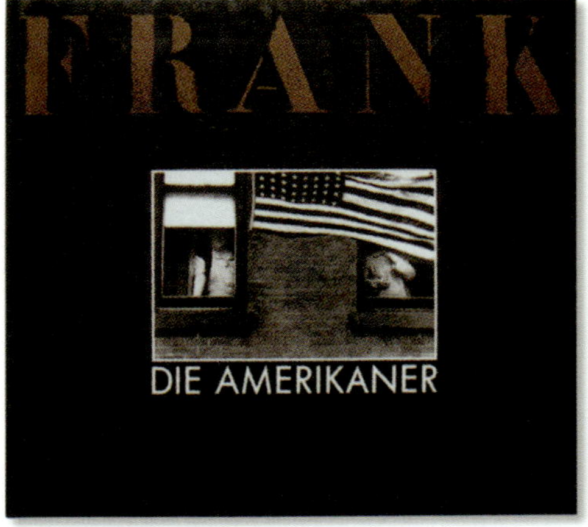

Scalo, 1993

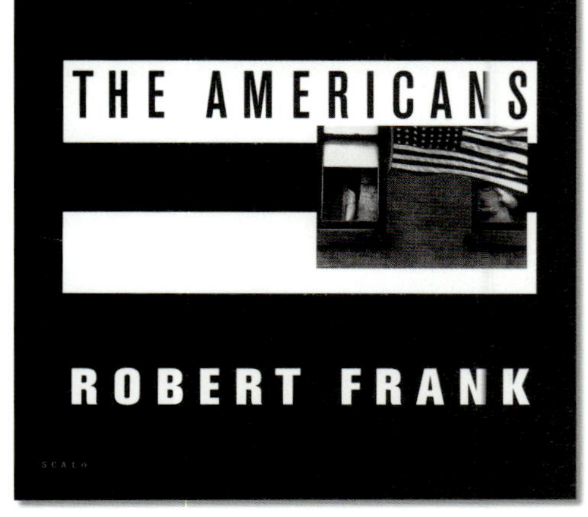

Scalo, 2000

A Short Publishing History of *The Americans*

Monte Packham

Robert Frank's *The Americans* was first published on 15 May 1958 by Robert Delpire in Paris. It featured 83 of Frank's photographs taken in America in 1955 and 1956, accompanied by writings in French on American political and social history selected by Alain Bosquet. Delpire's *Les Américains* formed part of the "Encyclopédie essentielle" series, which presented foreign countries to a French audience. Each of Frank's photographs in this edition is placed on a right-hand page, with the texts on the left-hand pages.

The first English edition of *The Americans* was published in 1959 by Grove Press in New York. It showed the same photographs as the Delpire edition, however a text by Jack Kerouac replaced the French writings. The book begins with Kerouac's introduction, followed by Frank's photographs in the same sequence as the Delpire edition. On the left-hand pages are short captions which describe the respective locations on the right-hand pages.

Since 1959 *The Americans* has been reprinted by different publishers, in multiple languages and formats; Frank had varying influence on these editions and some were printed without his approval.

In July 2007 the Steidl edition of *The Americans* was printed. Frank was involved in every step of its design and production. The 83 photographs were scanned at Steidl from vintage prints in Frank's collection, which confirmed that many images in past editions were crops of the originals. For the new book Frank reviewed each composition and in numerous cases enlarged the crops of the Delpire and Grove Press editions.

The Steidl edition also reproduces two photographs printed from negatives different to those used in the 1958 and 1959 books. These images depict the same two subjects ("Metropolitan Life Insurance Building—New York City" and "Assembly Line—Detroit"), but from slightly different perspectives.

Kerouac's text and Frank's captions remain unaltered from the Grove Press edition, the typography however was redesigned. As well as revising the book's design, Frank chose the paper, endpapers and book linen. He opted for a thread-stitched book, and conceived a new dust jacket made from the same paper as in the book (Xantur 170 g from Scheufelen), sealing it with a simple varnish. Frank personally oversaw the tritone printing on 18 July 2007, inspecting and approving each sheet on Steidl's press in Göttingen.

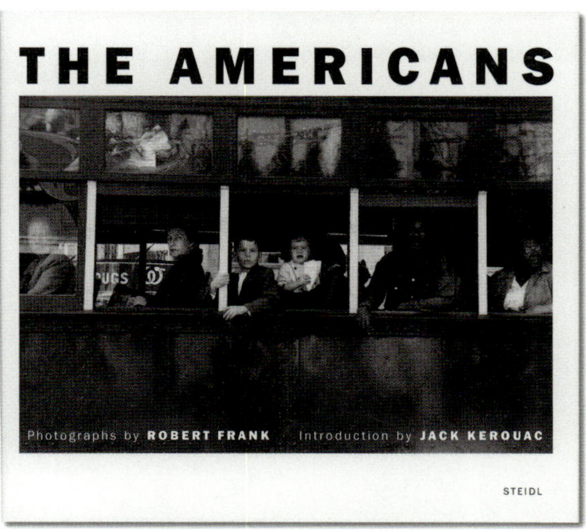

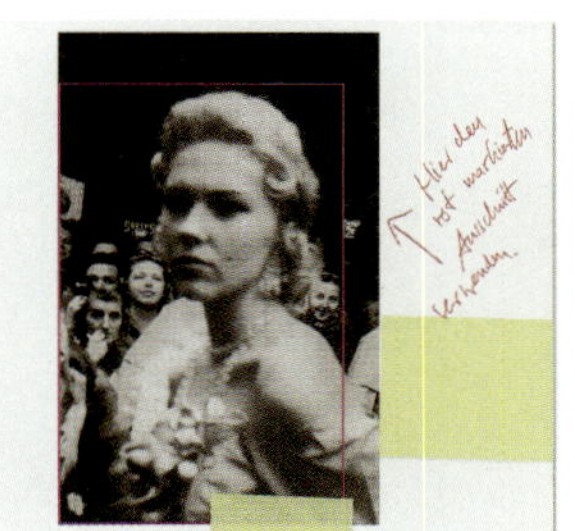
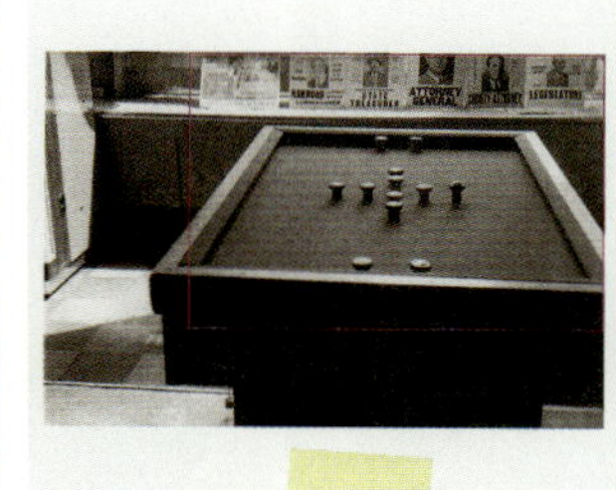
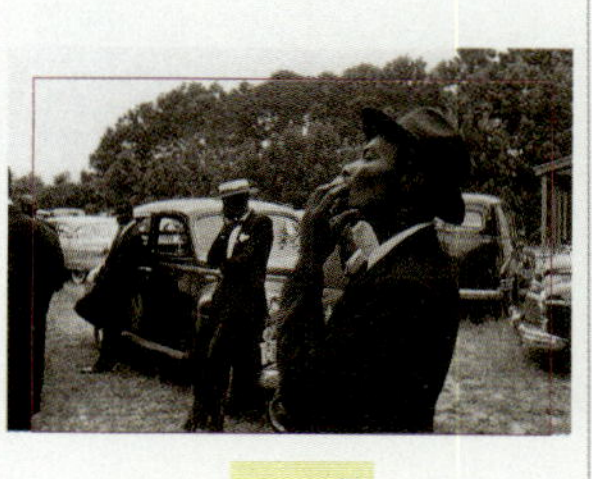
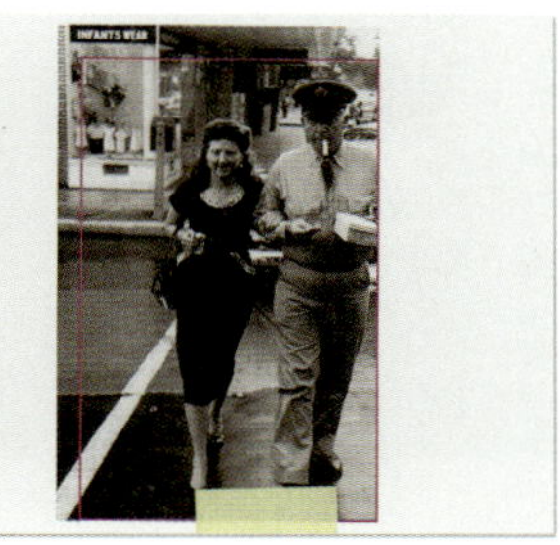
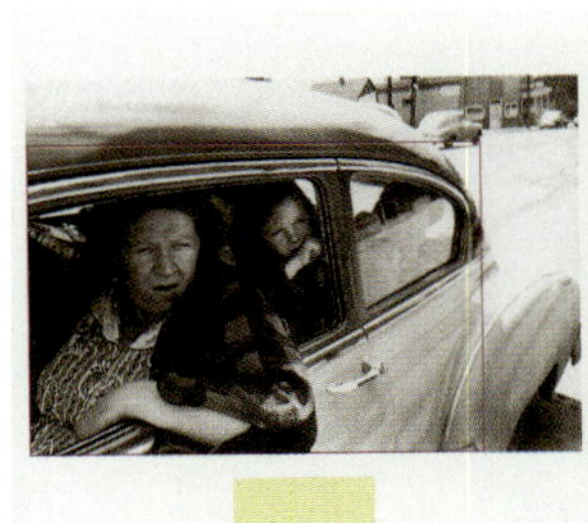
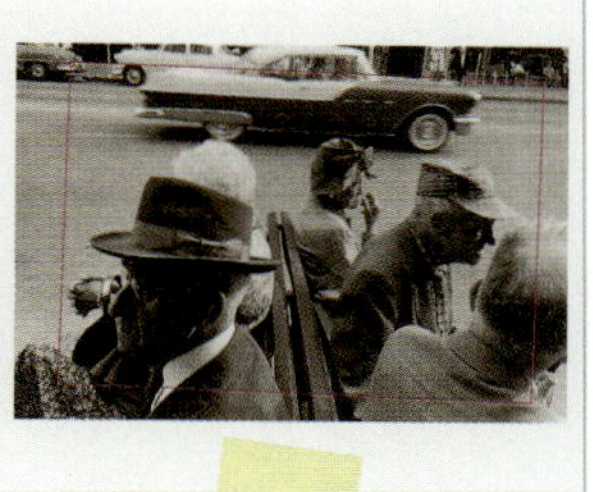

Pages from a handmade maquette, showing the full size of the scanned vintage prints. The red rectangles show the crops in the Delpire and Grove Press books, many of which Frank altered for the Steidl edition.

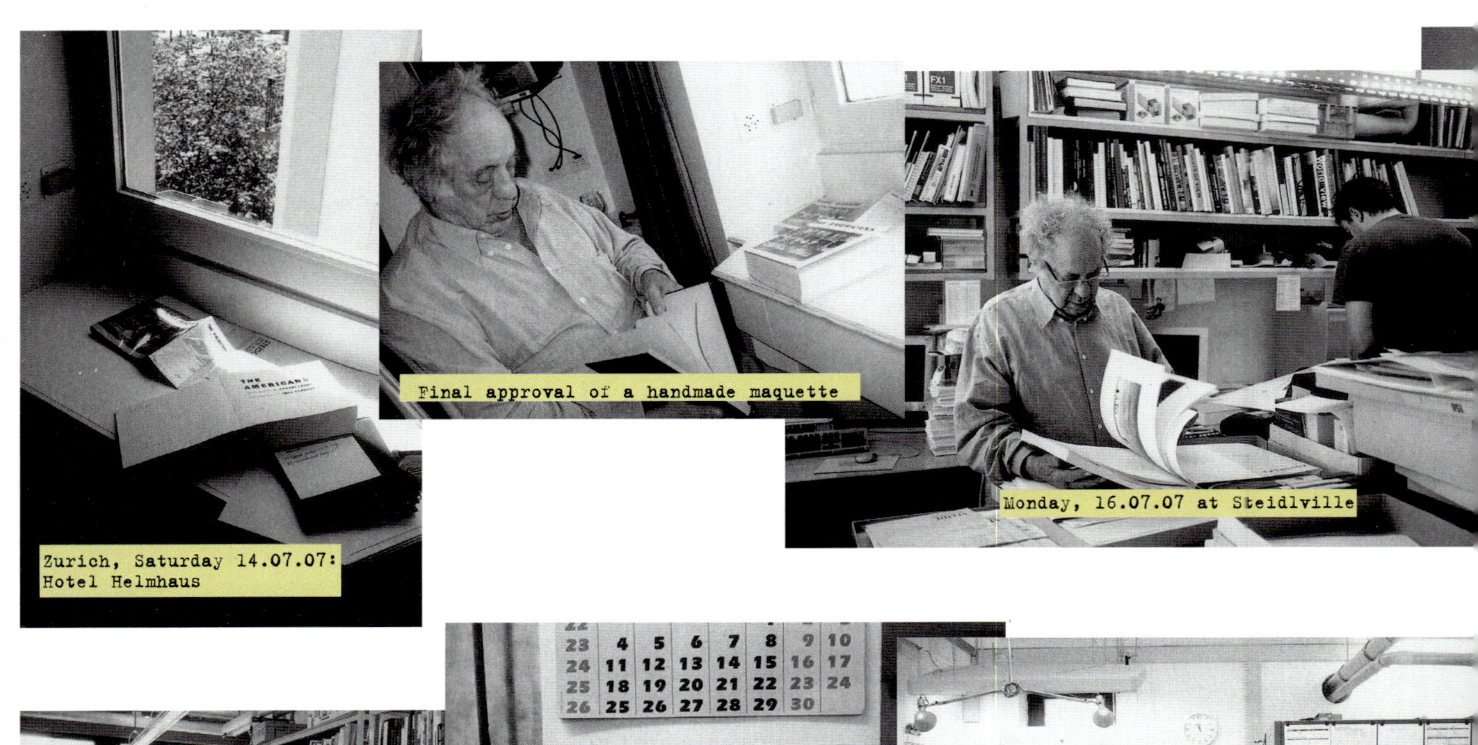
Final approval of a handmade maquette
Monday, 16.07.07 at Steidlville
Zurich, Saturday 14.07.07:
Hotel Helmhaus

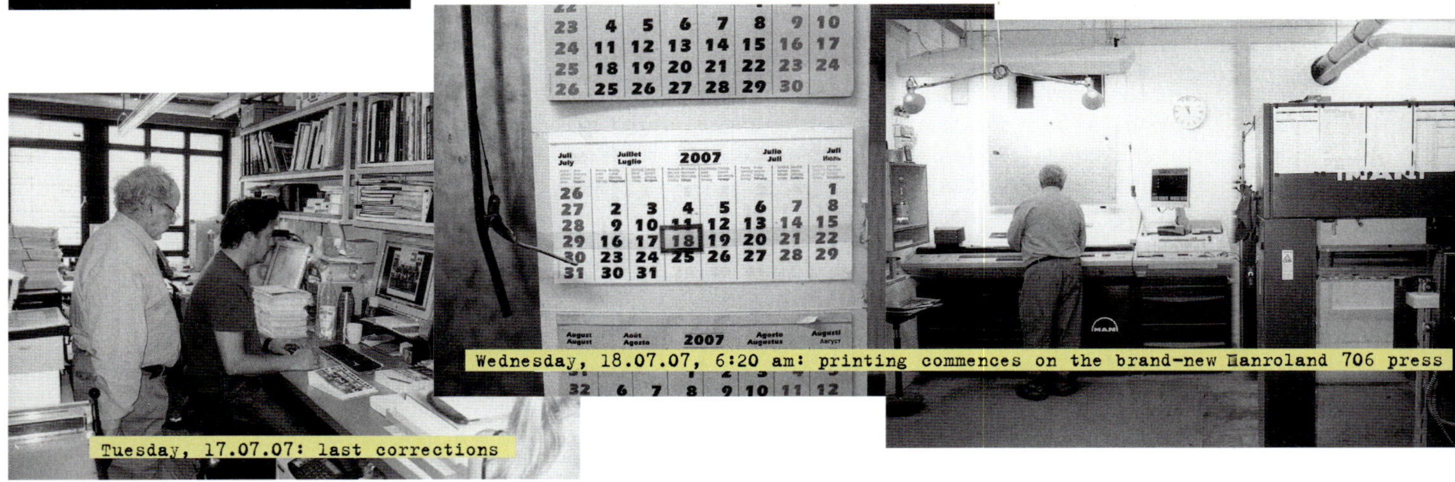
Wednesday, 18.07.07, 6:20 am: printing commences on the brand-new Manroland 706 press
Tuesday, 17.07.07: last corrections

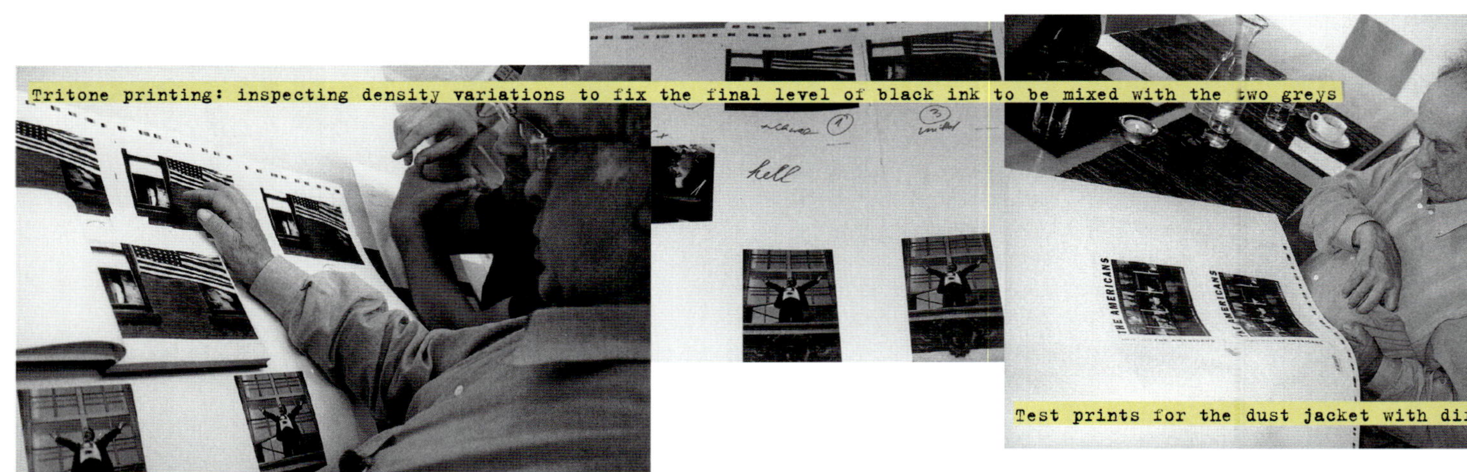
Tritone printing: inspecting density variations to fix the final level of black ink to be mixed with the two greys
hell
Test prints for the dust jacket with dif

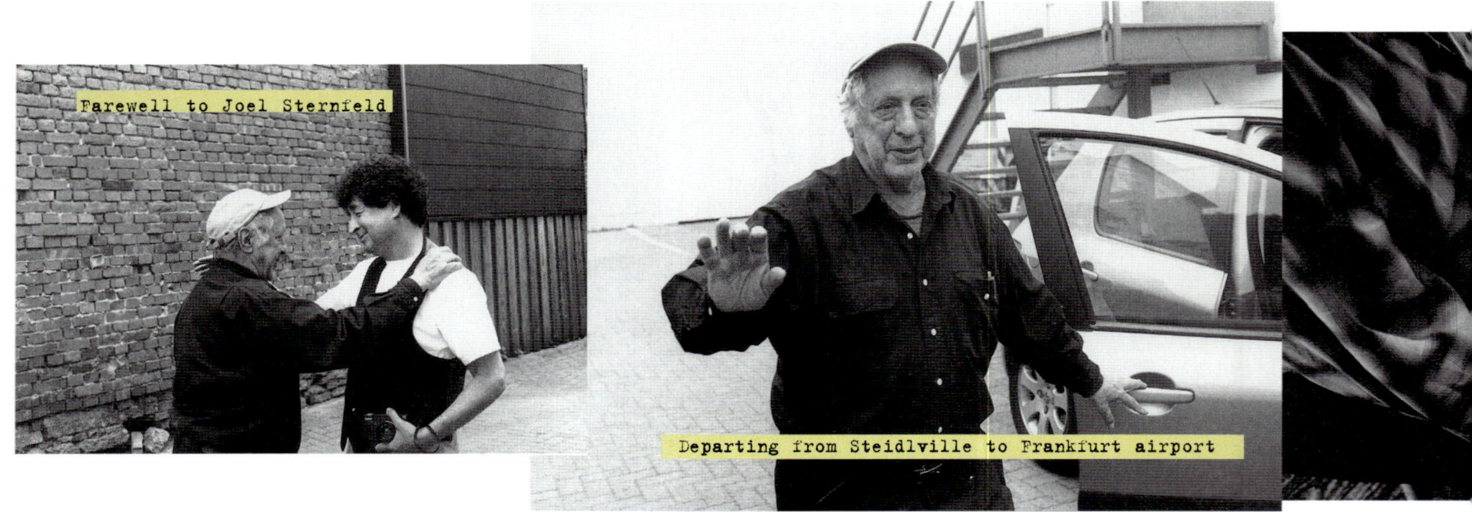
Farewell to Joel Sternfeld
Departing from Steidlville to Frankfurt airport

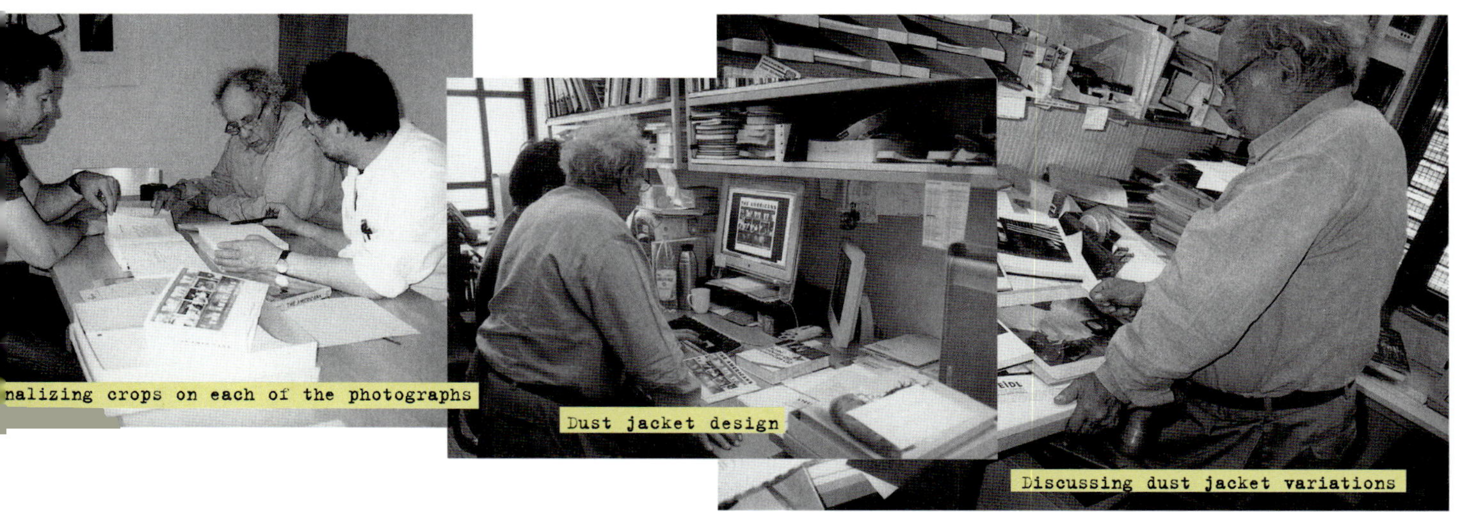

nalizing crops on each of the photographs

Dust jacket design

Discussing dust jacket variations

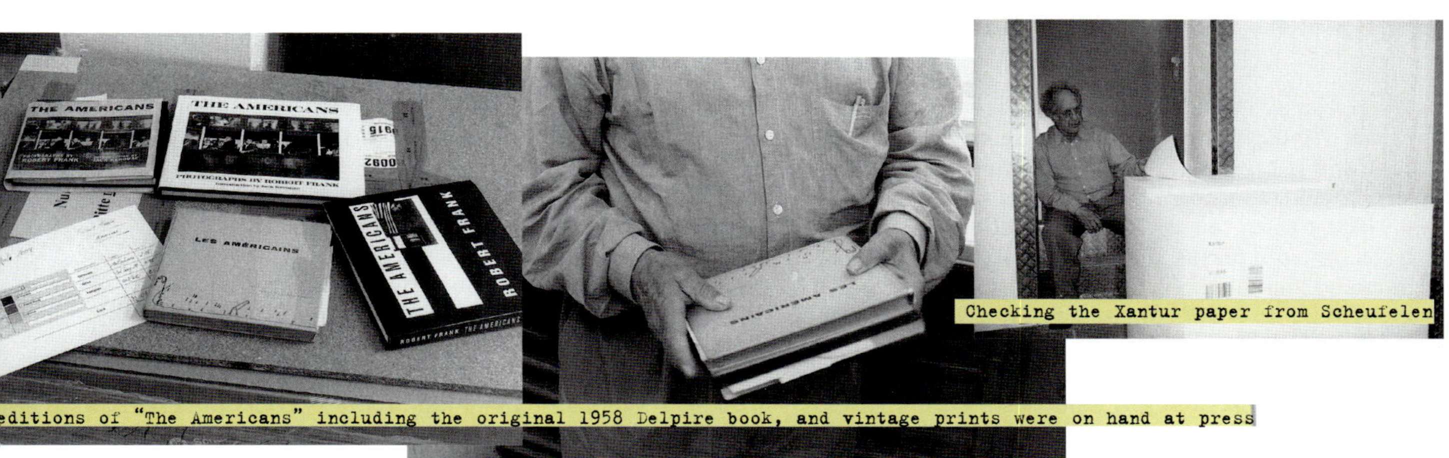

Checking the Xantur paper from Scheufelen

editions of "The Americans" including the original 1958 Delpire book, and vintage prints were on hand at press

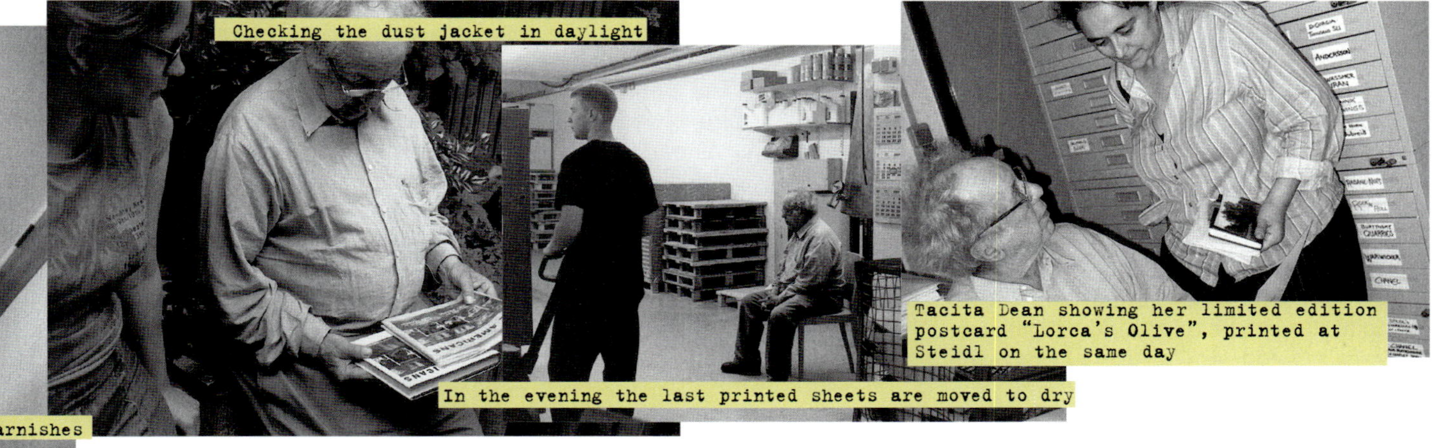

Checking the dust jacket in daylight

Tacita Dean showing her limited edition postcard "Lorca's Olive", printed at Steidl on the same day

In the evening the last printed sheets are moved to dry

varnishes

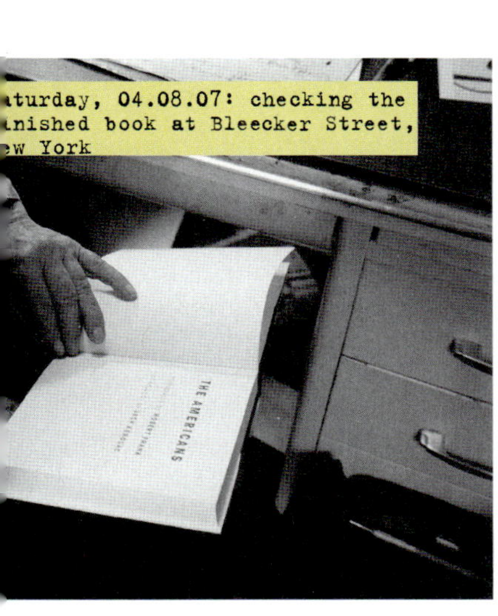

aturday, 04.08.07: checking the nished book at Bleecker Street, ew York

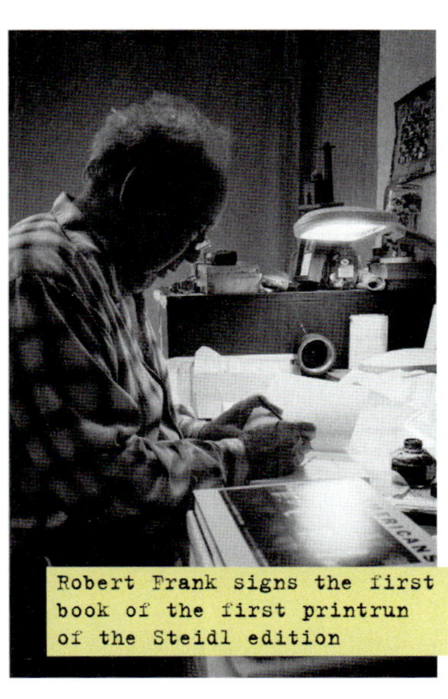

Robert Frank signs the first book of the first printrun of the Steidl edition

Photos by Gerhard Steidl

The Winding Creative Road to *The Americans*

Monte Packham

For the thousandth time, it must be said that pictures speak for themselves, wordlessly, visually—or they fail. Walker Evans, "Robert Frank" in *U.S. Camera Annual 1958*

From Robert Frank's beginnings as a photographer in the 1940s, the photobook—one with little or no text and a primary focus on the images and their sequence—was central to his art. And nowhere is Frank's desire for such an unapologetically visual book, as well as his engagement with the dynamic between image and text, as evident as in the publishing history of *The Americans*. Frank took the photos that would become this, his most famous book, in 1955 and '56, yet it is his first three books, pre-dating these travels, that form the creative blueprint for *The Americans*.

In 1946 Frank crafted *40 Fotos*, a unique spiral-bound volume consisting of 40 gelatin silver prints (of his photos as well as some by other photographers which he had retouched), and no text. The book relies purely on the images and their juxtapositions on opposite and consecutive pages to convey meaning.

In 1948 Frank made two copies of *Peru*, a spiral-bound volume with 39 silver gelatin prints of photos he had taken that year in Peru (the two versions of the book contain the same images but in different sequences). Like *40 Fotos*, *Peru* contains no text and presents photos in multiple formats; yet *Peru*'s layout is even more experimental, with some images bleeding to the page's edge, others crossing the spine, and Frank's bold irregular use of white space around the photos.

Black White and Things of 1952, designed by Frank's friend Werner Zryd and realized by the photographer in three handmade copies with 34 original prints, includes minimal text and anticipates the relationship between image and text that shapes *The Americans*. At the beginning of the book is a (now famous and overused) quote from Antoine de Saint-Exupéry's *The Little Prince* of 1943: "it is only with the heart that one can see rightly / what is essential is invisible to the eye." Below this is Frank's commentary on the three sections of the book "black," "white," and "things": "somber people and black events / quiet people and peaceful places / and the things people have come in contact with / this, I try to show in my photographs." (Frank would later re-visit such suggestive fragmentary statements in *The Lines of My Hand* [1972] and his visual diaries [2010–17].) At the beginning of each section is a list of the photos that follow, composed of short captions in the format "Parade / Valencia 1952" that prefigure those in *The Americans*.

Today, the seminal relationship between image and text in *The Americans* seems so straightforward that we take it for granted. Yet the various editions of the book published since 1958—with their different formats, croppings, cover motifs and designs, texts (both in terms of content and their placement in the book) as well as typography—show that Frank's road to simplicity was a long and rough one.

The book was originally published in 1958 as *Les Américains* by Robert Delpire in Paris, as the fifth volume in his "Encyclopédie essentielle" series (1957–68) which presented encyclopedic perspectives on art, history and science to a French audience. At his distributor's request to encourage sales of *Les Américains*, Delpire commissioned an anthology of old and new writings on America, compiled by Alain Bosquet. These sociological and anecdotal texts were included in the book against Frank's will, and their effect was to largely reduce his photos to illustrations (the texts are on the left-hand pages, the photos on the right). Frank also wanted one of his photos to appear on the book's cover, yet Delpire instead chose a stylized whimsical drawing by Saul Steinberg of New York—a design with little in common with Frank's photos, and a decision Delpire would later rectify when he reprinted *Les Américains* with a photo on the cover in the 1986 and subsequent editions. The 1959 Italian *Gli Americani*, published by Il Saggiatore in Milan, follows the design and content of the Delpire book.

For the 1959 English edition, published by Grove Press in New York, Frank realized his wish for a photo on the book's cover and no running text; the photo sequence is the same as the Delpire edition. Instead of the French texts is Jack Kerouac's introduction, and short captions on the left-hand pages opposite the photos. Kerouac's text, which Frank asked him to write following their first meeting in September 1957 (the same month in which Kerouac's *On the Road* was published), seeks not to explain Frank's photos but capture a sense of his restless ambitious undertaking, both critical and celebratory, in seemingly spontaneous, unpretentious and sometimes capricious prose that mirrors the mood and tone of Frank's photos and even defends them: "Anybody doesnt like these pitchers dont like potry, see?" The captions follow the style of those in *Black White and Things* and appear neutral in tone, though some become ironic in the context of the photos they describe, for

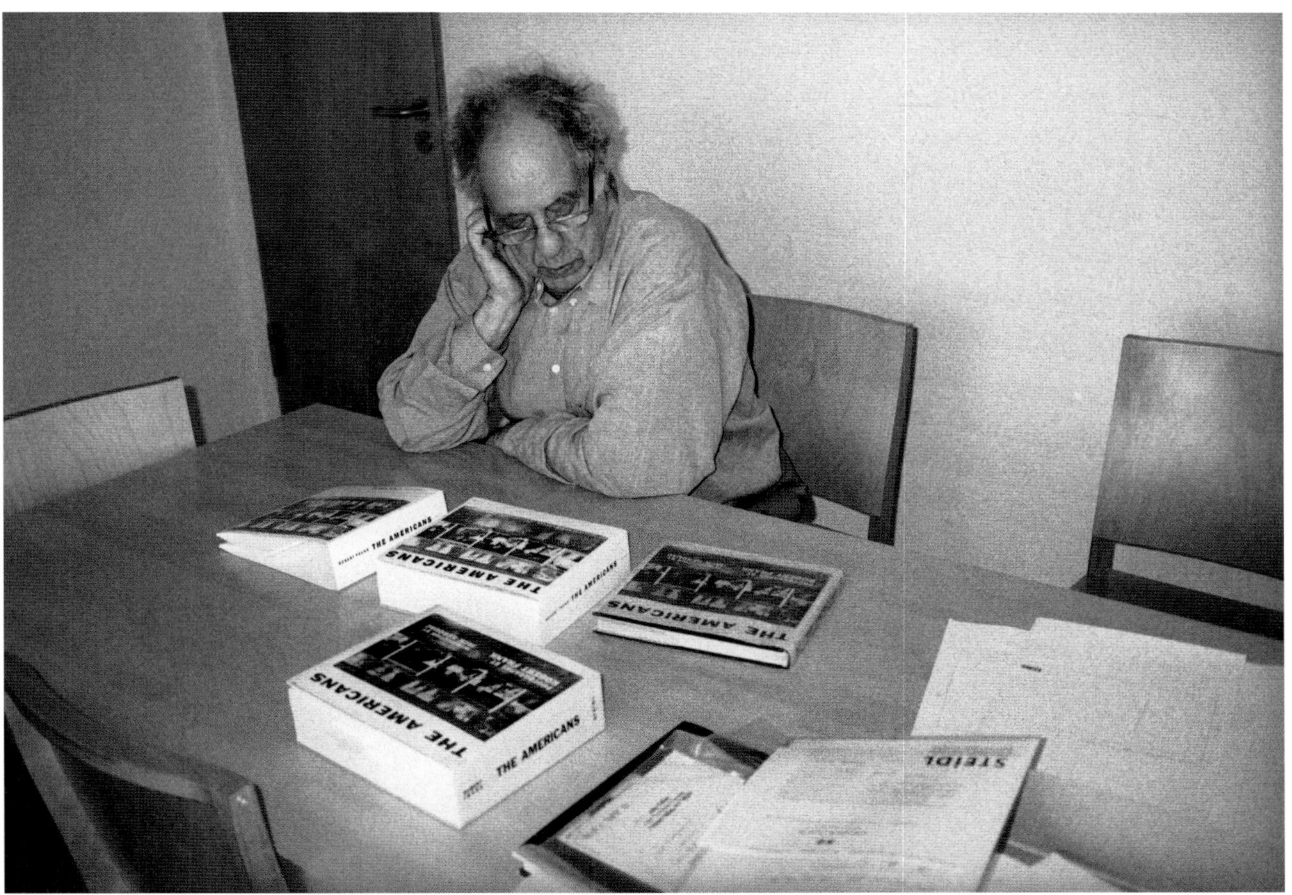

Frank checking cover variations for
The Americans, Göttingen, 2007

example "Car accident—U.S. 66, between Winslow and Flagstaff, Arizona," which shows the post-accident mundaneness of a blanket-covered corpse and four onlookers.

In the more than 20 editions of *The Americans* that have now been published, the photo sequence and introduction of the Grove Press edition have been maintained. In nearly all editions the captions are also present, though in some books they are not placed opposite the photos but in a consolidated list separate to the image sequence. The cover motif has varied (although most editions retain Grove's "Trolley—New Orleans"), as have croppings of the photos within the book.

Despite these irregularities and the shifting tensions between image and text they create, at the heart of *The Americans* remain Frank's photos and their vital, tenacious sequence—the elegant links and contrasts from page to page; the play between hushed stillness and dynamism; the filmic pacing; the engrossing combination of intimacy and detachment, revelation and implication, clarity and ambiguity. These are photos that record specific moments in 1950s America, and yet which express themes of commonality and difference that still shape America and beyond today.

It is most likely the proven ability of *The Americans* to succeed on primarily visual terms that made Robert Frank contemplate in 2007, when he oversaw the redesign and production of the last edition of the book at Steidl in Göttingen, to remove both Kerouac's introduction and the captions. This would have marked a return to Frank's pure bookmaking beginnings, to a solely visual photobook in the manner of *40 Fotos* and *Peru*. And yet Frank finally decided to retain the introduction and captions, acknowledging that they had, over a period of more than half a century, become an integral part of *The Americans*' complex message. The intricate, self-renewing dance between image and text had taken on a life of its own.

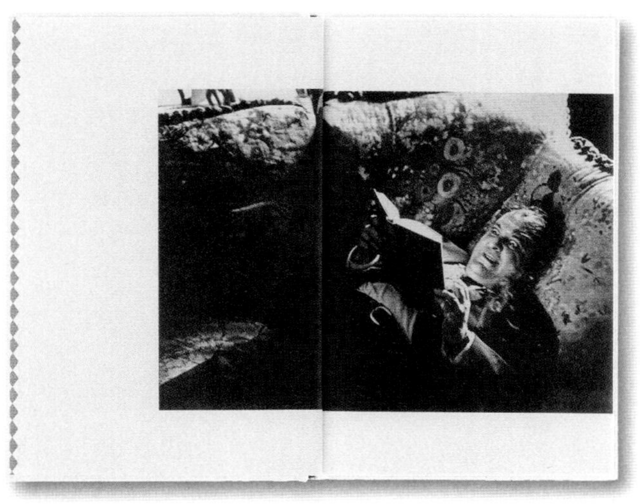

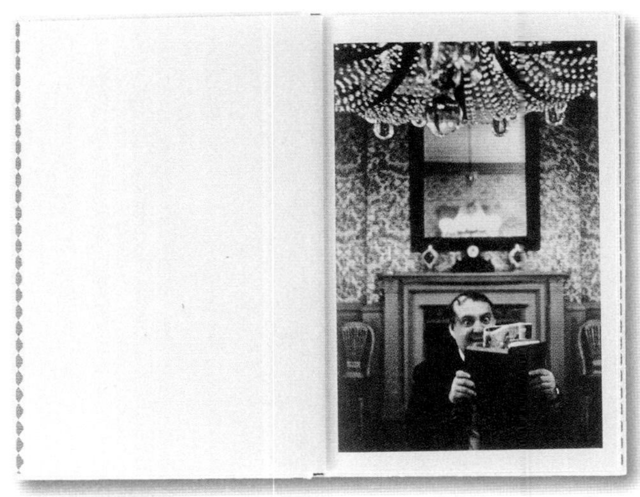

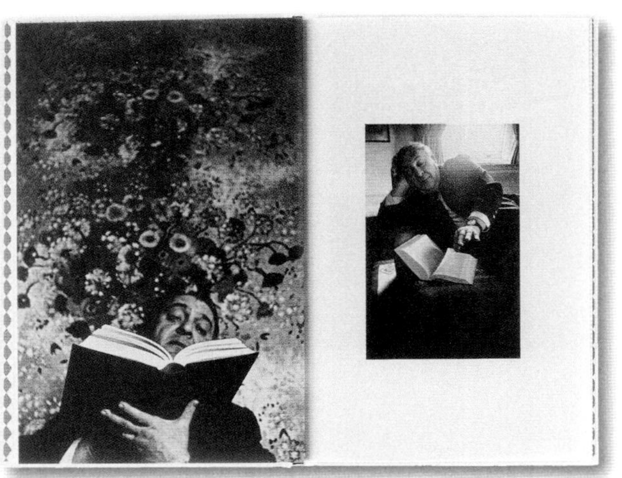

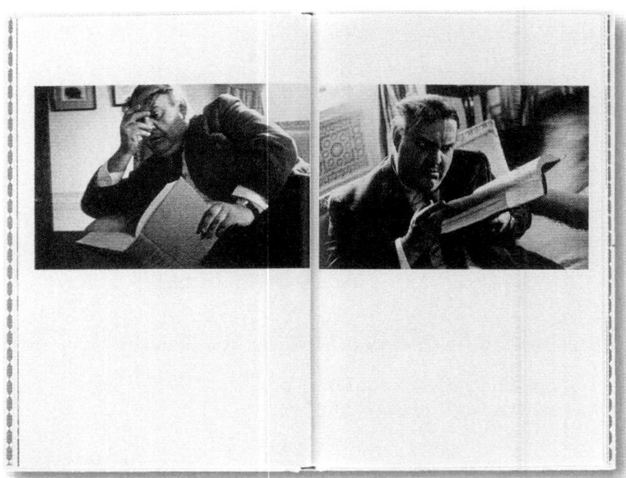

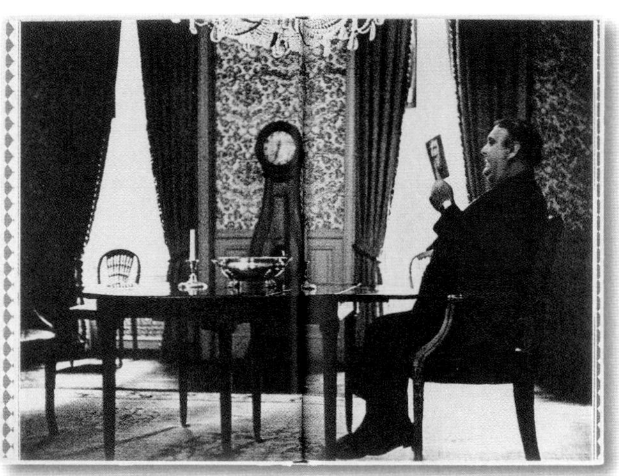

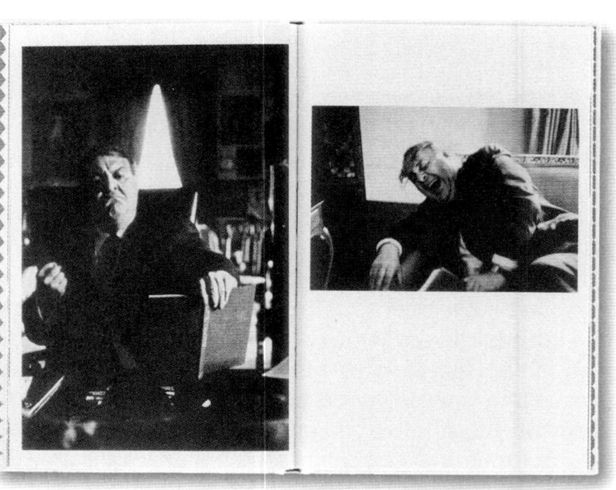

**Zero Mostel
Reads a Book**

First edition published by
The New York Times, 1963
Published by Steidl, 2008

Zero Mostel

reads

a book

When Robert Frank had completed his first two films, he accepted a commission for a photobook from *The New York Times*, which became *Zero Mostel Reads a Book*. In it Frank takes the comic actor Zero Mostel (1915–1977) for his subject, and depicts him in cartoonish dimensions—bemused, baffled and apoplectic, as he makes his way through an unidentified hardback volume, seated at a table or on a sofa.

Originally published "for the fun of it" in 1963 and dedicated to the American bookseller, the book was intended as a present for customers yet it never reached the book market. It has been a collector's item since. *Zero Mostel Reads a Book* references a series of theatrical and playful vignettes in which Mostel's most famous roles— Tevye in *Fiddler on the Roof*, Pseudolus in *A Funny Thing Happened on the Way to the Forum*, and Max Bialystock in *The Producers*—are clearly signaled. It is a delightful moment of slapstick in Frank's œuvre, and directly reflects his emphasis on the moving image at the time.

Uncredited text
Book design by Robert Frank
and Gerhard Steidl
40 pages
5.7 × 8.5 in. / 14.4 × 21.5 cm
36 black-and-white photographs
Tritone
Hardcover

ISBN 978-3-86521-586-4

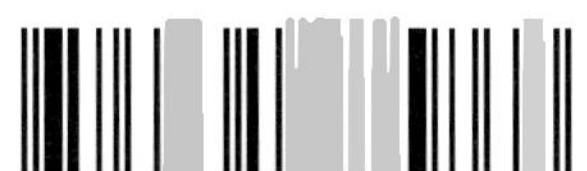

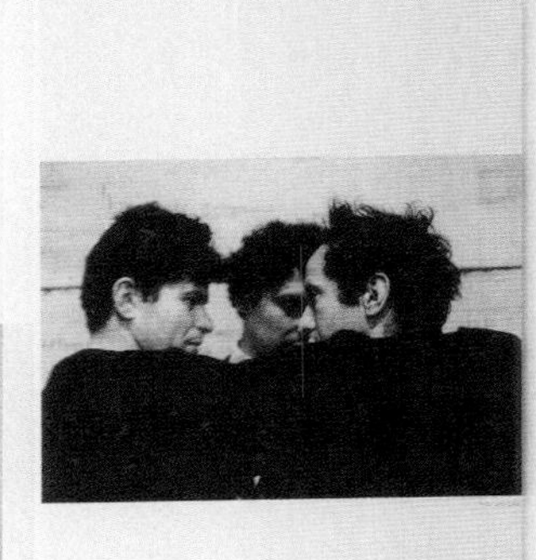

CAST

The Bishop	Mooney Peebles
Allen Ginsberg	Himself
Gregory Corso	Himself
Peter Orlovsky	Himself
Girl in Bed	Denise Parker
Milo	Larry Rivers
The Bishop's Mother	Alice Neal
The Bishop's Sister	Sally Gross
Carolyn	Beltiane
Little Boy	Pablo Frank
Pat Mezz McGillicuddy	David Amram

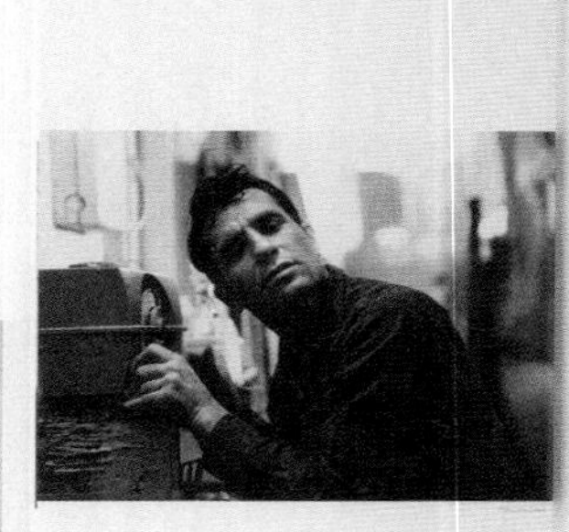

PULL MY DAISY
TIP MY CUP
ALL MY DOORS ARE OPEN
CUT MY THOUGHTS FOR COCO␣UTS
ALL MY EGGS ARE BROKEN

HOP MY HEART SONG
HARP MY HEIGHT
SERAPHS HOLD ME STEADY
HIP MY ANGEL
HYPE MY LIGHT
LAY IT ON THE NEEDY

Pull My Daisy
Lyrics by Jack Kerouac and Allen Ginsberg
Music by David Amram
Singer: Anita Ellis

Rob my locker	say my oops
lick my rocks	ope my shell
leap my cock in school	Bite my naked nut
Rack my lacks	Roll my bones
lark my looks	ring my bell
jump right up my hole	call my worm to sup
Whore my door	Pope my parts
beat my boor	pop my pot
eat my snake of fool	raise my daisy up
Craze my hair	Poke my pap
bare my poor	pit my plum
asshole shorn of wool	let my gap be shut

Allen Ginsberg & Jack Kerouac

Generation, an unproduced play by Jack Kerouac. They had one camera, one spotlight, one professional performer (the beautiful girl who plays the wife). The interior was Leslie's loft at Fourth Avenue and 12th Street; a Brooklyn warehouse near the East River served for the brief exteriors. Shooting took two weeks—"with interruptions." The cost was $15,000 including cast salaries; nobody worked for nothing except Frank and Leslie.

Pretty soon they began to depart from the written script. Too much good stuff wasn't getting in. Thereafter it went like this, as described by Robert Frank: "You're in a room where people are sitting around. You see something and swing the camera." (If you pay close attention when watching the movie you will see that the camera always swings to the right—clockwise—as the eye does in reading.) "Then Alfred did the directing in his editing. Because after two days of rushes we sort of gave up on the story. It is in this way that it is to my mind a pure film rather than an acting film."

Finally there came the matter of Kerouac's sound track. "Jack had seen the picture twice, silent. He thought he was ready to supply something"—an ad-libbed text along only the sketchiest of predetermined lines—"and we tried it at his house. No good. So we brought him down to a sound studio and put the picture on. He was wearing earphones, feeling great, listening to unrelated jazz. We went through it in three-sections, reel by reel, at that one sitting."

So here we are at the heart of the matter. Kerouac's sound track (and "narration" of same) for *Pull My Daisy*. It is without any doubt at least a minor if not major masterpiece and the most honest and honestly funny piece of beatthink within my (however limited) experience. It is also an epic poem, a self-appraisal, a stoicism, a plain unvarnished delight. Nothing but hearing him do it could recapture his fantastic acting ability and mimicry; but of course you may hear him do it when-ever and wherever you next get a chance to catch the film. It is also, like the movie, an ugly poem—ugly for its pull-downs, its woman-hatred, its sexual squareness (all beat sex is square), its holier-than-thou infantile anarchies. This too is part of its honesty, ...and its beauty—and, inversely, its joy. As with the entirety of *Pull My Daisy*. For the motion picture did not begin, as some think, with *Pull My Daisy*. Nor, as others think, did it end there. It merely moved, as with Vigo's *Zero de Conduite* of twenty-eight years ago, toward "pure film," spontaneity, freedom. That in itself is all one may properly ask for.

(1961)

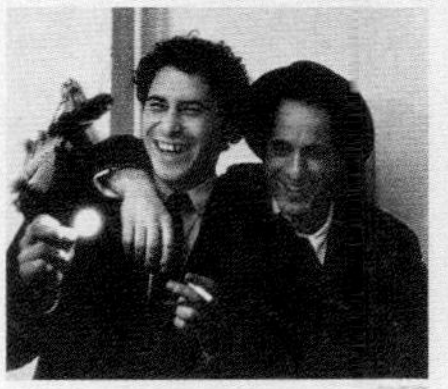

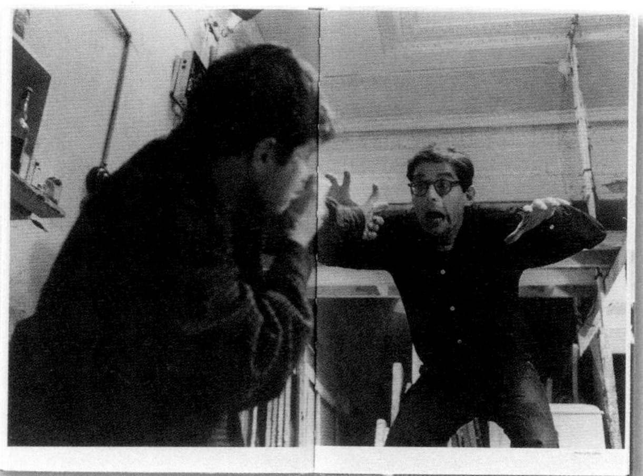

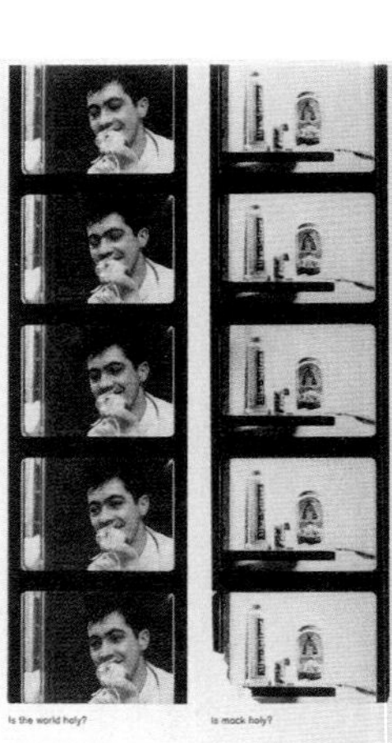
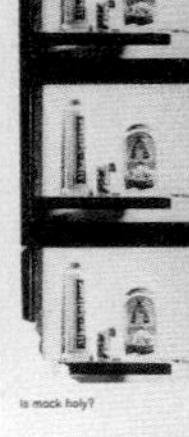

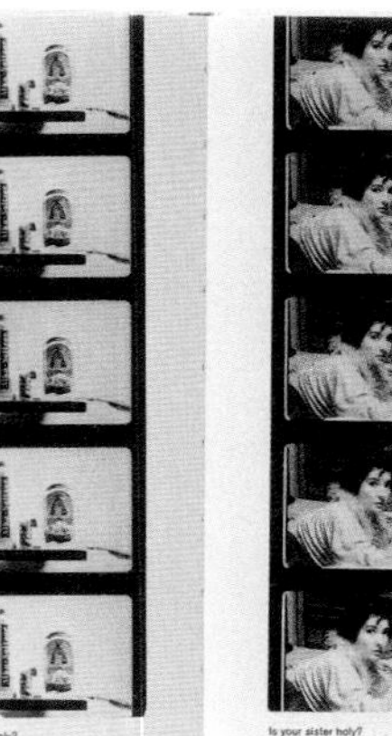
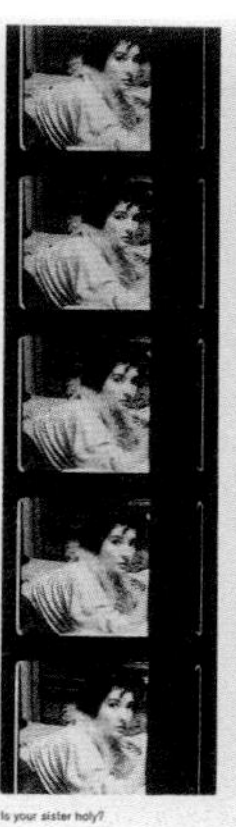
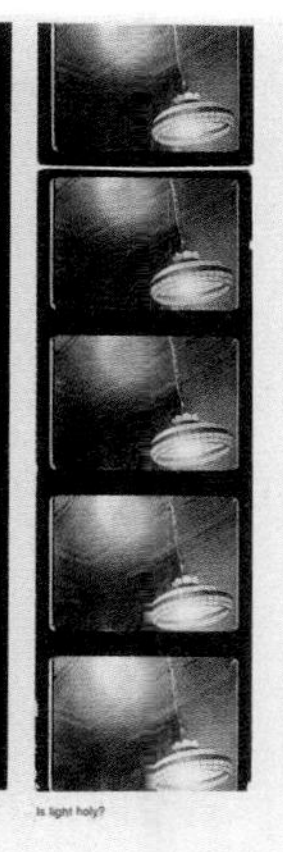

Pull My Daisy

Published by Steidl, 2008

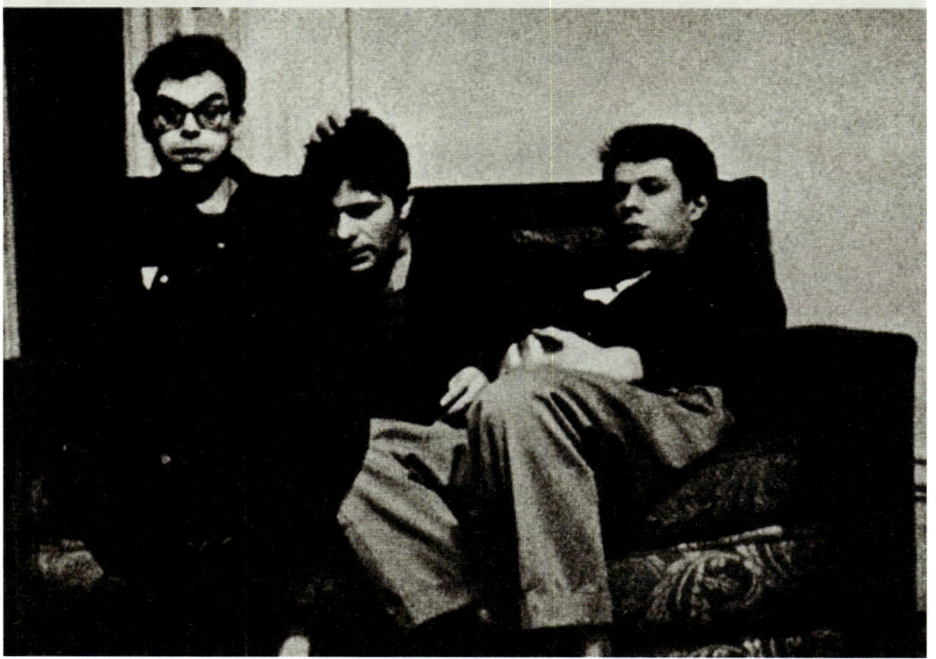

Introduction by Jerry Tallmer
Text by Jack Kerouac
Book design by Robert Frank,
Gerhard Steidl and Rukminee
Guha Thakurta
64 pages
5.3 × 7.9 in. / 13.5 × 20 cm.
55 black-and-white photographs
and film stills
Tritone
Hardcover

ISBN 978-3-86521-673-1

Pull My Daisy is a 1959 short film that typifies the Beat Generation. Directed by Robert Frank and Alfred Leslie, *Pull My Daisy* was adapted by Jack Kerouac from the third act of a stage play he never finished titled *Beat Generation*. Kerouac also provided improvised narration. It starred Allen Ginsberg, Gregory Corso, Larry Rivers, Peter Orlovsky, David Amram, Richard Bellamy, Alice Neel, Sally Gross and Pablo Frank, Robert Frank's then-infant son.

This book interweaves a transcript of Kerouac's narration from the film with film stills and also includes an introduction by Jerry Tallmer written in 1961.

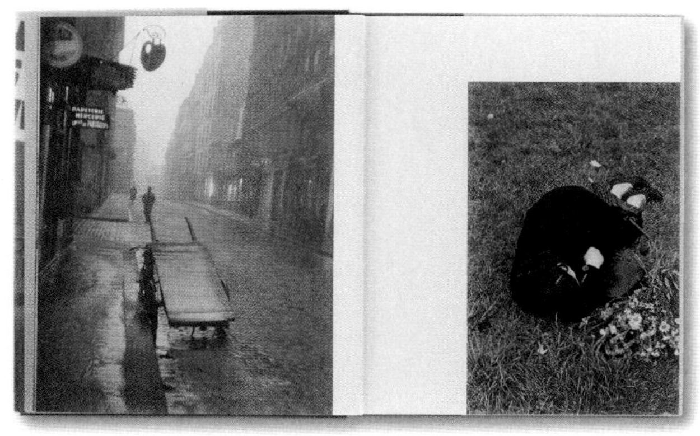

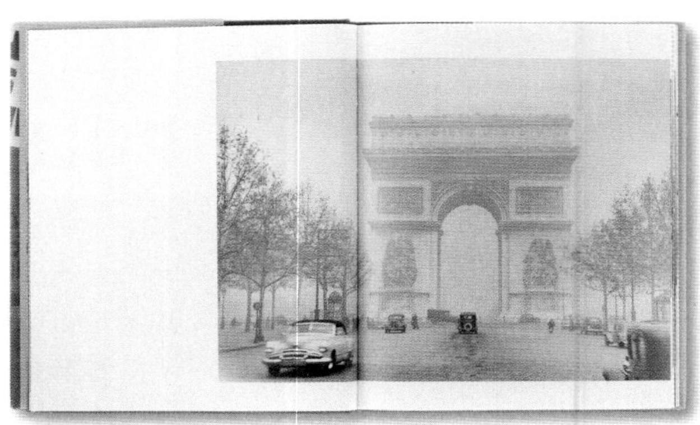

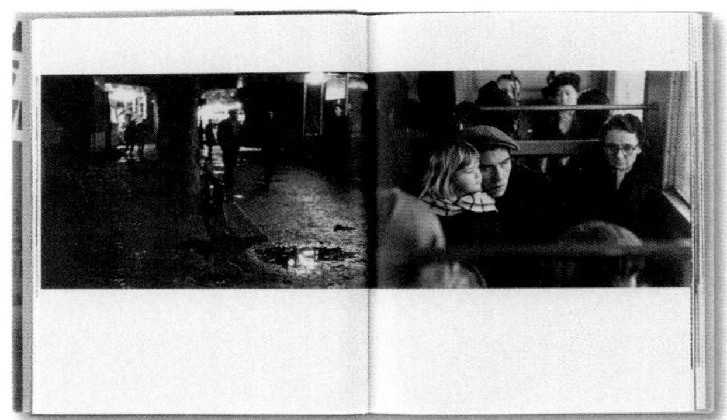

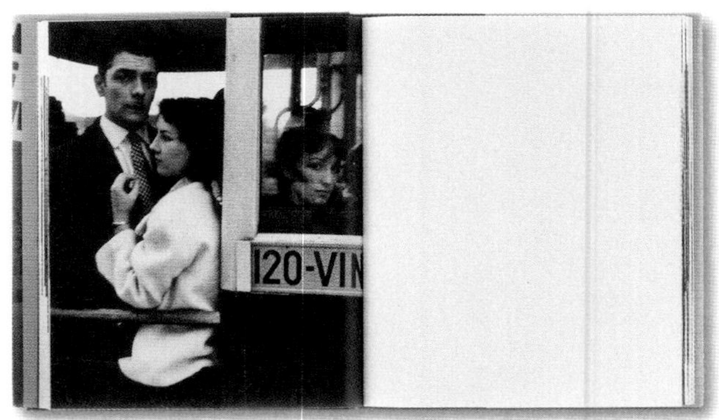

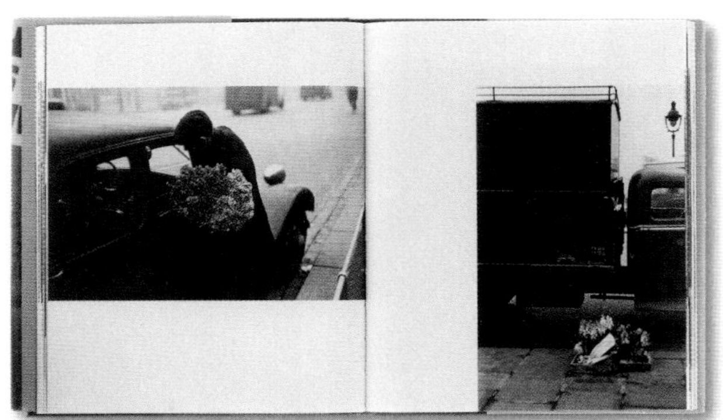

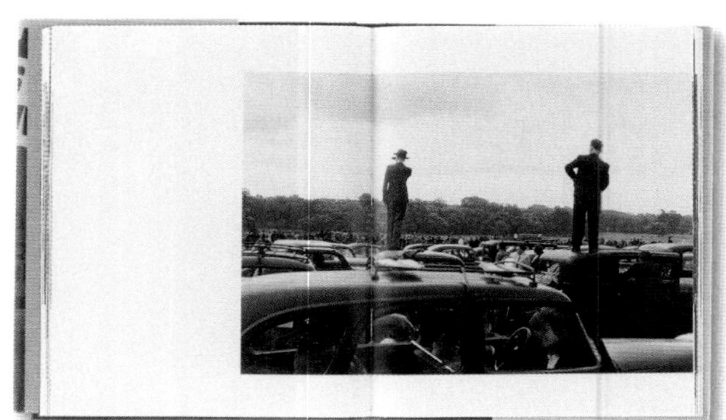

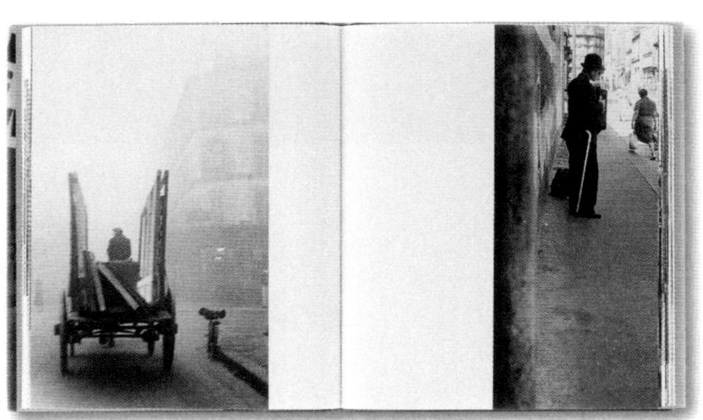

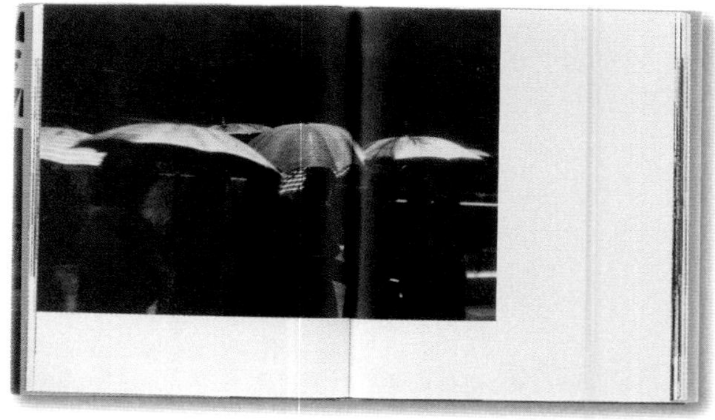

Paris

Published by Steidl, 2008

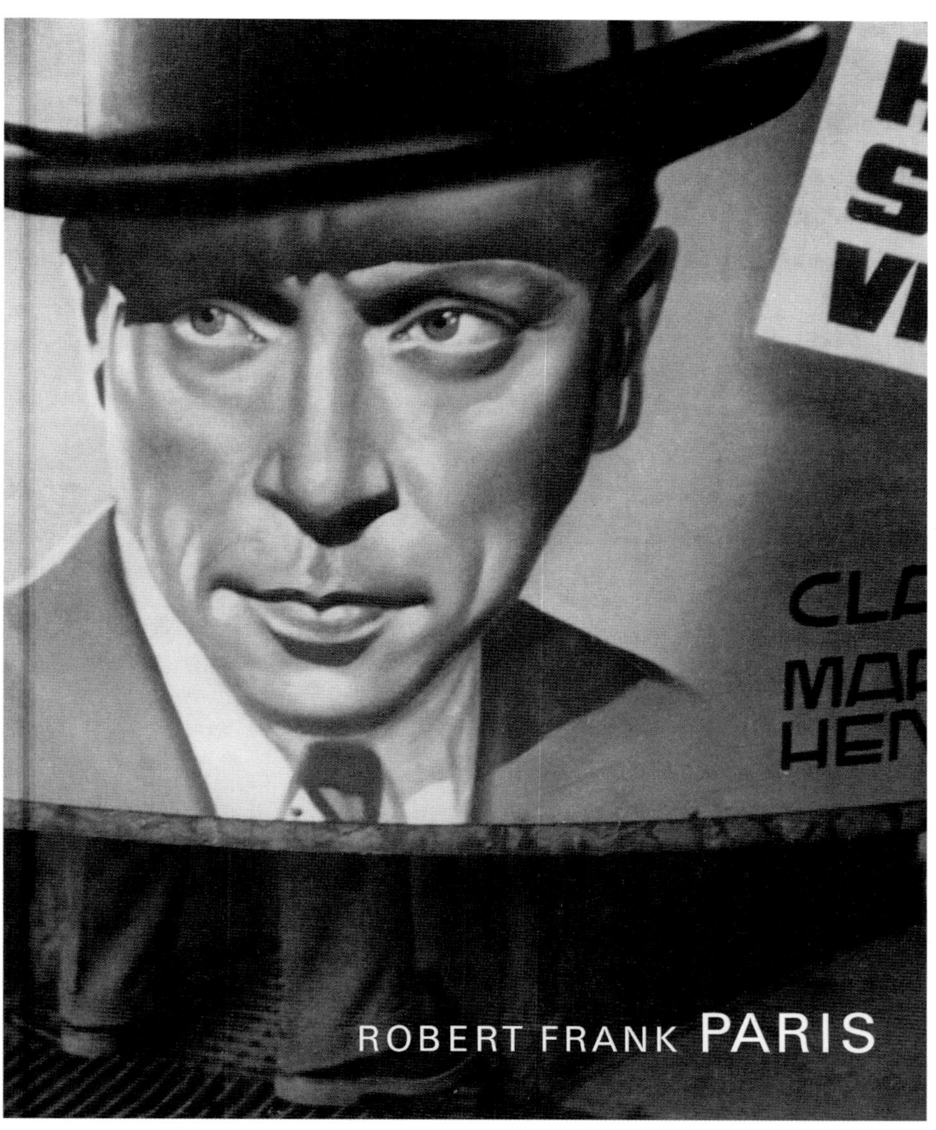

Edited by Robert Frank
and Ute Eskildsen
Book design by Gerhard Steidl
and Sarah Winter
108 pages
7.2 × 8.7 in. / 18.5 × 22 cm
69 black-and-white photographs
Tritone
Clothbound hardcover in
dust jacket

ISBN 978-3-86521-524-6

Paris marks the first time that the significant body of photographs which Robert Frank made in Paris in the early 1950s is presented in a single book. His visit to Paris in 1951 was his second return to Europe after he had settled in New York City in 1947, and some of the images he made during this visit have since become iconic in the history of the medium.

The photographs selected by Robert Frank and Ute Eskildsen here suggest that Frank's experience of the "new world" had sharpened his eye for European urbanism. He saw the city's streets as a stage for human activity and focused particularly on the flower sellers. His work clearly references Eugène Atget and invokes the tradition of the flâneur.

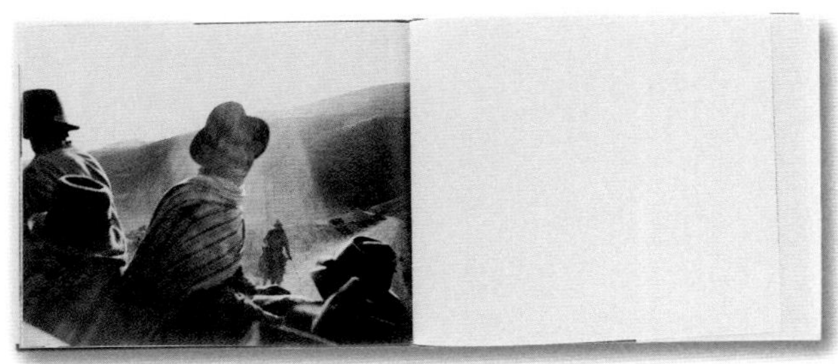
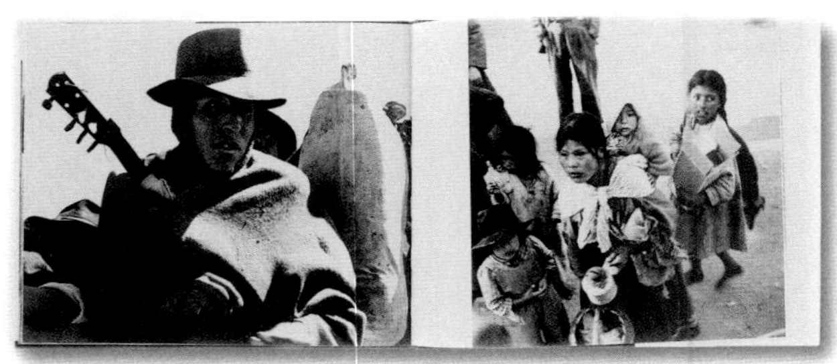
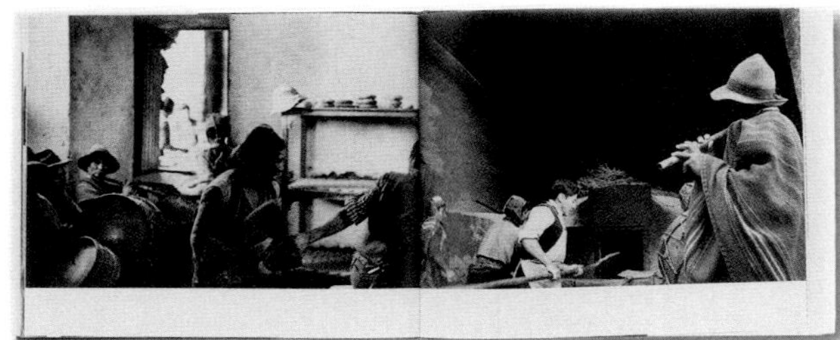
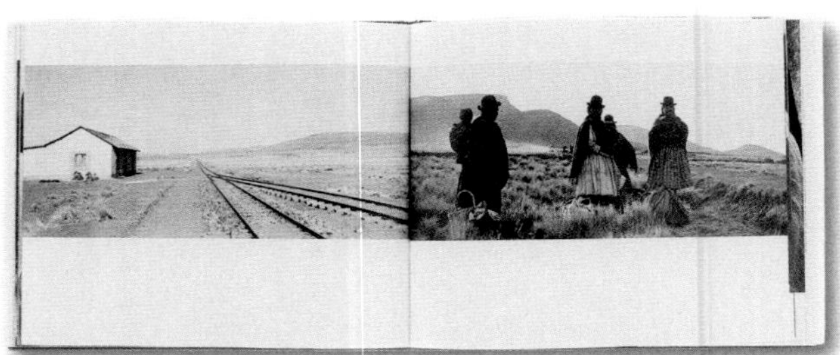
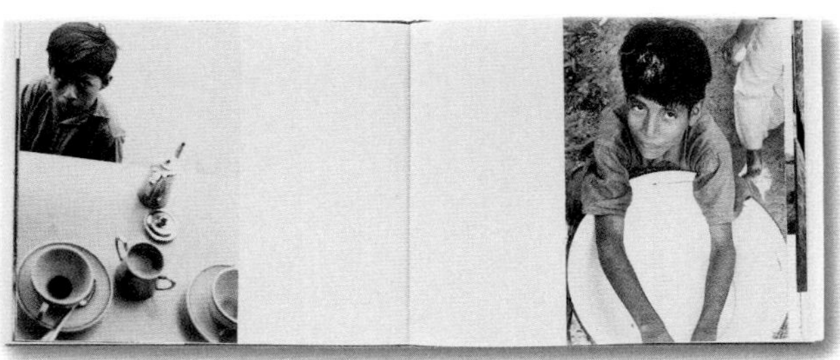
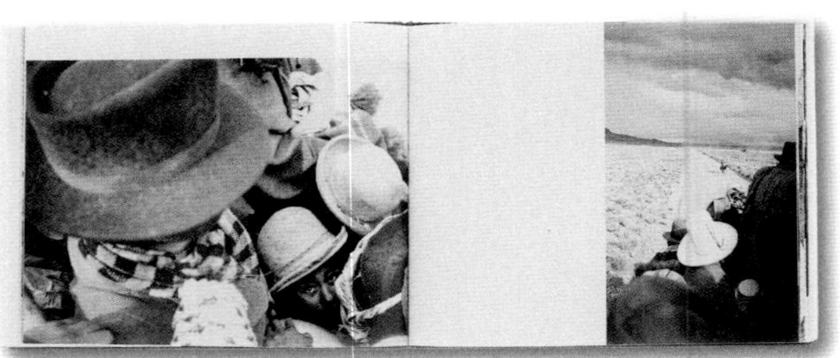
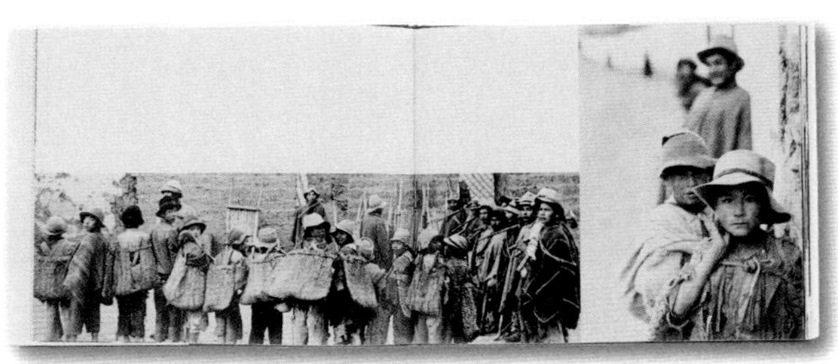
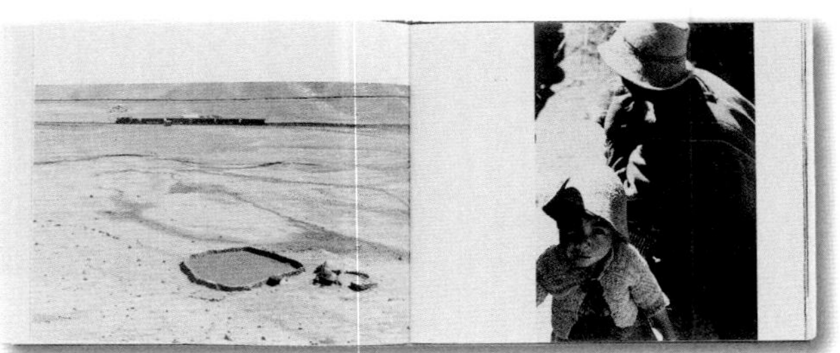
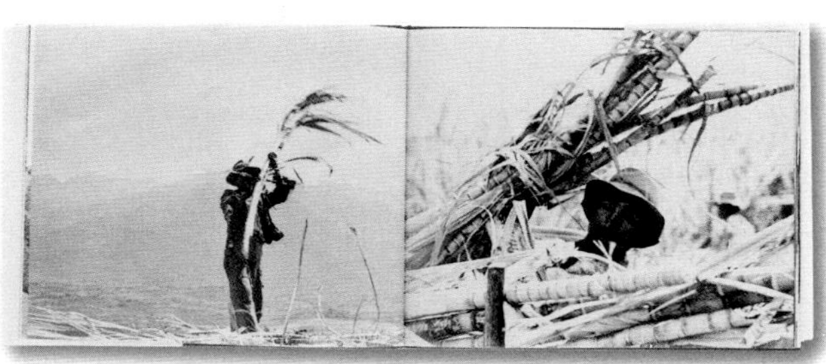
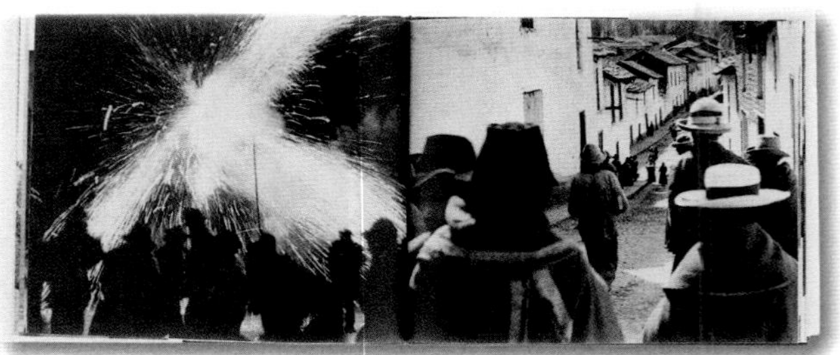

Peru

Published by Steidl, 2008

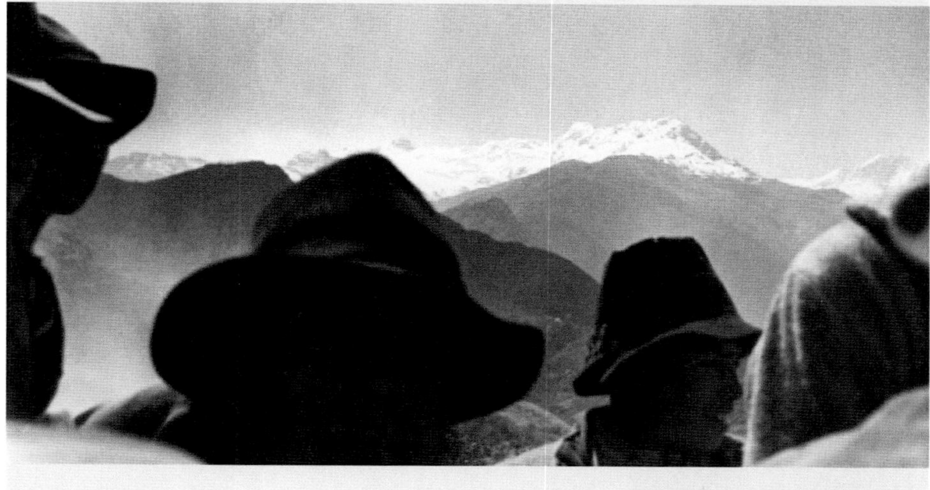

Book design by Robert Frank
and Gerhard Steidl
48 pages
9.8 × 7.9 in. / 25 × 20 cm
39 black-and-white photographs
Tritone
Clothbound hardcover with
dust jacket

ISBN 978-3-86521-692-2

Writing from New York in March 1949, Robert Frank sent home to his mother in Switzerland a birthday gift of a book maquette of a series of photographs he had made during a visit to Peru in 1948. A few of these images became well-known in Frank's œuvre, but previously the entire series had only been seen by a small number of people. *Peru* presents for the first time the complete sequence of images, based on the original book Frank had conceived, and realized under his direction.

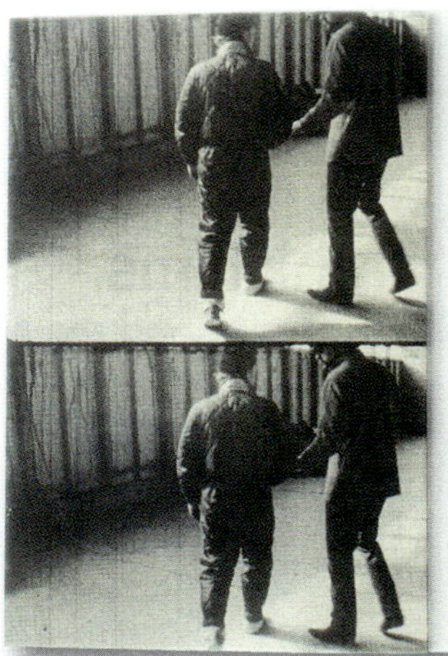
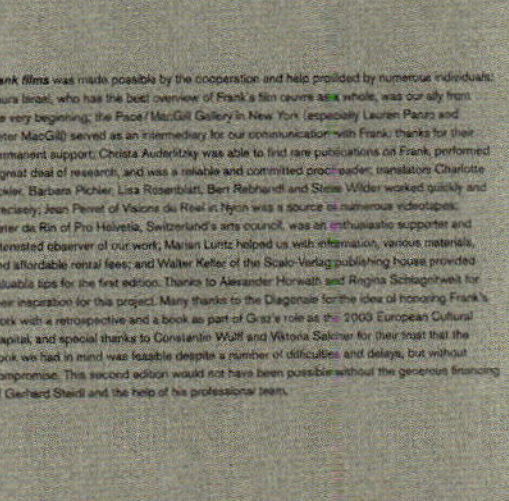
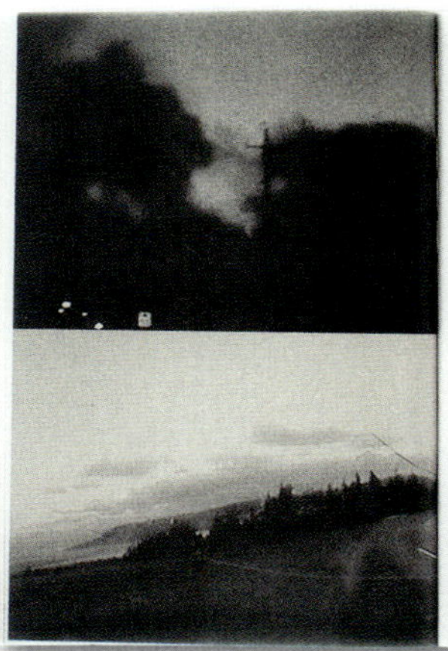
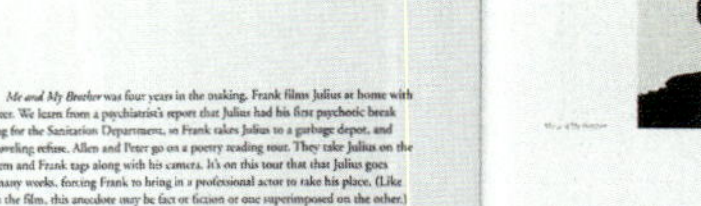
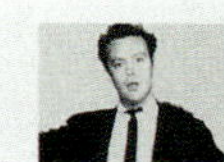
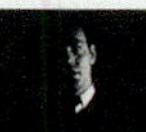
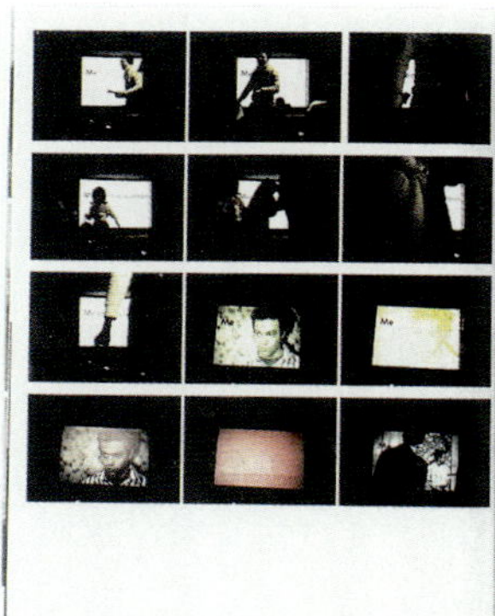
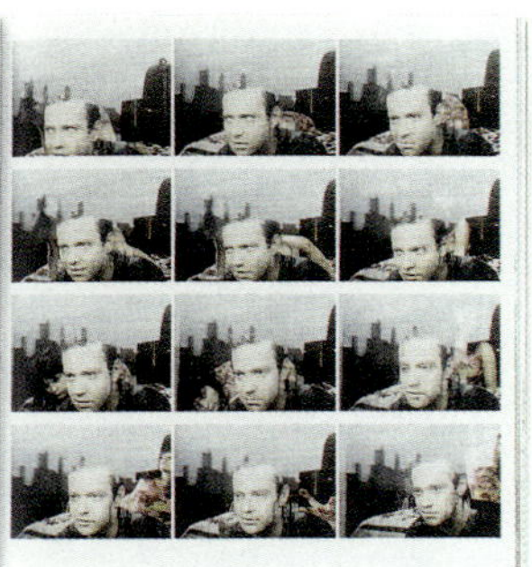
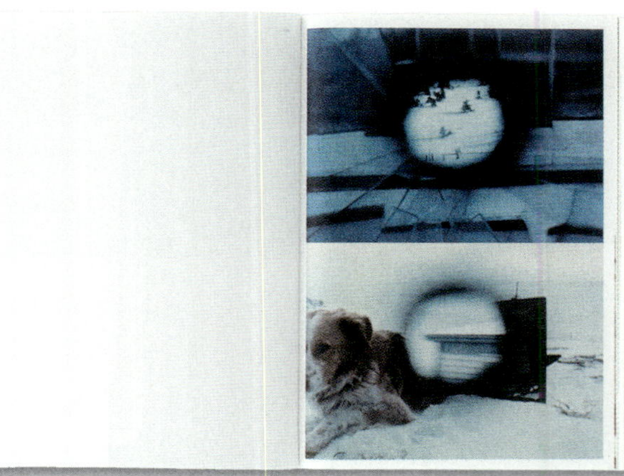
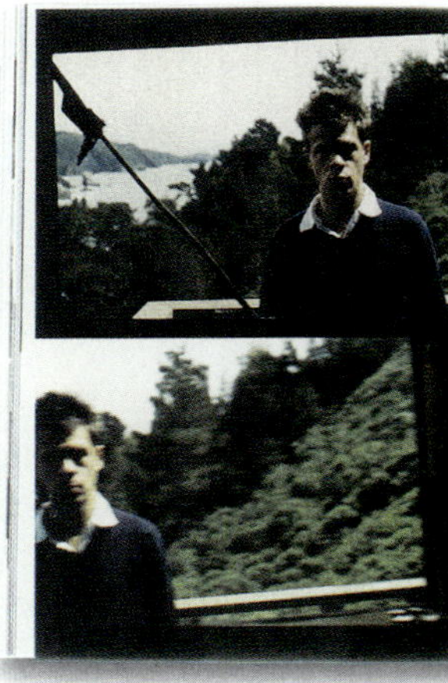
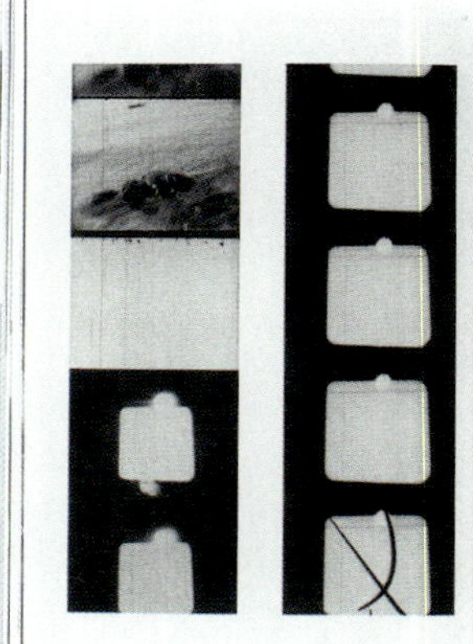
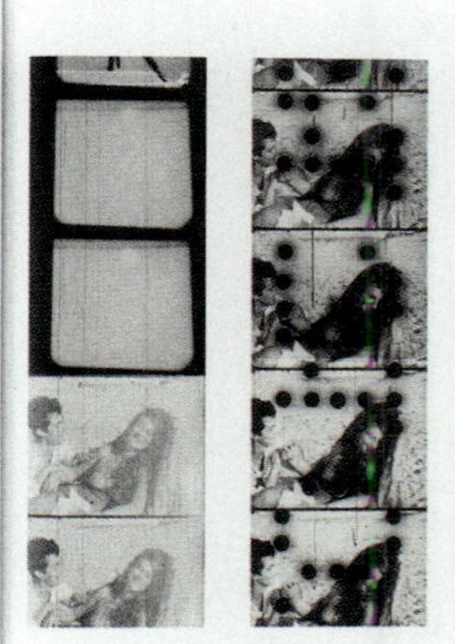

**Frank Films.
The Film
and Video
Work of
Robert Frank**

First edition published by
Scalo, 2003
First Steidl edition, 2009

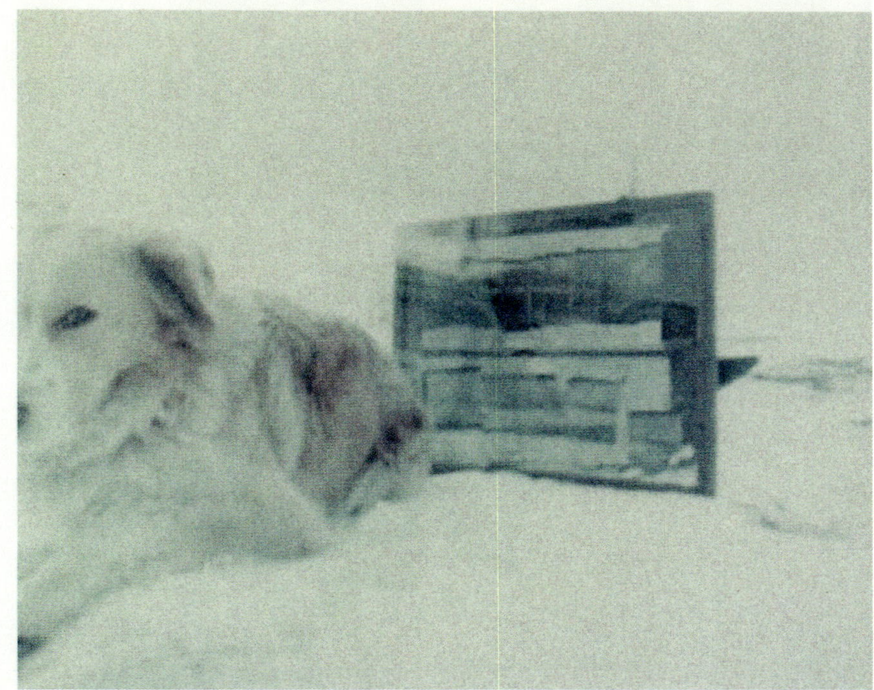

Edited by Brigitta Burger-Utzer
and Stefan Grissemann
Texts by Michael Barchet,
Philip Brookman, Brigitta
Burger-Utzer, Stefan
Grissemann, Kent Jones,
Thomas Mießgang, Pia Neumann,
Bert Rebhandl, Amy Taubin
Book design by Karl Ulbl
272 pages
6.7 × 9.4 in. / 17 × 24 cm
432 black-and-white and
81 color film stills
Four-color process
Softcover

ISBN 978-3-86521-815-5

Robert Frank turned to filmmaking at the end of the 1950s. Although he made around 30 films, the work has largely remained a well-kept secret. Frank approached each film project as a new experience, challenging the medium and its possibilities at every turn, amalgamating documentary, fiction and autobiography, cutting across genres.

This book offers a visually innovative approach to Frank's films: only new stills taken from videotapes have been used and they add up to a visual essay on Frank's cinema that establishes an engaging dialogue with his photographic work. Each film is introduced with detailed analysis, discussing the history and the aesthetics of Frank's film work. An interview with Allen Ginsberg provides an insider view.

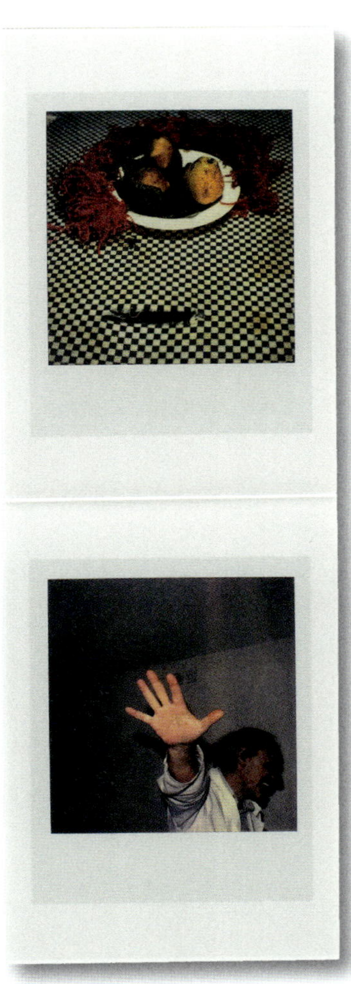

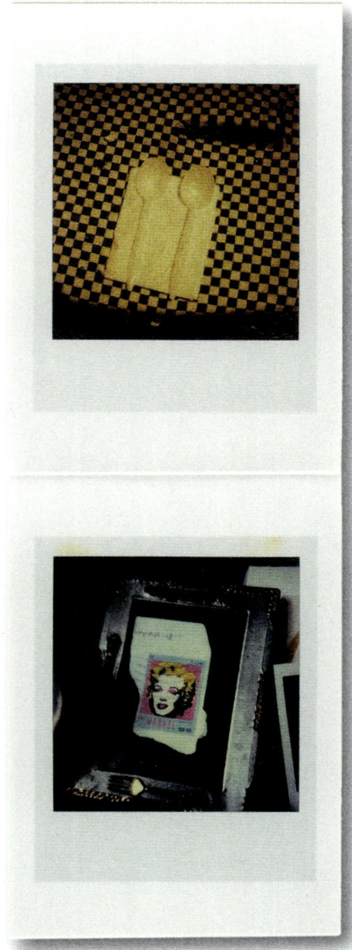
Depuis "LES JACKETS" 1985
Salut R.

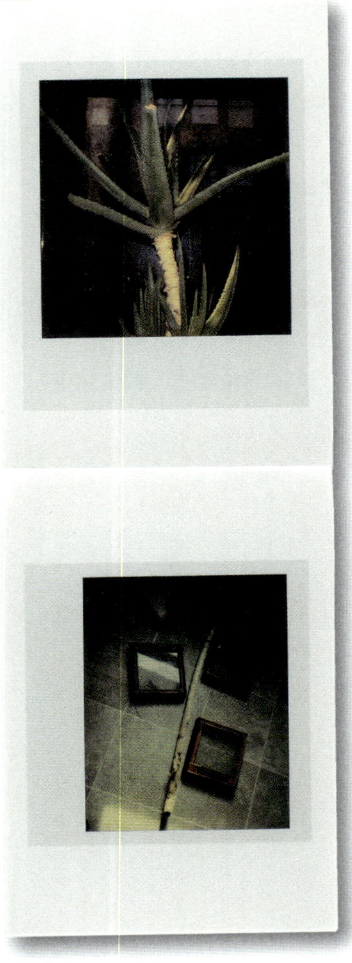

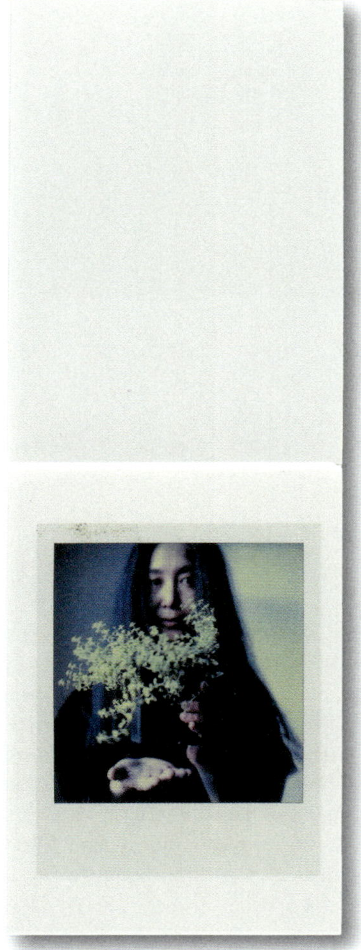

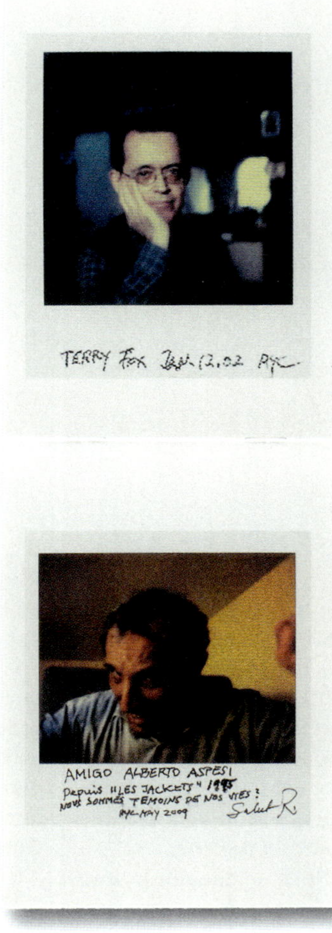
TERRY FOX Jan 12.02 NYC
AMIGO ALBERTO ASPESI
Depuis "LES JACKETS" 1985
NOUS SOMMES TEMOINS DE NOS VIES!
NYC-NY 2009
Salut R.

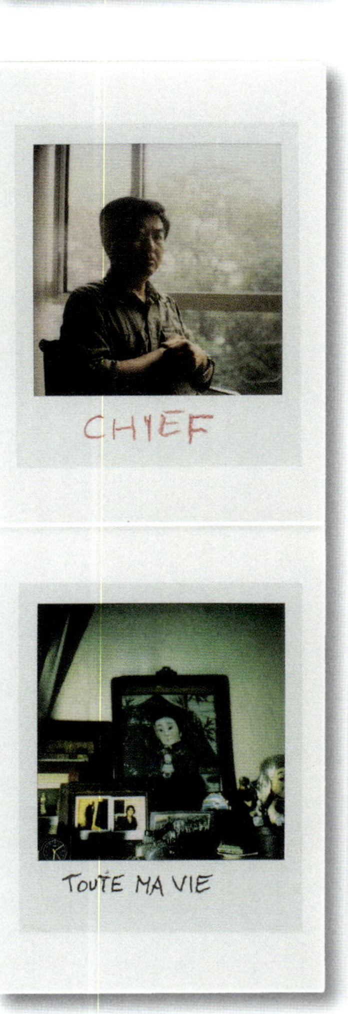
CHIEF
TOUTE MA VIE

Seven Stories

Published by Steidl, 2009

Robert Frank

Seven Stories

Steidl

Book design by Robert Frank,
A-chan and Gerhard Steidl
124 pages
5.5 × 3.9 in. / 14 × 10 cm
16 black-and-white and
71 color photographs
Four-color-process with
a glossy UV varnish
7 stapled booklets in a slipcase

ISBN 978-3-86521-789-9

In his later years Robert Frank worked almost exclusively with Polaroids, exploring the collage and assemblage possibilities of the instant photograph. *Seven Stories* brings together sequences of single images which Frank compiled to create books of new work. As always the photographs and stories relate Frank's life and milieu, his home in Mabou and New York, or a trip to China or Spain. *Seven Stories* is an important precursor to his visual diaries (2010–17); see page 87.

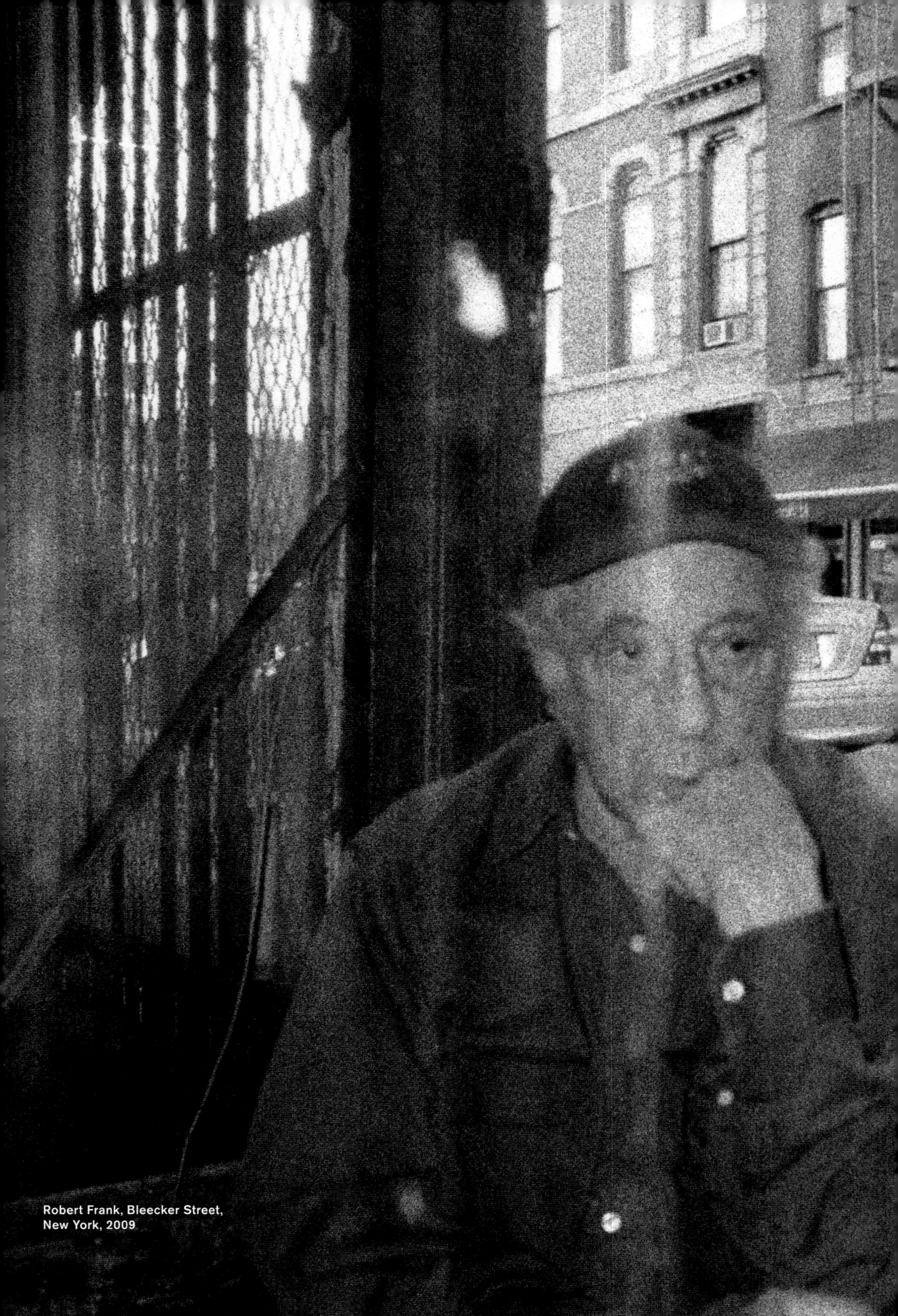

Robert Frank, Bleecker Street,
New York, 2009

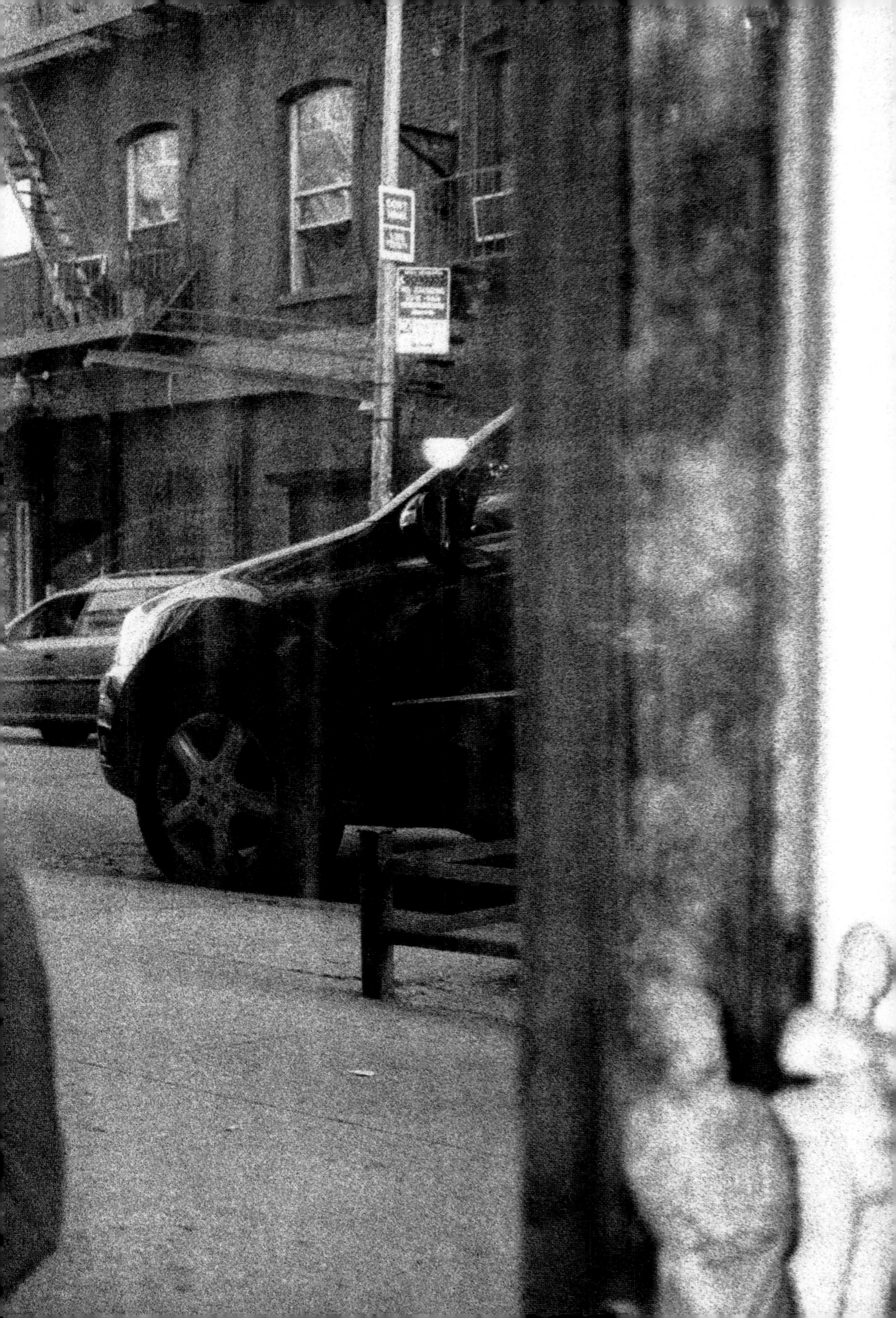

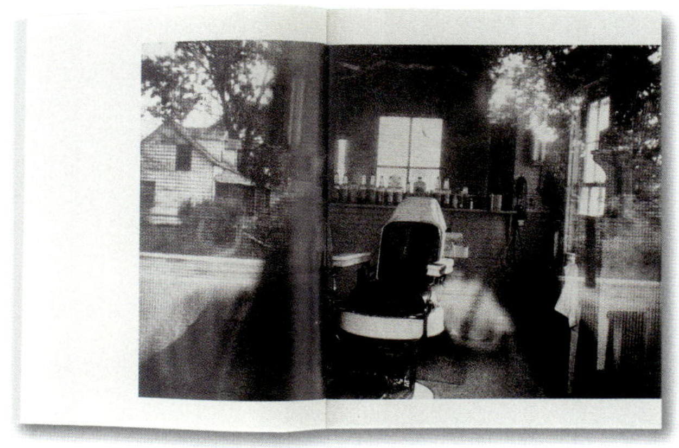
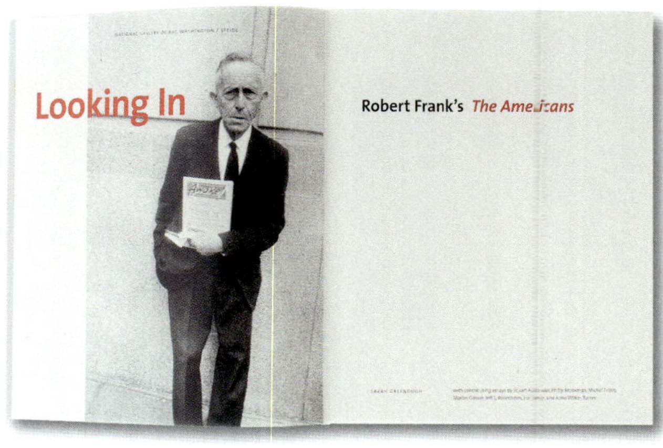
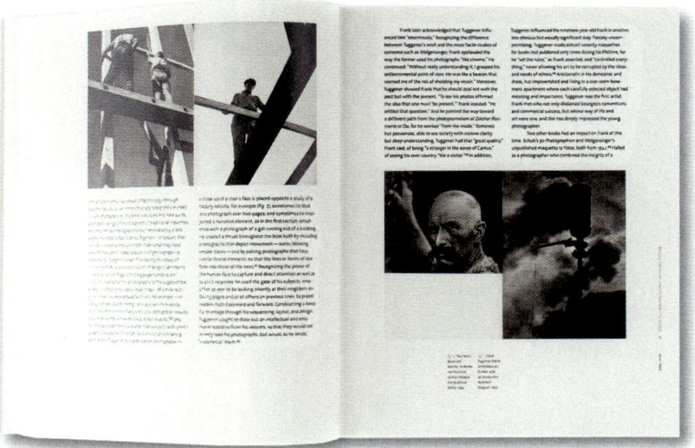
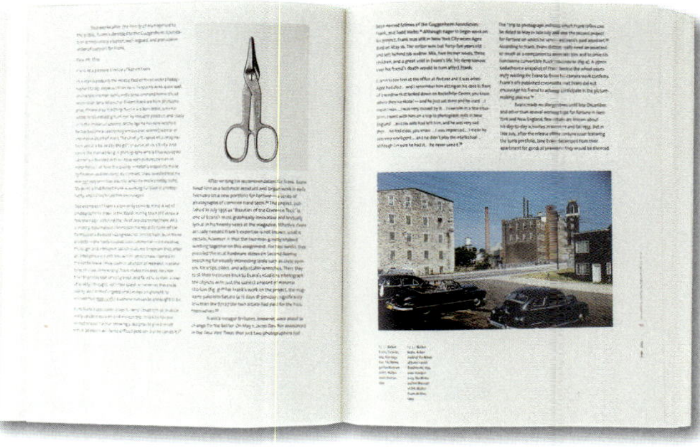
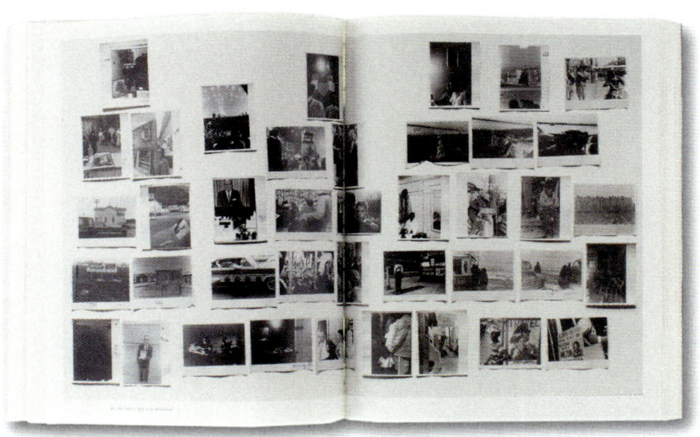
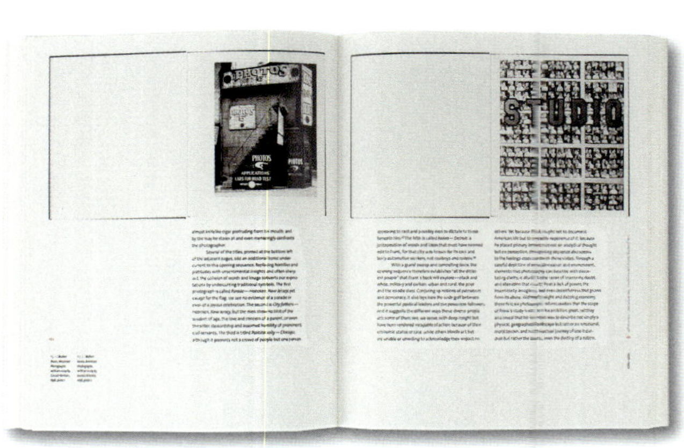
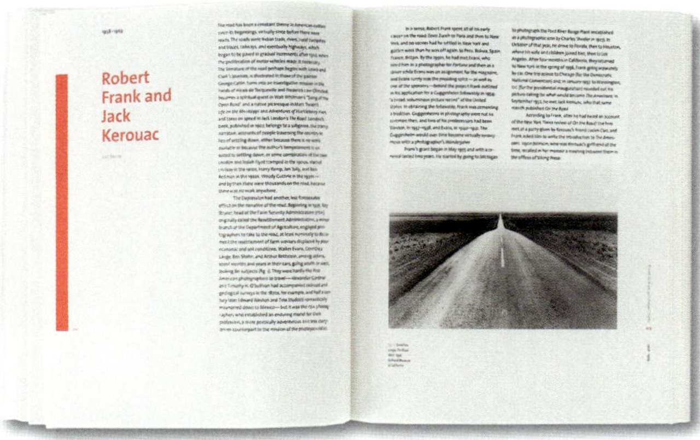
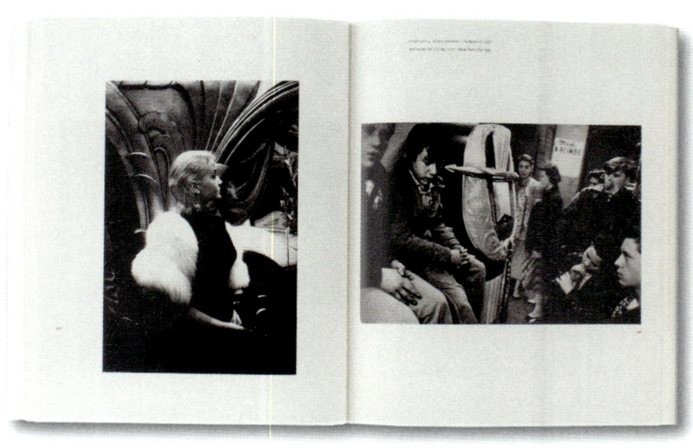

Looking In:
Robert Frank's
The Americans

Published by Steidl, 2009

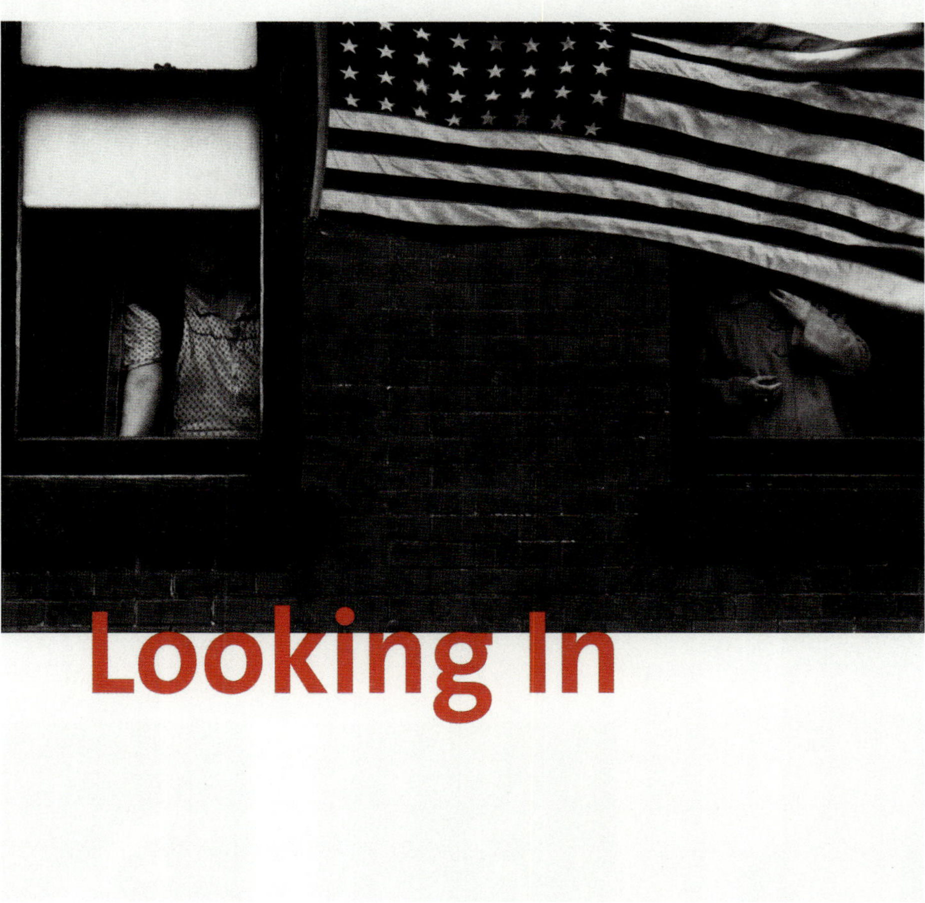

Edited by Sarah Greenough
Texts by Stuart Alexander, Philip
Brookman, Michel Frizot, Martin
Gasser, Sarah Greenough,
Jeff L. Rosenheim, Luc Sante
and Anne Wilkes Tucker
Book design by Margaret Bauer
506 pages
9.1 × 11.5 in. / 23.2 × 29.2 cm
452 black-and-white and
2 color photographs, and
49 illustrations
Tritone and four-color process
Clothbound hardcover with
dust jacket

ISBN 978-3-86521-806-3

Published on the occasion of a major exhibition on Robert Frank's *The Americans* at the National Gallery of Art, Washington D.C., in 2009, *Looking In: Robert Frank's The Americans* is the definitive source of information on Frank's seminal book. It presents a wealth of materials including essays and photographs, all of Frank's vintage contact sheets related to *The Americans*, a section that re-creates his preliminary sequence and presents variant croppings of the first and subsequent editions of the book, a map and chronology, as well as letters and manuscript materials by Frank, Walker Evans and Jack Kerouac related to Frank's Guggenheim fellowship, his travels around the United States in 1955–56 and his construction of the book.

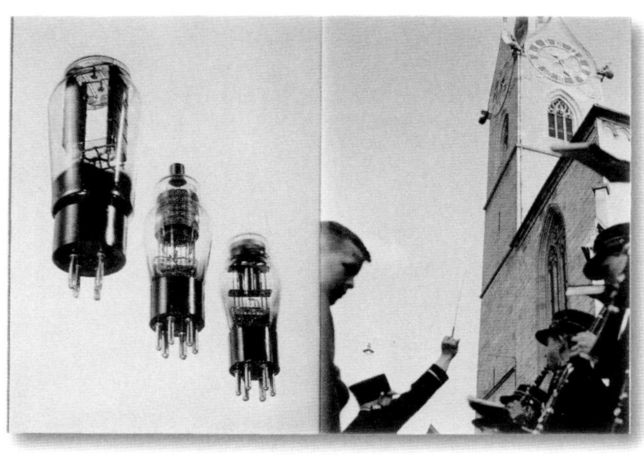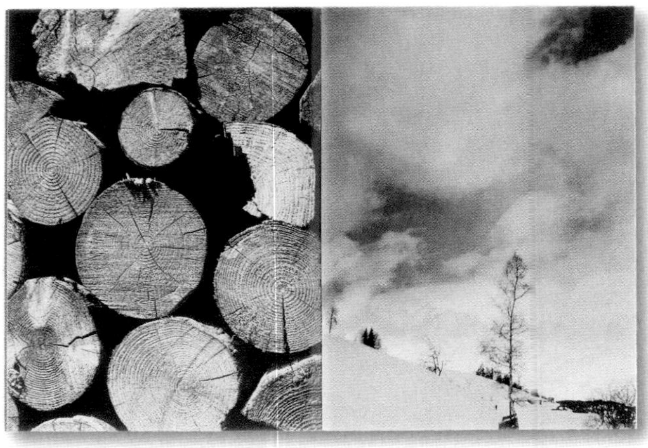
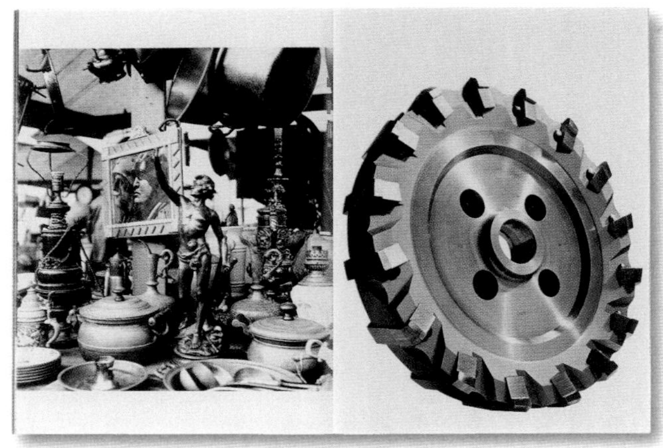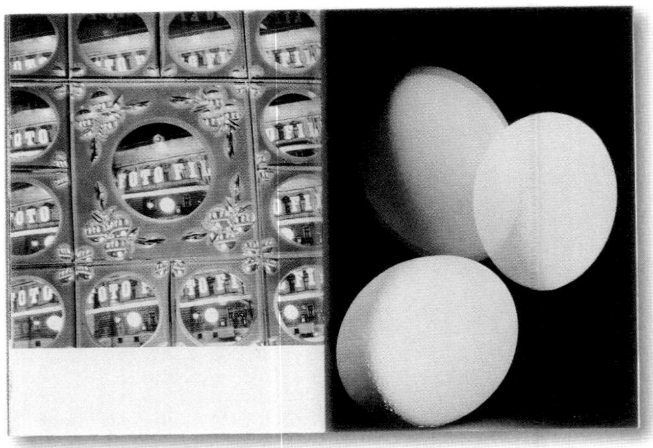
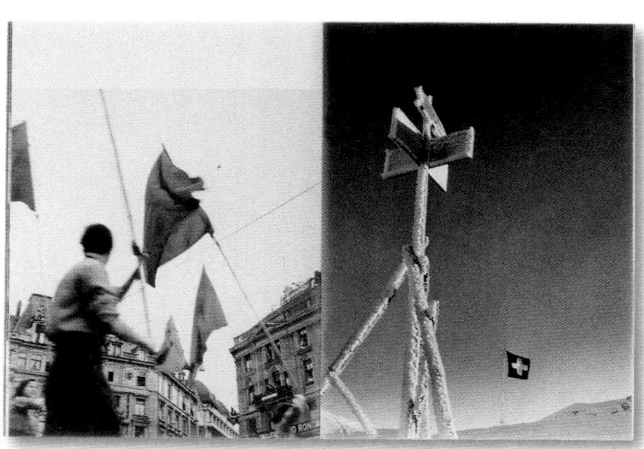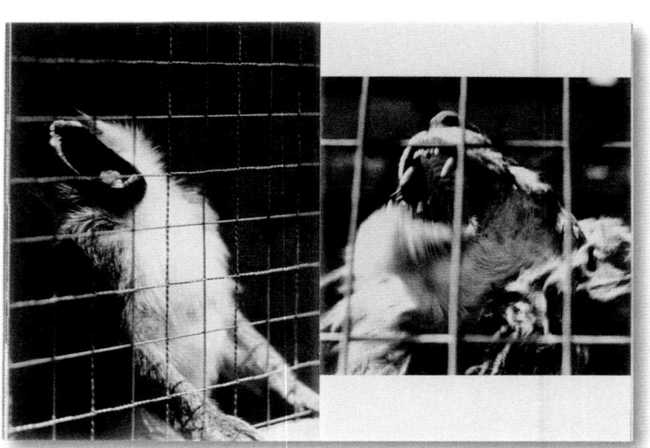
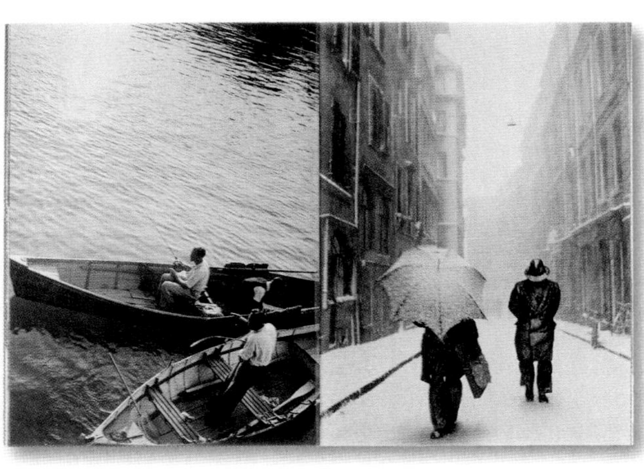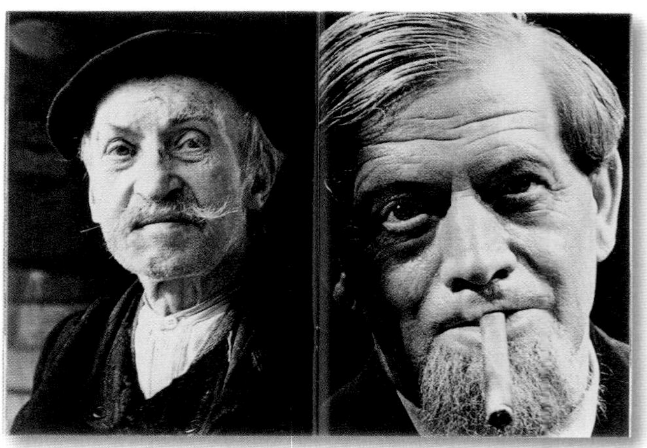

Portfolio.
40 Photos
1941 / 1946

Published by Steidl, 2009

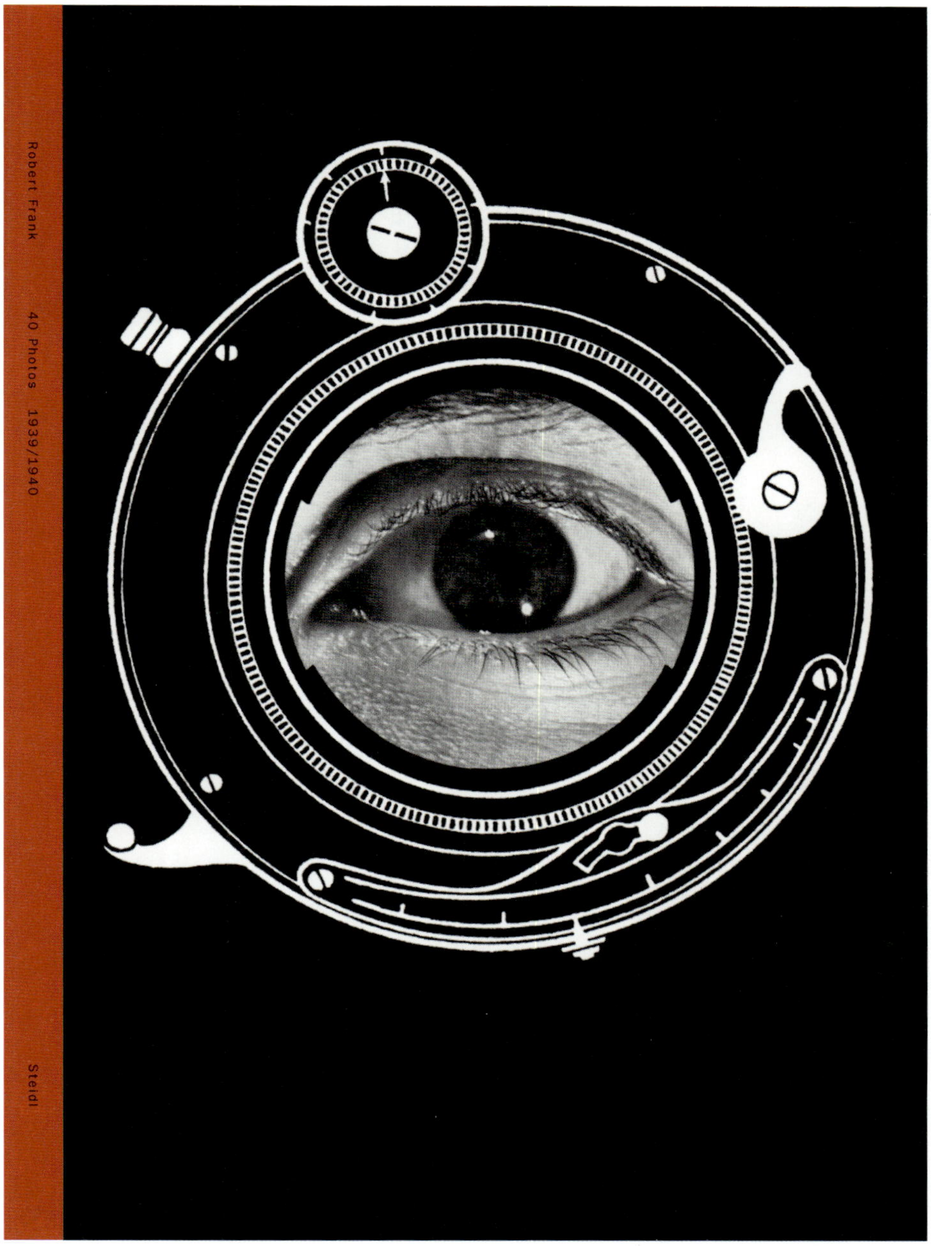

Book design by Robert Frank
and Gerhard Steidl
40 pages
8 × 10.7 in. / 20.5 × 27.3 cm
39 black-and-white photographs
Tritone
Softcover

ISBN 978-3-86521-813-1

When Robert Frank immigrated to New York from Zurich in 1947, the aspiring young photographer brought along his portfolio of 40 photos to help him secure employment. *Portfolio* is the facsimile version of this fascinating object.

Containing Frank's earliest original photographs as well as the work of other photographers which he had retouched, the portfolio presents images of rural life in Switzerland and alpine landscapes, alongside cityscapes and still lifes.

Portfolio contains the seeds of a career of such scope and influence which even the ambitious 23-year-old Robert Frank could not have anticipated.

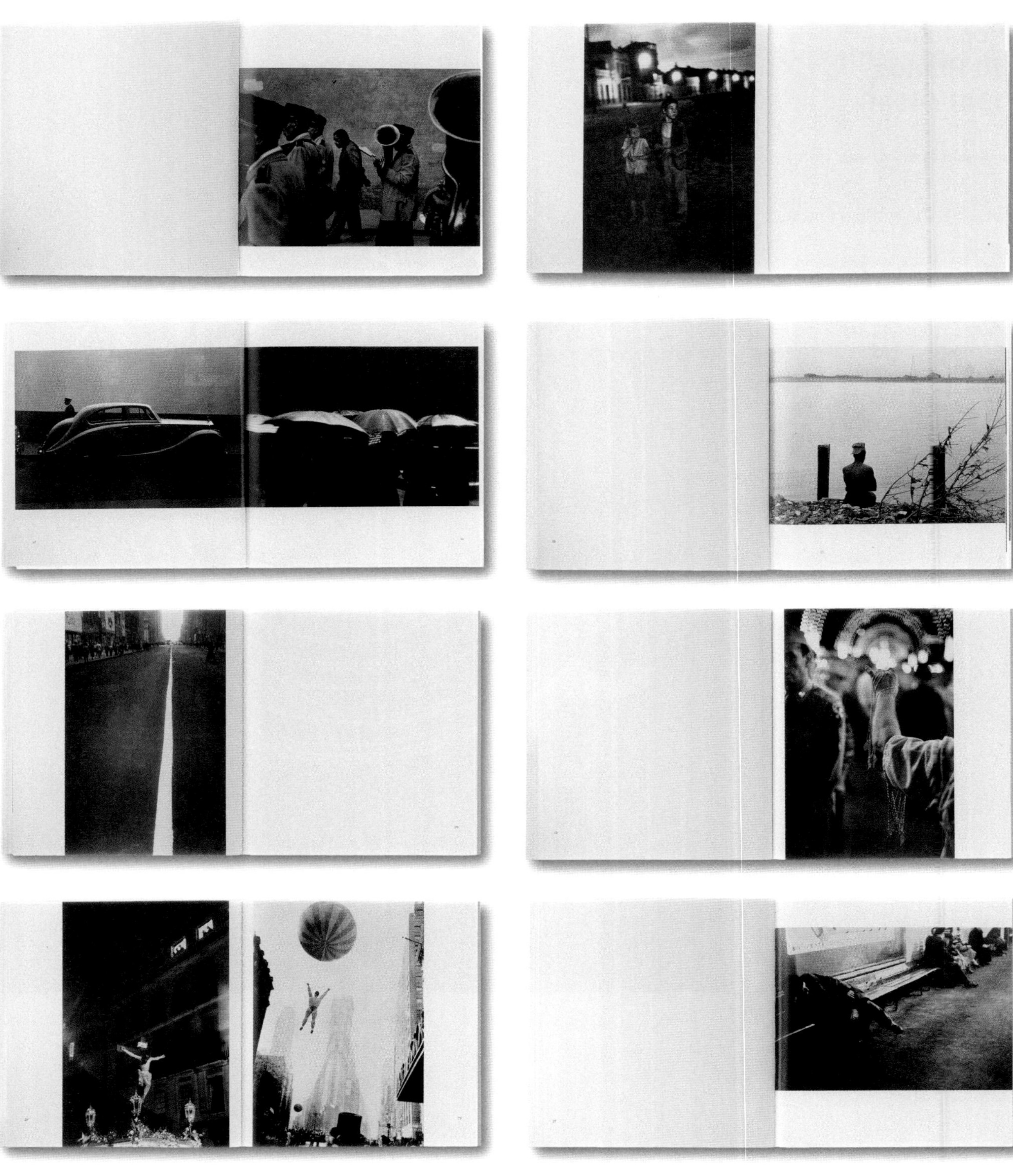

Black White
and Things

First edition published by
Scalo, 1994
First Steidl edition, 2009

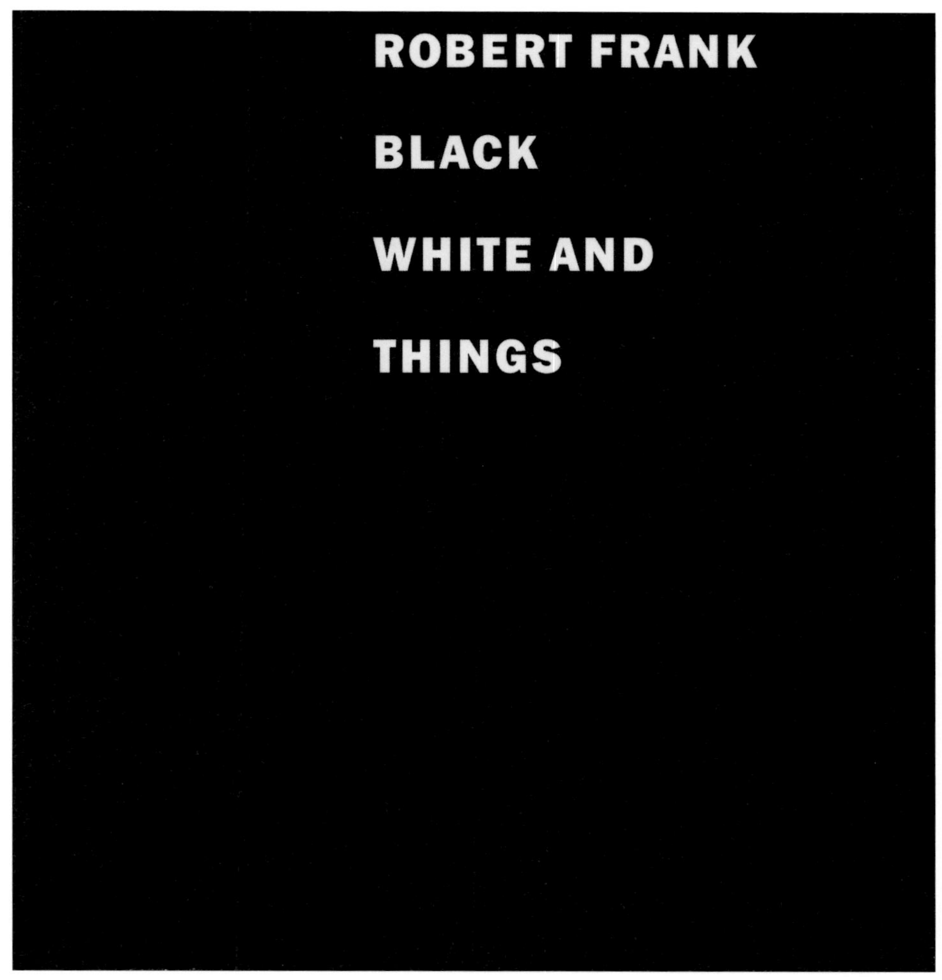

Book design by Werner Zryd
and Robert Frank
76 pages
8.3 × 8.5 in. / 21 × 21.6 cm
39 black-and-white photographs
Tritone
Softcover

ISBN 978-3-86521-808-7

Containing photographs taken between 1948 and 1952, *Black White and Things* was in its original form a book hand-crafted by Robert Frank in 1952. Frank made three identical copies designed by Werner Zryd, each with spiral binding and original photographs.

Separated into three categories "black," "white," and "things," which are shaped more by mood than subject matter, the book traces Frank's travels to cities such as Paris, New York, Valencia and St. Louis.

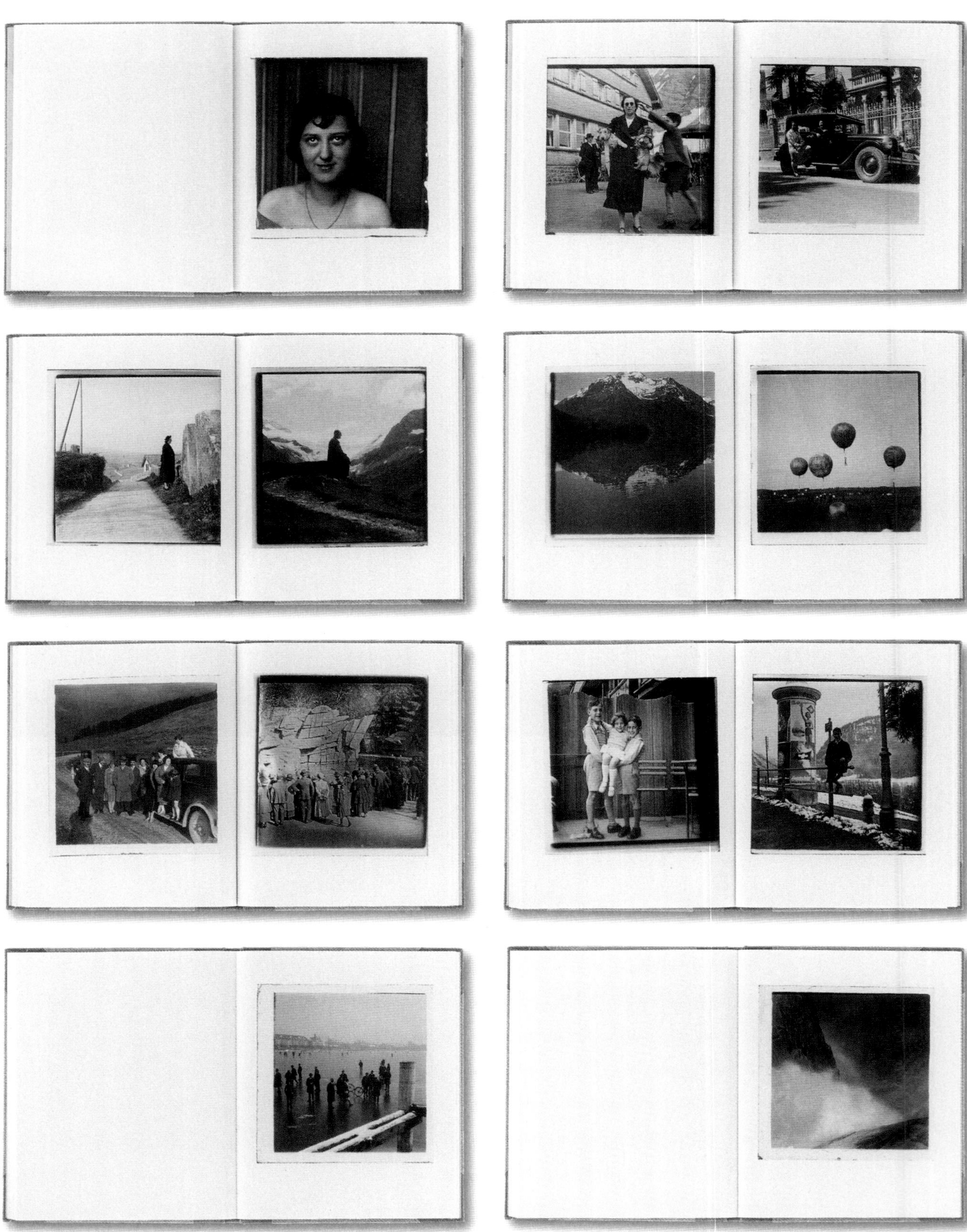

Henry Frank,
Father
Photographer

Published by Steidl, 2009

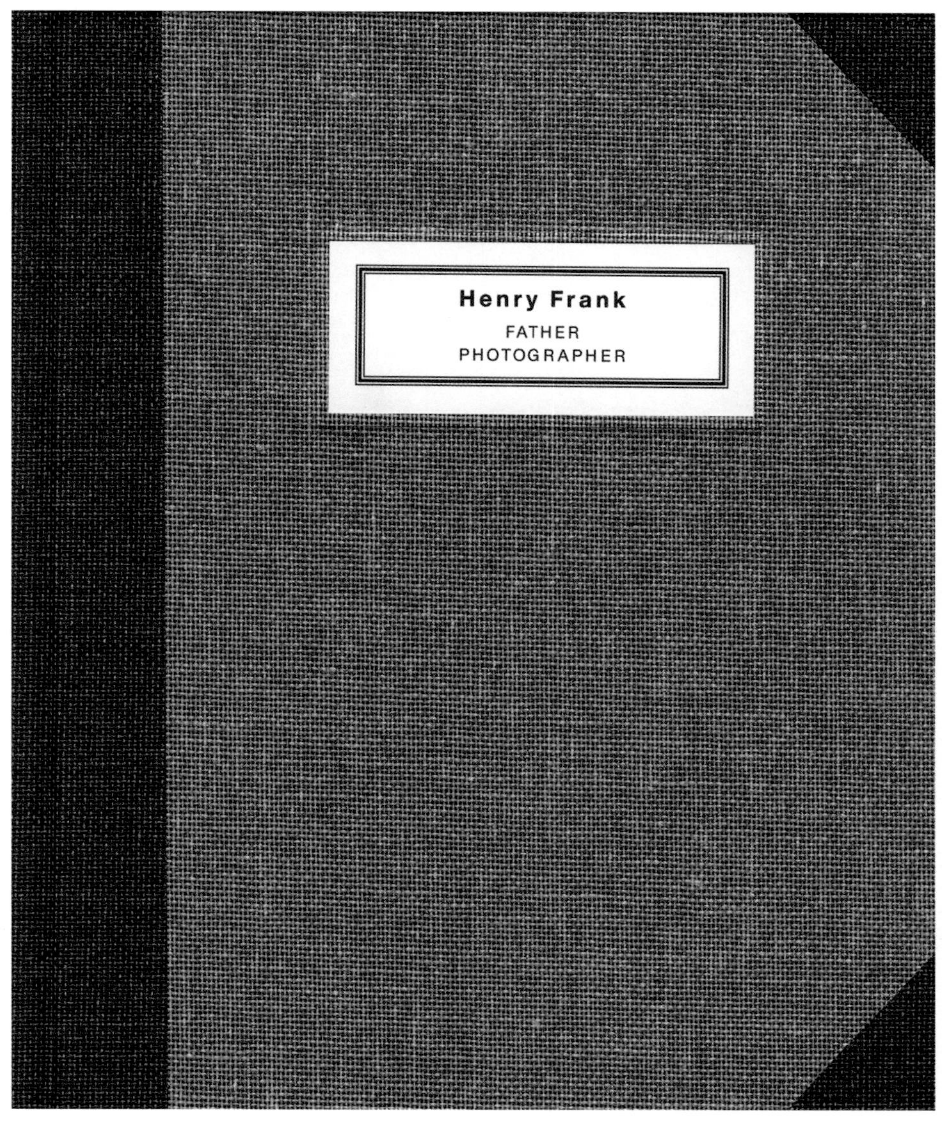

Edited by Robert Frank and
François-Marie Banier
Text by Robert Frank
Book design by Robert Frank,
François-Marie Banier,
Gerhard Steidl and Sarah Winter
88 pages
5.5 × 6.5 in. / 14 × 16.5 cm
48 black-and-white photographs
Tritone
Clothbound hardcover

ISBN 978-3-86521-814-8

Robert Frank's father, Henry (1890–1976), was both the proprietor of a bicycle shop in Zurich, and a keen amateur photographer. *Father Photographer* makes public for the first time a selection of Henry Frank's photographs including landscapes, family portraits, still lifes and cityscapes.

When Robert Frank immigrated to the United States in 1947, a wooden box containing his father's stereophotographs was one of the few objects he brought with him. In 2008 that box and the fragile photographic glass plates within it were hand-escorted to Steidl and scanned in preparation for this book.

Designed by Robert Frank, *Father Photographer* reveals Henry Frank to be both a talented photographer and an avid traveller. His pictures include snow-capped Alps and lakes in Switzerland, views of Venice, Pisa and Florence, and depictions of his family and friends including the young Robert. Henry Frank also reveals a passion for modern means of transport in images of aeroplanes, ships, hot-air balloons, and a car fair at the Grand Palais in Paris.

Father Photographer is a revelation of the unknown photographer Henry Frank, a historical photographic document of the early twentieth century, as well as a singular chapter in Robert Frank's bookmaking.

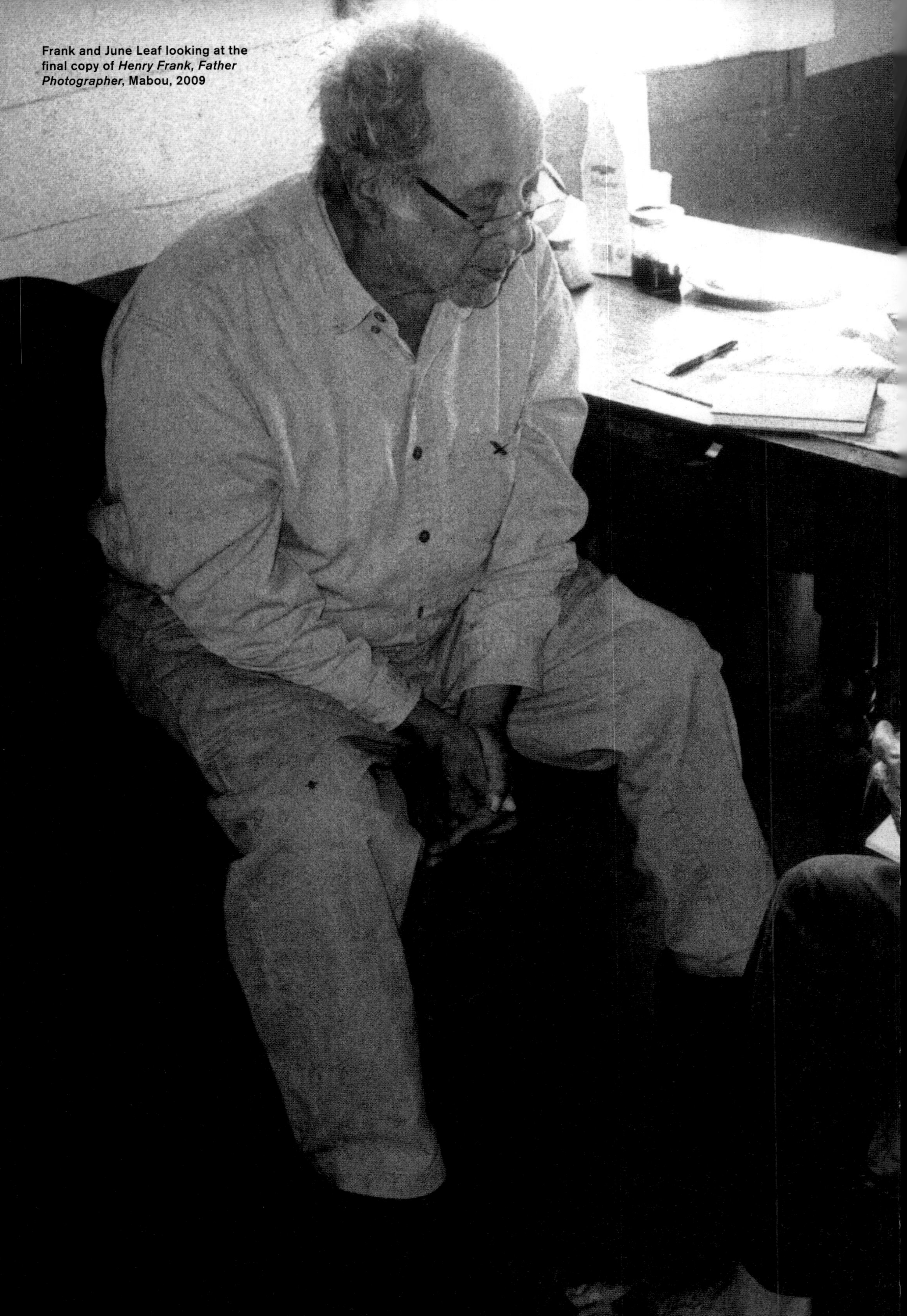

Frank and June Leaf looking at the final copy of *Henry Frank, Father Photographer*, Mabou, 2009

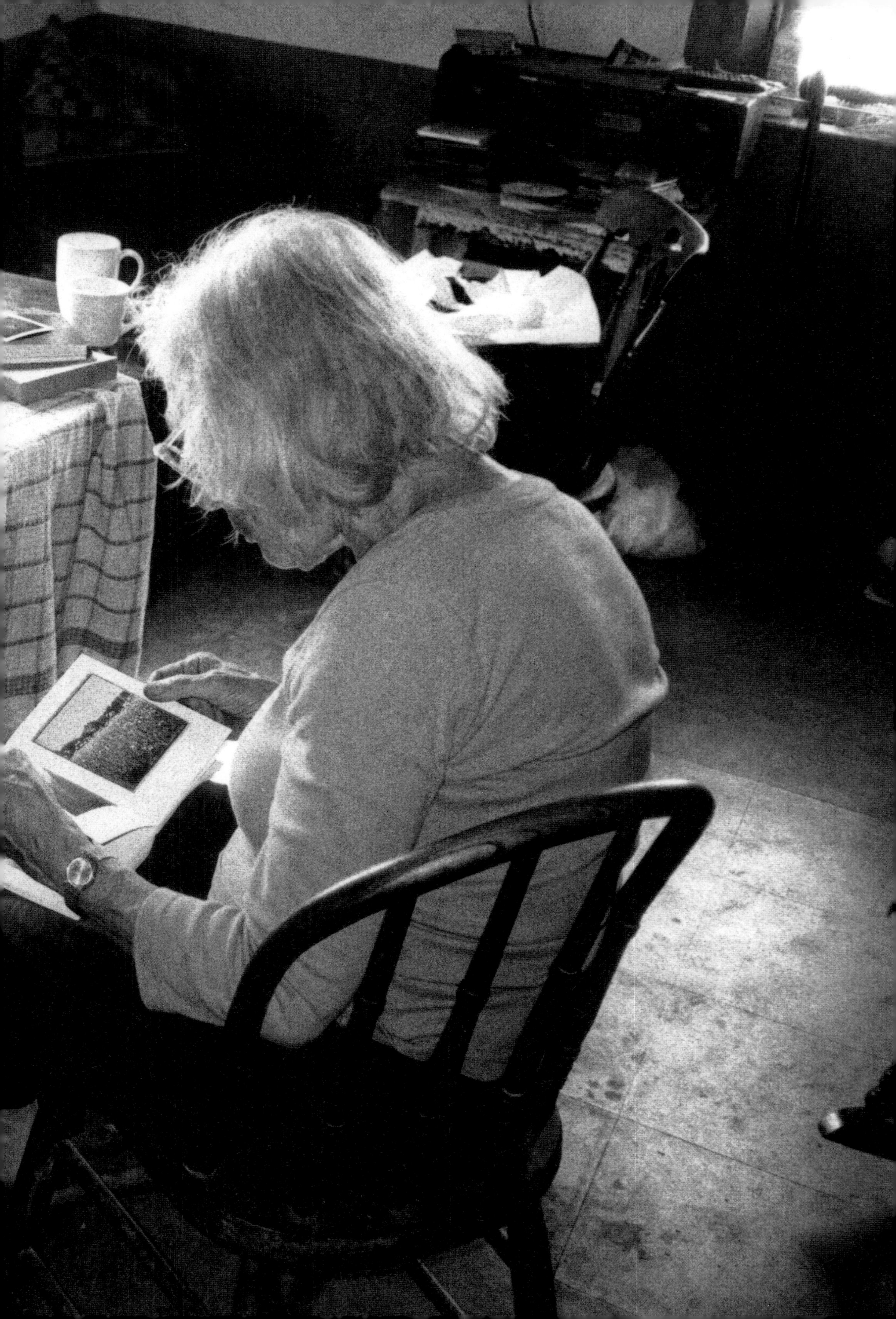

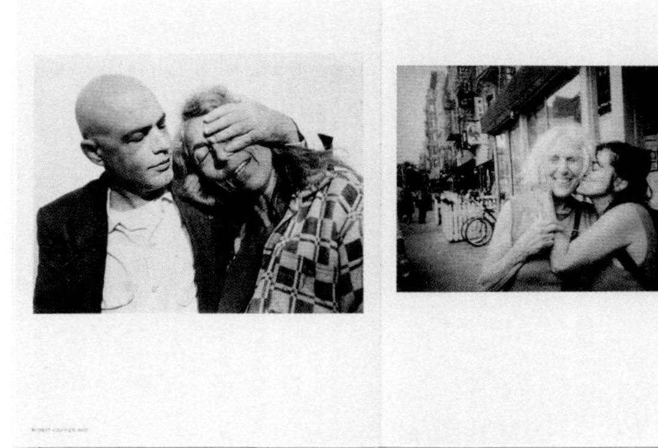

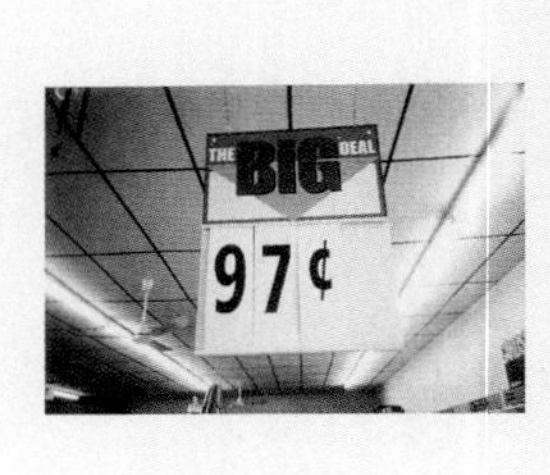

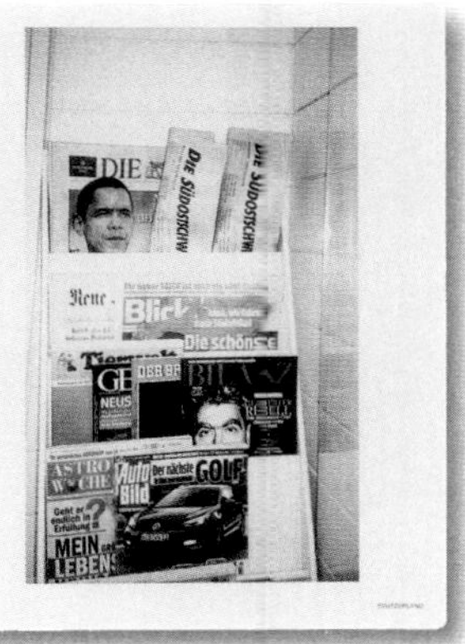

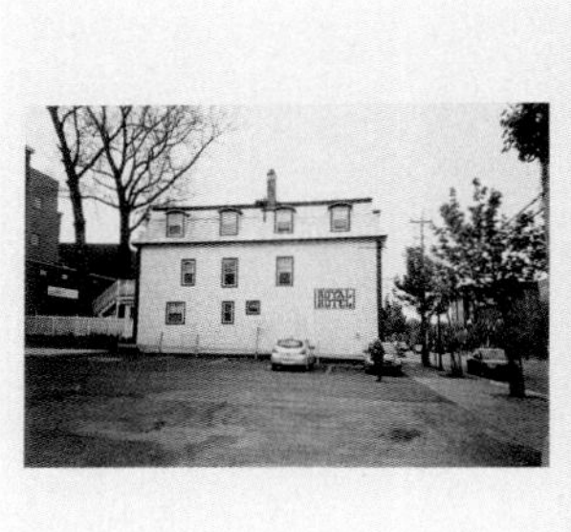

Up seven steps to the door of Royal Hotel Sidney Nova Scotia.
Narrow reception desk big windows Moosehead above fire place.
Pay-Telephone in booth, dog on carpet sleeping.
Ring buzzer the owner Irene or Burt will come to
take your name give you key and Room 4.

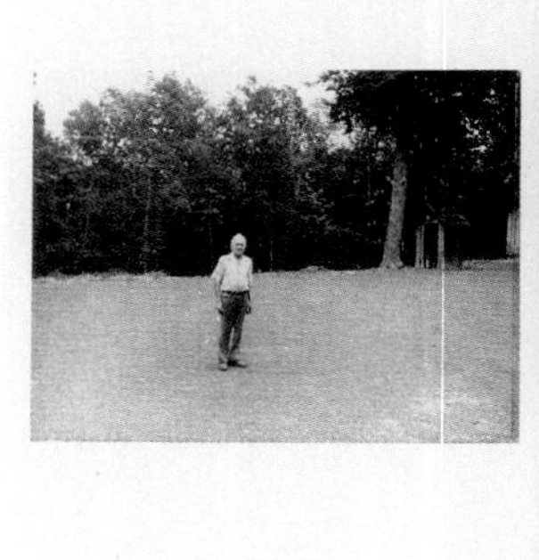

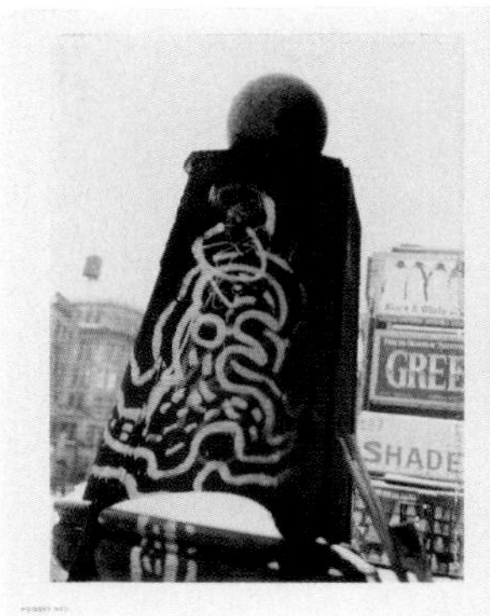

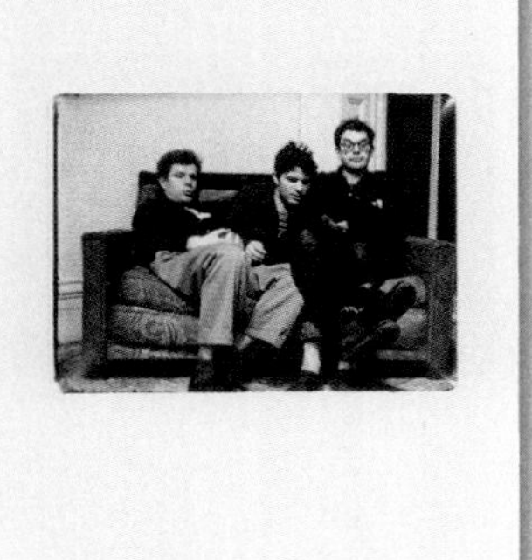

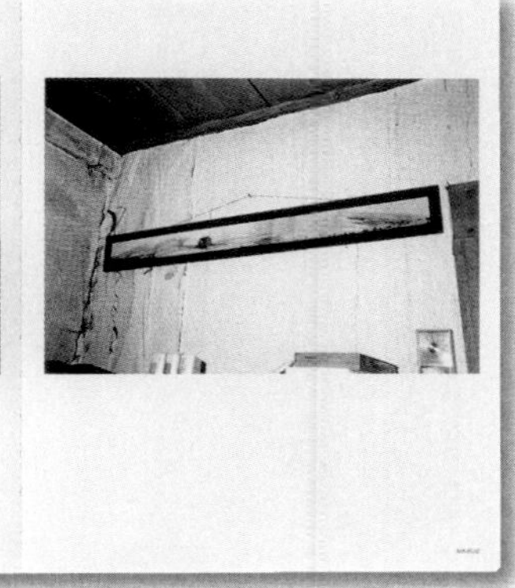

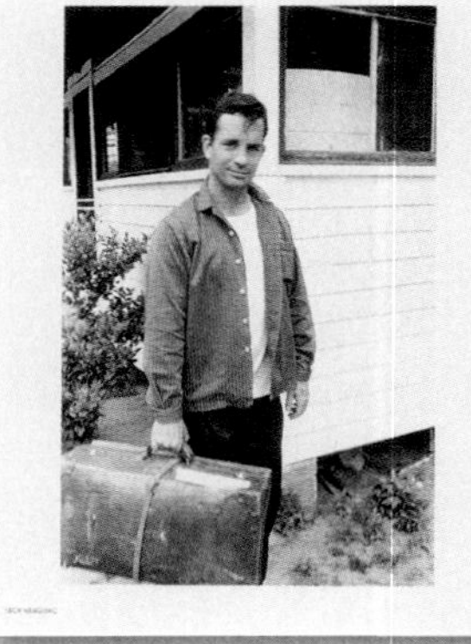

Tal Uf Tal Ab

Published by Steidl, 2010

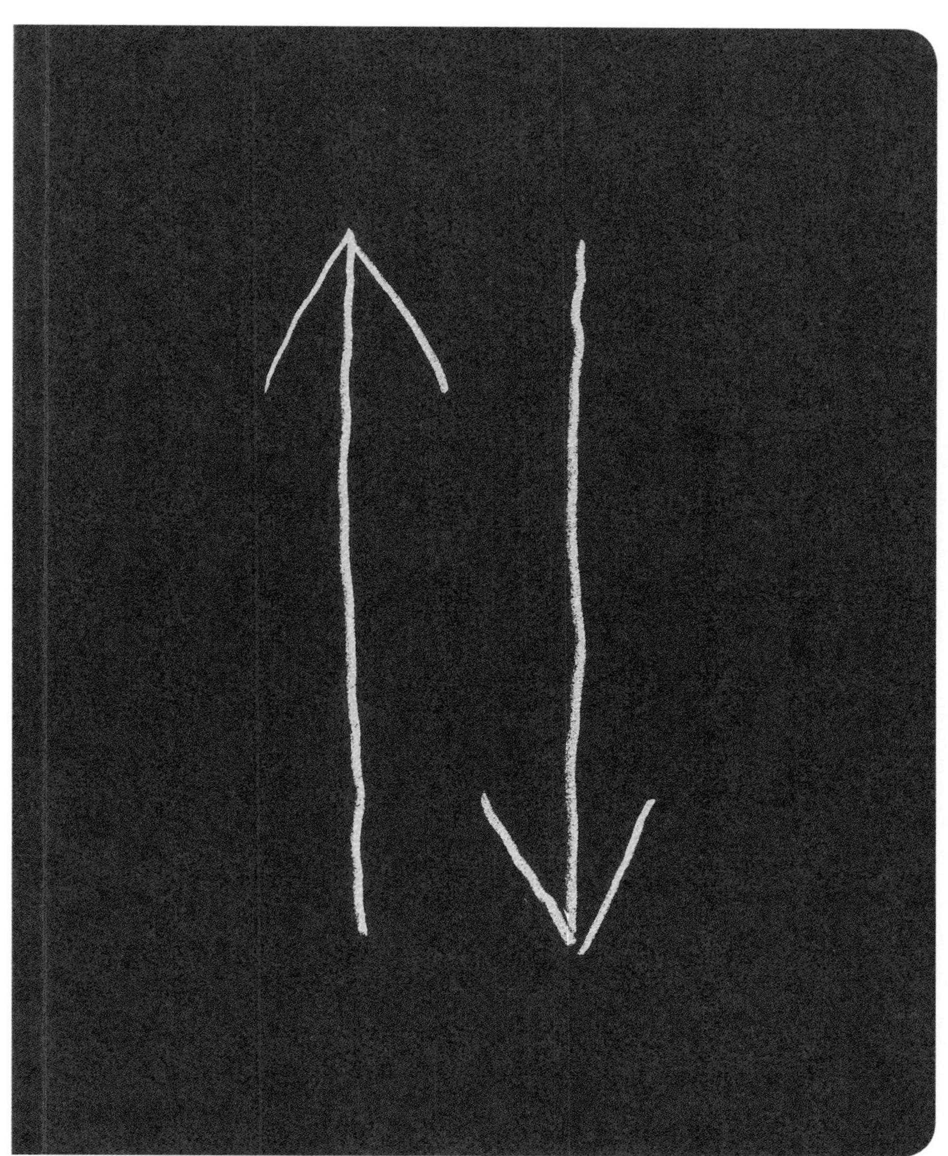

Text by Robert Frank
Book design by Robert Frank,
A-chan and Gerhard Steidl
40 pages
8 × 9.8 in. / 20.5 × 25 cm
29 black-and-white photographs
Tritone
Otabind softcover in a slipcase

ISBN 978-3-86930-101-3

Tal Uf Tal Ab shows how Robert Frank's life was an inquisitive existence shaped by memory, and includes photographs of newsstands, streetscapes, friends, his wife June Leaf, interiors, as well as a self-portrait. Among these images are scattered ones from Frank's past, for example a candid portrait of Jack Kerouac. As with all Frank's publications, *Tal Uf Tal Ab* is an understated yet important progression in the medium of the photobook.

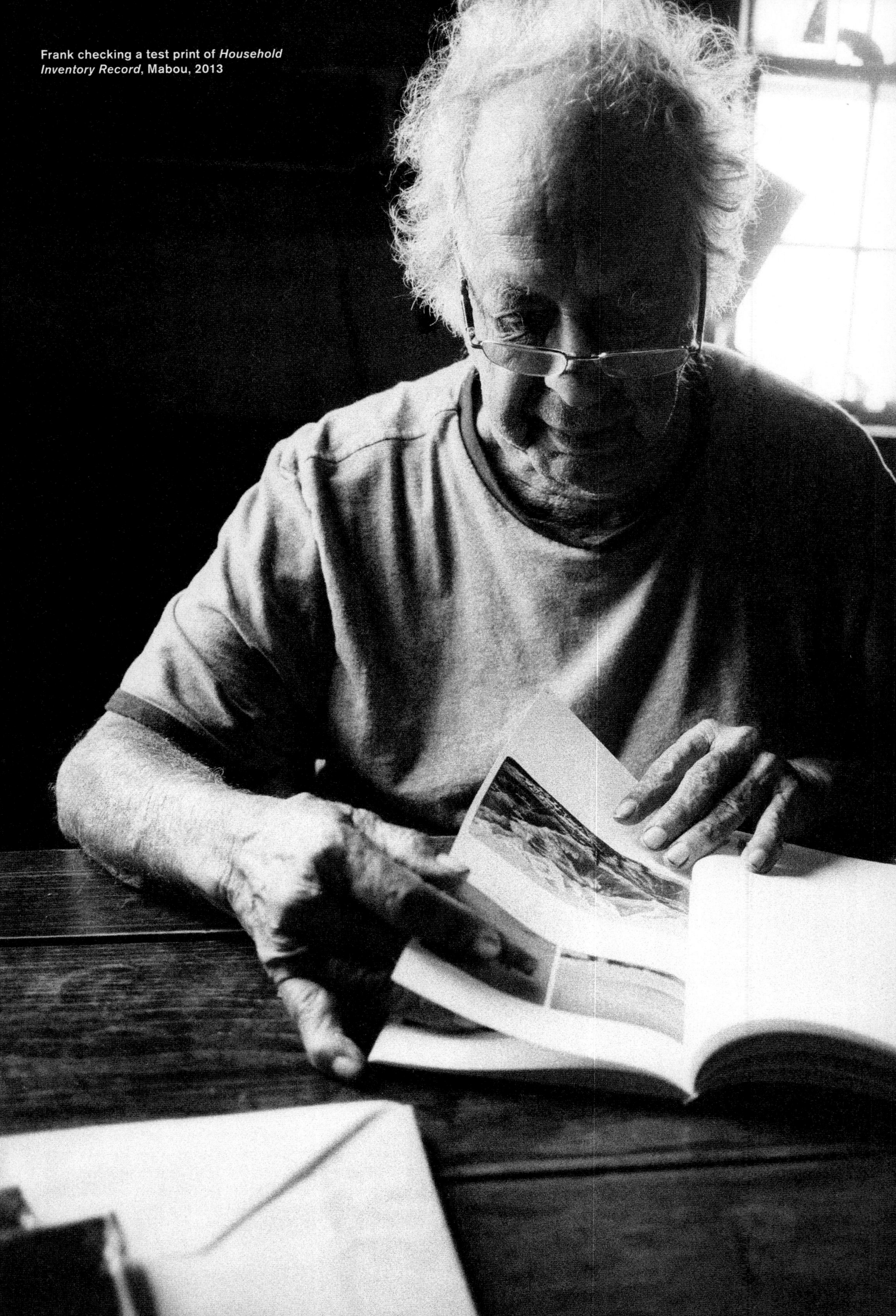

Frank checking a test print of *Household Inventory Record*, Mabou, 2013

The Visual Diaries

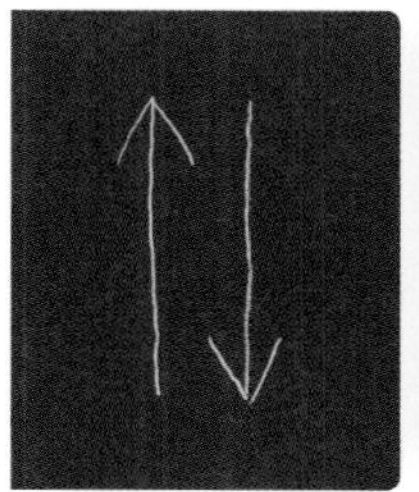
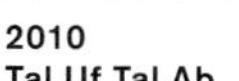

2010
Tal Uf Tal Ab

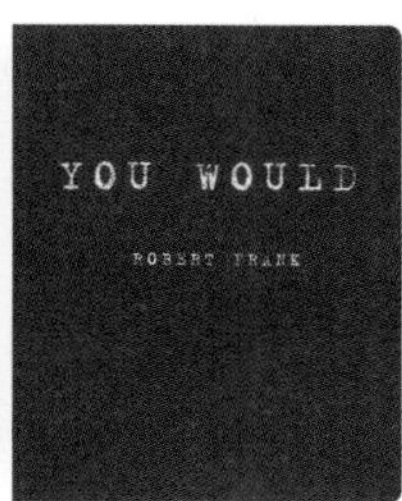

2012
You Would

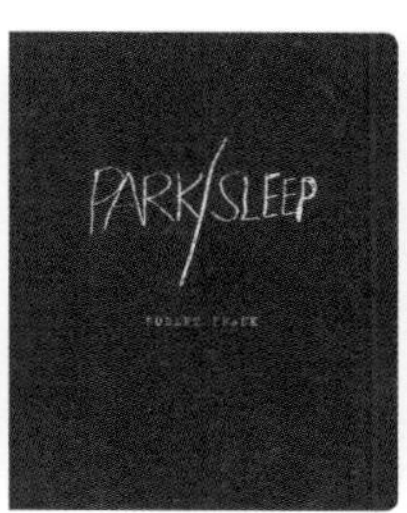

2013
Park / Sleep

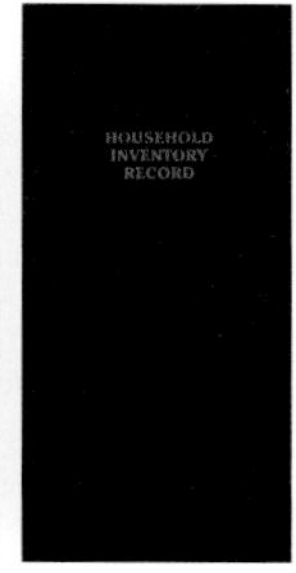

2013
Household Inventory
Record

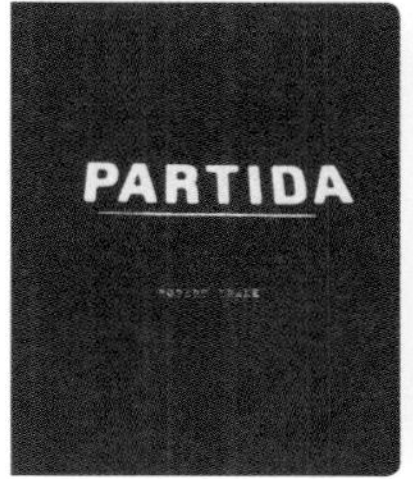

2014
Partida

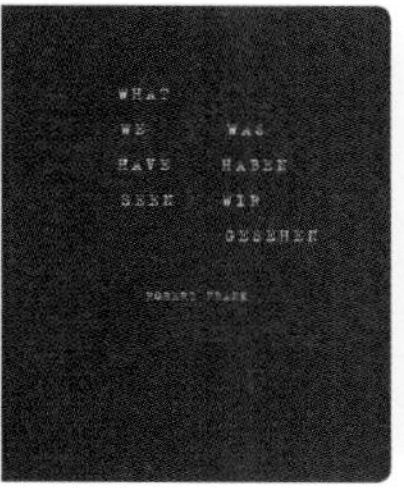

2016
Was haben wir
gesehen / What we
have seen

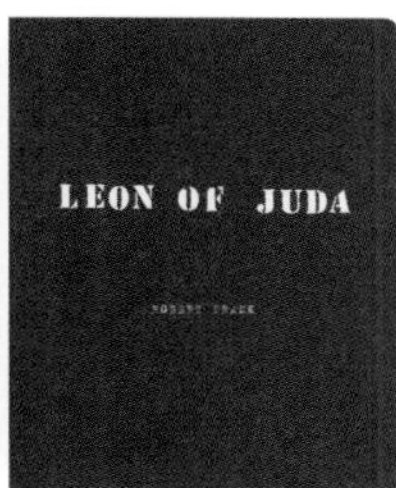

2017
Leon of Juda

Known as his visual diaries, these seven humble introspective volumes, published between 2010 and 2017, are the most important in Robert Frank's late bookmaking practice.

The books imaginatively combine iconic photos from Frank's early career with the more private pictures he made in later life. Black-and-white photos taken on 35mm film, including some from *The Americans*, mix with contemporary photos, often color Polaroids. Quiet still lifes, contemplative landscapes and urban scenes, self-portraits, and spontaneous endearing shots of friends, colleagues and the photographer's wife artist June Leaf show the life he lived in their homes in Bleecker Street, New York, and Mabou, Nova Scotia.

With these images Frank created seemingly casual layouts that recall the look and spirit of a private album or scrapbook, and comment on memory and the passage of time. Factual captions and short, sometimes cryptic texts are scattered throughout the books—Frank's thoughts, fragments of conversations, poems, notes.

When making the first of the books *Tal Uf Tal Ab* in 2010, Robert Frank and Gerhard Steidl decided all in the series would be simple softcover volumes with an approachable size of 20.5 × 25 cm and a modest page-count. All books would be bound in a dark grey, leather-like cardboard, and housed in an inexpensive cardboard slipcase to create an archival feel.

But how many books would there be? Frank and Steidl decided that each volume should have different colored endpapers, and Steidl suggested Fedrigoni's Tintoretto Ceylon 140 g, which was then available only in six colors. And so it was an easy decision for Frank: six books at this size there would be—each a self-contained visual diary, but conceived together as chapters in a larger story. (The seventh diary, *Household Inventory Record* of 2013, is a readymade and an exception in the series. Here Frank took a real inventory book as his template, and the final publication recreates its size and haptic qualities.)

Robert Frank's highly personal approach to all these books suggests how the past tempered his present, and shows how his life was not only documented in but shaped by bookmaking. The visual diaries are without doubt a reflection upon his later life and past, but even when he was looking back he was looking towards the future. Right up until his passing in 2019, Frank remained as innovative and ambitious as ever, and the book was the primary expression of his steadfast artistic curiosity.

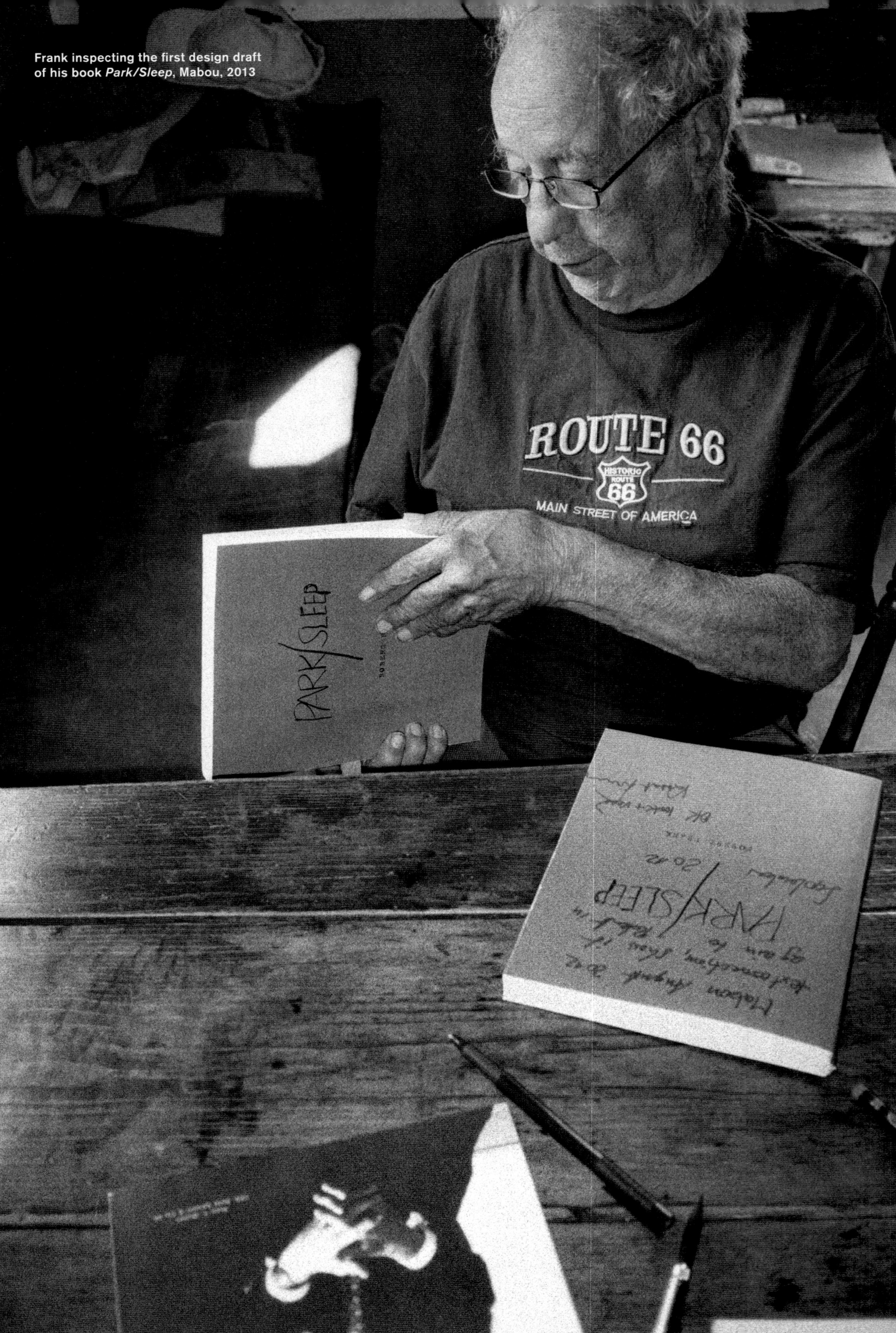

Frank inspecting the first design draft of his book *Park/Sleep*, Mabou, 2013

Fragments of Living:
The Poetry of Robert Frank's Visual Diaries

John Farrel

In 2013, Michail Mersinis, a tutor in the Fine Art Photography Department at the Glasgow School of Art, sent an email to Robert Frank. The email was written on behalf of Mersinis' students and requested a "donation of words" that could be included in that year's class exhibition catalogue. In his email, Mersinis made mention of an impassioned discussion that arose during a class lecture the week before. The discussion revolved around Frank's seminal 1989 work, *Hold Still, Keep Going*. Much to everyone's surprise, a few weeks later, a reply came for "a donation of words":

Your familiarity with my work suggests that you understand that I have long run out of words. I am left with only photographs now. To satisfy the urgency of your letter and the care that your letter on behalf of your students suggests, please tell them this: tell them to make work that is close to their heart. It seems to me that no one can expect more than this. I hope this is enough.
Regards, Robert

Make work that is close to your heart. This simple notion seems to me to be the prevailing spirit that runs throughout most, if not all, of Frank's work. This is especially evident in a recent series of publications, collectively known as the "visual diaries," that Frank has been making in close collaboration with his long-time publisher Gerhard Steidl. The most recent, *Was haben wir gesehen / What we have seen*, was published earlier this year.

Frank was born in Zurich, Switzerland, in 1924 and moved to New York City in 1947 with a portfolio of photographs in the hope to make a new life. He quickly found work at *Harper's Bazaar*, which enabled him to travel, first around Peru and Bolivia, followed by a brief return to Europe, where he travelled around Spain and France in 1949. It was in Paris that Frank first met with Robert Delpire, the acclaimed French publisher that would later publish *Les Américains* in 1958.

In New York City Frank struck up friendships with the poet Allen Ginsberg, writers Jack Kerouac, William S. Burroughs, and others of the Beat Generation, which would have a lasting impact on his work. Much like Kerouac and his novel *On the Road*, Frank is best known for *The Americans.* This iconoclastic publication's legacy still reverberates to this day, made almost 60 years ago, it has influenced generations of photographers and artists, people such as Ed Ruscha, Nan Goldin, Duane Michals and JH Engström, to name but a few.

In 1959, Frank put down his Leica and picked up a movie camera and began making films, beginning with *Pull My Daisy*, a half-hour short film written and narrated by Kerouac. Frank would spend the majority of the next decade working on film projects until the publication of his next major book work, 1972's *The Lines of My Hand.* This book heralded a different kind of revolution in picture making—Frank's photographs from this period are much more direct, poetic, and deeply personal.

Working with a Polaroid camera and pack film, Frank scratched and painted words and phrases over the images, giving the photographs a tactile immediacy and tacit emotional depth. Throughout *The Lines of My Hand,* we are faced by powerful, singular works in which Frank has taped, nailed, or glued images and text together; filmstrips are combined with still images and printed or pasted together on boards and scrawled over. It is in this work that we see, for the first time, what will become the central themes of Frank's work. His mantra of never looking back is belied by the fact that the first half of the book dredges through the earliest part of his career. *The Lines of My Hand* is very much a book in two halves—the inclusion of early photographs from London, Paris, Spain, Peru, and iconic images from *The Americans* in the book's first half serve only to emphasize the dramatic shift in style and tone of the pictures in the book's second half.

The post-1970s aesthetic may have been informed not just by the dramatic changes in locale, from Bleecker Street to rural Nova Scotia, but by a number of personal tragedies. The death of his close friend Danny Seymour, with whom Frank collaborated on a number of his early films, had a profound effect on him. This was followed shortly thereafter by the death of Frank's daughter Andrea in 1974. Andrea, along with his son Pablo, were Frank's only children born out of his first marriage to artist Mary Frank. Andrea was killed in a plane crash in Guatemala at aged 23, and the wealth of works addressed or dedicated to his daughter is testament to her passing's impact on Frank. His son Pablo, who had battled with drug addiction and mental illness for many years, took his own life in 1994, aged just 43. His relationship with his son was fraught, and a number of film works in which Pablo featured testify to this: the films *Conversations in Vermont* (1969), *Life Dances On* (1980), and *Home Improvements* (1985) clearly demonstrate the difficult, often strained relationship between father and son and the deterioration of Pablo's mental and physical well-being. The diaristic mode Frank adopted as a film and picture maker at this time is evident throughout his later work.

Frank's charged articulation of his own life and family form the visual diaries that have been published since 2010. Publisher Gerhard Steidl worked closely with Frank on these books, as well as on a number of classic book reprints. Frank and Steidl have forged a trusted working relationship which has culminated in this new series of book works; beautiful, small paperback volumes that have been published almost annually since 2010. The first volume was *Tal Uf Tal Ab,* in which Frank combined previously unseen photographs from his extensive archive with photographs made in recent years.

"Tal Uf Tal Ab" is Swiss-German. It means direction up the valley—down the valley. Now I live and wait and think mostly in the places I live—New York and Nova Scotia.

Throughout this series of new publications, of which there are six to date, similar themes indeed recur and conscious attention is paid to the passing of time. Old friends, long gone, reappear. Images of Burroughs, Ginsberg, and Kerouac taken from film stills and informal portraits are sequenced alongside photographs of neighbours and visitors. Also present are a number of still lifes and photographic constructs, as well as portraits of June Leaf, of A-chan; Frank's co-editor and printer, Gerhard Steidl and of Pablo and Mary Frank. Interiors from Mabou and New York feature heavily, as do photographs of everyday objects and sparse, cryptic writings.

In *Was haben wir gesehen / What we have seen* (2016), we repeatedly encounter a number of visual markers: the Empire State Building, the Statue of Liberty, doorways, windows, and the sea. These act as visual devices that set the book's pace, much like the way in which the jukebox or the American flag set the pacing in *The Americans.* Frank's visual acuity permeates each of the visual diaries and there is a slightness and potency to these pictures that confronts the viewer and demands a closer reading. In each volume, we are confronted by a litany of visual devices and codes that demand both the viewer's attention and time, in order for them to reveal themselves. Perhaps it is the seemingly abstruse nature of the pictures that has allowed these later works to slip through relatively unnoticed within the discourse of Frank's work. The photographs still share all the outsider inquisitiveness of Frank's earlier pictures, but the feeling within them is far more oblique and poetic. Frank seems concerned only with satisfying his own vision when making these pictures. He is not trying to offer us as viewers, or indeed to indulge himself in, anything other than an experience of pure looking. Frank leaves the photographs to speak for themselves. That there is little to no captioning of his work, save for the occasional name of a person or place, reinforces the importance placed on the pure visual experience.

Throughout the books, regular themes and symbols recur; photographs of doorways, window frames, the sky, and the shoreline appear over and over in almost every book. This visual continuity works in a kind of performative modus operandi, binding the books together in such a way that they can be viewed both independently, or as one larger, extended body of work.

The small photographic series of three color photographs of the sky that appear near the end of *Partida*

(2014) provides an interesting example of the performative qualities within these later works. Not unlike a series of film stills, Frank repeatedly photographs this skyline as perfectly white clouds encroach upon a brilliant blue sky, appearing just above the treeline. The subtlety of the blue sky set against the near pure white clouds, along with the repeated exposure, are arranged and composed so as to appear as three nearly identical photographs. The informal, almost accidental, editing perfects the performative nature of Frank's photography, emphasizing the tides of time, an idea that echoes throughout the visual diaries. In *Household Inventory Record* (2013), the cloud work re-appears, this time as a single image set against a photograph of the black reverse side of the Polaroid. Scratched onto its surface are the words "Porque? Quel Dia?," meaning "Why? This day?" Frank is asking more questions than he is offering answers to.

In these newer works, there is a definite feeling of reflection upon the life of the artist, though this does not mean he is simply counting waves. Even in his ninth decade, Frank is continually striving to arrive at new places within his work, constantly moving forward even when he is looking back. Despite the somewhat sombre and reflective nature of some of the photographs, there is no indication that Frank is any less radical now in his later years than he was in his youth. His intention is even more vital now than in his earlier years, his famously restless spirit still emanates from these photographs...

Frank deftly combines older pictures from his archive with new and previously unseen photographs, creating a time shift and tension that permeates each of the books. He has become increasingly more prosaic in terms of how he makes pictures, opting instead for a directness that is at once poetic, often gestural, but without ever being didactic. These notions are reflected by some of Frank's own musings throughout the books:

I suppose my photographs are of things I don't
want to forget
My instinct tells me that they are important
They are quiet
They demand no attention
They are not empty

Within these lines, Frank has described the essential qualities of these books. Reflective and seemingly simplistic, they are not the loaded, genre-defining images of *The Americans,* nor are they the emotionally charged, morose Polaroids of *The Lines of My Hand.* Frank is an artist who is not content with a single style or vision. Instead he is an artist that continues to work according to his own intuition, moving his work thoughtfully forward, making work that is close to the heart.

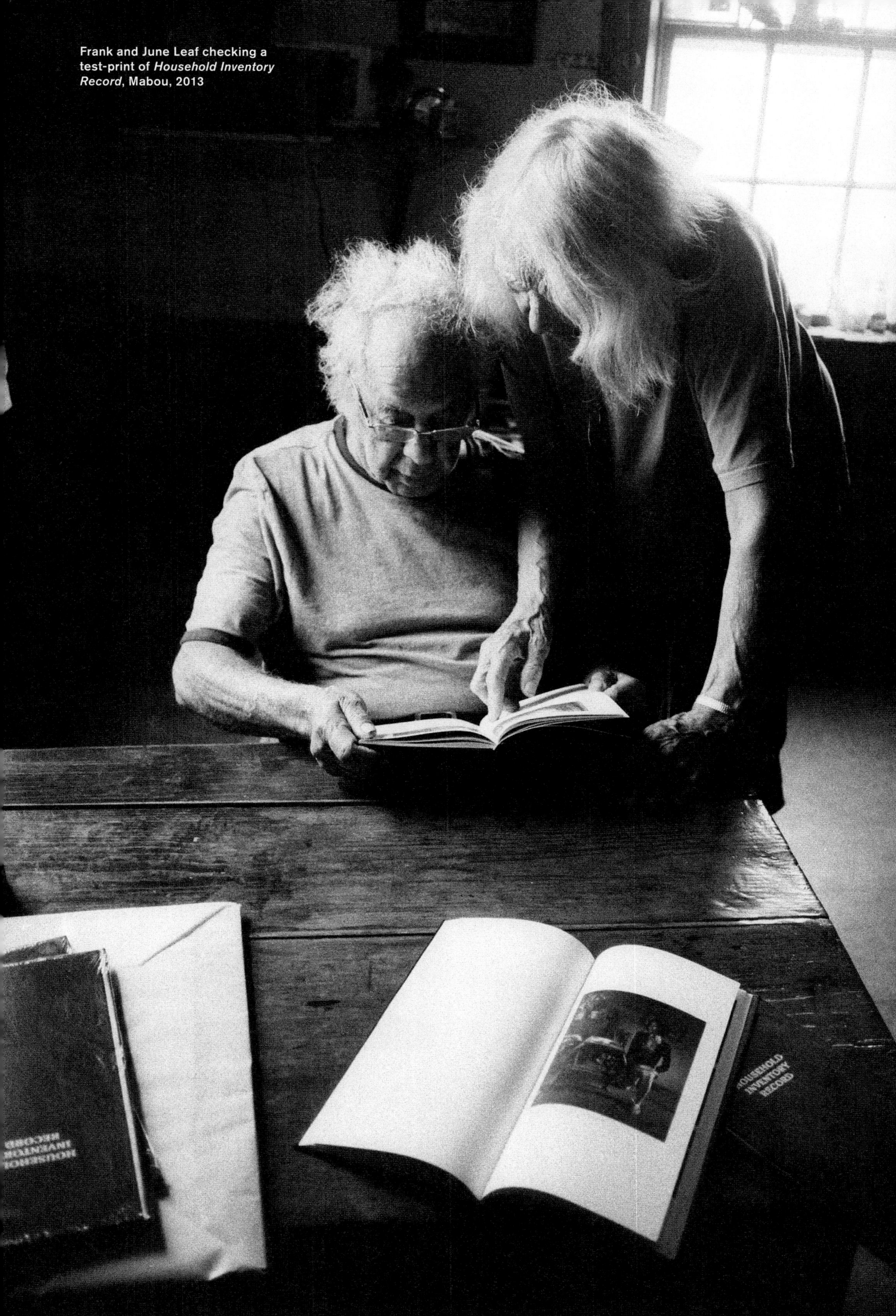

Frank and June Leaf checking a test-print of *Household Inventory Record*, Mabou, 2013

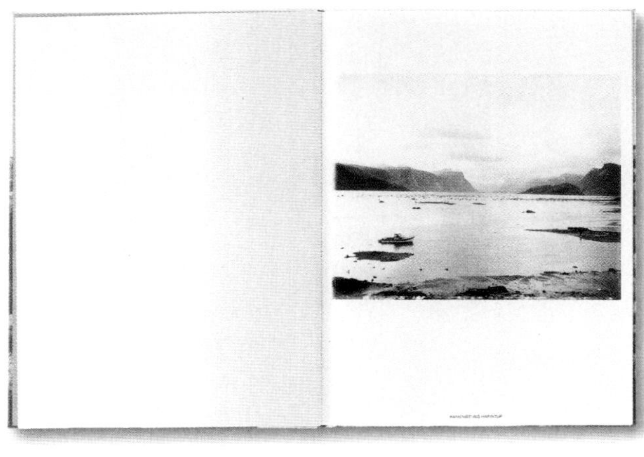

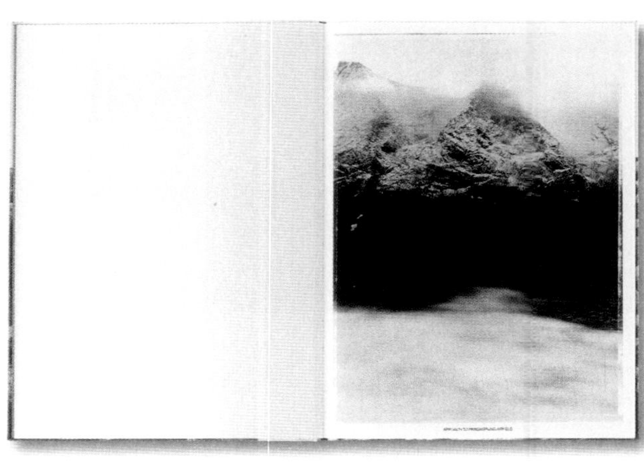

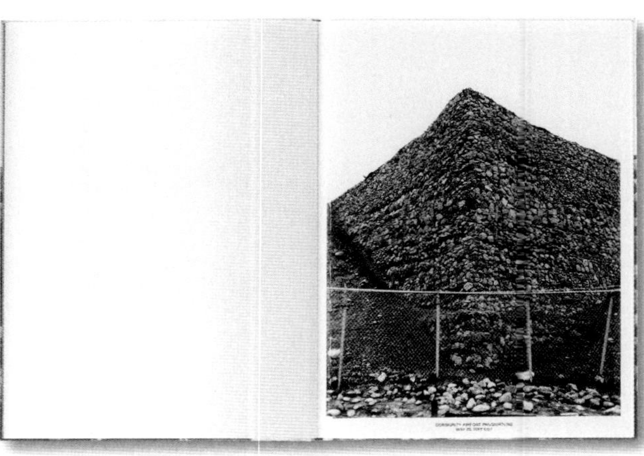

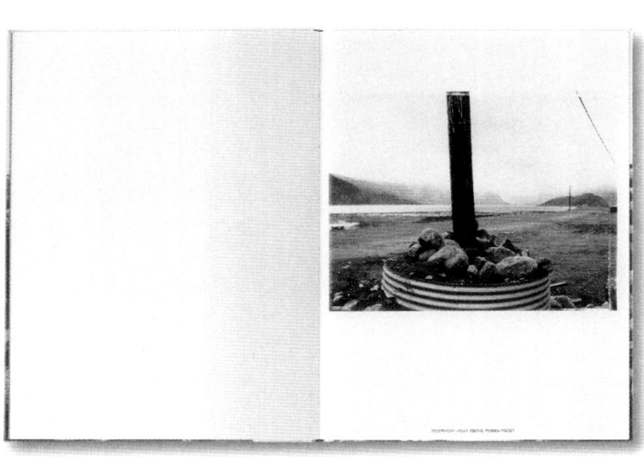

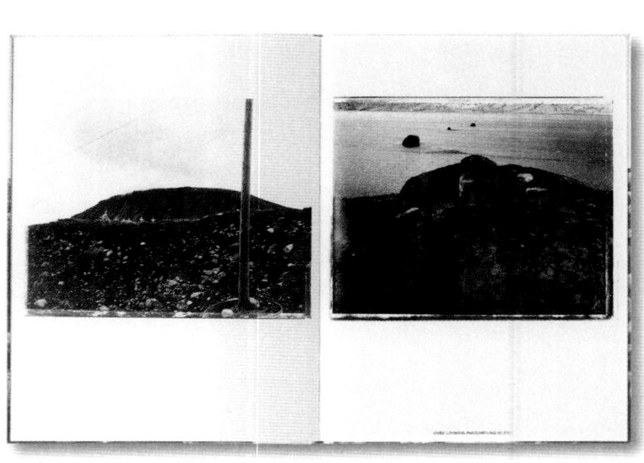

After 1 hour flight from Iqaluit (Formerly Frobisher Bay)
A four passenger plane lands at Pangnirtung airport.

The people's language is   INUKTITUT
One Man: INUK
More – the people   INUIT

I stay with friends at their house in Pangnirtung.
A remarkable quiet visit of 8 days.

Prefabricated homes along the main road in Pangnirtung.
At times a decorated window – reflections inside or outside.
Stones – maybe the balance of a big sky above...

R.F.

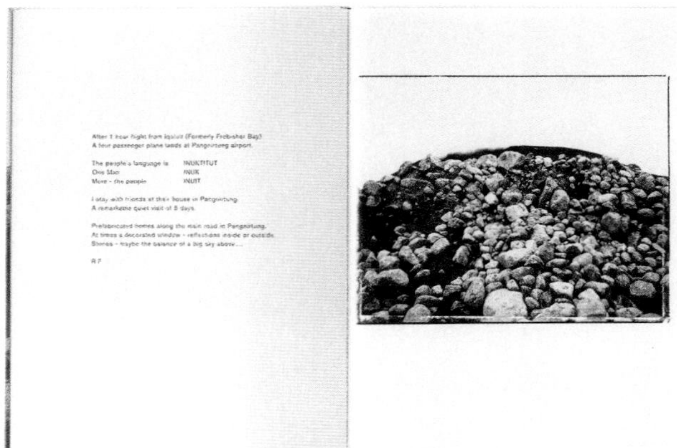

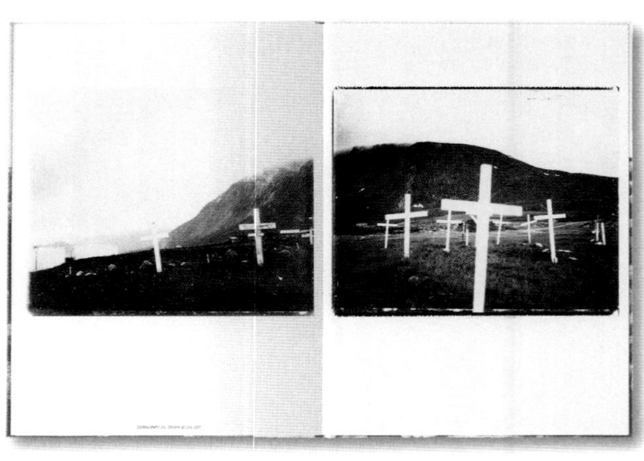

Pangnirtung

Published by Steidl, 2011

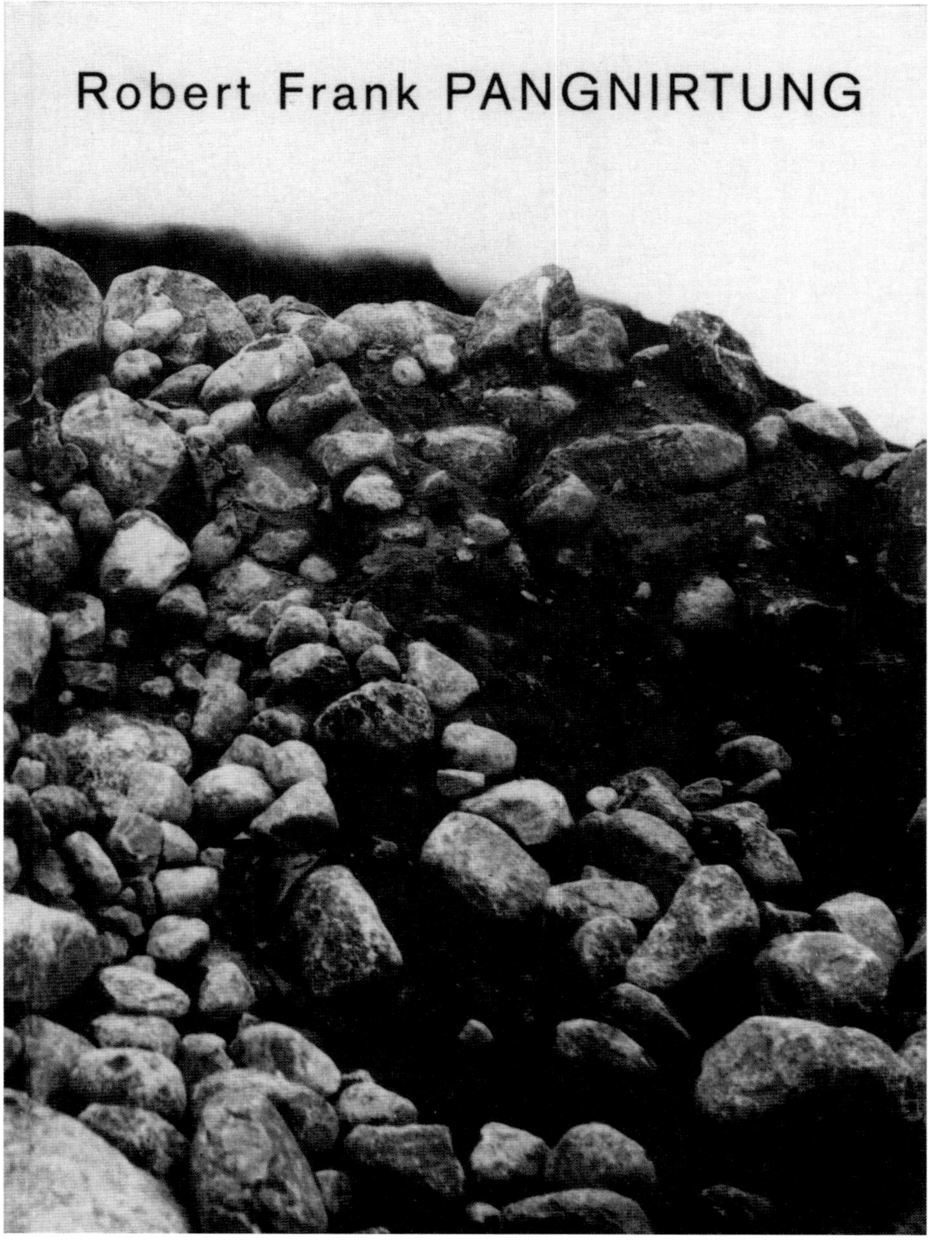

Text by Robert Frank
Book design by Robert Frank,
A-chan and Gerhard Steidl
40 pages
9 × 12 in. / 23 × 30.5 cm
27 black-and-white photographs
Tritone
Clothbound hardcover

ISBN 978-3-86930-198-3

In August 1992 Robert Frank's good friend Reginald Rankin invited Frank on a trip to Pangnirtung, a village of around 1,300 Inuit inhabitants in the Arctic Circle. This book is Frank's documentation of the five-day sojourn. Curiously Frank depicts Pangnirtung void of its people: the still harbor, public housing, a convenience store, a telephone post. Sincere without being sentimental, the photos are shaped by a short text from Frank himself: "Prefabricated homes along the main road in Pangnirtung. At times a decorated window—reflections inside or outside. Stones—maybe the balance of a big sky above…"

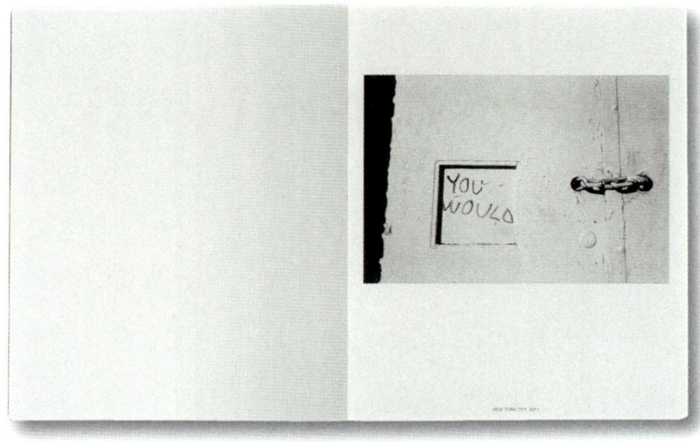
YOU
WOULD

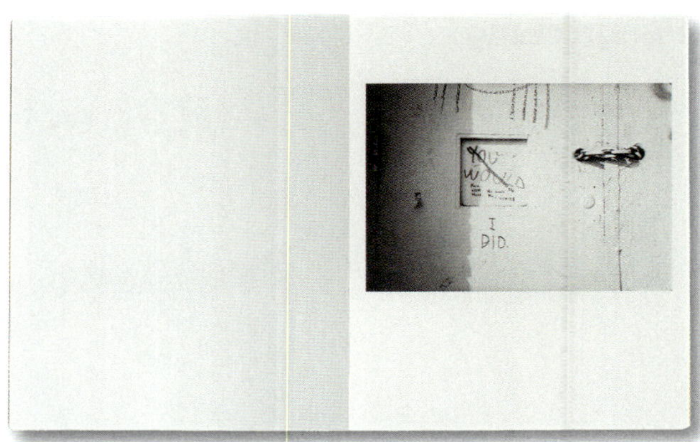
YOU
WOULD
I
DID.

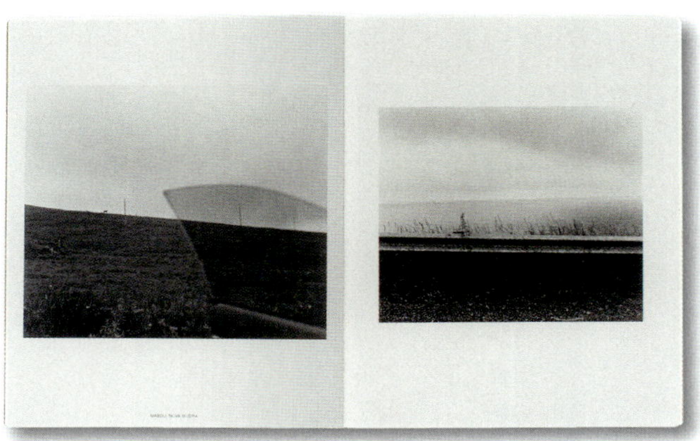

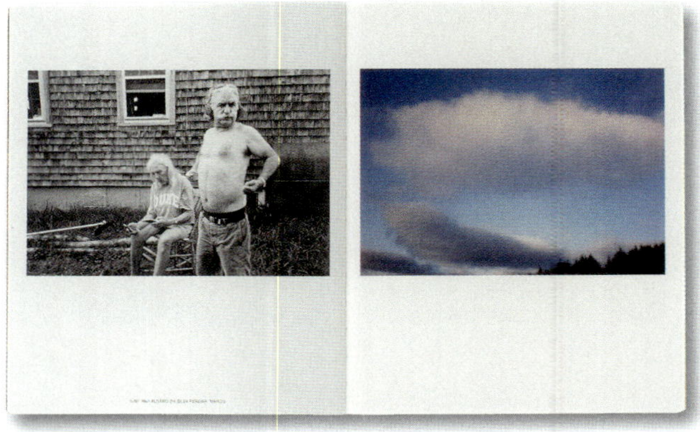

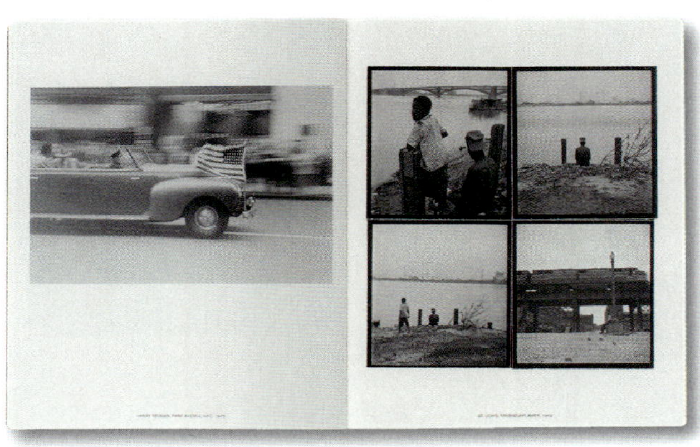

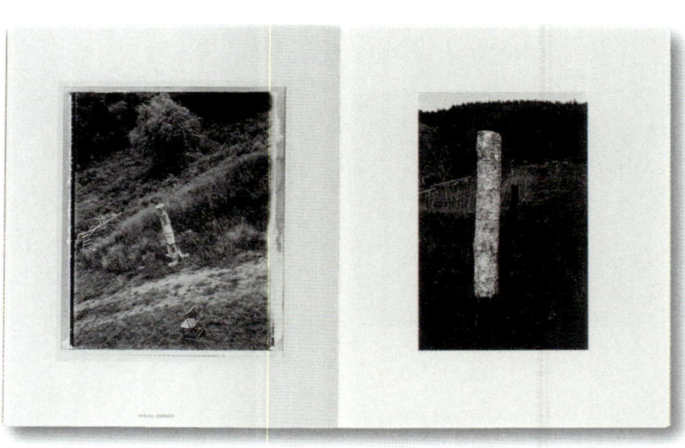

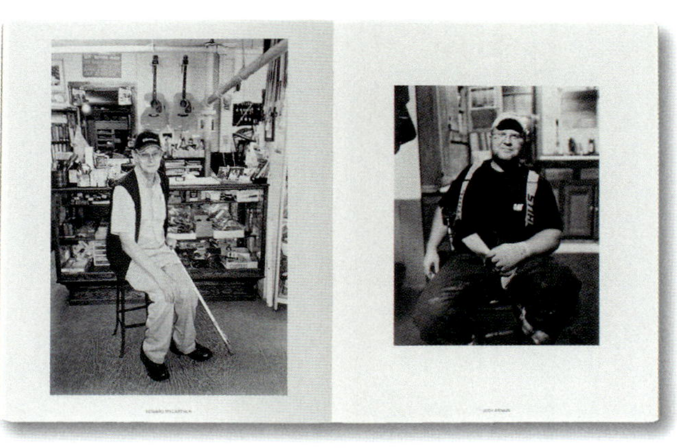

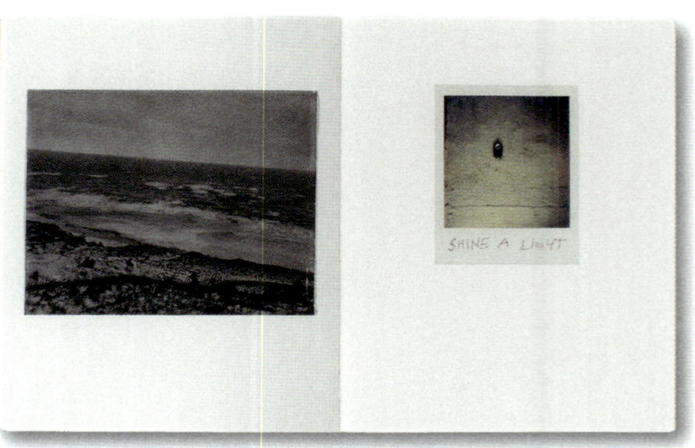
SHINE A LIGHT

You Would

Published by Steidl, 2012

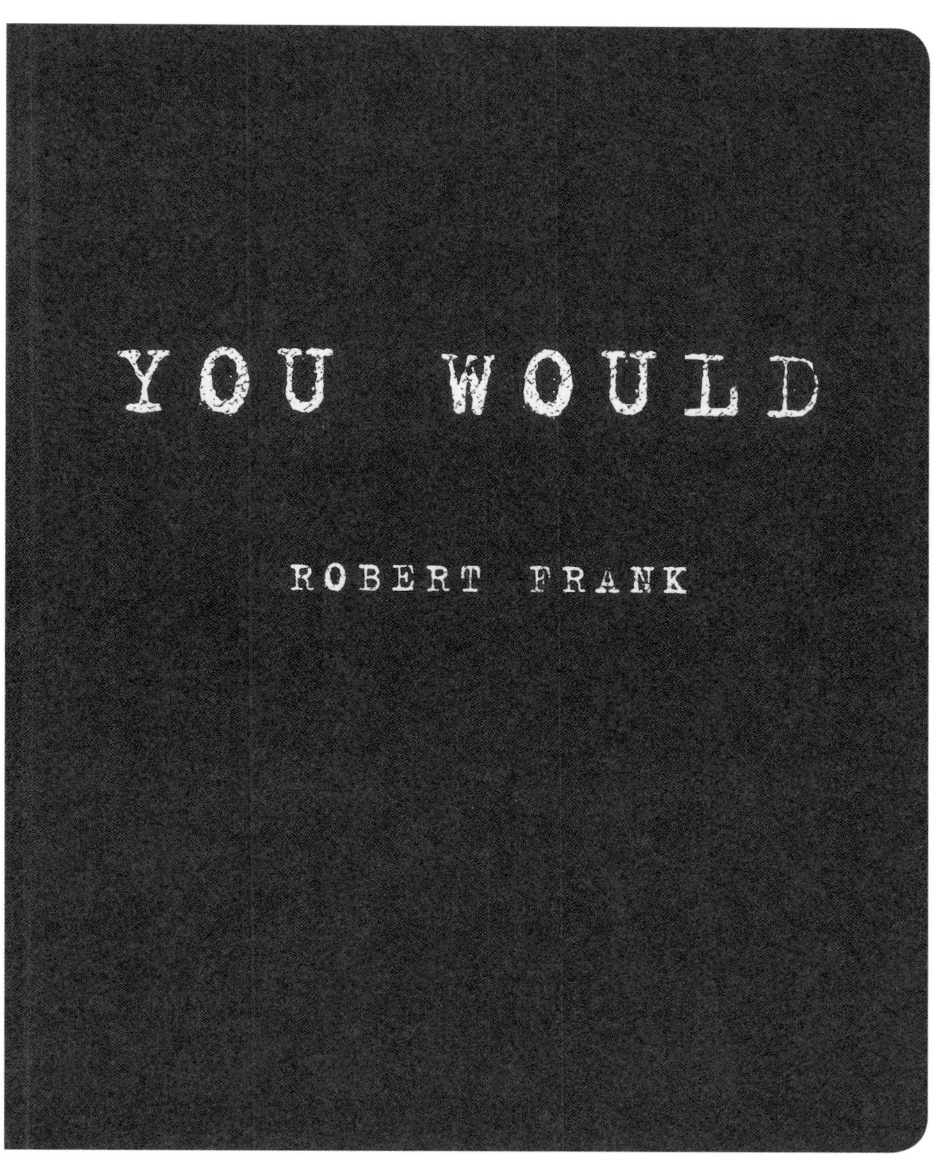

Text by Robert Frank
Book design by Robert Frank,
A-chan and Gerhard Steidl
48 pages
8 × 9.8 in. / 20.5 × 25 cm
34 black-and-white and
4 color photographs
Tritone and four-color process
Otabind softcover in a slipcase

ISBN 978-3-86930-418-2

You Would is a sequel to Robert Frank's original visual diary, *Tal Uf Tal Ab* of 2010. *You Would* contains contemporary images, some shot on 35 mm, others Polaroids, of Frank's friends, acquaintances and surroundings in New York and Mabou, Nova Scotia. In the book are also iconic images from earlier in Frank's career such as a photo of Delphine Seyrig and Larry Rivers on the set of Frank's 1959 film *Pull My Daisy,* creating a careful edit of old and new.

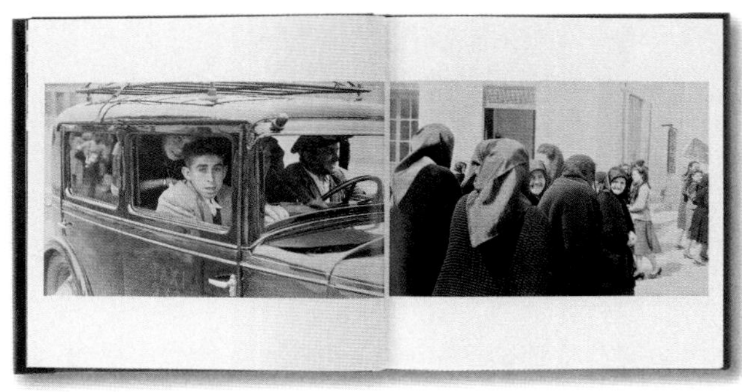

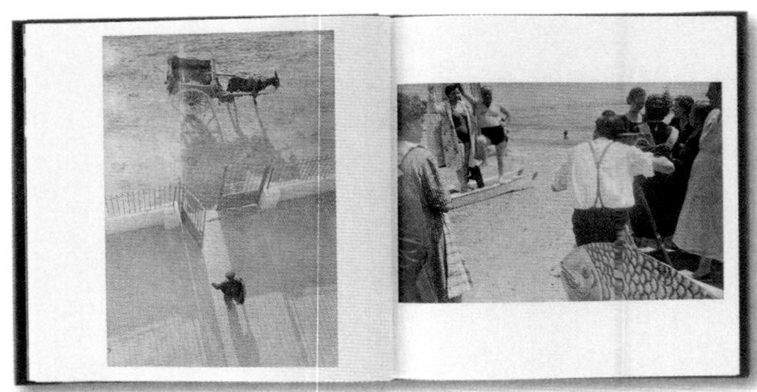

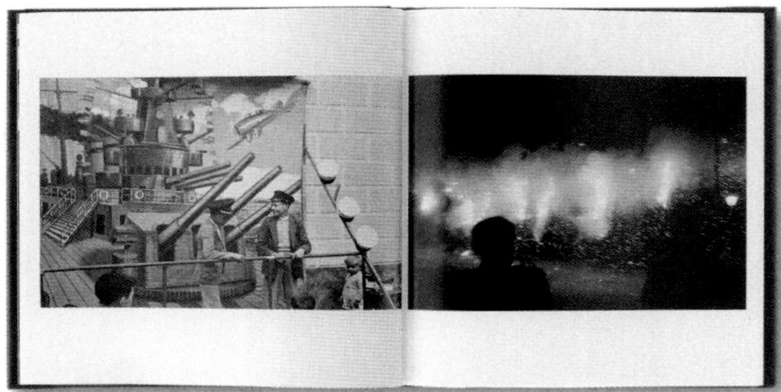

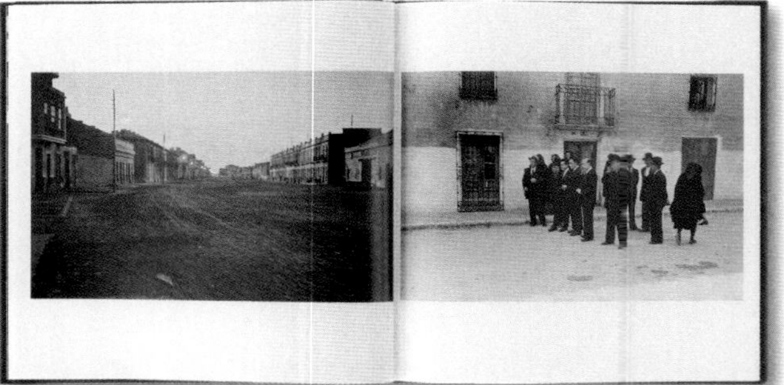

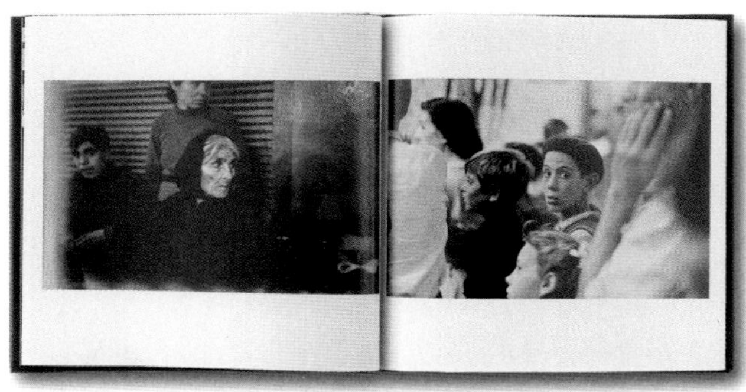

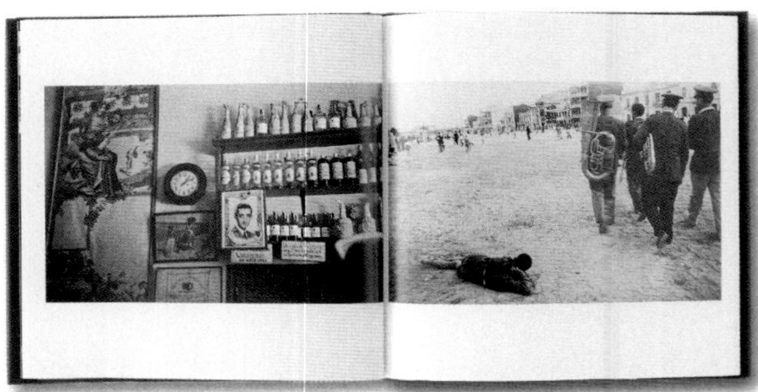

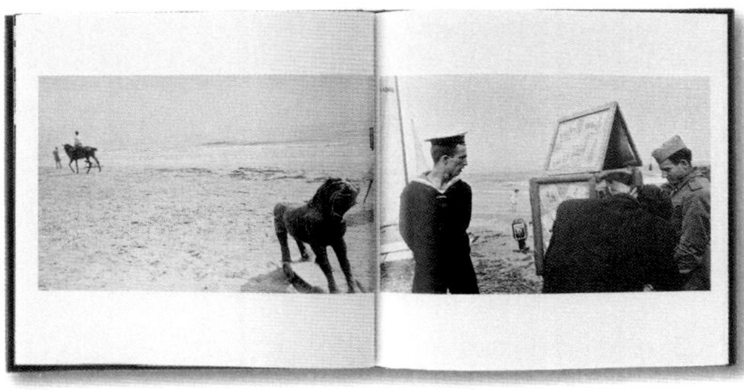

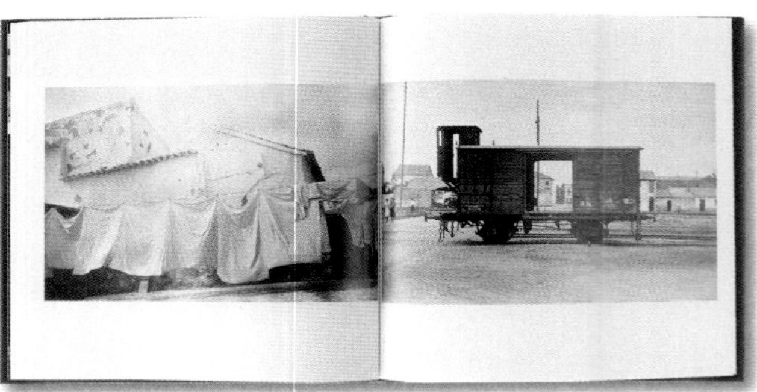

Valencia 1952

Published by Steidl, 2012

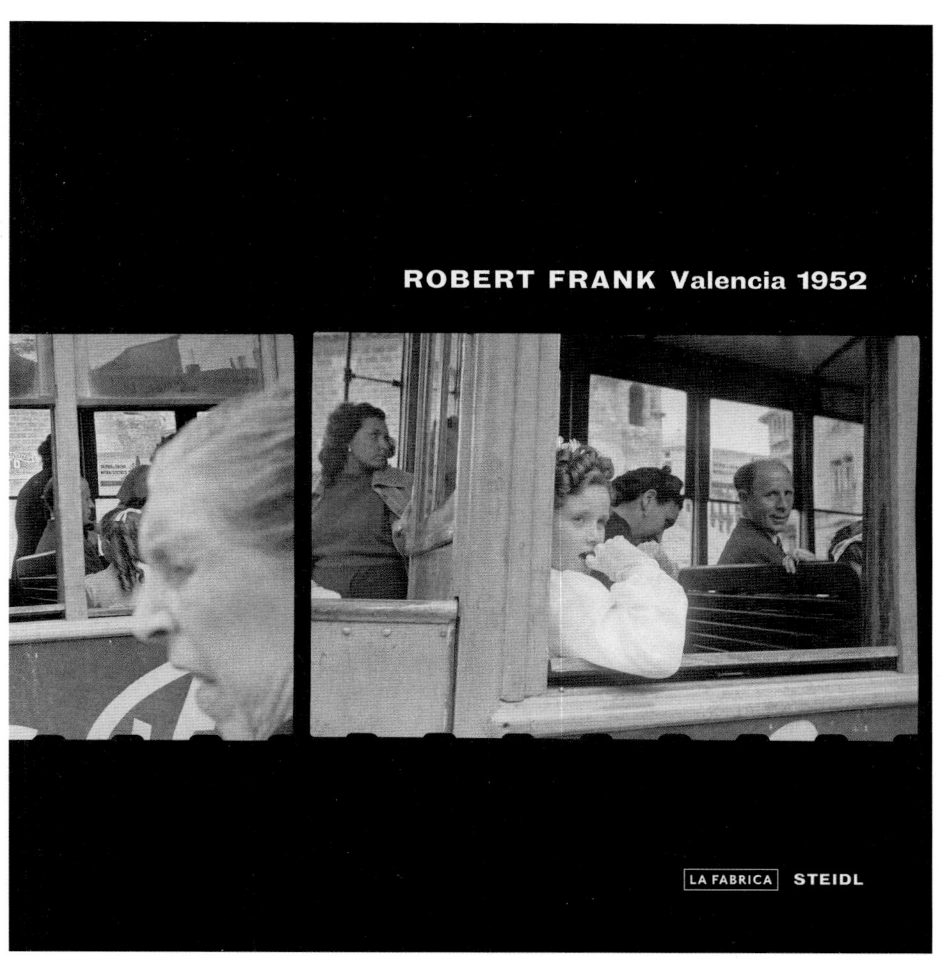

Edited by Robert Frank
and Vicente Todolí
Conversation between Sarah
Greenough, Vicente Todolí
and Peter MacGill
Book design by Fernando Gutiérrez
64 pages
10 × 10 in. / 25.3 × 25.3 cm
44 black-and-white photographs
Tritone
Clothbound hardcover in
dust jacket

ISBN 978-3-86930-502-8

In 1950 Robert Frank left his job as a photographer in New York to travel through Europe with his family. That summer he arrived in Valencia, which at the time was a humble, bleak place enduring the austere conditions of the postwar period like the rest of Spain. The pictures Frank took of Valencia depict the daily life of a fishing village. His portrayal is so natural and clear that further verbal explanation seems superfluous; they simply reflect, in the photographer's words, "the humanity of the moment," allowing dignity to override poverty.

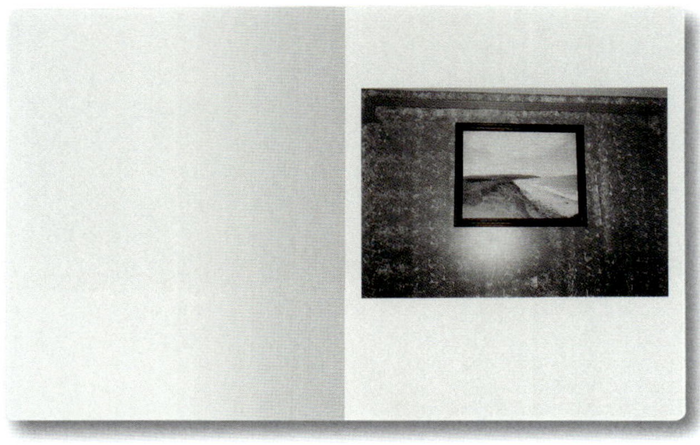

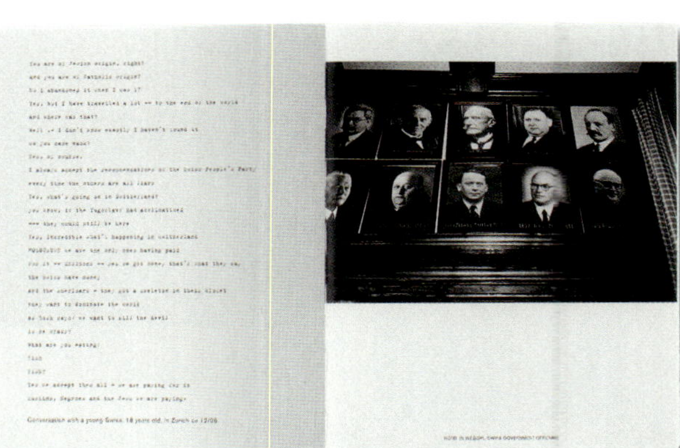

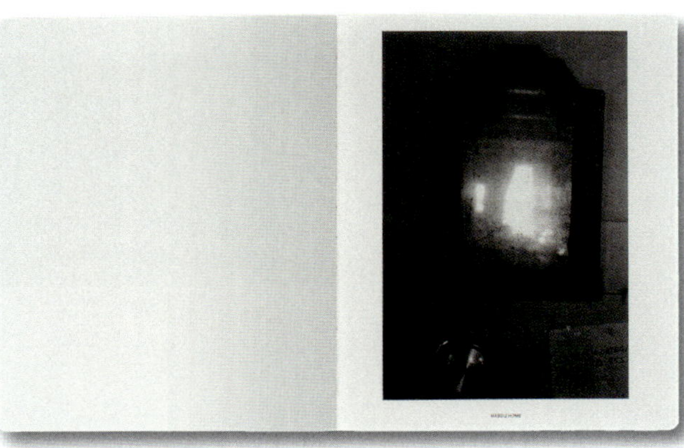

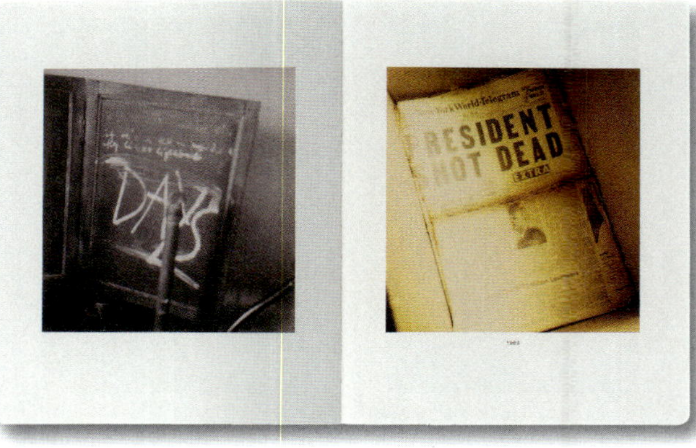
New York World-Telegram
PRESIDENT
SHOT DEAD
EXTRA

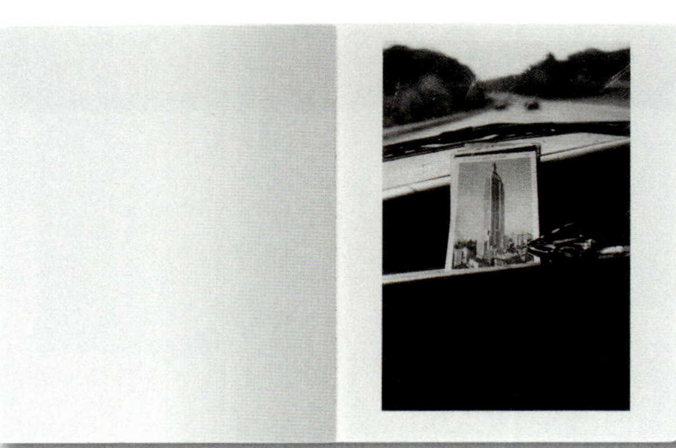

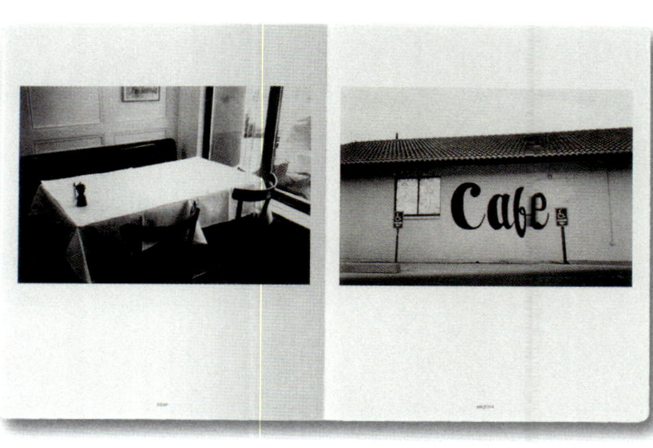
Cafe

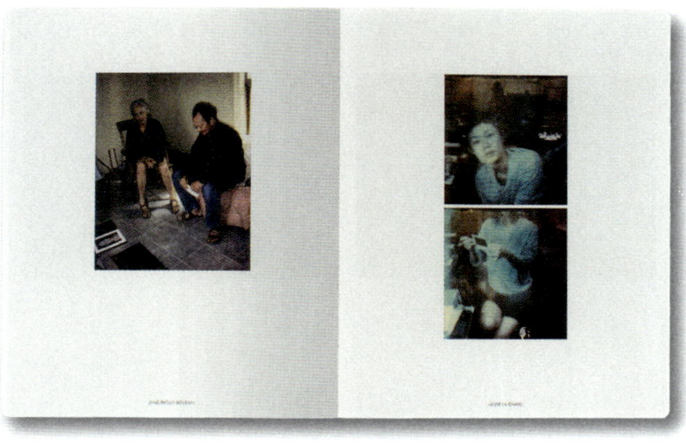

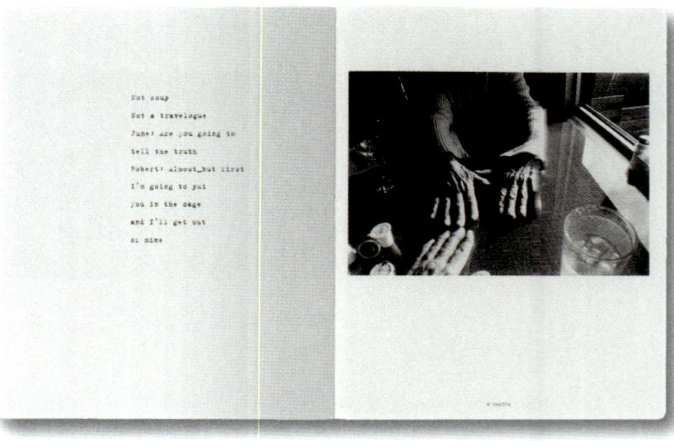

Park/Sleep

Published by Steidl, 2013

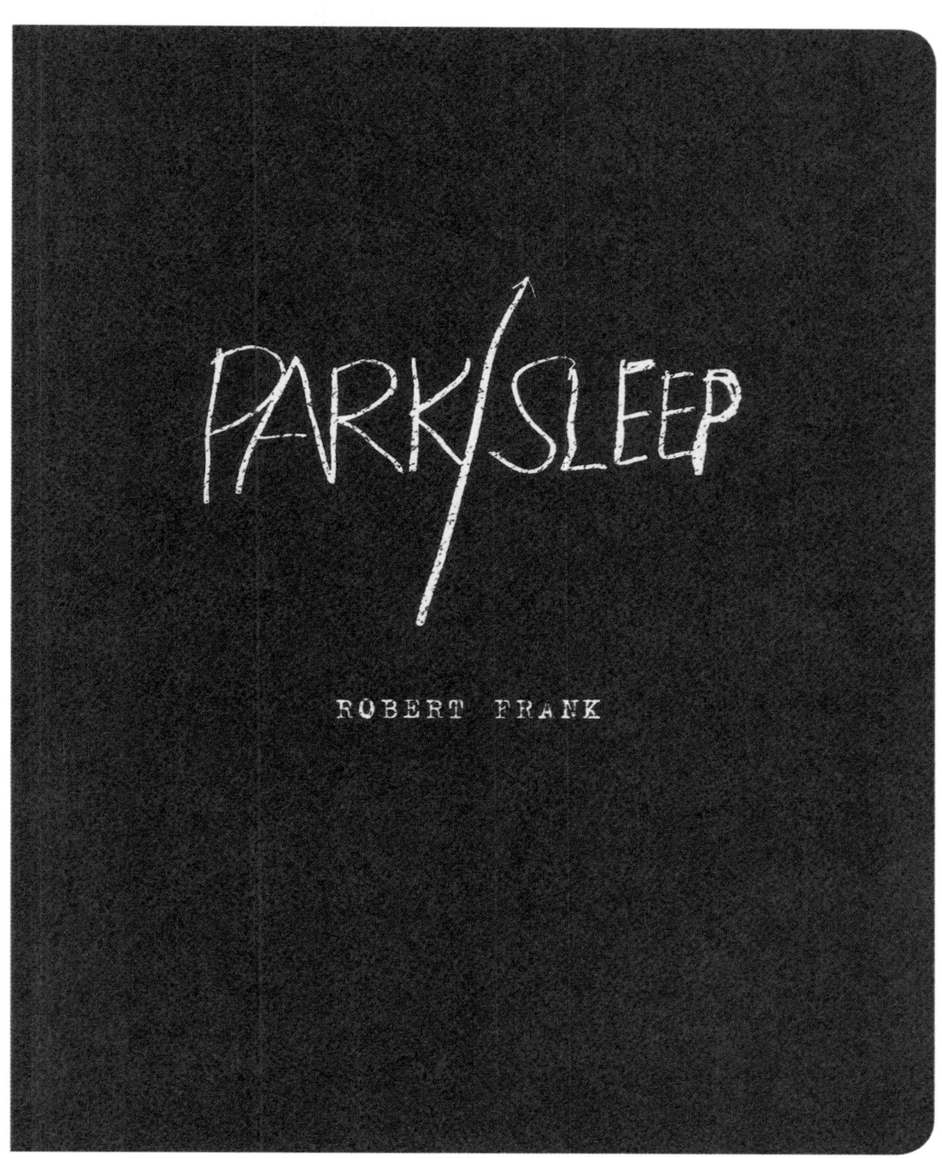

Text by Robert Frank
Book design by Robert Frank,
A-chan and Gerhard Steidl
52 pages
8 × 9.8 in. / 20.5 × 25 cm
30 black-and-white and
4 color photographs
Tritone and four-color process
Otabind softcover in a slipcase

ISBN 978-3-86930-585-1

Following its predecessors *Tal Uf Tal Ab* (2010) and *You Would* (2012), *Park/Sleep* is the third in the series of Robert Frank's visual diaries. It takes up his familiar collage technique, combining recent and older snapshots, mainly of Frank's friends, family, and home/studio, but also scenic and urban settings and interiors. The images are accompanied by short texts—notes, pieces of conversations, poems and thoughts.

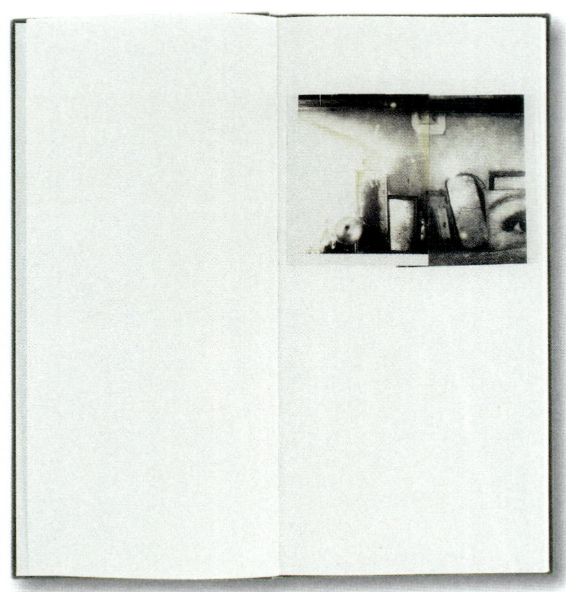
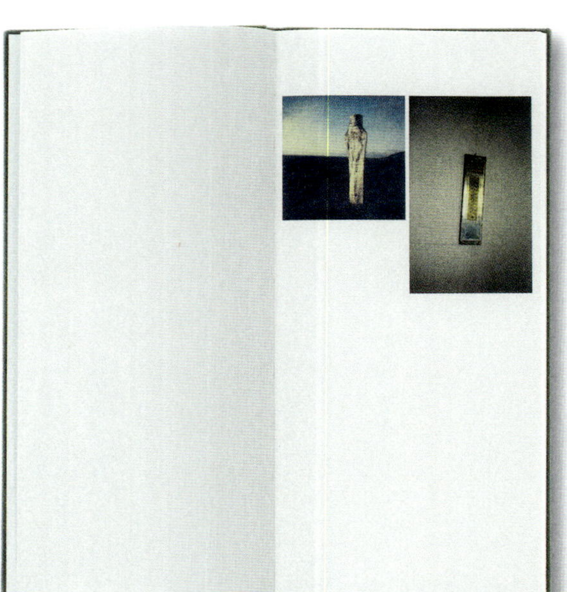
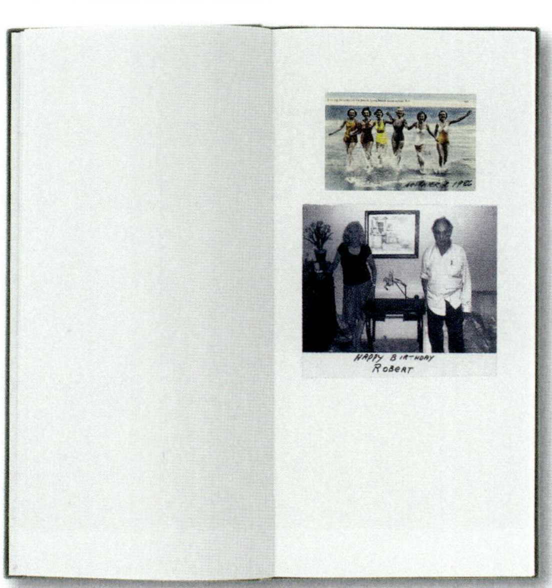
HAPPY BIRTHDAY
ROBERT
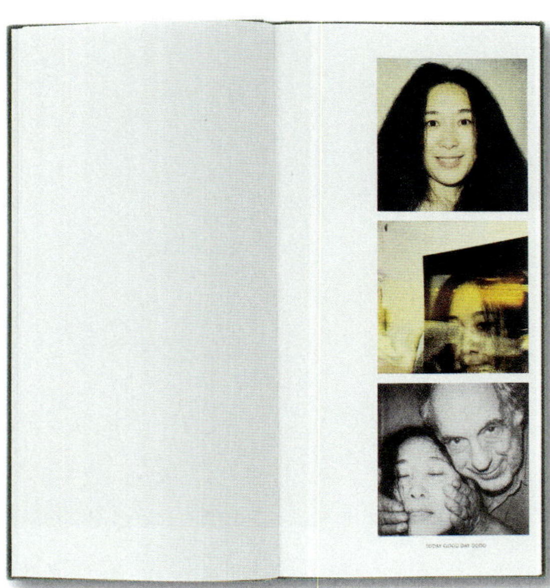
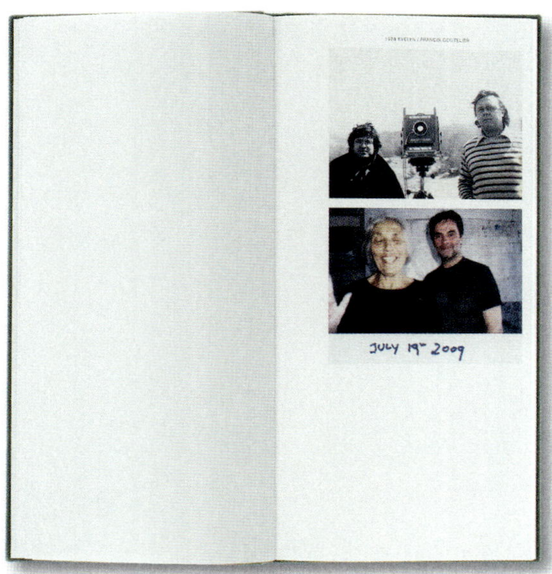
JULY 19th 2009
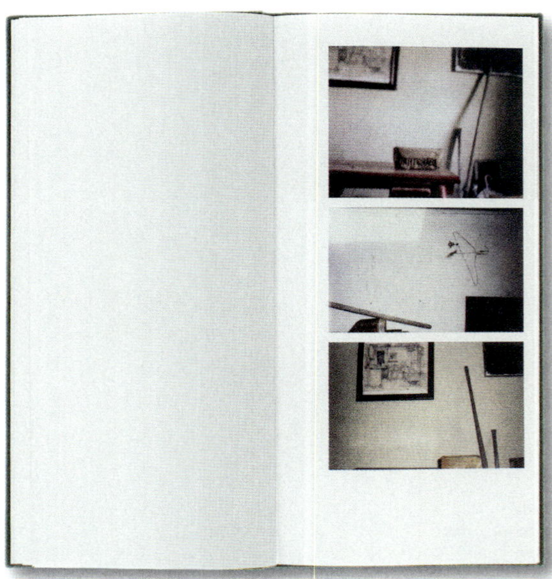

Household Inventory Record

Published by Steidl, 2013

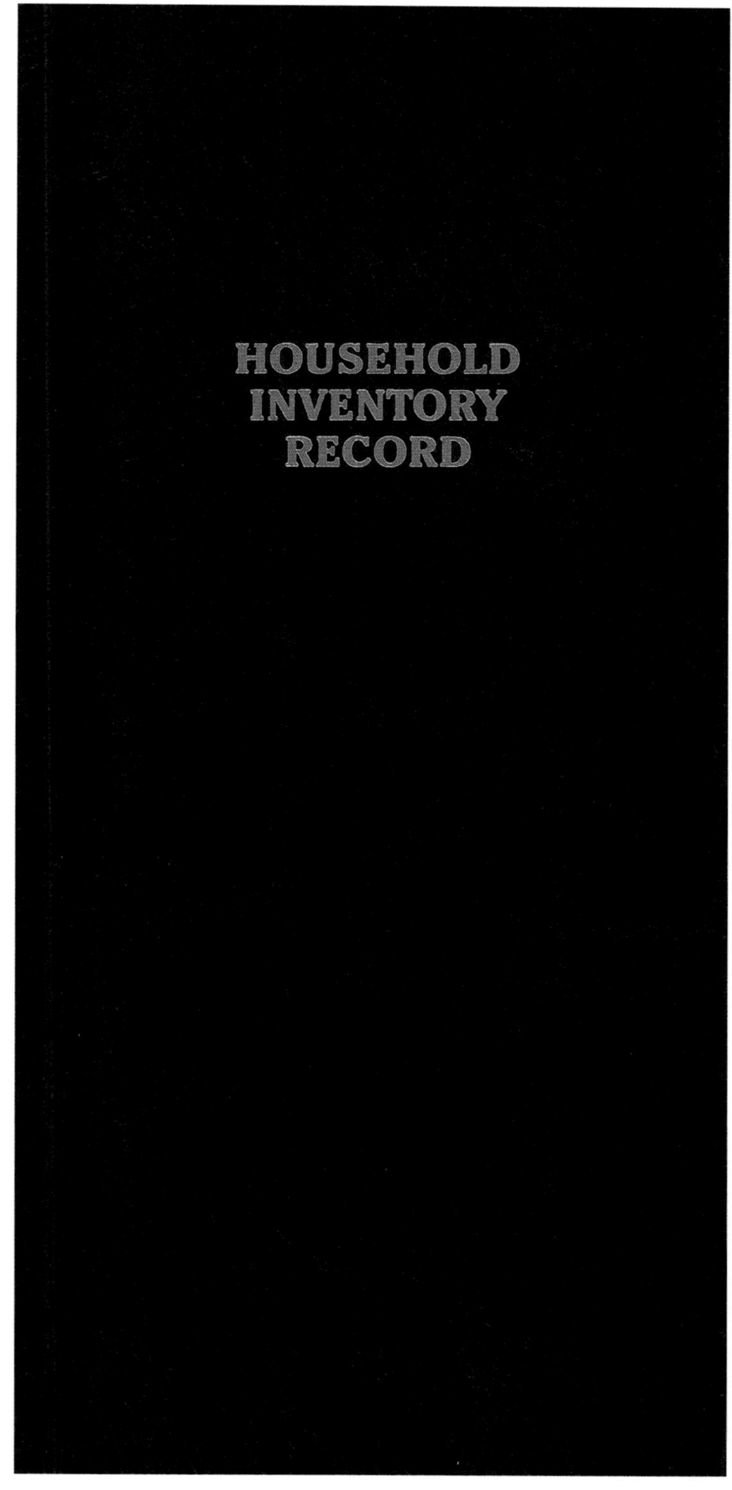

Text by Robert Frank
Book design by Robert Frank,
A-chan and Gerhard Steidl
88 pages
5.5 × 11.4 in. / 14 × 28.9 cm
20 black-and-white and
68 color photographs
Four-color process
Imitation-leather hardcover

ISBN 978-3-86930-660-5

Household Inventory Record is a ready-made in the series of Robert Frank's visual diaries. Composed of Polaroids, the thin and upright volume continues the journey into Frank's personal realm and imagery, showing us snapshots from his travels, of his friends and everyday curiosities.

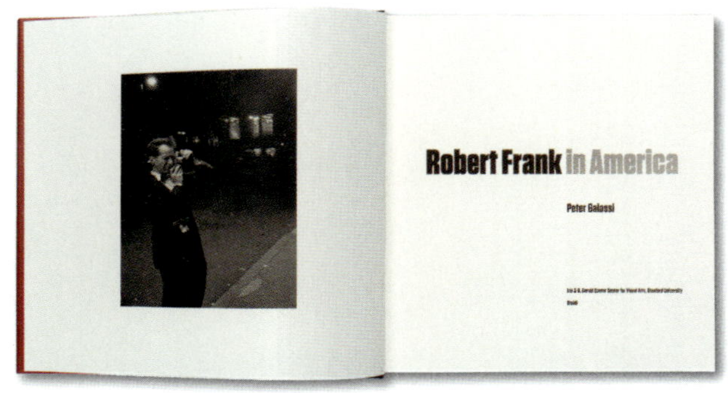
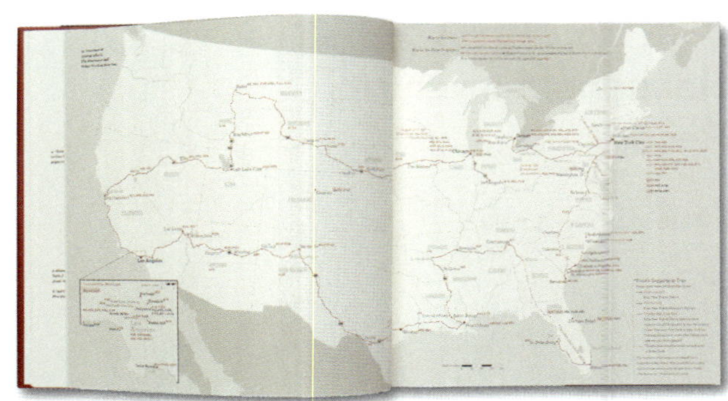
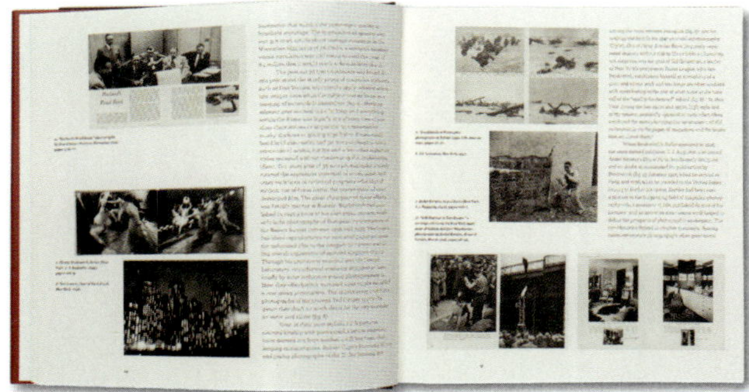
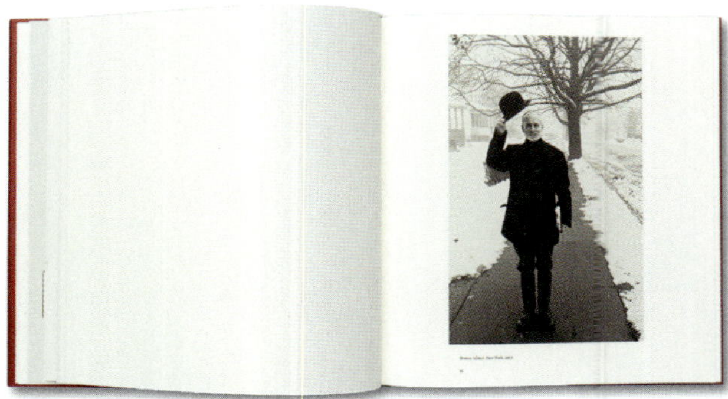
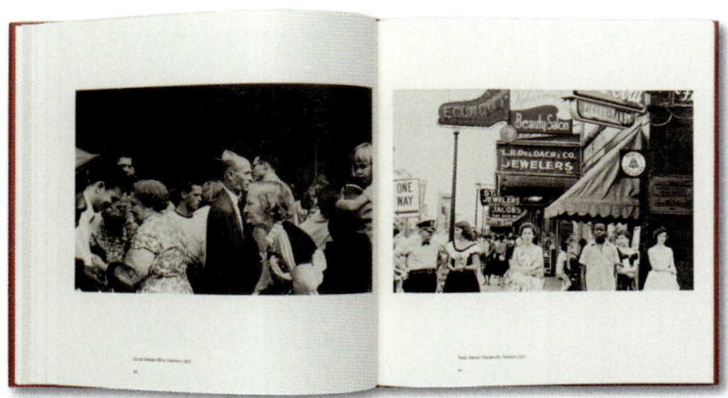
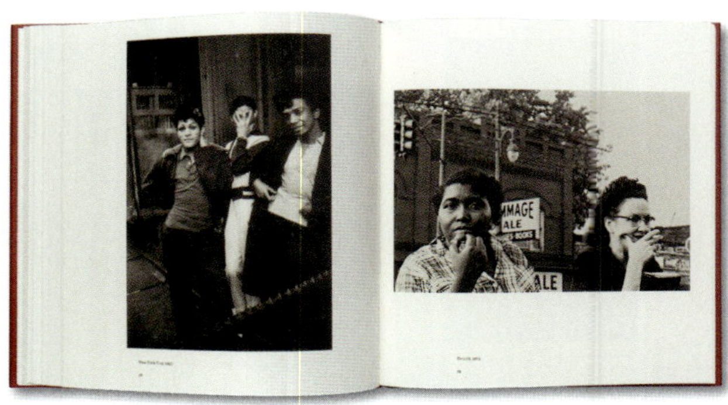
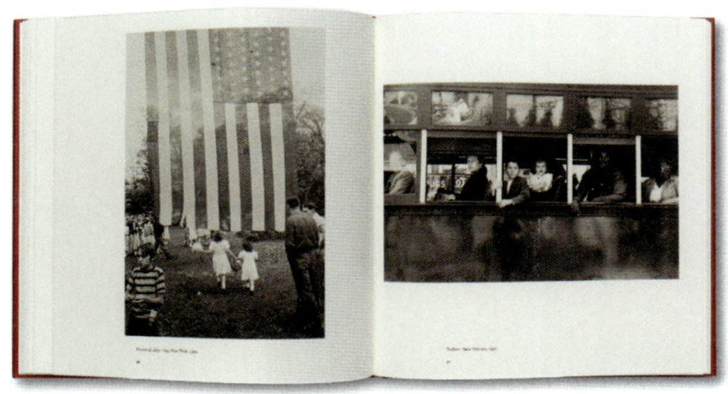
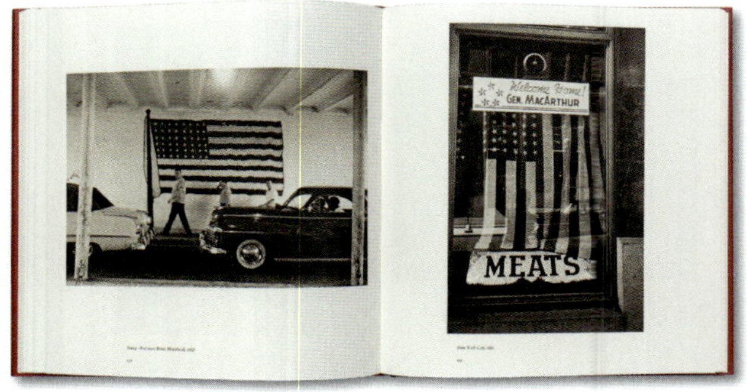

In America

Published by Steidl, 2014

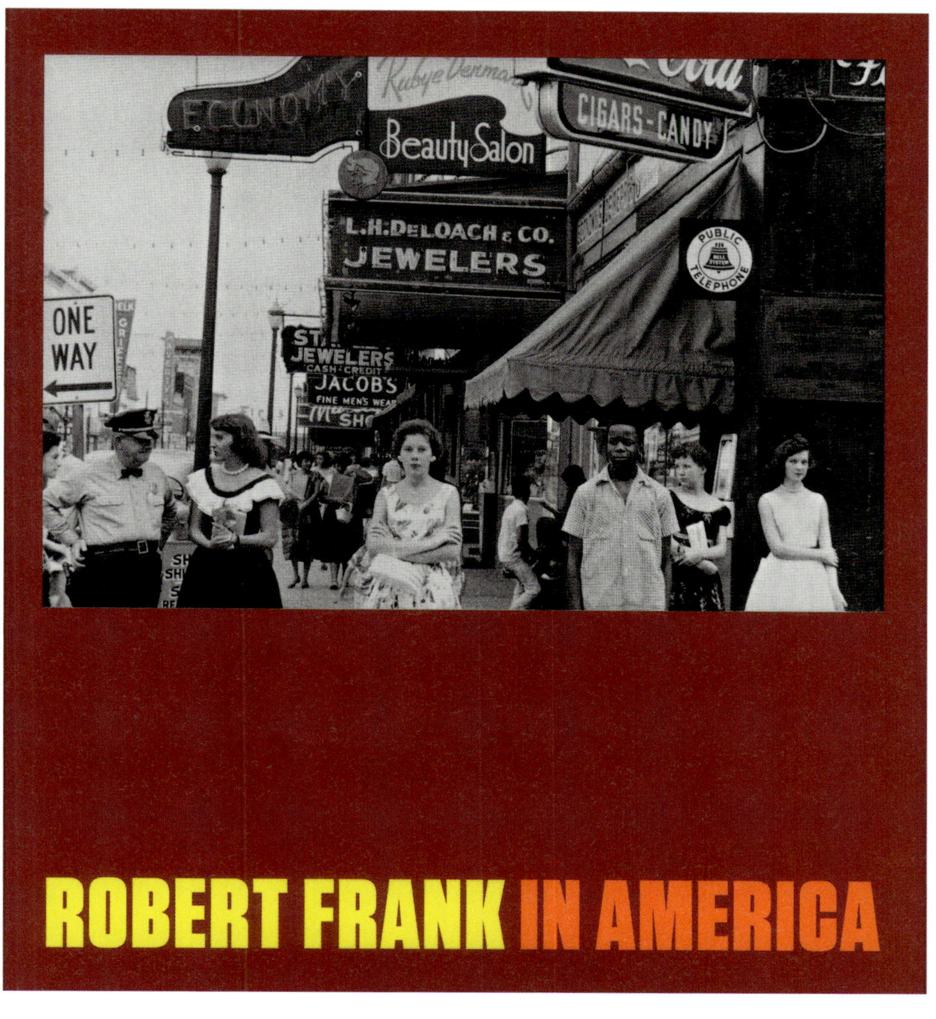

Edited by Peter Galassi
Texts by Peter Galassi
and Connie Wolf
Book design by Katy Homans
196 pages
9 × 9.6 in. / 23 × 24.5 cm
138 black-and-white
photographs
Tritone
Clothbound with dust jacket

ISBN 978-3-86930-735-0

Because of the importance of Robert Frank's *The Americans*; because he turned to filmmaking in 1959, the same year the book appeared in the United States; and because he made very different kinds of pictures when he returned to still photography in the 1970s, most of Frank's American work of the 1950s is poorly known. This book, based on the important Frank collection at the Cantor Arts Center at Stanford University, is the first to focus on that work. Its careful sequence integrates photographs from *The Americans* with more than 100 unknown or unfamiliar images to chart the major themes and pictorial strategies of Frank's work in the United States in the 1950s. Peter Galassi's text presents a thorough reconsideration of Frank's first photographic career and examines in detail how he used the full range of photography's vital 35mm vocabulary to reclaim the medium's artistic tradition from the hegemony of the magazines.

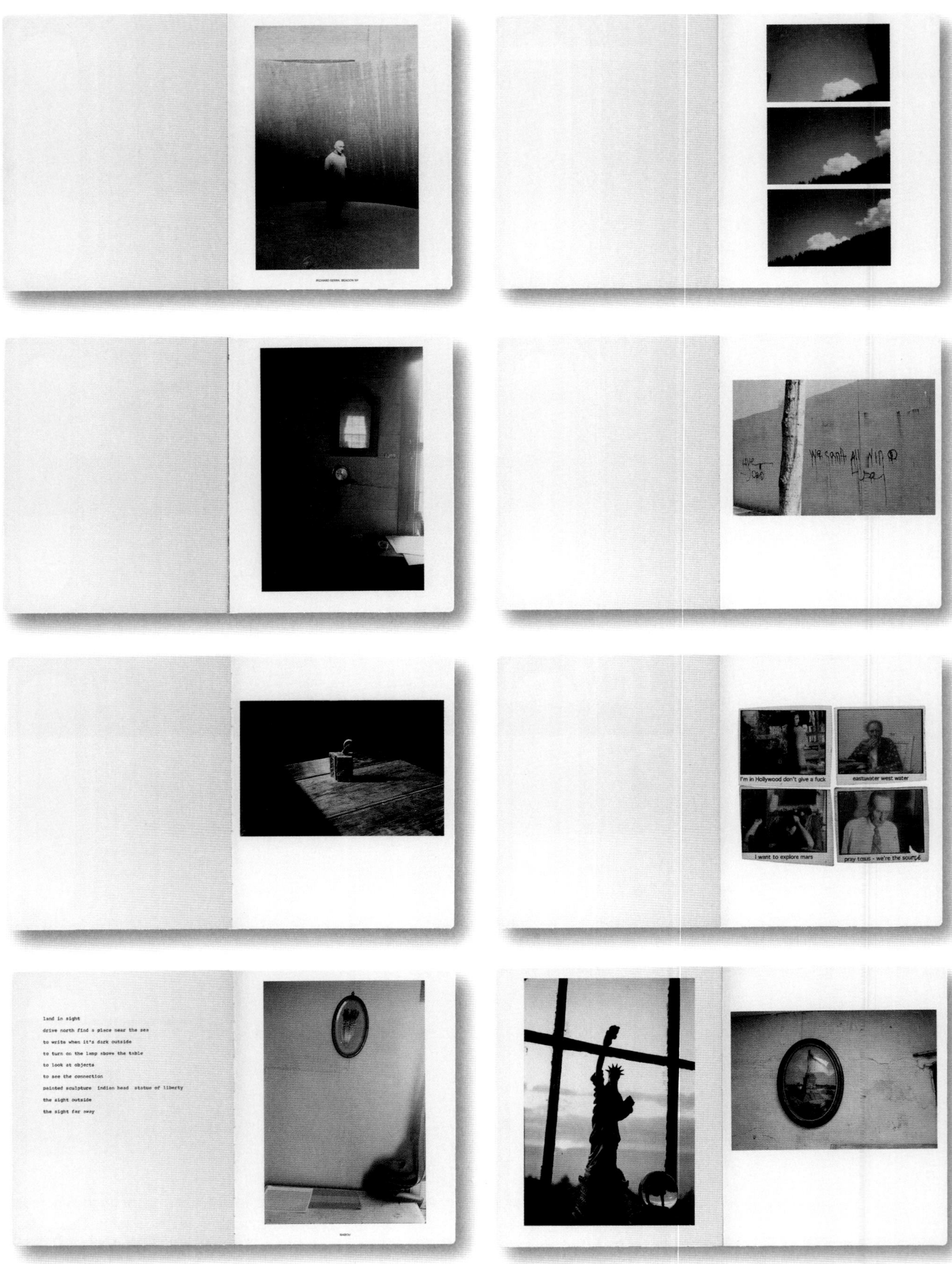
land in sight
drive north find a place near the sea
to write when it's dark outside
to turn on the lamp above the table
to look at objects
to see the connection
painted sculpture indian head statue of liberty
the sight outside
the sight far away
I'm in Hollywood don't give a fuck
eastwater west water
i want to explore mars
pray tcaus - we're the source

Partida

Published by Steidl, 2014

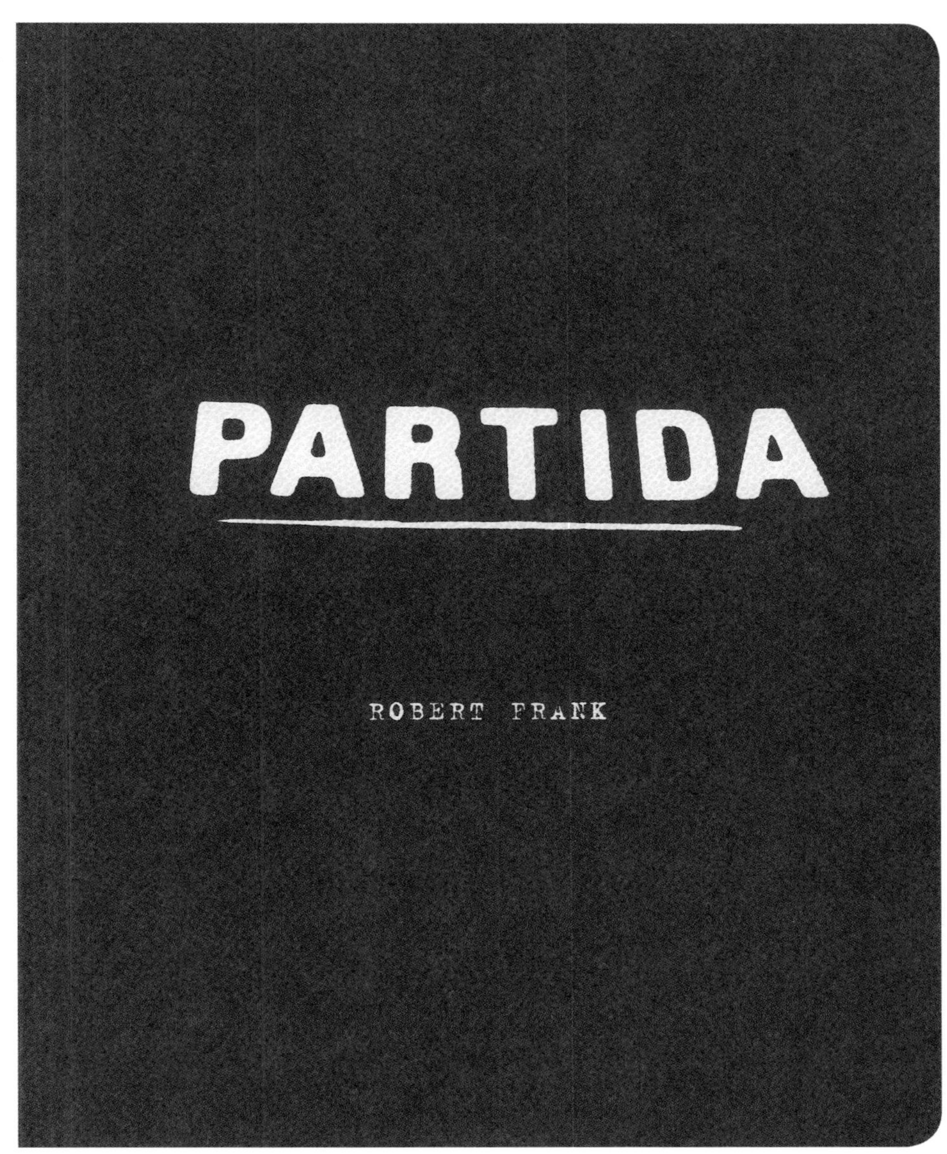

Text by Robert Frank
Book design by Robert Frank,
A-chan and Gerhard Steidl
56 pages
8 × 9.8 in. / 20.5 × 25 cm
30 black-and-white and
5 color photographs
Tritone and four-color process
Otabind softcover in slipcase

ISBN 978-3-86930-795-4

In *Partida* Robert Frank continued the exploration of his archives, presenting an intuitive series of images of friends, colleagues, interiors, of quiet still lifes and snapshots of both ordinary and unexpected objects and situations. As often in his visual diaries, Frank's ambiguous text fragments hint at his deeper ambitions: "to look at objects / to see the connection … the sight outside / the sight far away."

"My whole life is in this newspaper."

Robert Frank

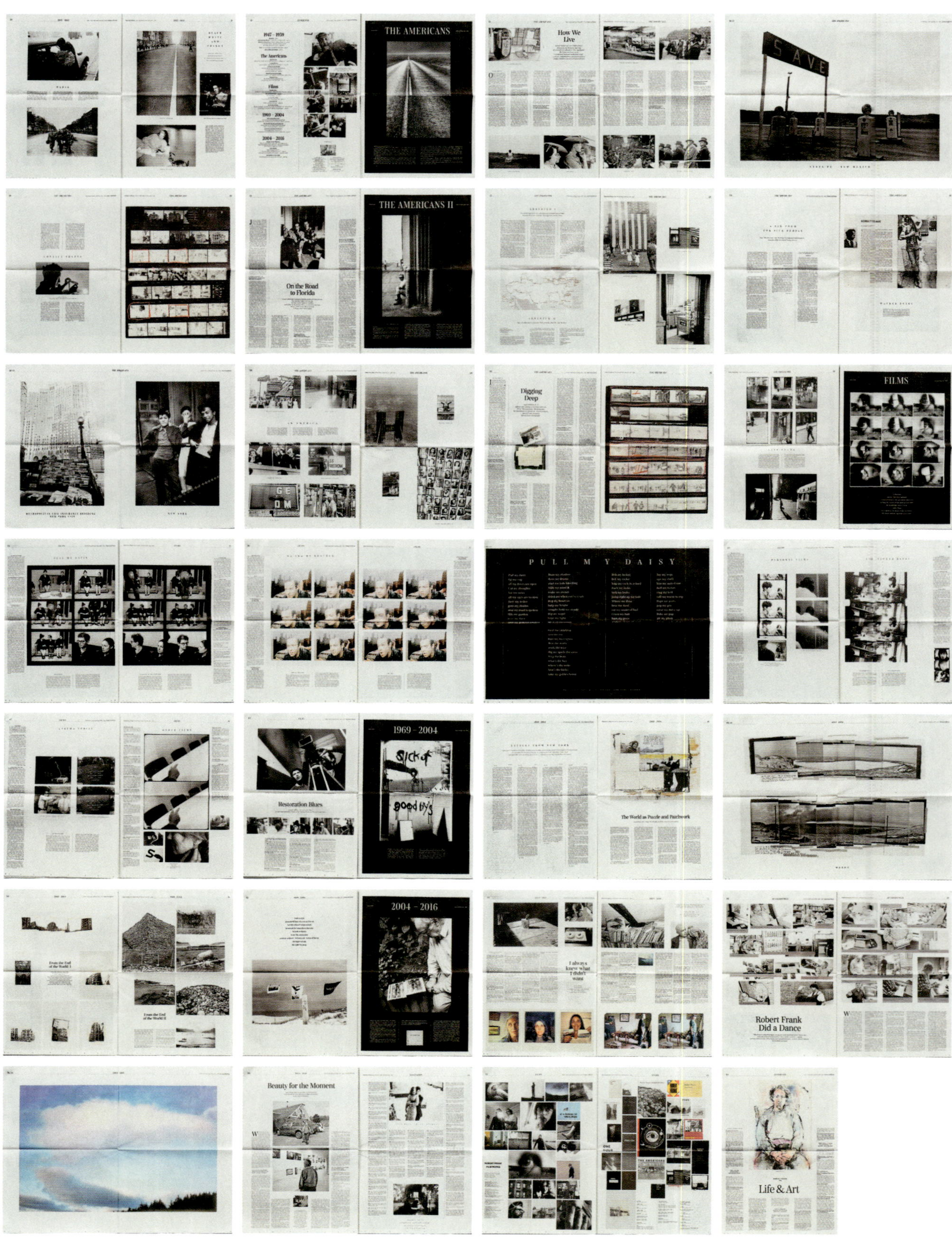

Robert Frank: Books and Films, 1947–2016

Published by Steidl and the *Süddeutsche Zeitung*, 2016

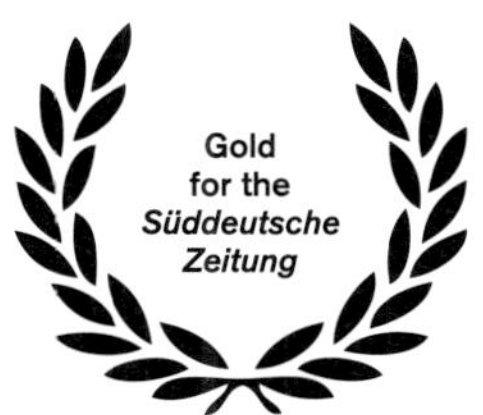

Gold
for the
*Süddeutsche
Zeitung*

Lead Awards
Lead Newspaper of the Year

Germany 2015

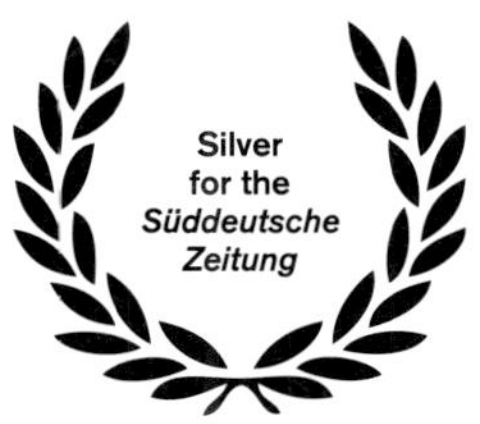

Silver
for the
*Süddeutsche
Zeitung*

Lead Awards
Portfolio of the Year

Germany 2015

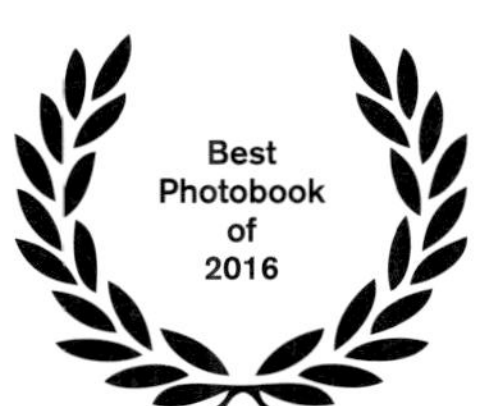

Best
Photobook
of
2016

Time Magazine
New York

November 2016

Concept by Robert Frank,
Alex Rühle and Gerhard Steidl
Edited by Alex Rühle
Texts by Philip Brookman,
Ute Eskildsen, Robert Frank,
Sarah Greenough, Stefan
Koldehoff and Gerhard Steidl
Book design by Stefan Dimitrov
and Christian Tönsmann
64 pages
15.9 × 10.8 in. / 40.4 × 27.5 cm
168 black-and-white and
26 color photographs, and
35 illustrations
Four-color rotary on newsprint

ISBN 978-3-95829-026-6

This is the unconventional catalogue of the travelling exhibition "Robert Frank: Books and Films, 1947–2016," a special edition of the German newspaper the *Süddeutsche Zeitung*—following its original design and format, and printed on newsprint.

Conceived by Robert Frank and Gerhard Steidl, the exhibition presents Frank's iconic images in the context of his life, creative processes and wider cultural history. Here Frank's books and films are seen against the backdrop of his photographs, which are presented in an immediate and straightforward way: printed on up to three-meter-long sheets of newsprint and installed directly onto the wall, without frames.

The newspaper catalogue recreates the raw, innovative approach of the exhibition. Featuring interviews, essays, letters and opinion pieces alongside rich picture sequences, *Robert Frank: Books and Films, 1947–2016* is an unpretentious and accessible printed object—or in Frank's own words: "Cheap, quick and dirty, that's how I like it!"

HALIFAX INTERNATIONAL AIR
ada
ada Jazz
al Airlines
Life is good.

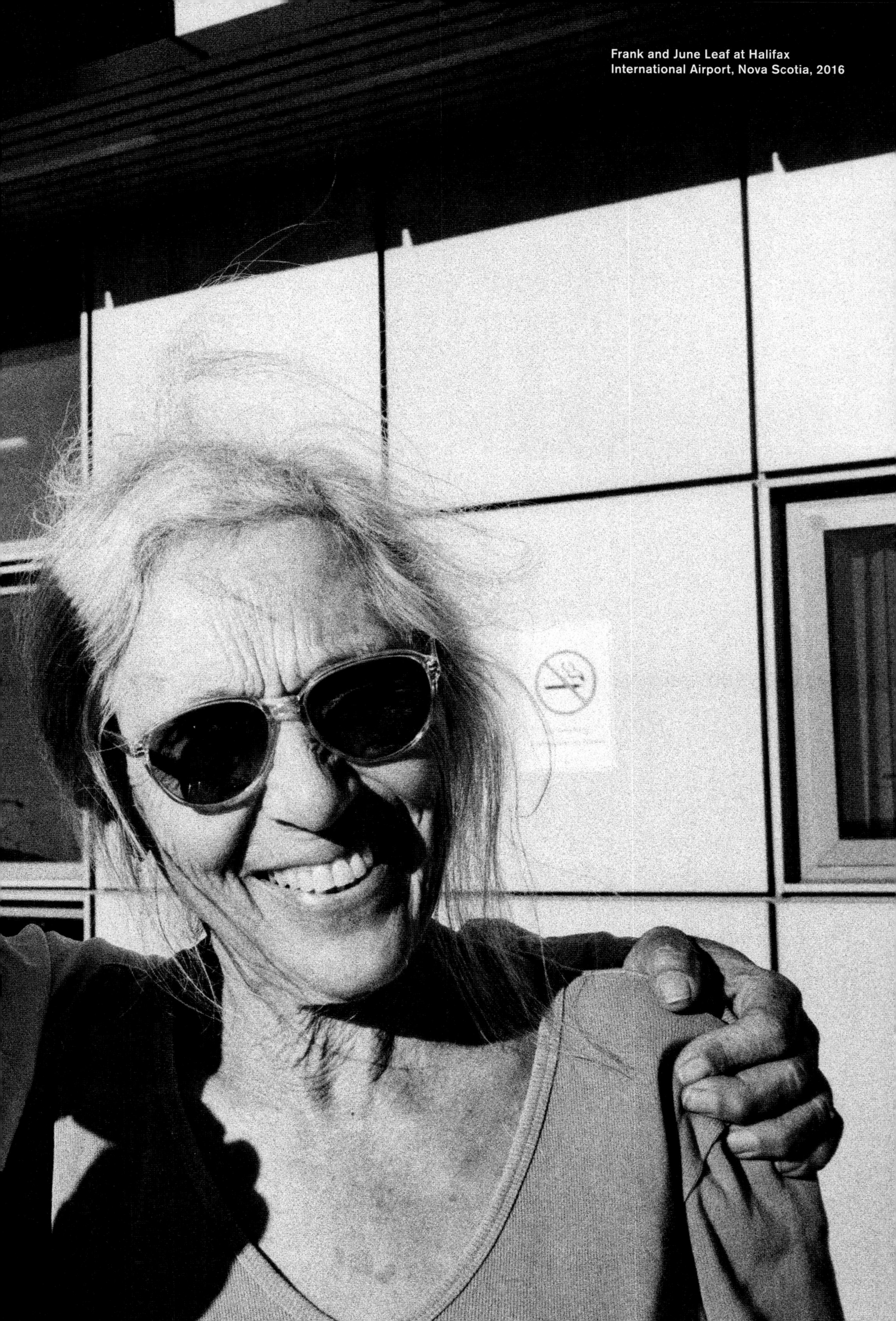
Frank and June Leaf at Halifax
International Airport, Nova Scotia, 2016

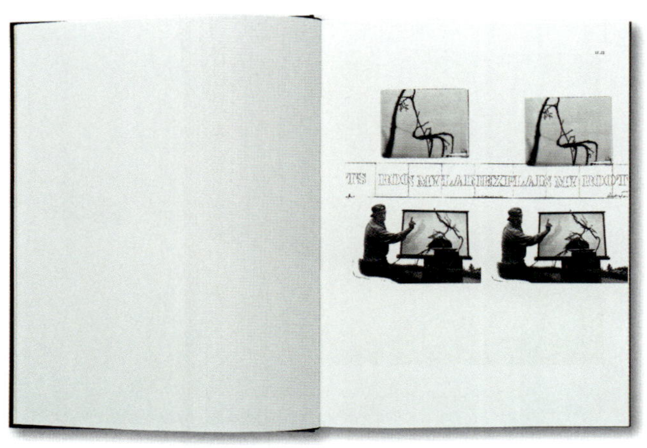
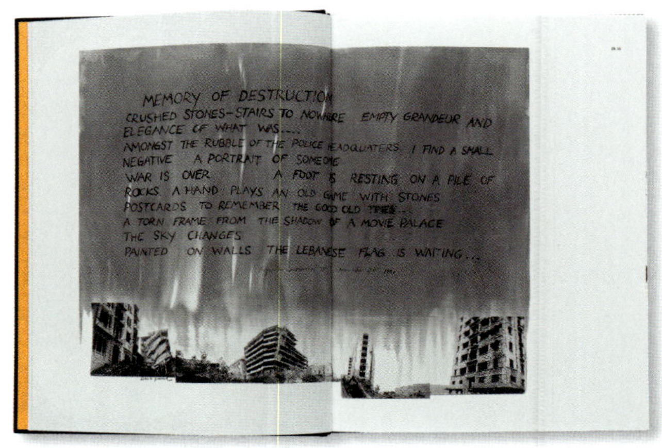
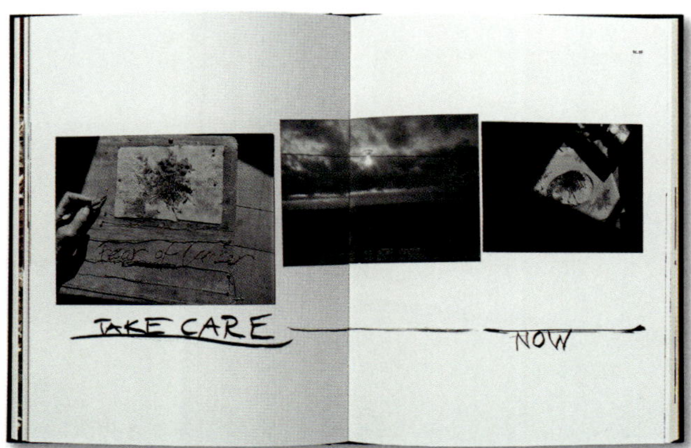
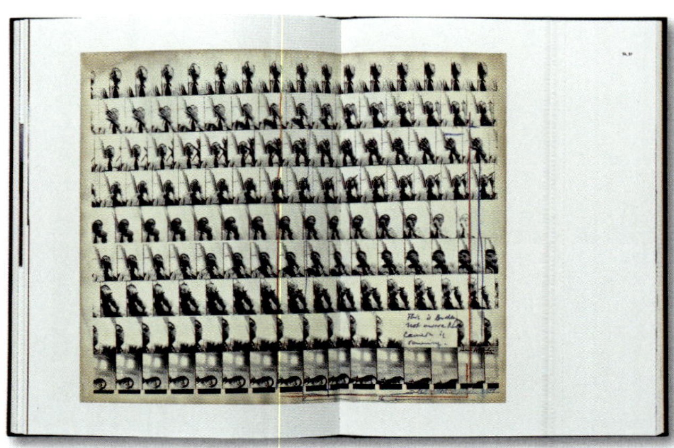
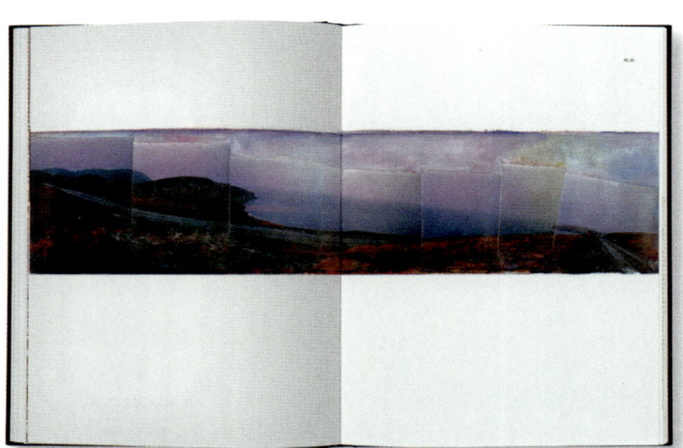
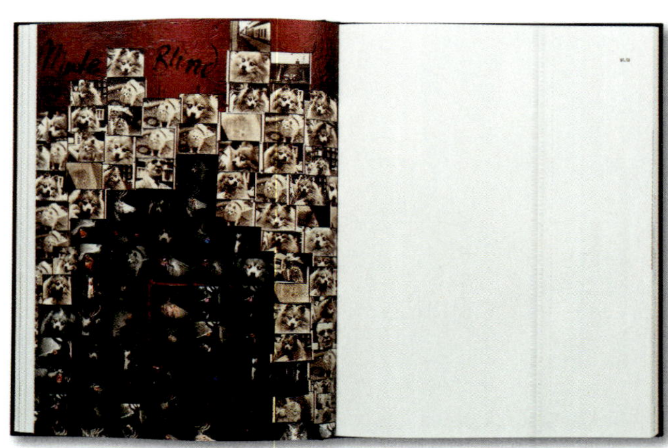
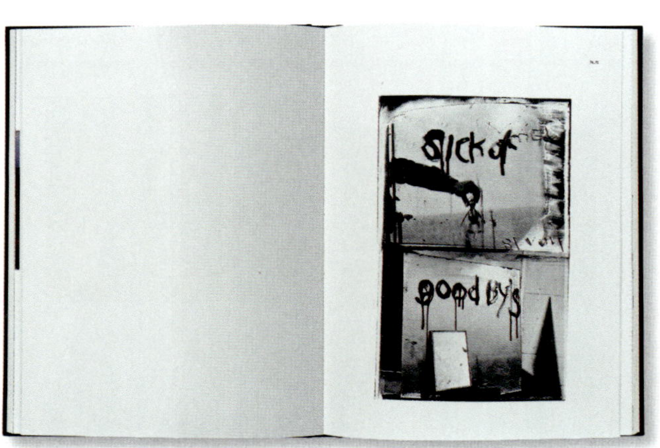
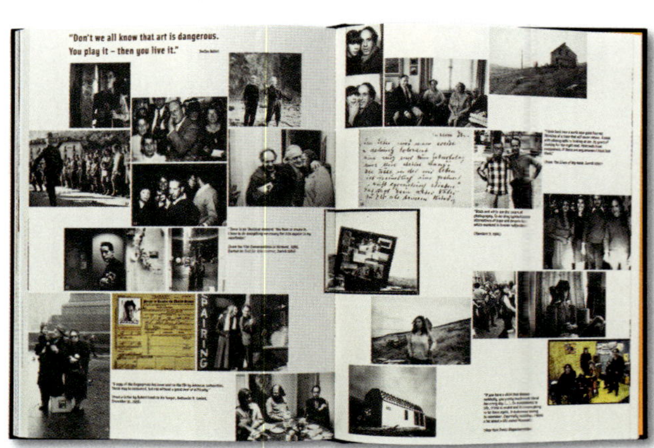

HOLD STILL—
keep going

First edition published by
Scalo, 2001
First Steidl edition, 2016

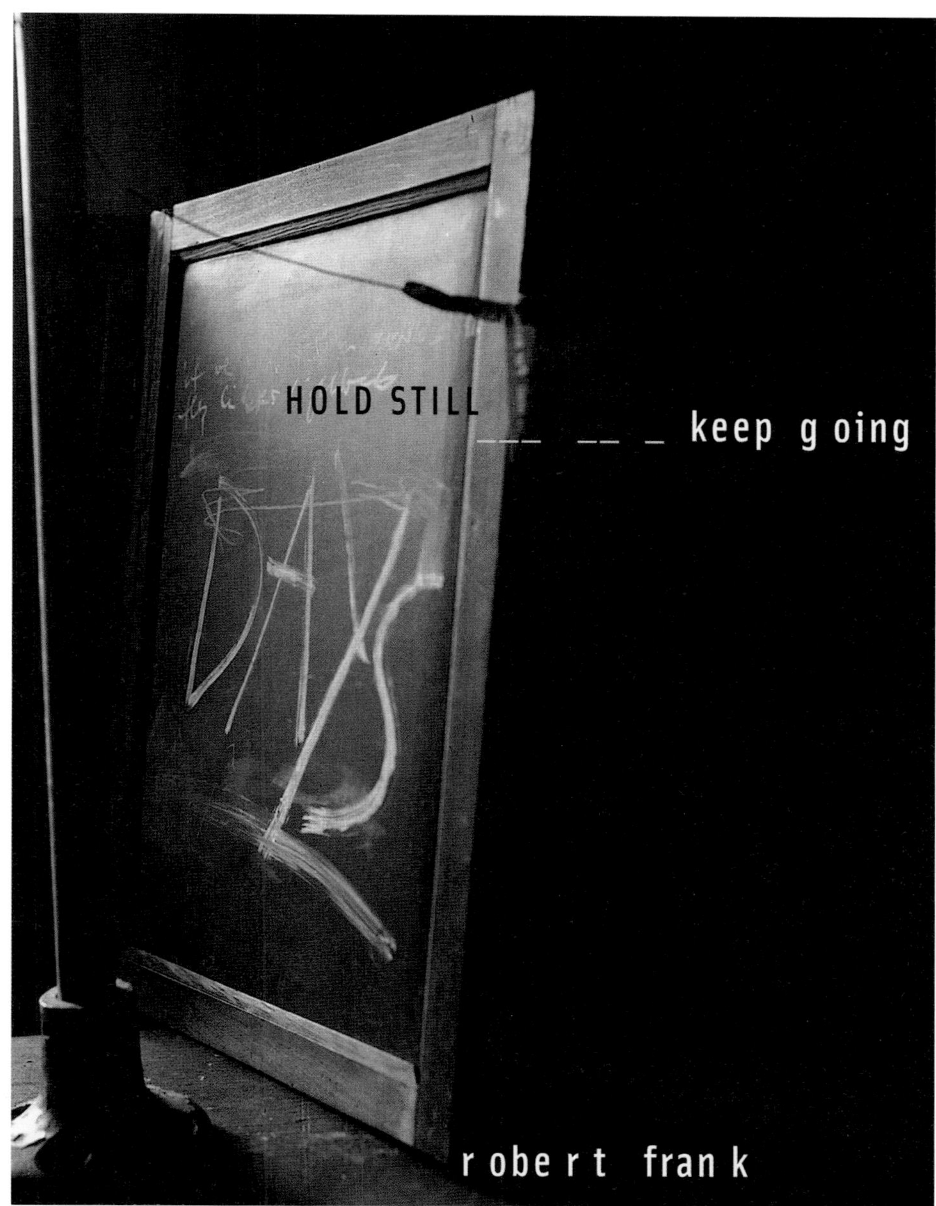

Texts by Wolfgang Beilenhoff,
Ute Eskildsen and
Christoph Ribbat
Book design by Sabine an Huef
168 pages
8 × 10.4 in. / 20.5 × 26.5 cm
87 black-and-white and
13 color photographs
Tritone and four-color process
Clothbound hardcover with
dust jacket

ISBN 978-3-86930-904-0

HOLD STILL—keep going is the long-awaited reprint of the catalogue to Robert Frank's 2001 exhibition of the same name at Museum Folkwang in Essen. The book explores the role of film in Frank's work and the interaction between the still and moving image that engaged him since the late 1950s. *HOLD STILL—keep going* adopts a non-chronological approach, including photographs, film stills, 35mm filmstrips, as well as photo-montages that present his most famous series alongside less-known work. Text, from handwritten phrases on photographs (of which "HOLD STILL—keep going" is but one example) to the dialogues in his films, emerges as a crucial tool, one also central to Frank's visual diaries.

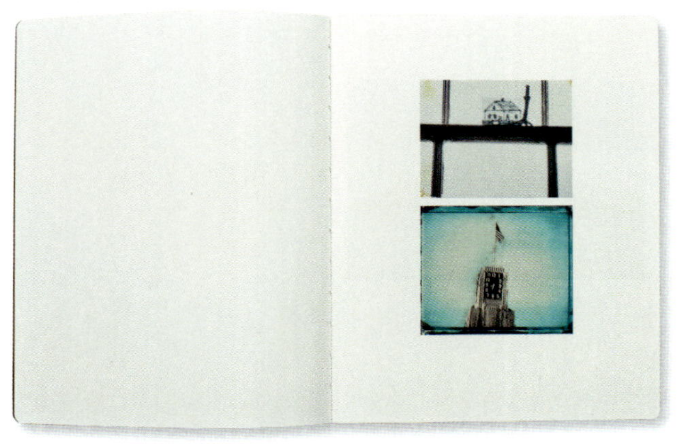
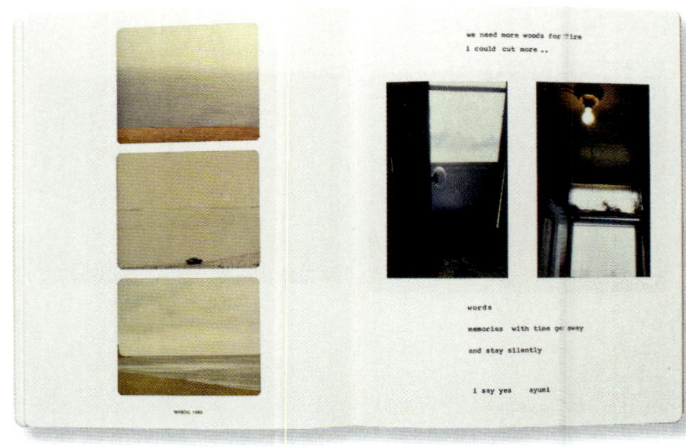
we need more woods for fire
i could cut more ..
words
memories with time go away
and stay silently
i say yes   ryuei
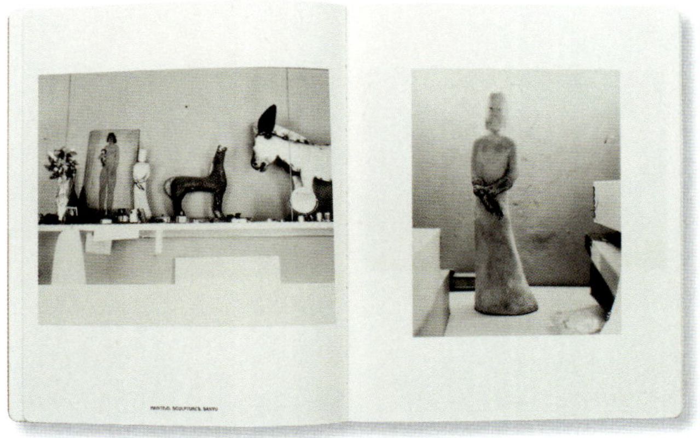
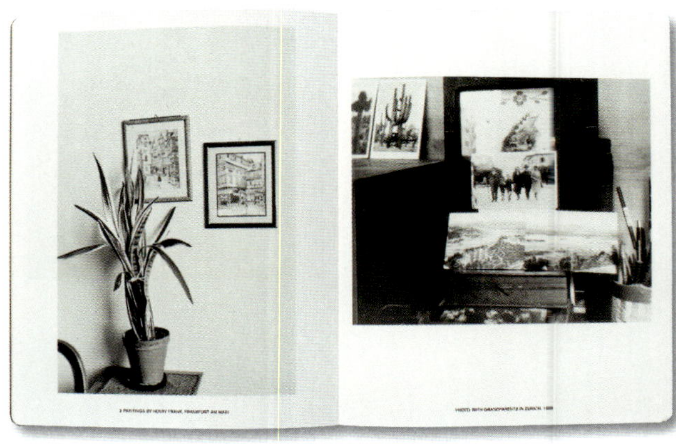
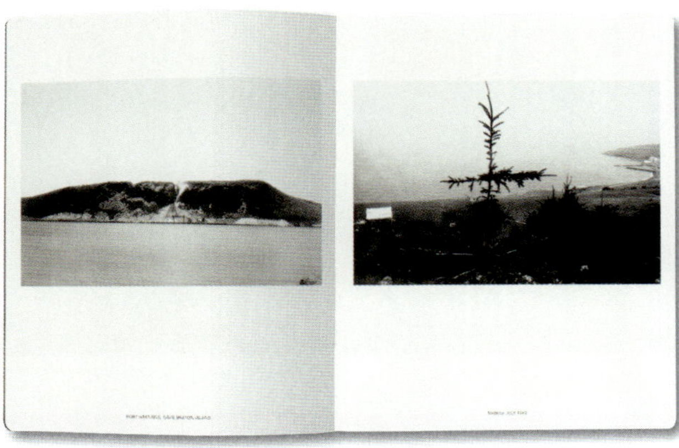
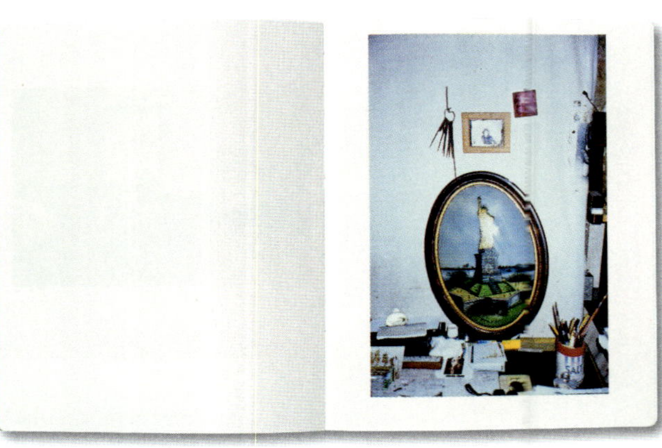
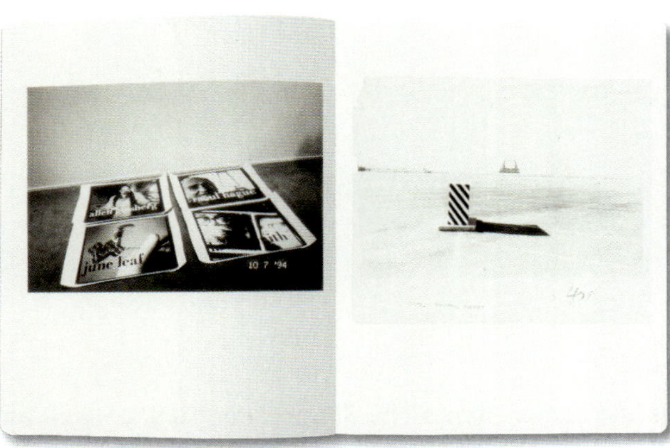
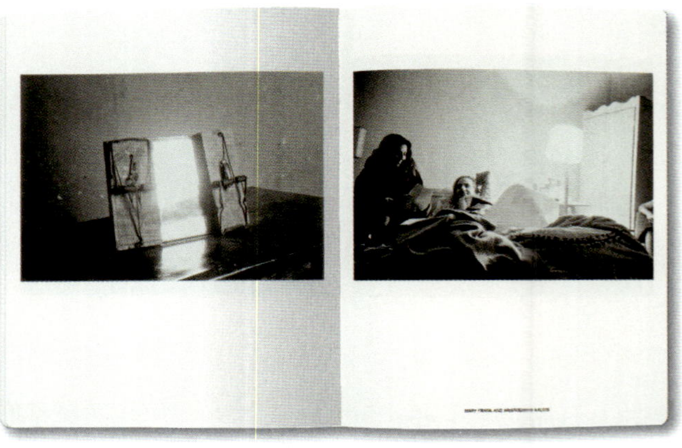

Was haben wir gesehen / What we have seen

Published by Steidl, 2016

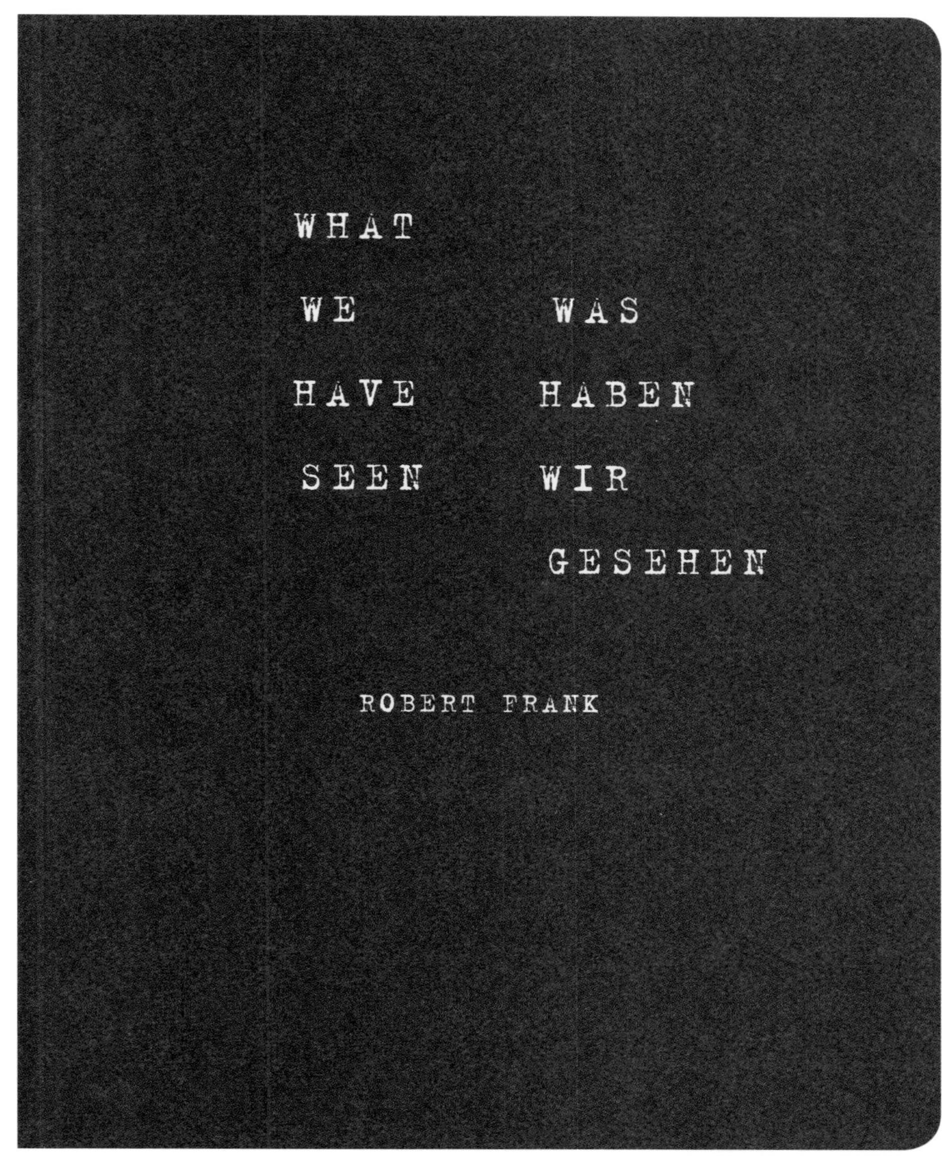

Text by Robert Frank
Book design by Robert Frank,
A-chan and Gerhard Steidl
48 pages
8 × 9.8 in. / 20.5 × 25 cm
28 black-and-white and
14 color photographs
Tritone and four-color process
Otabind softcover in slipcase

ISBN 978-3-95829-095-2

Yet another volume in his series of visual diaries, *Was haben wir gesehen / What we have seen* is all about people and places in the life of Robert Frank. Auspiciously opening and closing with the zoom on the dial of a clock tower, serving as a reminder of the silent but constant passage of time, the book explores memories and old photographs. Like a leitmotif carrying us through the images, the word "souvenir" pops up under a magnifying glass positioned on a French text as a reading device. Frank's house in Mabou is once again portrayed as a popular hideaway for his friends, while Jack Kerouac, Allen Ginsberg and William S. Burroughs greet us from the past.

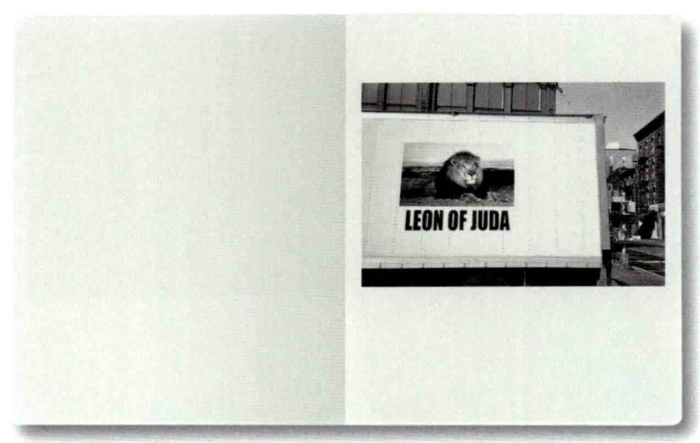

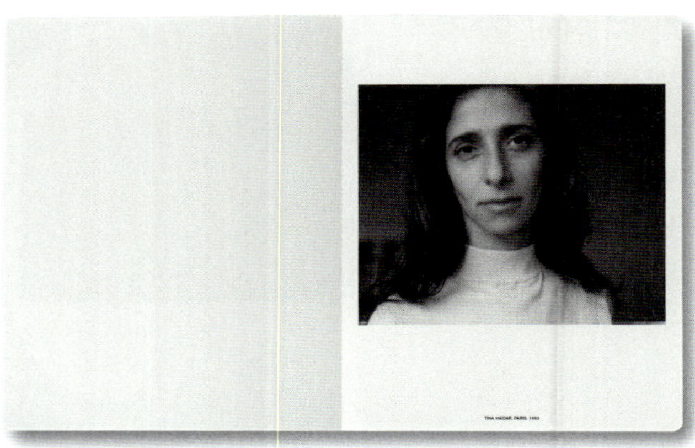

TINA HAIDAR, PARIS. 1993

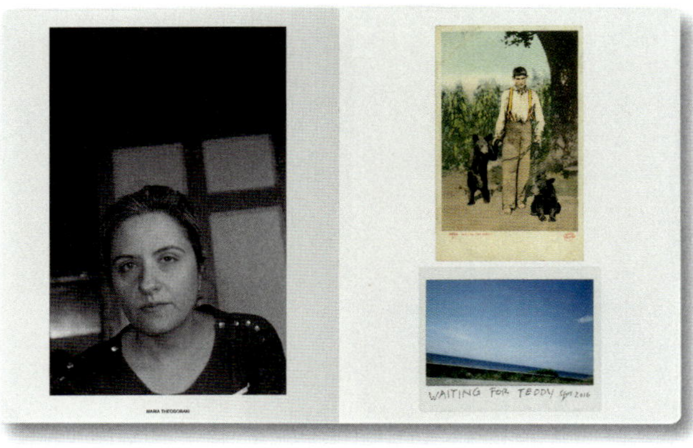

MARIA THEODORAKI

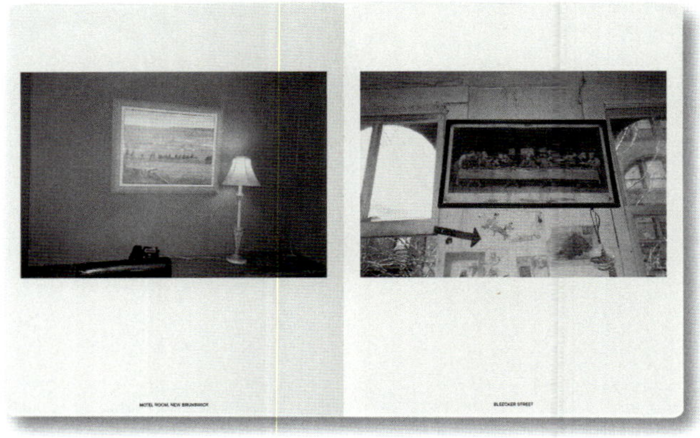

MOTEL ROOM, NEW BRUNSWICK

BLEECKER STREET

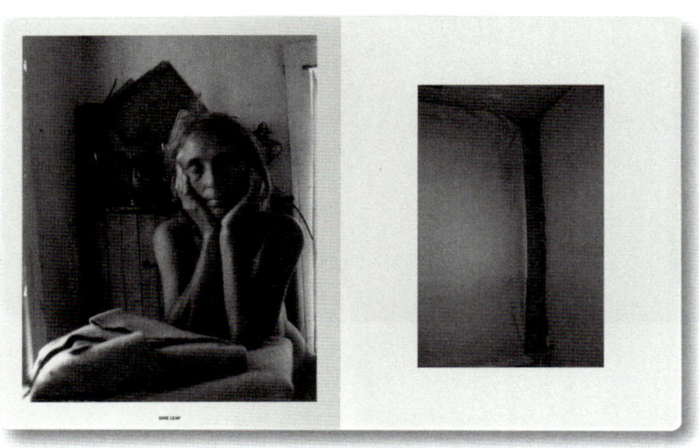

SIRE LEAF

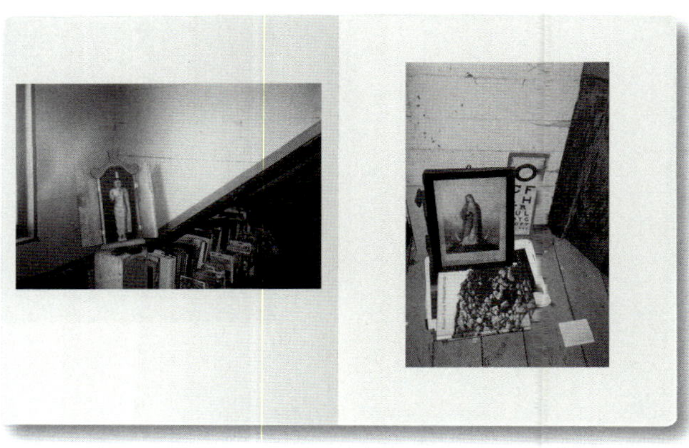

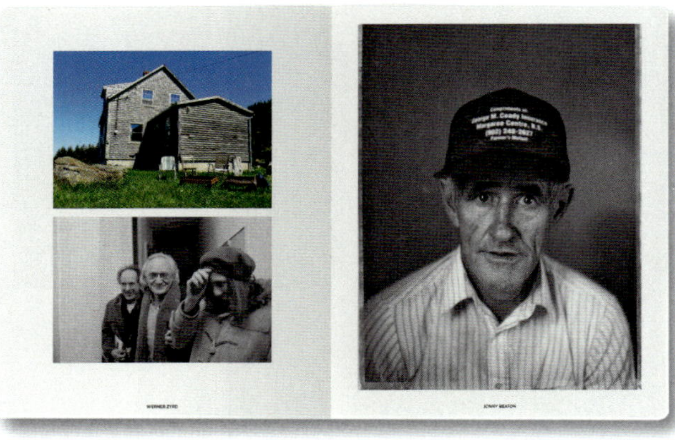

WERNER ZYRD

JONNY BEATON

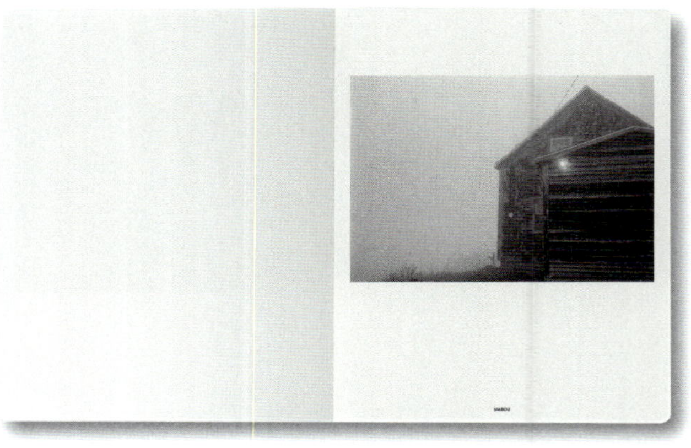

MABOU

Leon of Juda

Published by Steidl, 2017

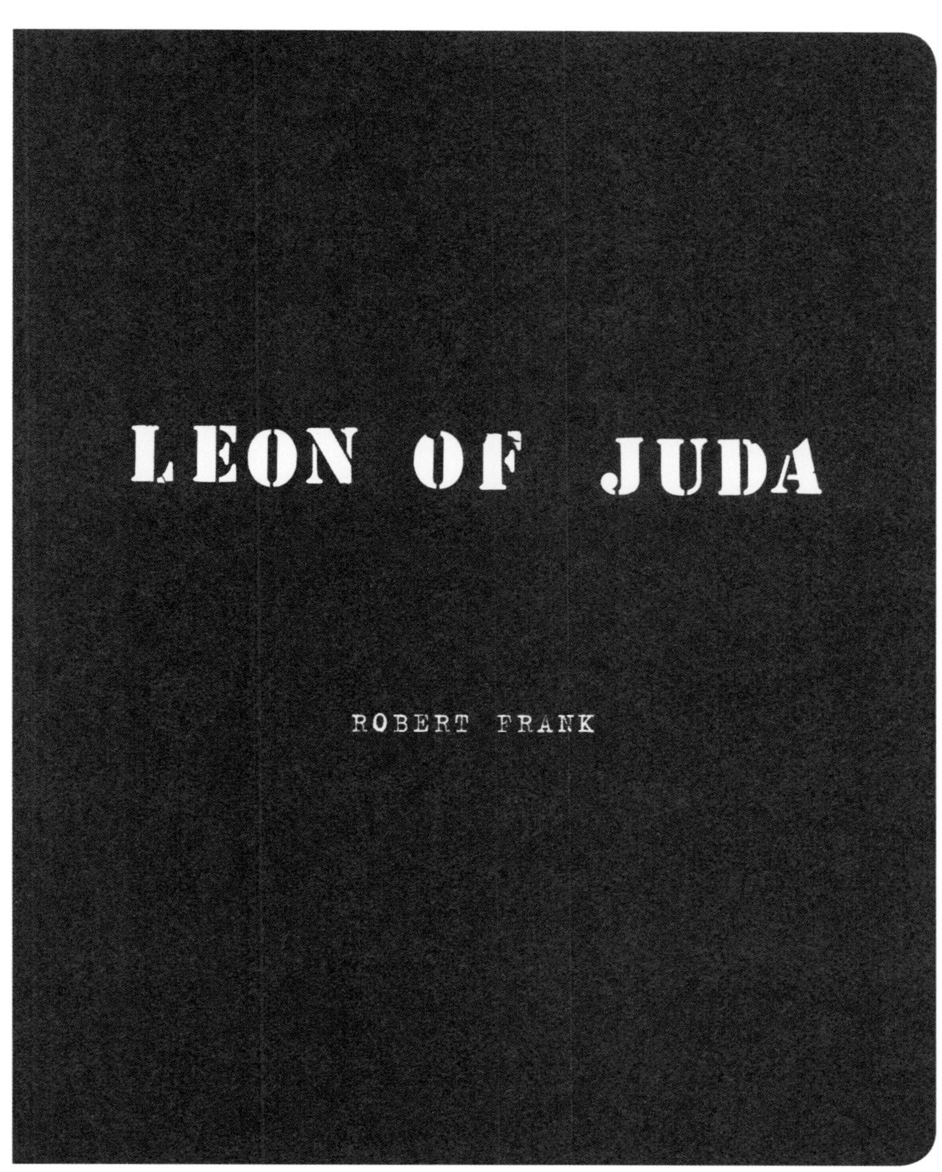

Text by Robert Frank
Book design by Robert Frank,
A-chan and Gerhard Steidl
52 pages
8 × 9.8 in. / 20.5 × 25 cm
30 black-and-white and
8 color photographs
Tritone and four-color process
Otabind softcover in slipcase

ISBN 978-3-95829-311-3

Leon of Juda is the last of Robert Frank's visual diaries, which combine iconic photos from throughout his career with the more personal pictures he made in later life. Here still lifes taken in Frank's home in Bleecker Street and landscapes around his house in Mabou jostle alongside spontaneous portraits of friends, colleagues and his wife artist June Leaf, as well as vintage postcards. Equally humble and ambitious, *Leon of Juda* shows how the past and present shaped Frank's bookmaking.

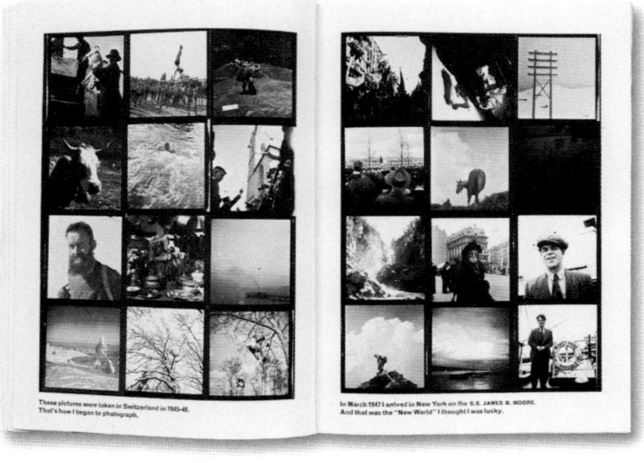
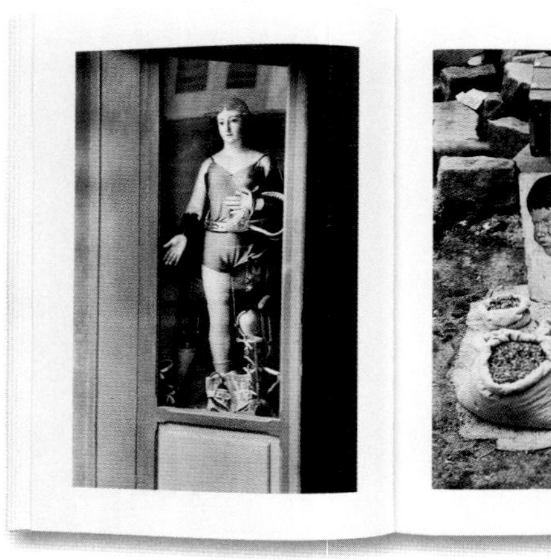
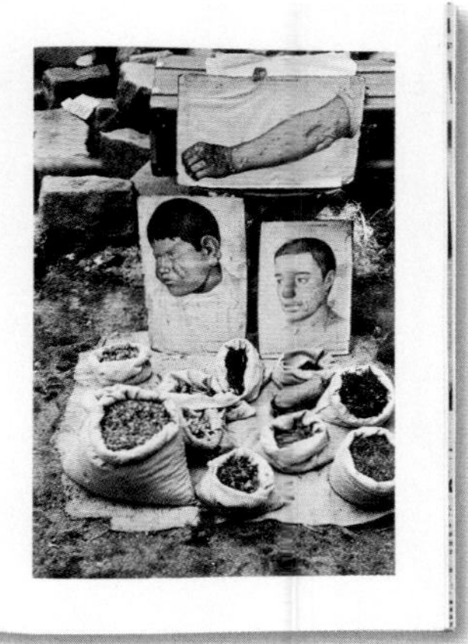
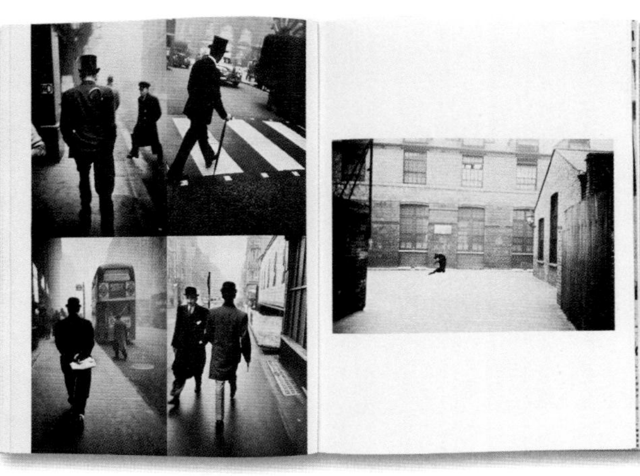
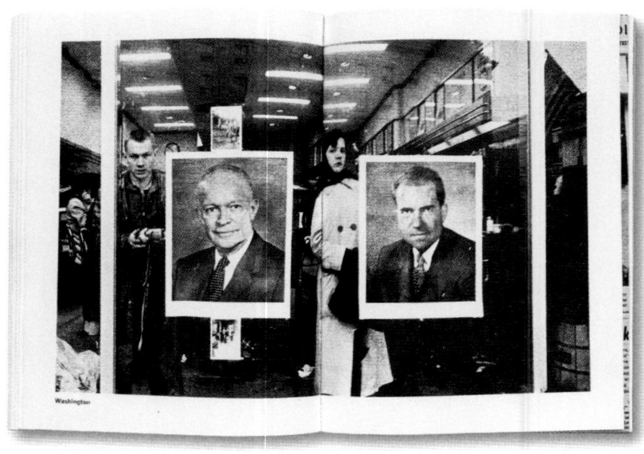
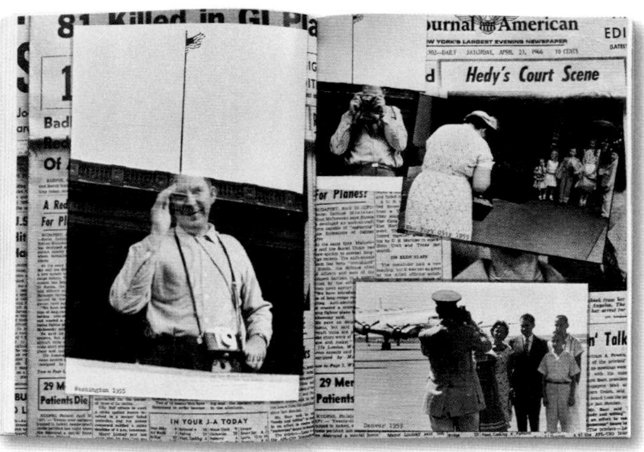
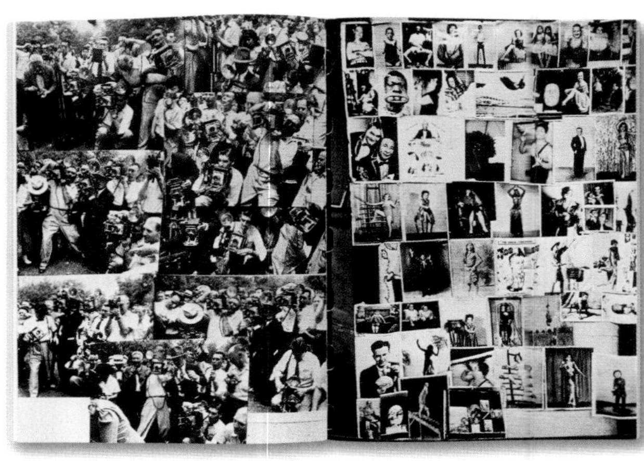
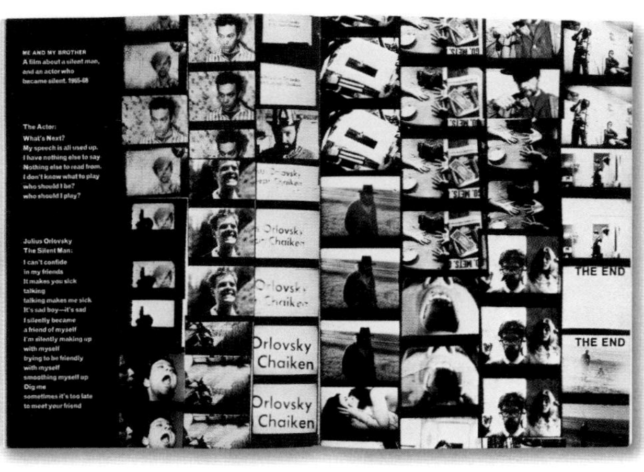
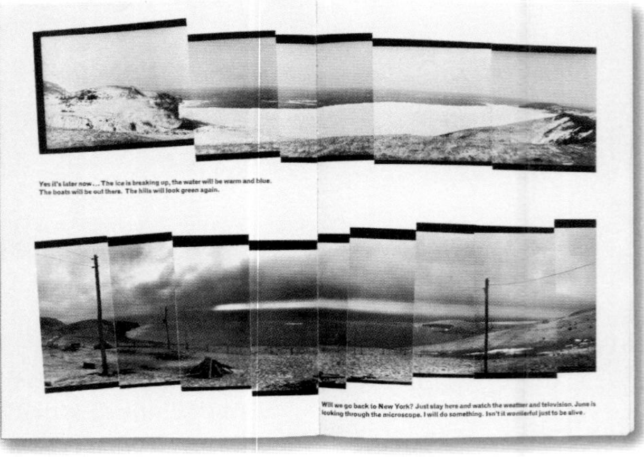

The Lines
of My Hand

First edition published by Lustrum
Press, 1972
First Steidl edition, 2017

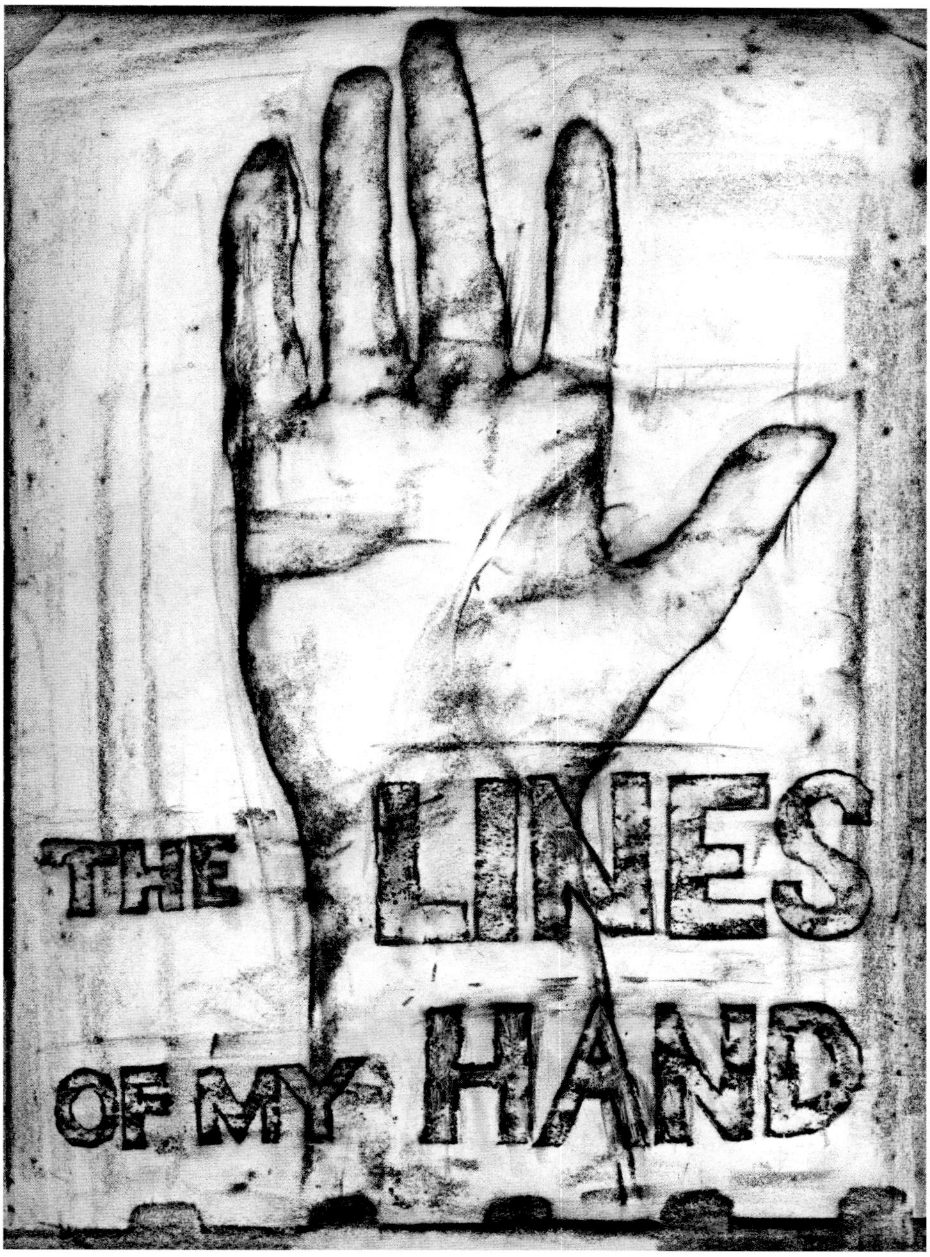

Text by Robert Frank
Cover by June Leaf
112 pages
8.9 × 12 in. / 22.5 × 30.4 cm
101 black-and-white
photographs
Tritone
Otabind softcover

ISBN 978-3-95829-320-5

After *The Americans*, *The Lines of My Hand* is arguably Robert Frank's most important book and without doubt the publication that established his autobiographical, sometimes confessional, approach to bookmaking. The book was originally published by Yugensha in Tokyo in 1972, and this Steidl edition, made in close collaboration with Robert Frank, follows and updates the first US edition by Lustrum Press of 1972.

The Lines of My Hand is structured chronologically and presents selections from every stage of Frank's work until 1972—from early photos in Switzerland in 1945–46, to images of his travels in Peru, Paris, Valencia, London and Wales, and to contact sheets from his 1955–56 journey through the United States that resulted in *The Americans* and made him famous. Here too are intimate photos of Frank's young family, later photo-collages and stills from films including *Pull My Daisy* (1959) and *About Me: A Musical* (1971). This structure itself mirrors the rhythm of Frank's life but it is his short personal texts, like diary entries, that fully bring his voice into the book.

In its original combination of text and image, its fearless self-reflection, and its insistence on photography and film as equal though different aspects of the artist's visual language, *The Lines of My Hand* has become an inspiration for many photographers—not least Robert Frank himself, who continued and expanded this approach in his visual diaries.

"

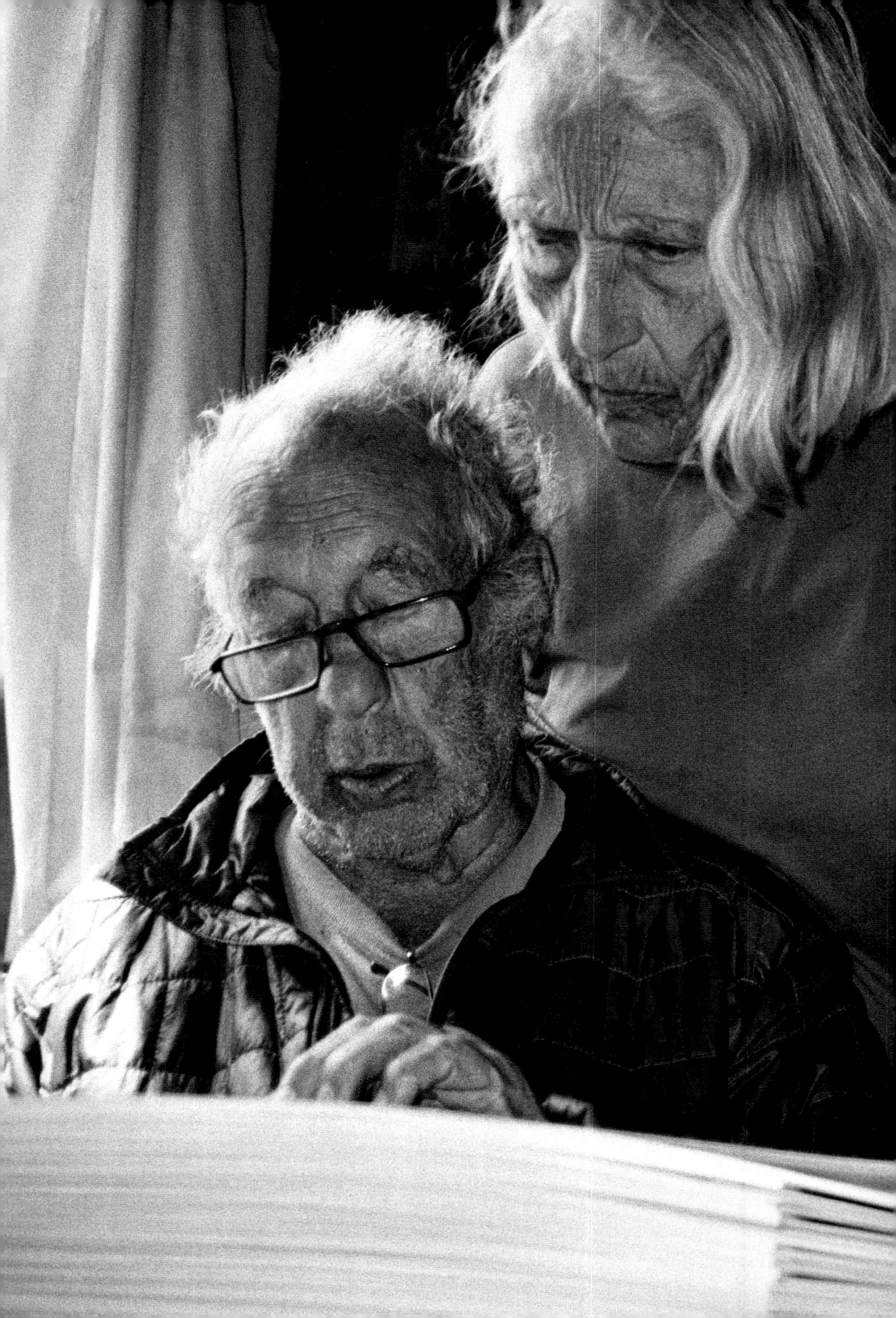

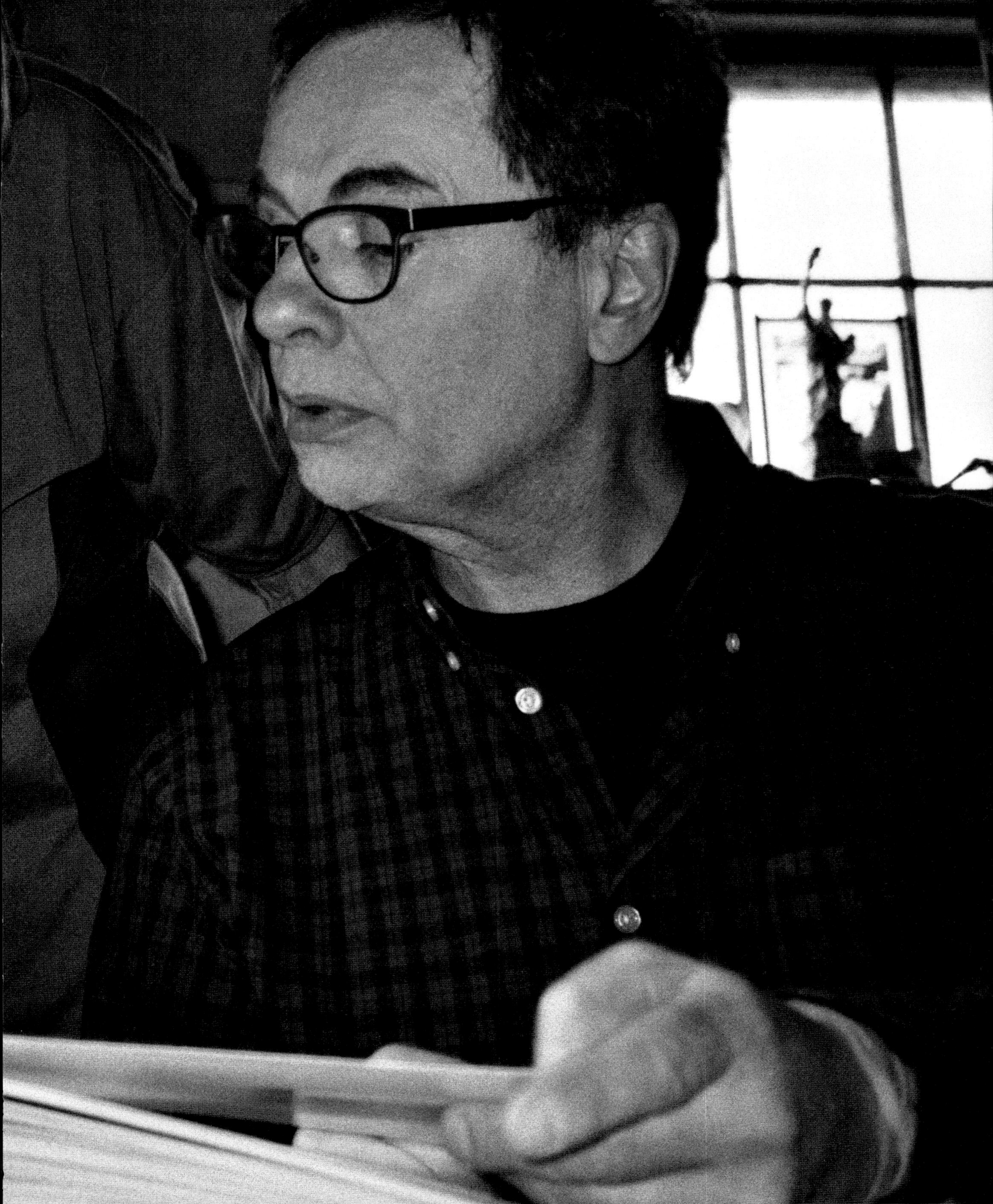

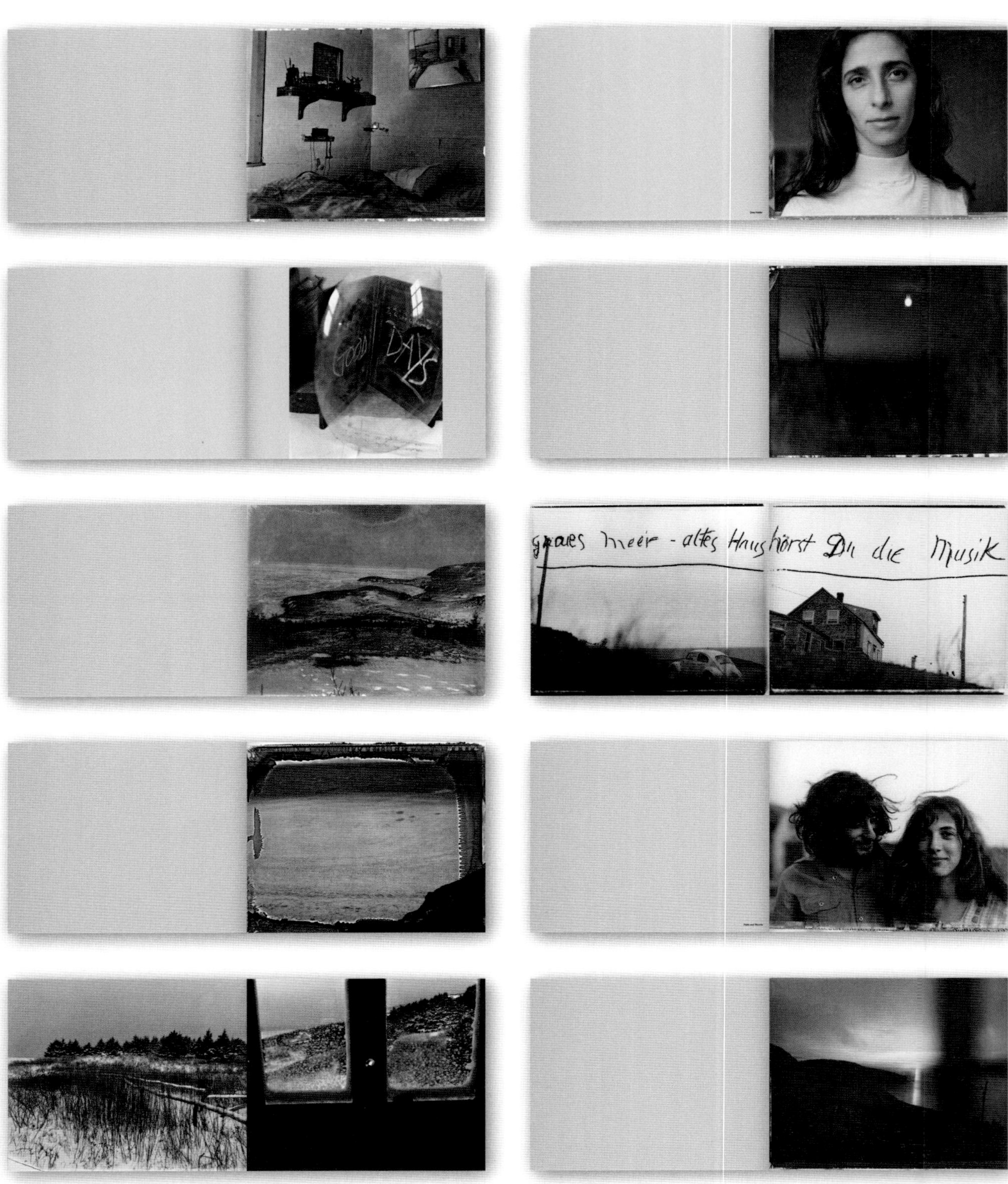
graues meer - altes Haus hörst Du die Musik

Good Days Quiet

Published by Steidl, 2019

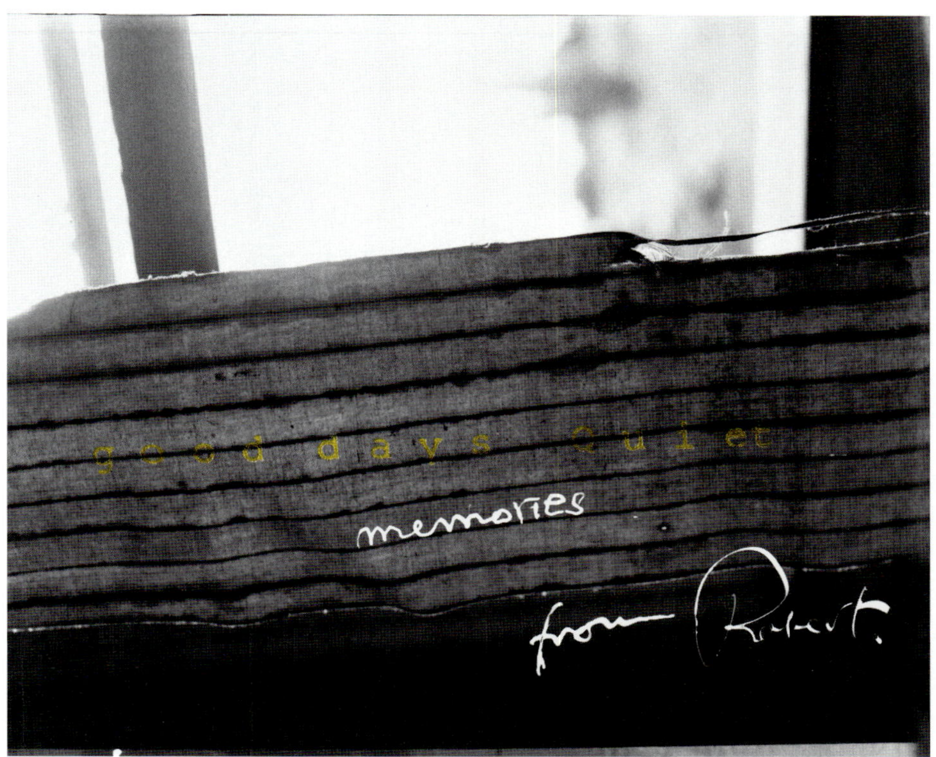
Book

Sleeve

Book design by Robert Frank,
A-chan, and Gerhard Steidl
64 pages
10 × 8 in. / 25.4 × 20.3 cm
37 black-and-white photographs
Tritone
Open-spine softcover in
a sleeve

ISBN 978-3-95829-550-6

In this, Robert Frank's last book, he both acknowledged and moved beyond his visual diaries (2010–17), which juxtapose photographs—past and present, iconic and unknown—with suggestive, often autobiographical text fragments.

In *Good Days Quiet* Frank's focus is life inside and outside his beloved weather-beaten wooden house in Mabou, where he spent summers for decades with his wife June Leaf. Among portraits of Leaf, Allen Ginsberg and Frank's son, are images of the house's simple interior with its wood-fuelled iron stove, humble furniture and bare light bulbs, as well as views of the land and sea by the house: snow-covered, windswept, stormy or lit by the dying sun.

Frank's Polaroids scanned for the book show various deliberate states of deterioration and manipulation at his hands, including texts that move from the merely descriptive ("watching the crows") to the emotive ("memories," "grey sea—old house / can you hear the music"). As always in Frank's books, his message lies primarily in the photos' lyrical sequence, an influential approach to the photobook he pinoeered over the decades of his practice.

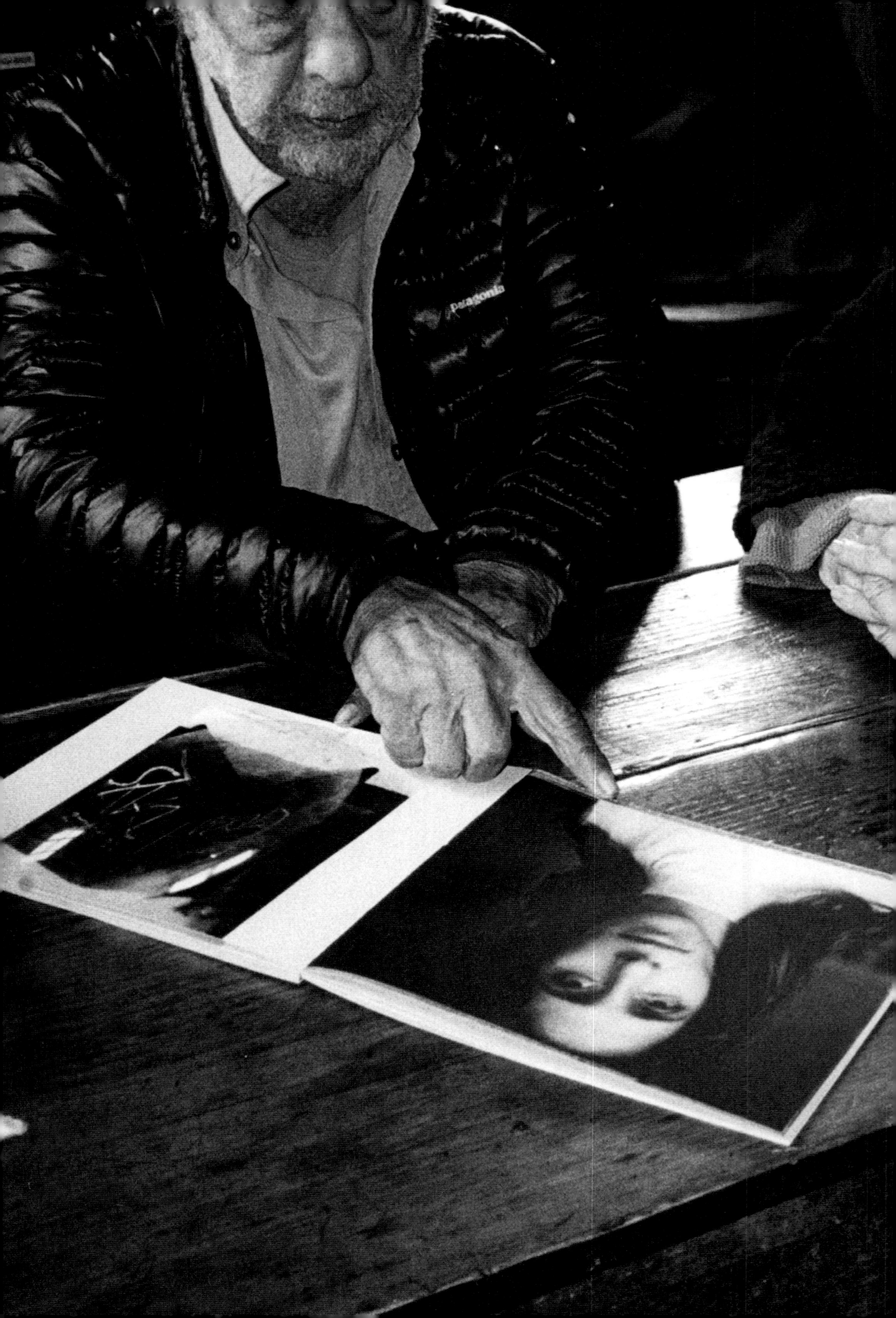

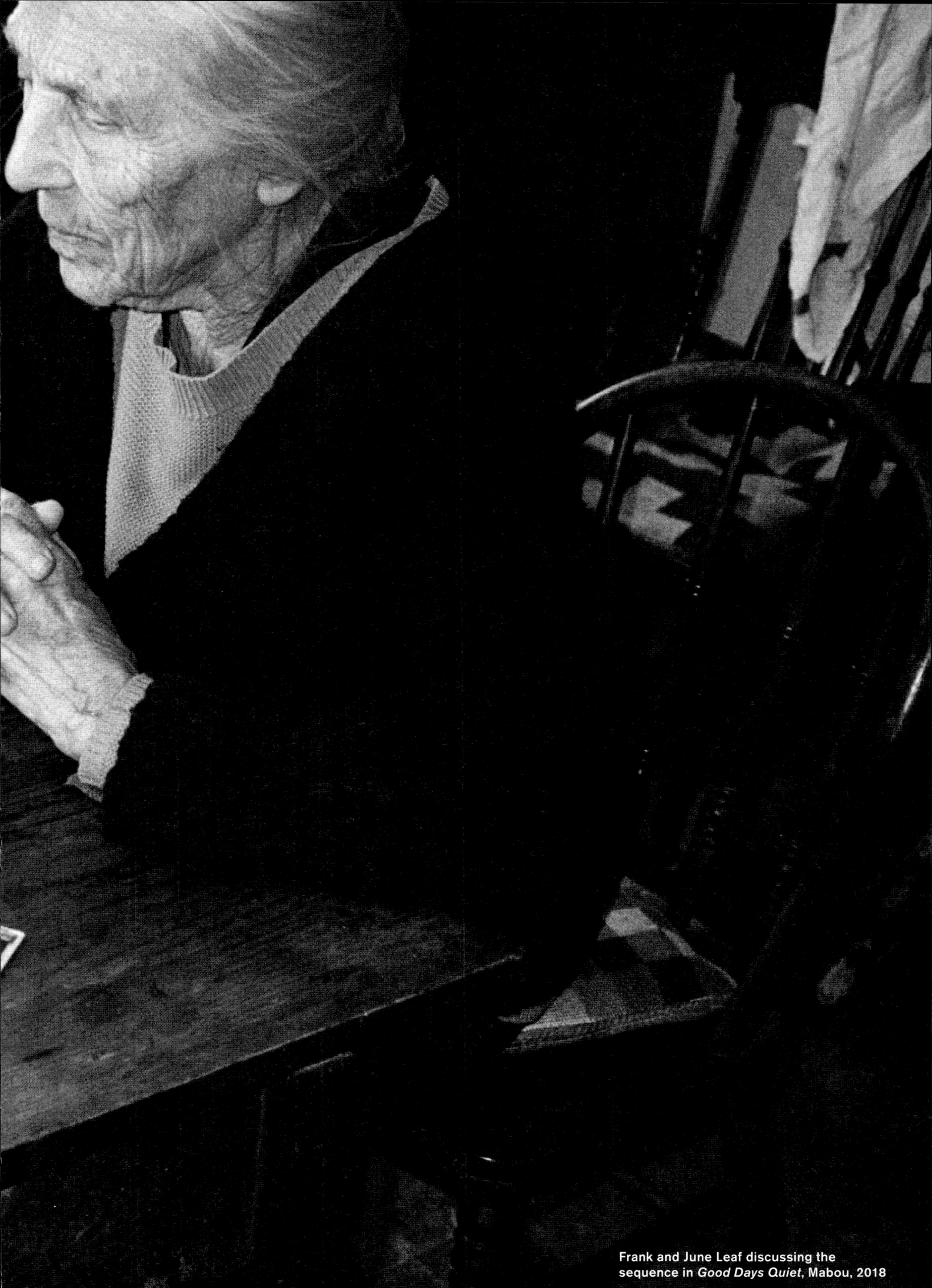

Frank and June Leaf discussing the sequence in *Good Days Quiet*, Mabou, 2018

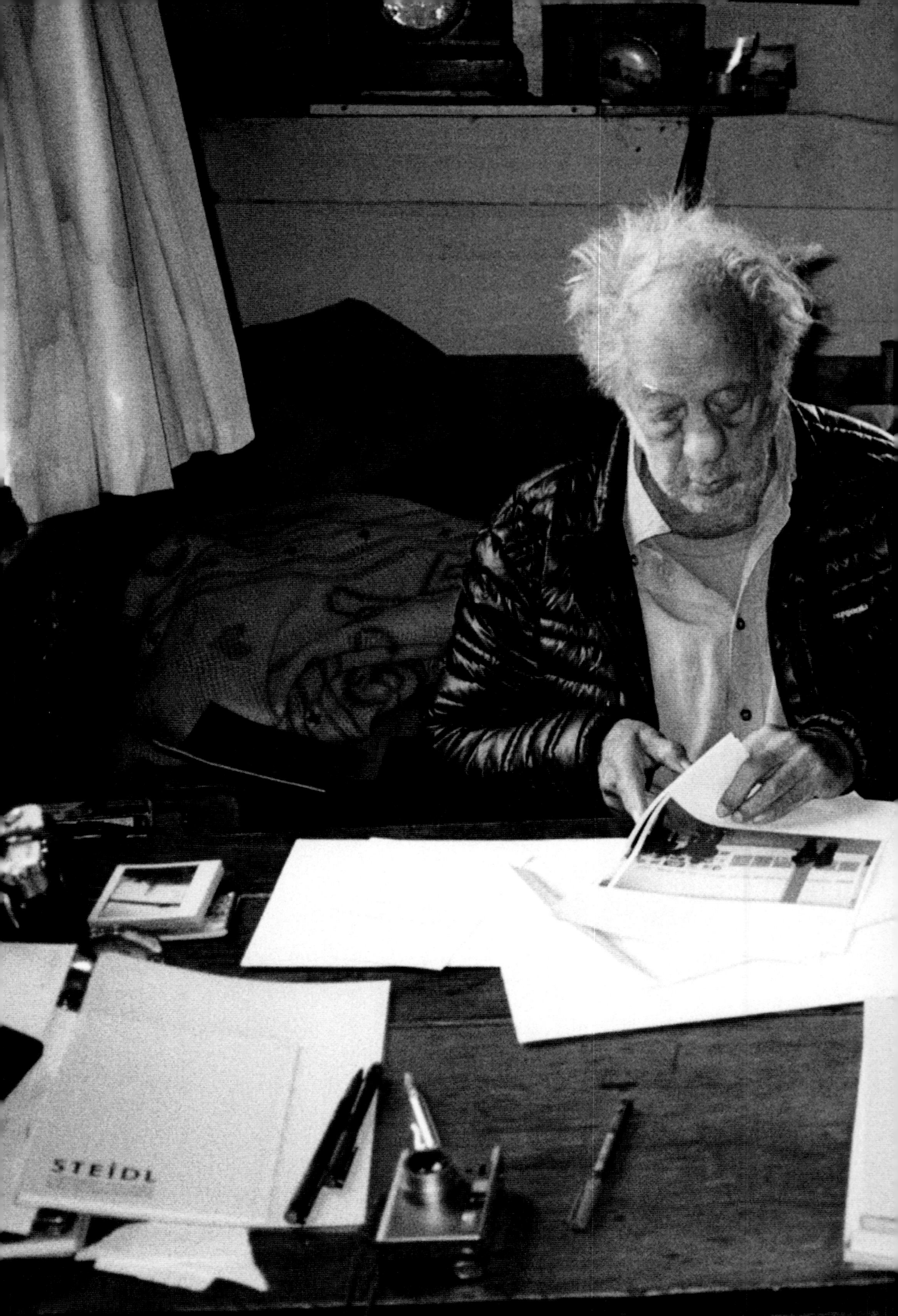

Frank approving *Good Days Quiet*
for printing, Mabou, 2018

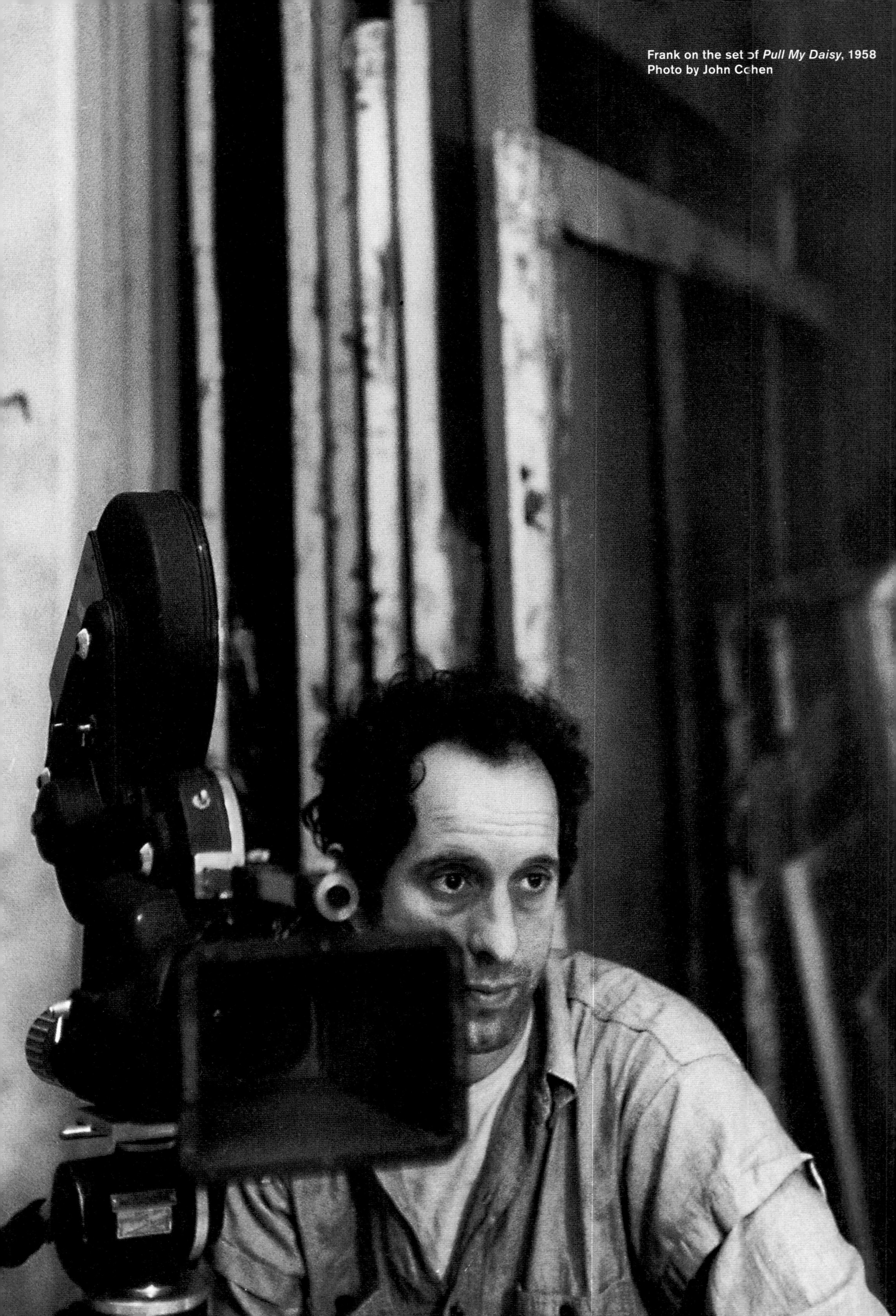

Frank on the set of *Pull My Daisy*, 1958
Photo by John Cohen

Films and Videos

1959–2008

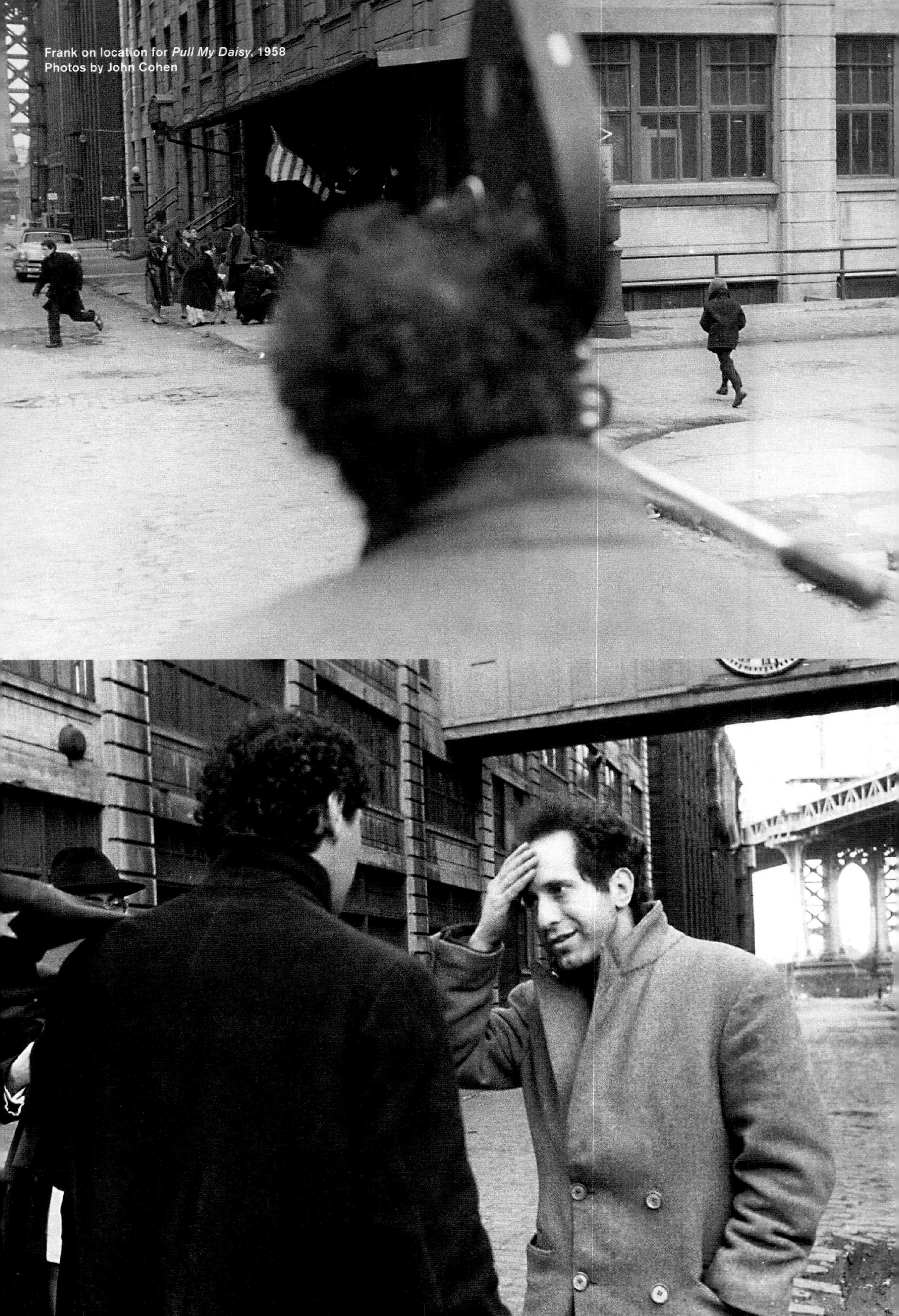

Frank on location for *Pull My Daisy*, 1958
Photos by John Cohen

Restoration Blues:
Survival in Films, the Survival of Films

An interview with Gerhard Steidl on the digital
restoration of Robert Frank's films

*Fritz Göttler: Who had the idea of restoring Robert
Frank's cinematic œuvre and thus making it accessible again?*
Gerhard Steidl: I started printing books for Robert
Frank in 1989, for the Scalo publishing house. When
it closed its doors in 2004, I acquired the rights and
continued printing the books. I sat down with Robert
and we made a plan for future editions: new editions
of books that were already in print, books for which
he had pasted together dummies but never found a
publisher, and new books from his material. His life's
work was thus available from Steidl … and so we
decided to also add the films.

*FG: What was the state of the source material, the
prints and negatives?*
GS: None of the films had ever been properly
archived; in other words, Robert had simply stacked
up the 16mm or 35mm film reels and the videos at his
home on Bleecker Street. Nothing was in the National
Gallery—it was all in his house. We then persuaded
Laura Israel to restore and digitize the films for us,
which took her ten years. She has a wonderful understanding of his work and has managed since 1994 to
digitize all of his film titles. She color-corrected the
pictures and cleaned up the audio tracks. Then Robert
watched the restored films and gave her tips on where
she might find various outtakes that were missing
from that particular version. He still had a collection of
cans on Bleecker Street, in the stairwell …

FG: So the prints were not in a final state.
GS: In some films, especially the short ones, there
were spots that had been dilettantishly patched
together; these spots in the film reel were then wrin-
kled or torn, and sometimes even crumbling. But they
only amount to seconds or minutes. That's simply his
attitude: people shouldn't treat my photos with so
much respect, he once said to me.

*FG: Were the films all unique pieces then? Weren't
there any prints that he had made for lending out?*
GS: Professional prints had only been made of very few
of his films. In our restoration work, we viewed the outtakes separately; sometimes they were then integrated
into the films, and sometimes not. I'm satisfied with this
film, Robert said, so nothing needs to be changed. The
famous example is of course *Cocksucker Blues*, where
he had a completely different vision for the film than
his client, the Rolling Stones. They had actually wanted
a music film, with lots of scenes on stage, and Robert
wanted to show more what went on behind the scenes.

FG: Is there then a definitive version?
GS: No, at some point work on it just stopped, Robert
then delivered a version to the Rolling Stones' management—it was after all a commission. Mick Jagger
actually liked the film, but the band's management
thought the public would be put off by it. That was the
official reason for banning it.

FG: And it's still banned today.
GS: I wrote Mick Jagger a few letters, and he replied
to one but didn't give his permission to release it.
The compromise is that we can now show the film in
exhibitions, but it won't be included in the digitized
complete edition. We put in a few outtakes that are
really good, but it's still a fragment. The other films, by
contrast, were all reviewed and authorized by Robert.

*FG: To what extent was Frank influenced by clients in
his films?*
GS: Sometimes those funding the films wanted to
have a say in their making. Even Alfred Leslie, the
co-director of *Pull My Daisy*. But in most cases Robert
was able to prevail in the end. He always made any
compromises very pragmatically, in order not to
alienate the people he had worked with all his life:
the partners who financed his films, his actors, his
printers in the darkroom, his publishers. So that they
could all survive. And so that the friendships didn't
break up.

*FG: And it didn't occur to any of them to restore all of
this material?*
GS: Robert himself doesn't have much drive in this
respect, because he's only interested in what he's
doing at this moment, on this very day. His galleries
weren't interested because there would be nothing
to sell. And a normal arthouse cinema or distributor
doesn't tackle projects like this. We made high-res-
olution digital files and we're now in the final stages.
These files can be used for archival purposes, digital
projection and for creation of DVDs.

FG: Is Frank still making films?
GS: Whether on Bleecker Street in New York or in
Mabou, there are cameras lying around everywhere:
16mm, Super 8, video cameras, all kinds of models,
and he still has cassettes and film cans scattered
around. And when he feels like it, he grabs a camera
and shoots a scene. I know a spot in his house where
there are piles of undeveloped film material.

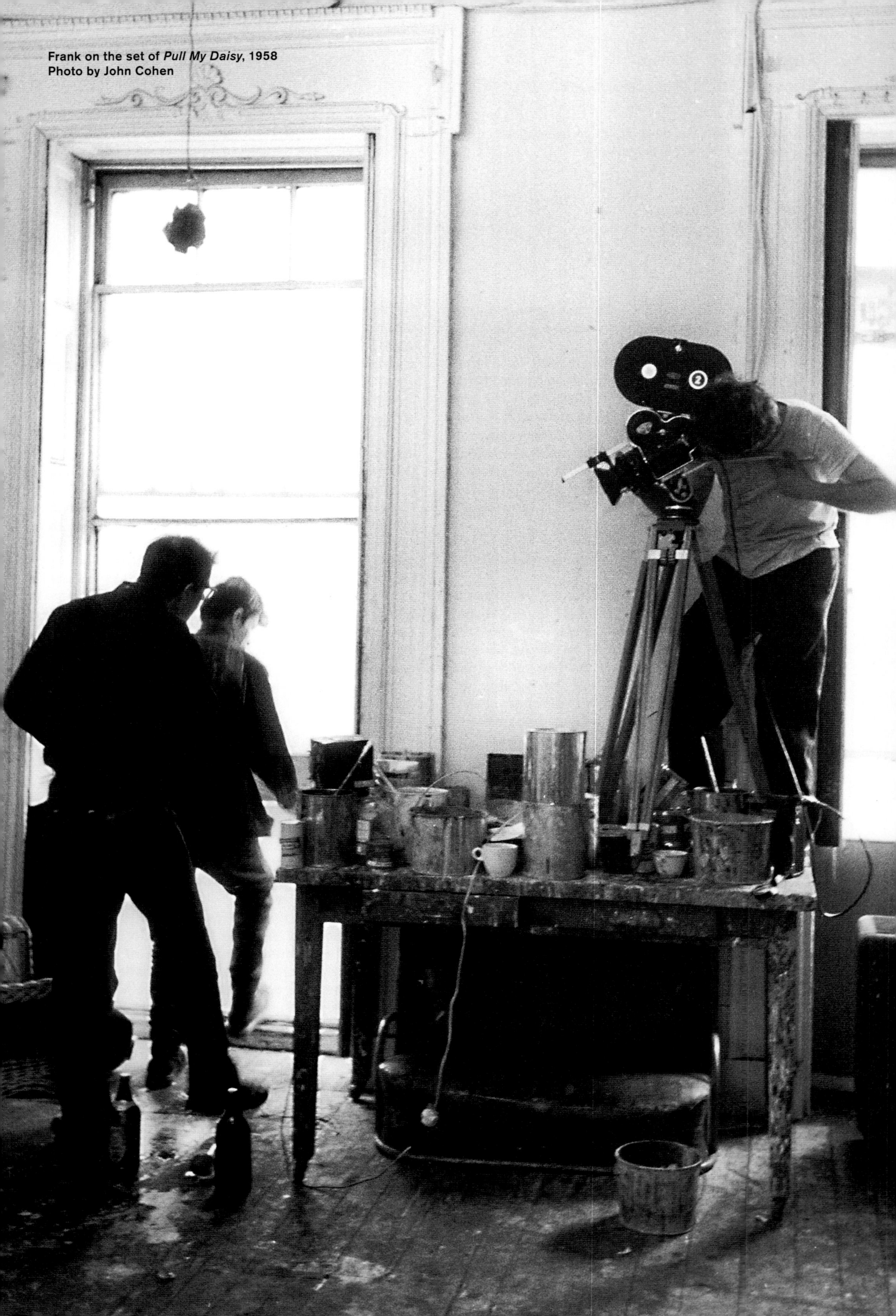

Frank on the set of *Pull My Daisy*, 1958
Photo by John Cohen

Robert Frank on making films:

"In 1958, right after finishing *The Americans*, I made my first film. I knew film was first choice. Nothing comes easy, but I love difficulties, and difficulties love me."

"A decision: I put my Leica in a cupboard. Enough of lying in wait, pursuing, sometimes catching the essence of the black and the white, the knowledge where God is. I make films. Now I speak to the people in my viewfinder. Not simple and not especially successful."

"Since being a filmmaker I have become more of a person. I am confident that I can synchronize my thoughts to the image, and that the image will talk back—well it's like being among friends. That eliminated the need to be alone and take pictures."

"I'm filming the outside in order to look inside."

"All will have to come from inside me. No help looking through the viewfinder and choosing the Decisive Moment. That's where it starts, the difference between doing stills and doing a film. I find it very difficult to organize, to control and to discipline my thinking before I step into the doing of it. I feel a film-maker must express first what he feels—what's happening to him."

"The truth is somewhere between the documentary and the fictional, and that is what I try to show. What is real one moment has become imaginary the next. You believe what you see now, and the next second you don't anymore."

"The films I have made are the map of my journey thru all this ... living. [...] I want you to see the shadow of life and death flickering on that screen."

Quotes taken from *Frank Films. The Film and Video Works of Robert Frank,* edited by Brigitta Burger-Utzer and Stefan Grissemann

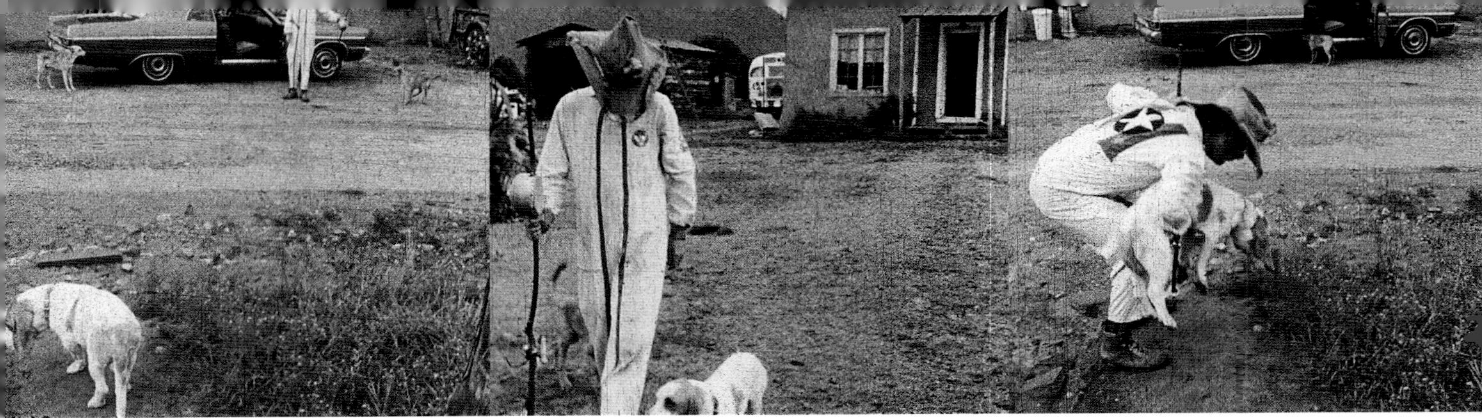

The Films

Pull My Daisy (1959)

Considered one of the most important works of avant-garde cinema, *Pull My Daisy*, made with Alfred Leslie, tells the story of a bishop and his mother who pay a visit to Milo, a railroad worker. At the same time his poet friends hang around quizzing the bishop about the meaning of life and its everyday relationship to art and poetry.

The Sin of Jesus (1961)

Robert Frank's second film is one of his most stylized and reflects Frank's increasingly sophisticated cinematographic eye. Based on a short story by Isaac Babel, this parable finds Jesus refusing mercy to a young woman, instead giving her a guardian angel that she seduces.

O.K. End Here (1963)

A day in the lives of a man and woman who live together in New York City. It is Sunday, a day without the distractions that keep people from facing each other and themselves.

Me and My Brother (1968)

Constantly delineating real and imaginary situations and moving back and forth between color and black and white, the film describes the inner and outer worlds of Julius, a catatonic, who silently observes the world around him.

Conversations in Vermont (1969)

Frank visits and interviews his son and daughter Pablo and Andrea who live in the countryside. A film about past and present and the story of a father's relationship with his two teenage children.

Life-Raft Earth (1969)

Frank's documentary about "The Hunger Show," a week-long fast staged by the Portola Institute in California which took place from 11 October to 18 October 1969 in a parking lot in Hayward. This was a "happening" designed to make the problem of world hunger and malnutrition a personal matter for participants and observers.

About Me: A Musical (1971)

Frank examines his life symbolically, by borrowing an actress to represent him, and questions the personal toll his work has taken and the value of his contribution as a photographer. His search for freedom is represented by the music.

S-8 Stones Footage From Exile on Main Street (1971)

A roll of Super 8 film footage of the Stones wandering around the Bowery in New York City. Individual frames were later enlarged to create the Stones album cover for *Exile on Main Street*. Original outtake footage, unedited, black and white, silent.

Keep Busy (1975)

A spontaneous, improvised story about a group of people living on an island near Cape Breton. Obsessed with daily aspects of their lives and the cycles of nature, the group is subjugated by a lighthouse keeper and his messenger, who have access to the only radio and therefore control the news. Frank's home in Nova Scotia serves as a backdrop.

Life Dances On (1980)

The film is dedicated to Frank's daughter Andrea and to his friend and collaborator Danny Seymour, both deceased. *Life Dances On* is composed of delicately balanced, intuitive moments that merge Frank's own sense of loss for two people close to him with several filmed portraits of those who share his life, including his family and people on the streets in New York City.

Energy and How to Get It (1981)

What began as a documentary film about Robert Golka, an engineer who was experimenting with ball lightening and the development of fusion as an energy force, was turned into a spoof on the documentary form, inserting fictional characters into the story such as the Energy Czar and a Hollywood agent.

This Song for Jack (1983)

The film is dedicated to Frank's late friend Jack Kerouac. Home-movie-like footage shot mostly on the Chautauqua lodge porch during a conference celebrating the 25th anniversary of *On the Road*, featuring Allen Ginsberg, William S. Burroughs, John Clellon Holmes, Gregory Corso, Herbert Huncke, Michael McClure, Edie Kerouac, Carl Solomon, Kens Kesey and Babbs, Abbie Hoffman, David Amram, Ann Charters, Joyce Johnson, Jack Micheline, Andy Clausen and others.

Ginsberg and Corso Reading (1984)

Frank had just bought his first video camera when he shot Allen Ginsberg and Gregory Corso reading their poetry at his home on Bleecker Street. Ginsberg reads "White Shroud," which like his earlier work, "Kaddish," was about his mother. Frank wanted to turn "Kaddish" into a film but eventually the project led to the making of *Me and My Brother*. In addition, Corso reads a poem he stayed up writing the night before as Ginsberg listens. Unedited original VHS video footage.

Home Improvements (1985)

A film diary which tells the story of how Frank's second wife June Leaf becomes ill and has to have surgery. With mixed feelings, Frank sets off to visit his son Pablo in a psychiatric clinic. His thoughts and actions all revolve around the past and his attempts to free himself of its remnants.

Hunter (1989)

An American in Germany's Ruhr valley. His name is Hunter, and he's touring the area around Duisburg. Somewhere between the Rhine and Ruhr rivers, in the country's industrialized midwest, he meets some locals. His attempts to establish contact with them are unsuccessful. But he keeps trying to understand how people cope living in this area.

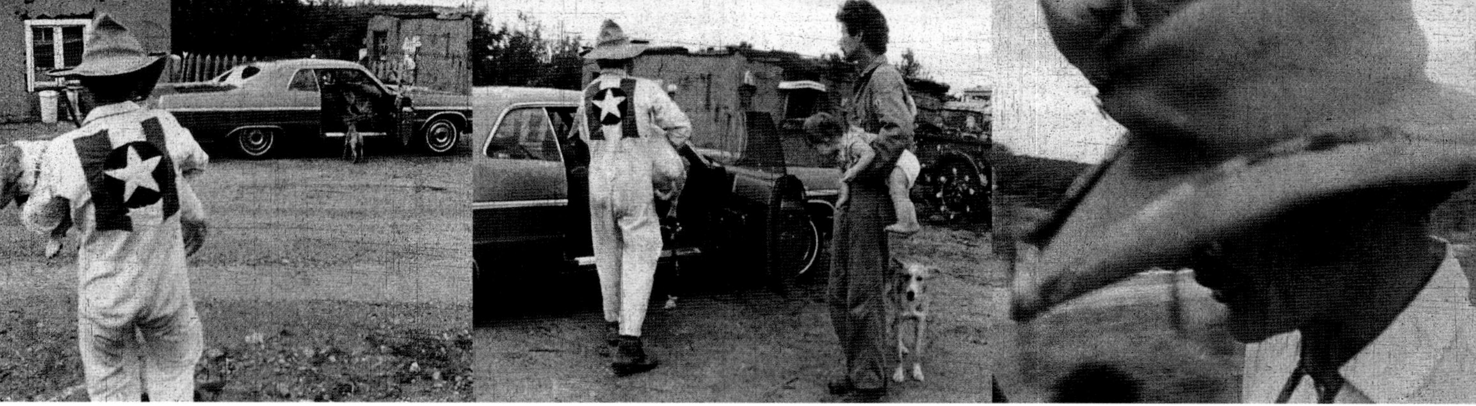

Film stills from *About Me: A Musical* (1971)

One Hour (1990)

A single-take account of Frank and actor Kevin O'Connor either walking or riding in the back of a mini-van through a few blocks of Manhattan's Lower East Side, capturing the somewhat uncanny coziness and intimacy of New York street life.

Last Supper (1992)

In an empty lot in Harlem, an elite group of New Yorkers prepares for a book-signing party given in honor of a writer who never shows up. Local residents, dealing with the practicality of life, look on as the guests obsess about identity, status and success. Finally, the writer's fears and doubts are understood, with ironic implications.

Moving Pictures (1994)

This silent work deals with Robert Frank's transition from photography to film and his search for a "solid form of expression." Frank assembled his own photographs in temporal and spatial sequences: one is laid atop another, photo albums are flipped through; strips of prints are filmed with a slow and probing gaze.

The Present (1996)

An attempt to connect with the things, people, animals, with events in front of the camera—and with the film's potential viewers.

Flamingo (1996)

Laborers arrive to work on the house in Nova Scotia where Frank lives with his wife June Leaf. An addition to the house is planned to provide an even better view of the ocean. In the film routine movements, the precision and speed with which they work, become organic shapes and processes, similar to a stack of paper fluttering in the wind.

What I Remember from My Visit (with Stieglitz) (1998)

Frank questioned his role as a photographer and filmmaker through the alter ego of other artists on various occasions. In this case, he borrows the identities of the great American photographer Alfred Stieglitz (played by Frank) and his wife, painter Georgia O'Keeffe (played by Frank's wife June Leaf), with whom he shared a similar life story. In this film Frank evokes once again his own biography, private life and work as a photographer.

Sanyu (2000)

In Paris and Taiwan Robert Frank sets off on a search for traces of a friend, the painter Sanyu, who died in 1966 at the age of 65. A requiem which documents the story of the film's own production.

Fragments (2000)

A video installation created to accompany the photo exhibition *HOLD STILL—keep going*. Underneath footage of a snake handler from a zoo in Egypt runs text from a letter written to Robert Frank from Dominique Edie, anticipating their meeting in Beirut and collaboration on a film that was never finished.

Paper Route (2002)

The filmmaker once again sets off on a journey, this time a paper route: he accompanies Bobby McMillan, a wiry, high-spirited paperboy, on his evening route around Mabou, Nova Scotia. 158 subscribers, each with a name and a story, and Bobby knows every one of them.

The Tunnel (2005)

Commissioned to premiere under the Swiss Alps at an event held during final blasting through the midpoint of the 21-mile Lötschberg Tunnel in 2005.

True Story (2004/08)

Speaking in voiceover, the artist narrates scenes shot in his homes in New York and Nova Scotia. His rambling commentary returns to familiar themes of memory, and the loss of friends and family members. Brief excerpts from earlier films are shown, along with Frank's photographs, the art of his wife, June Leaf, and extraordinarily detailed letters written by his son, Pablo (1951–94). Alternately poignant, reflective, self-mocking and angry, this candid autobiography reveals Frank's late career preoccupations.

Fernando (2008)

An homage to Frank's lifelong friend Fernando, a Swiss artist who passed away.

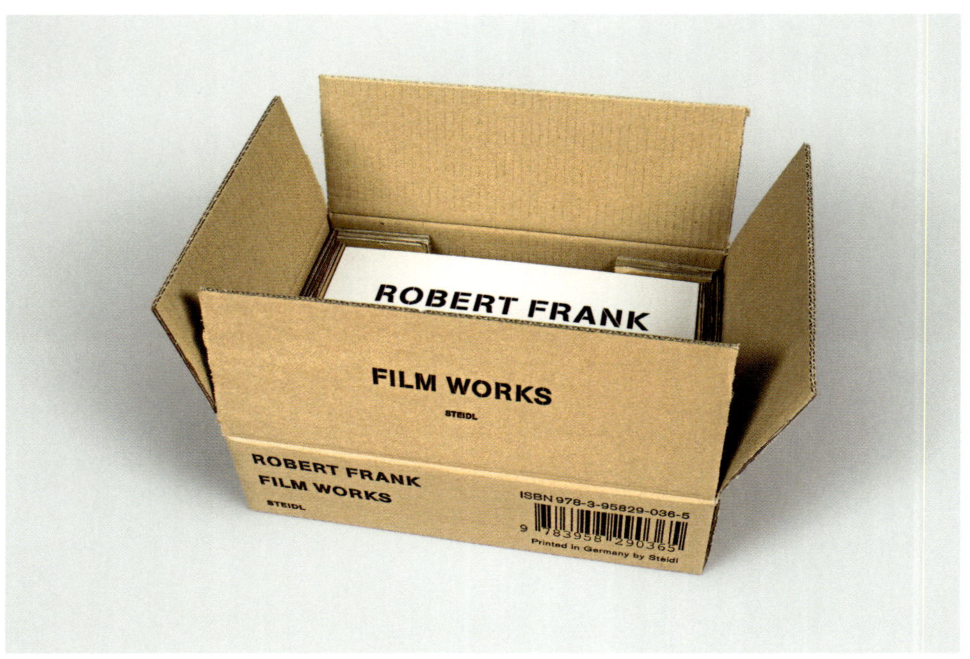

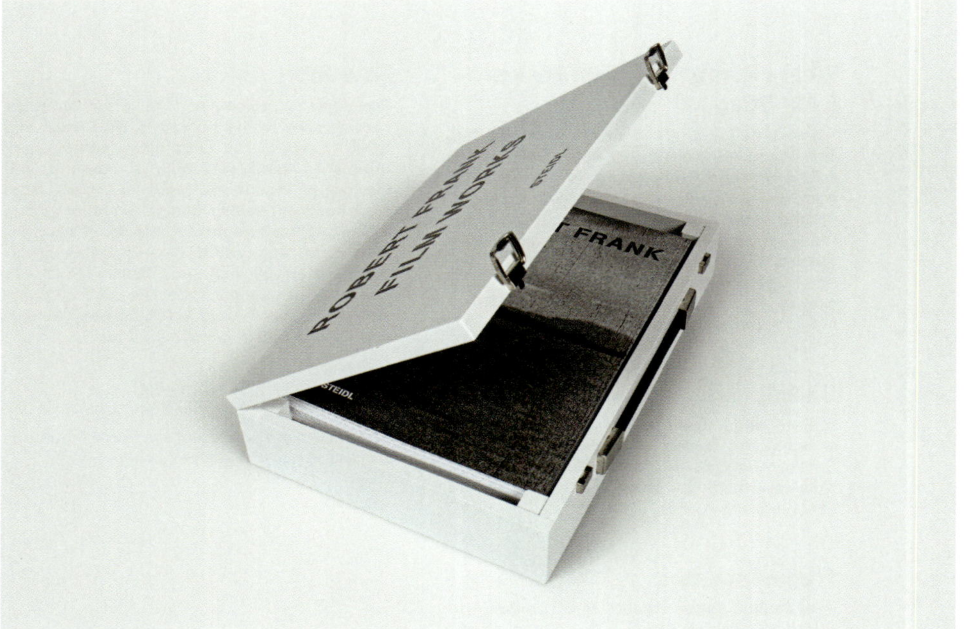

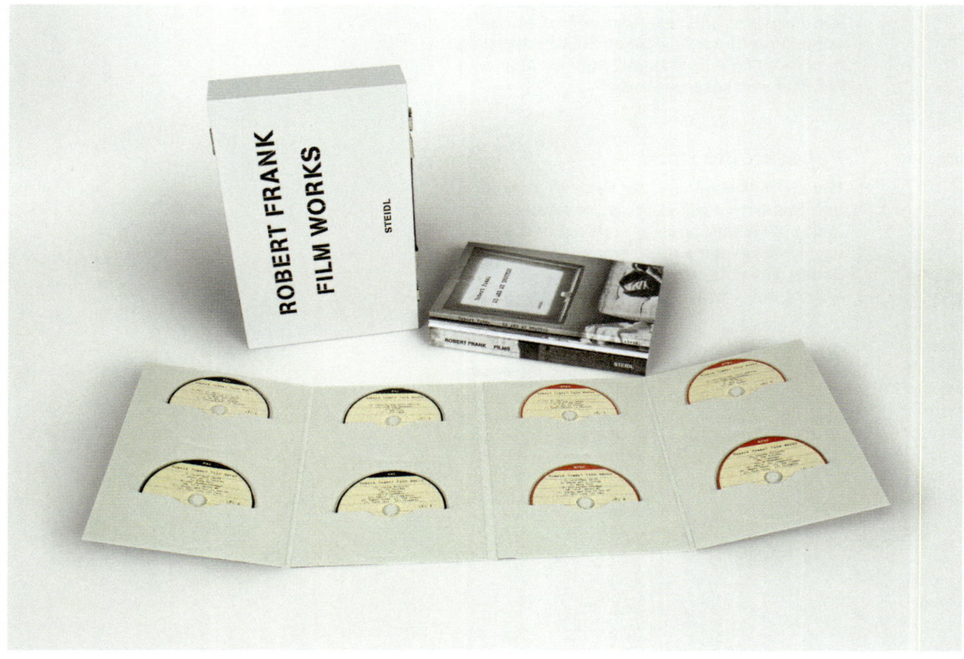

Film Works

Published by Steidl, 2016

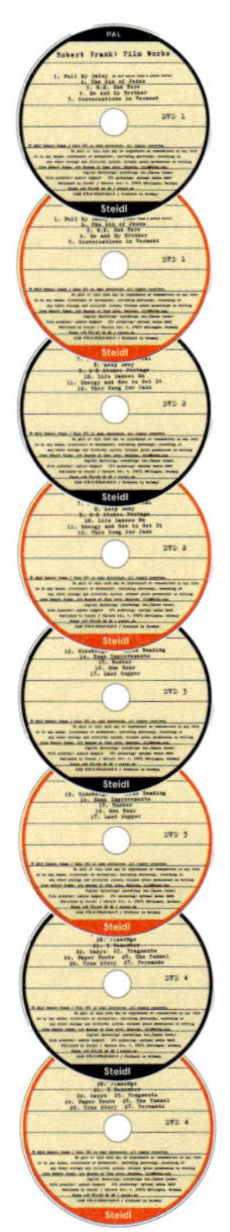

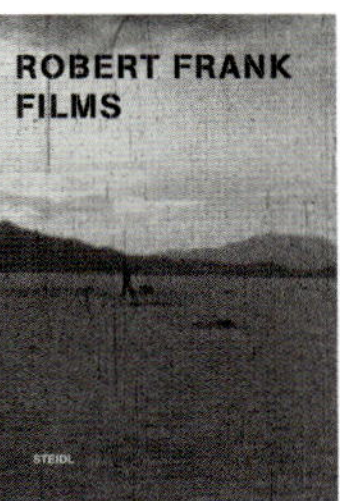
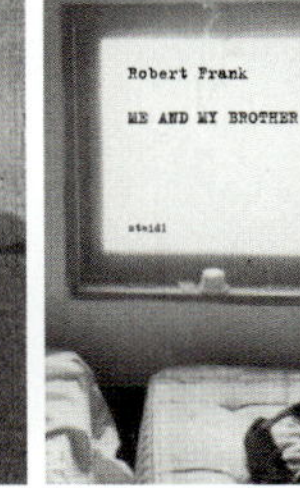
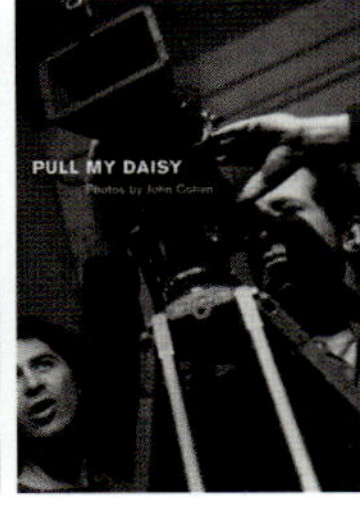
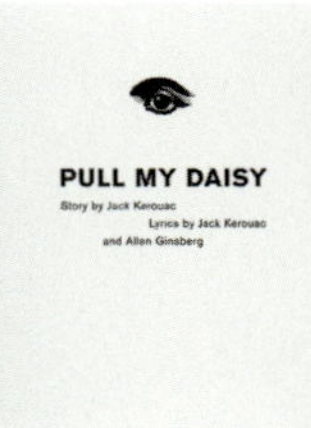
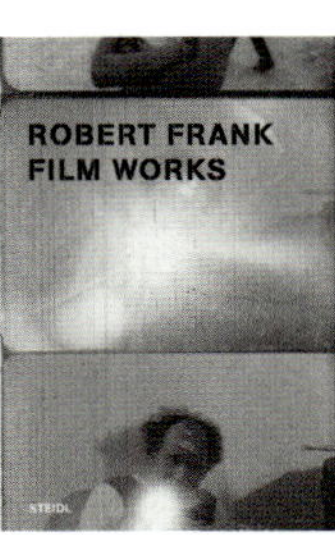

DVDs	Book: *Me and My Brother*	Book: *Pull My Daisy* (photos)	Book: *Pull My Daisy* (texts)	Book: *Film Works*

Films

Disc 1 / 210 mins
1 *Pull My Daisy* (1959), 28 mins
2 *The Sin of Jesus* (1961), 38 mins
3 *O.K. End Here* (1963), 33 mins
4 *Me and My Brother* (1968), 85 mins
5 *Conversations in Vermont* (1969), 26 mins

Disc 2 / 204 mins
6 *Life-Raft Earth* (1969), 33 mins
7 *About Me: A Musical* (1971), 30 mins
8 *Keep Busy* (1975), 45 mins
9 *S-8 Stones Footage From Exile on Main Street* (1971), 8 mins

10 *Life Dances On* (1980), 30 mins
11 *Energy and How to Get It* (1981), 31 mins
12 *This Song for Jack* (1983), 27 mins

Disc 3 / 191 mins
13 *Ginsberg and Corso Reading* (1984), 20 mins
14 *Home Improvements* (1985), 24 mins
15 *Hunter* (1989), 36 mins
16 *One Hour* (1990), 62 mins
17 *Last Supper* (1992), 49 mins

Disc 4 / 157 mins
18 *Moving Pictures* (1994), 17 mins
19 *The Present* (1996), 23 mins
20 *Flamingo* (1996), 10 mins [English and Swedish]
21 *What I Remember from My Visit (with Stieglitz)* (1998), 4 mins
22 *Sanyu* (2000), 27 mins
23 *Fragments* (2000), 10 mins
24 *Paper Route* (2002), 24 mins
25 *The Tunnel* (2005), 4 mins
26 *True Story* (2004/08), 26 mins
27 *Fernando* (2008), 12 mins

Books

Me and My Brother
Facsimile of the screenplay with notes and documentation of *Me and My Brother* (1968)
72 pages

Pull My Daisy
Photographs by John Cohen documenting the making of *Pull My Daisy* (1959)
56 pages
Tritone

Pull My Daisy
Screenplay of
Pull My Daisy (1959)
Introduction by Jerry Tallmer
Text by Jack Kerouac
32 pages

Frank Films
272 pages
Edited by Brigitta Burger-Utzer and Stefan Grissemann
Containing film stills, essays and summaries of each film, as well as comprehensive

bibliographic and technical data
Texts by Michael Barchet, Philip Brookman, Brigitta Burger-Utzer, Stefan Grissemann, Kent Jones, Thomas Mießgang, Pia Neumann, Bert Rebhandl, Amy Taubin

All books:
8.3 × 11.7 in / 21 × 29.7 cm
Tritone and four-color process
Softcovers

4 DVDs (both PAL and NTSC) with 4 books, housed in a hand-made plywood suitcase
13.8 × 9.2 × 2 in. / 35 × 23.4 × 5 cm

ISBN 978-3-95829-036-5

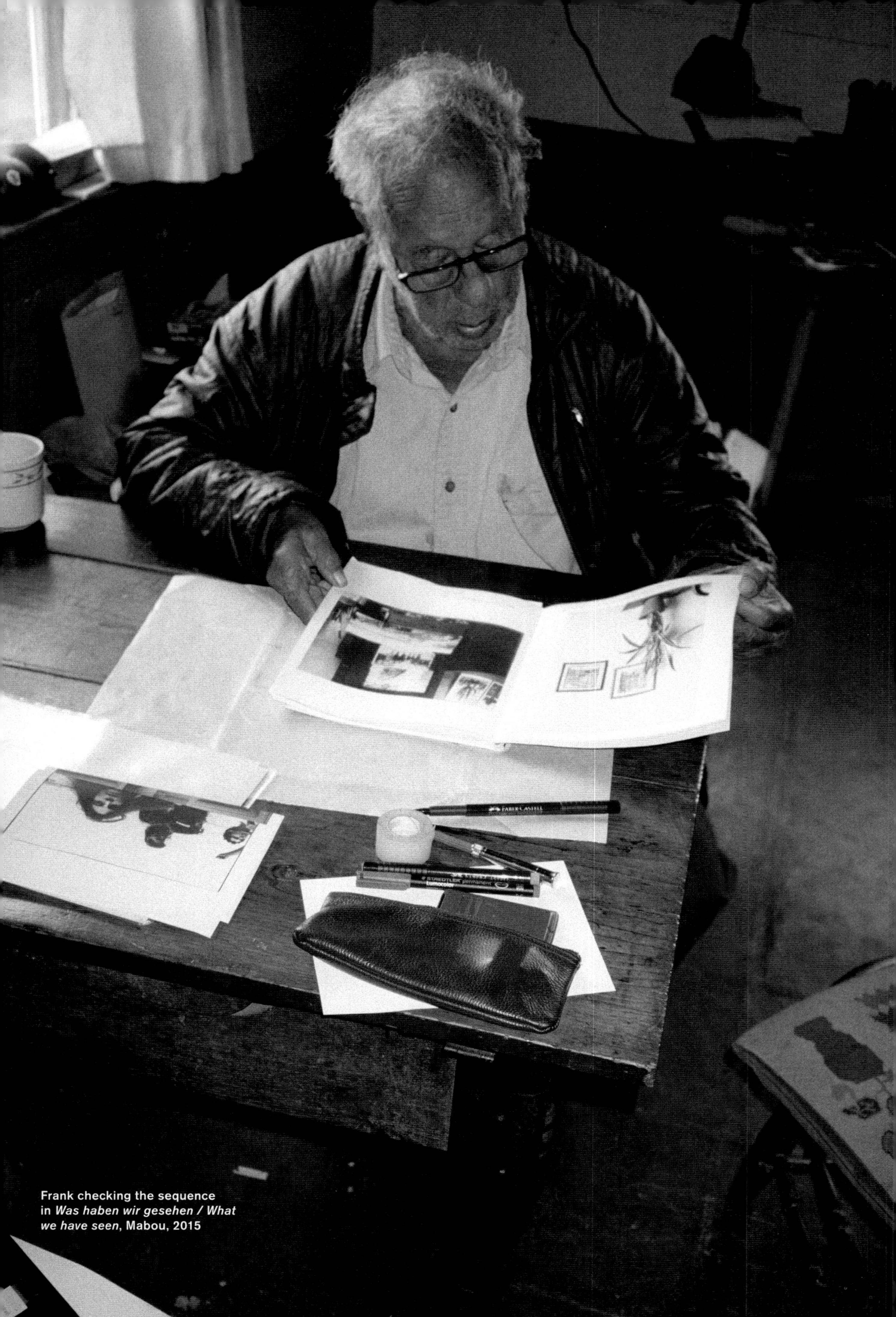

Frank checking the sequence
in *Was haben wir gesehen / What
we have seen*, Mabou, 2015

Robert Frank
Biography

1924
Born on 9 November in Zurich, Switzerland to Hermann and Rosa Frank. His father originated from a Jewish family from Frankfurt, Germany. Trained as an interior designer, Hermann Frank was the proprietor of a bicycle shop in Zurich, and a keen amateur photographer. Rosa Frank (née Zucker) was the daughter of a manufacturing family from Basel. Brother Manfred was born in 1922.

1940
Graduated from Lavater High School, Zurich. Studied French at Institute Jomini, Payerne.

1941
Apprenticeship with the photographer and graphic designer Hermann Segesser, Zurich (until March 1942). Frank's father and his sons had to apply for Swiss citizenship when the law on citizenship of the Reich proclaimed all German Jews stateless.

1942
Apprenticeship, then employment at the film- and photo-studio Michael Wolgensinger, Zurich.

1945
Swiss citizenship. Swiss military boot camp in Losone, Ticino.

1946
Worked for the graphic design studio Hermann Eidenbenz in Basel. First book *40 Fotos* with original prints.

1947
Left Europe for New York City.

Employed by Alexey Brodovitch at *Harper's Bazaar* as an assistant photographer.

1948
Travelled in Peru and Bolivia.

1949
Created two books, each with 39 original prints from Peru. Travelled to Europe for a year (France, Italy, Switzerland and Spain). Created a book with 74 original prints for Mary Lockspeiser.

1950
Return to New York City. Marriage to Mary Lockspeiser.

1951
Birth of son Pablo.

1952
Produced three copies of *Black White and Things* with 34 original prints each, designed by Werner Zryd.

1953
Photographed in Wales. Friendship with Walker Evans.

1954
Birth of daughter Andrea.

1955–56
Fellowship from the John Simon Guggenheim Memorial Foundation to pursue a photo project on the United States, resulting in *The Americans*.

1958
Robert Delpire published *Les Américains* in Paris.

1959
Grove Press, New York City, published *The Americans,* with a preface by Jack Kerouac. Co-directs first film *Pull My Daisy* with Alfred Leslie.

1961
First solo exhibition *Robert Frank, Photographer,* Art Institute of Chicago.

1963
American citizenship.

1969
Separation from Mary Lockspeiser.

1970
Together with artist June Leaf, bought land and a house in Mabou, Nova Scotia, Canada.

1971
Cover of the Rolling Stones' album *Exile on Main St.*

1972
The Lines of My Hand published by Yugensha in Tokyo, and Lustrum Press in New York.

1974
In December his daughter Andrea died in a plane crash in Guatemala.

1975
Marriage to June Leaf.

1977
Film *Life Dances On* (completed in 1980).

1980
Retrospective *The New American Filmmakers Series: Robert Frank,* Whitney Museum of American Art, New York.

1986
Exhibition *Robert Frank: New York to Nova Scotia,* Museum of Fine Arts, Houston.

1987
Peer Award for Distinguished Career in Photography, Friends of Photography, San Francisco.

1988
Exhibition *The Lines of My Hand,* Museum für Gestaltung, Zurich.

1990
The National Gallery of Art, Washington, D.C., founded the Robert Frank Collection.

1991
Photographs in Beirut, Lebanon.

1993
Trips to Egypt and Russia.

1994
Black White and Things published by Scalo. Retrospective *Moving Out,* National Gallery of Art, Washington, D.C. Son Pablo died in November in Allentown, PA.

1995
Establishment of the Andrea Frank Foundation.

1996
International Photography Award from the Erna and Victor Hasselblad Foundation, Gothenburg.

1997
Trips to Taiwan and Copenhagen. Met Rita Wong with whom he later co-founded the Sanyu Scholarship Fund at Yale University.

1999
Honorary doctorate from the University of Gothenburg.

2000
Cornell Capa Award, International Center of Photography, New York City.

2002
Exhibition *What Am I Looking At,* Art Institute of Chicago.

2003
Exhibition *Robert Frank: London/Wales,* Corcoran Gallery of Art, Washington, D.C.

2004
Exhibition *Robert Frank — Storylines,* Tate Modern, London.

2007
Exhibition *Robert Frank: Films and Videos,* Centre George Pompidou, Paris.

2008
New editions of *The Americans* published by Steidl in English, German, Italian, Spanish and Mandarin, celebrating the 50th anniversary of the publication. Start of restoration and digitalization of all films and videos with Laura Israel.

2009
Exhibition *Looking In: Robert Frank's* The Americans, National Gallery of Art, Washington, D.C.

2010
Tal Uf Tal Ab, the first of the visual diaries, published by Steidl between 2010 and 2017.

2014
Inaugural exhibition *Robert Frank: Books and Films, 1947–2014,* Anna Leonowens Gallery, NSCAD University, Halifax.

2015
Honorary doctorate from NSCAD University, Halifax.

Don't Blink, documentary film on Robert Frank by Laura Israel.

2016
World tour of the pop-up exhibition *Books and Films, 1947–2016* begins.

2017
Exhibition *Robert Frank: Photos Books Films,* Art Institute of Chicago.

2019
Last book *Good Days Quiet* published by Steidl.

Died on 9 September at the age of 94, in Inverness, Cape Breton Island, Nova Scotia.

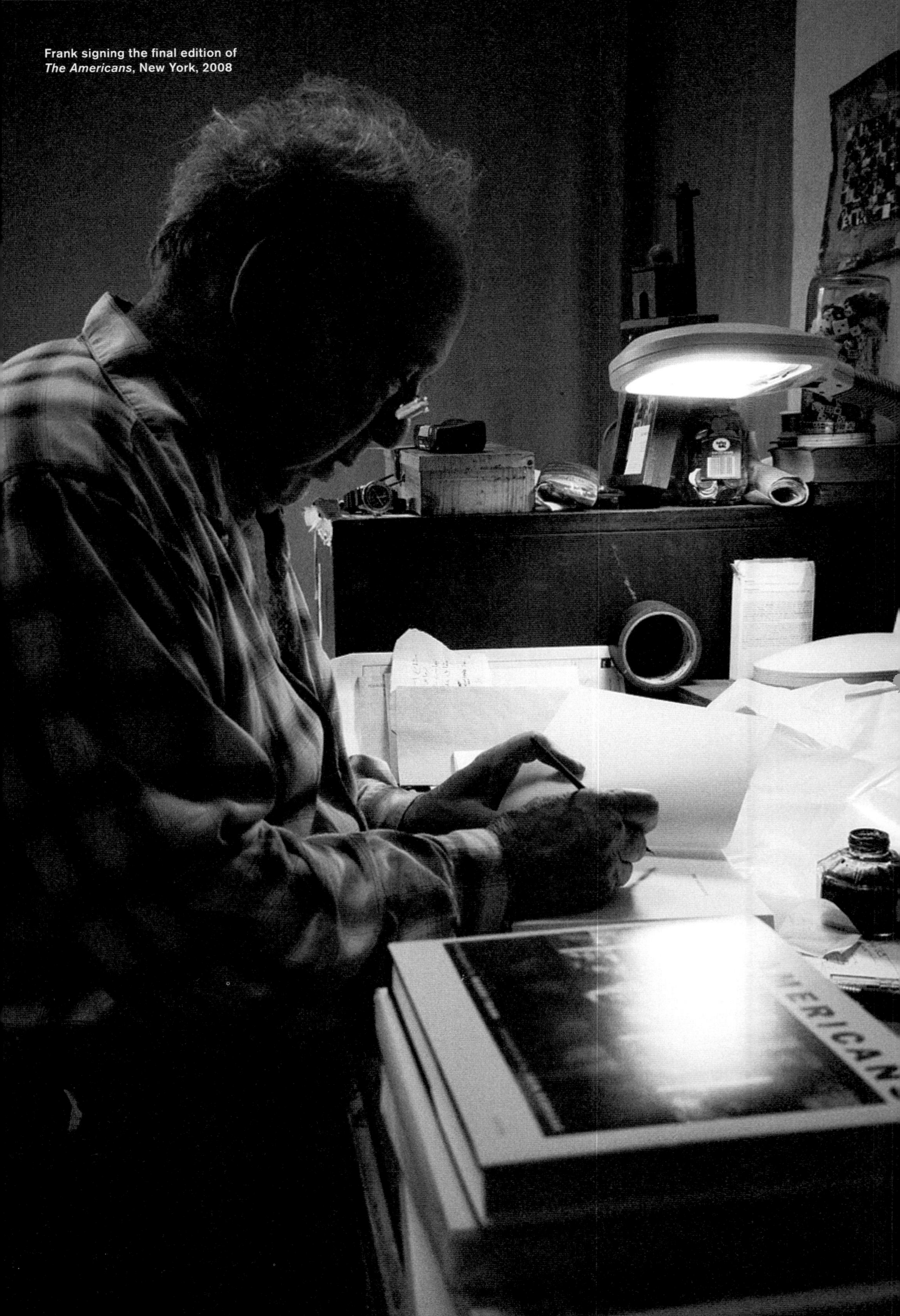

Frank signing the final edition of
The Americans, New York, 2008

Robert Frank
Bibliography

1946
First book *40 Fotos* with original prints
(Steidl, 2009)

1949
Two books, each with 39 original prints
from Peru (Steidl, 2008)
Book with 74 original prints for artist
Mary Lockspeiser

1952
Three copies of *Black White and Things*
with 34 original prints each, designed by
Werner Zryd (Scalo, 1994; Steidl, 2009)

1958
Les Américains, Robert Delpire

1959
The Americans with a preface by Jack
Kerouac, Grove Press (definitive edition:
Steidl, 2008)
New York is, The New York Times

1961
Pull My Daisy, illustrated film script with
49 film stills and 8 set photographs by
John Cohen (Steidl, 2008)

1963
Zero Mostel Reads a Book commissioned by *The New York Times* (Steidl, 2008)

1968
Me and My Brother combining the film
script with film stills and set photographs (Steidl, 2007)

1972
The Lines of My Hand, Yugensha,
Lustrum Press, 1972 (Scalo, 1989; Steidl, 2017)

1976
*Robert Frank: The Aperture History of
Photography Series* with a preface by
Rudy Wurlitzer, Aperture and Robert
Delpire

1986
New York to Nova Scotia, The Museum
of Fine Arts, Houston (Steidl, 2005)

1992
One Hour, Hanuman Books
(Steidl, 2007)

2001
HOLD STILL—keep going, Museum
Folkwang (Steidl, 2016)

2003
London/Wales, Scalo (Steidl, 2007)
Frank Films, Scalo (Steidl, 2009)

2004
Storylines, Steidl

2006
Come Again, Steidl

2007
One Hour, Steidl

2008
Pull My Daisy, Steidl
Paris, Steidl

2009
Seven Stories, Steidl
*Looking In: Robert Frank's The
Americans*, Steidl
Henry Frank, Father Photographer, Steidl

2010
Tal Uf Tal Ab, Steidl

2011
Pangnirtung, Steidl

2012
You Would, Steidl
Valencia 1952, Steidl

2013
Park/Sleep, Steidl
Household Inventory Record, Steidl

2014
In America, Steidl
Partida, Steidl

2016
*Was haben wir gesehen / What we
have seen*, Steidl
*Robert Frank: Books and Films,
1947–2016*, Steidl and the *Süddeutsche
Zeitung*
Film Works, Steidl

2017
Leon of Juda, Steidl
The Lines of my Hand, Steidl

2019
Good Days Quiet, Steidl

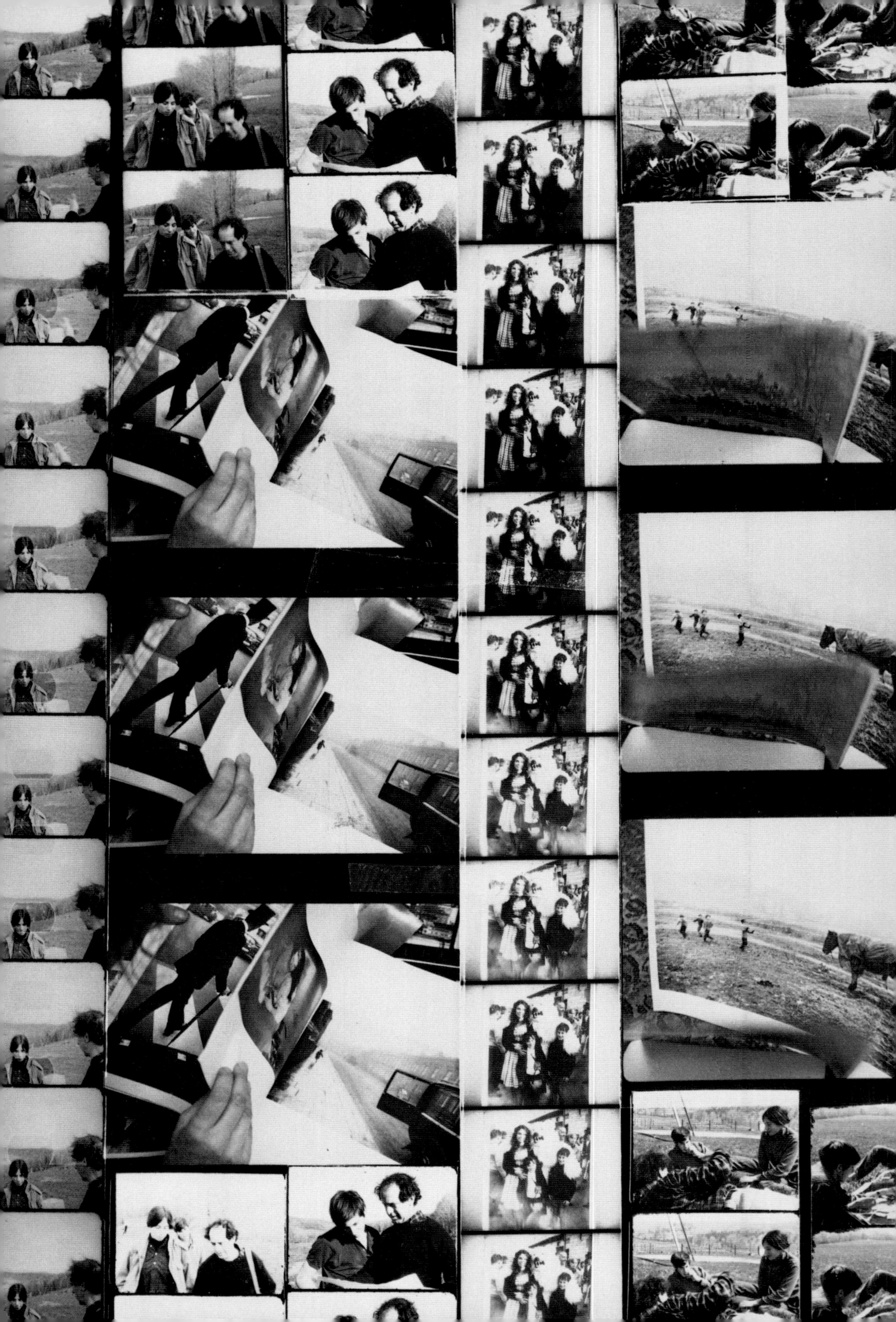

Robert Frank
Filmography

Photo-collage by Robert Frank

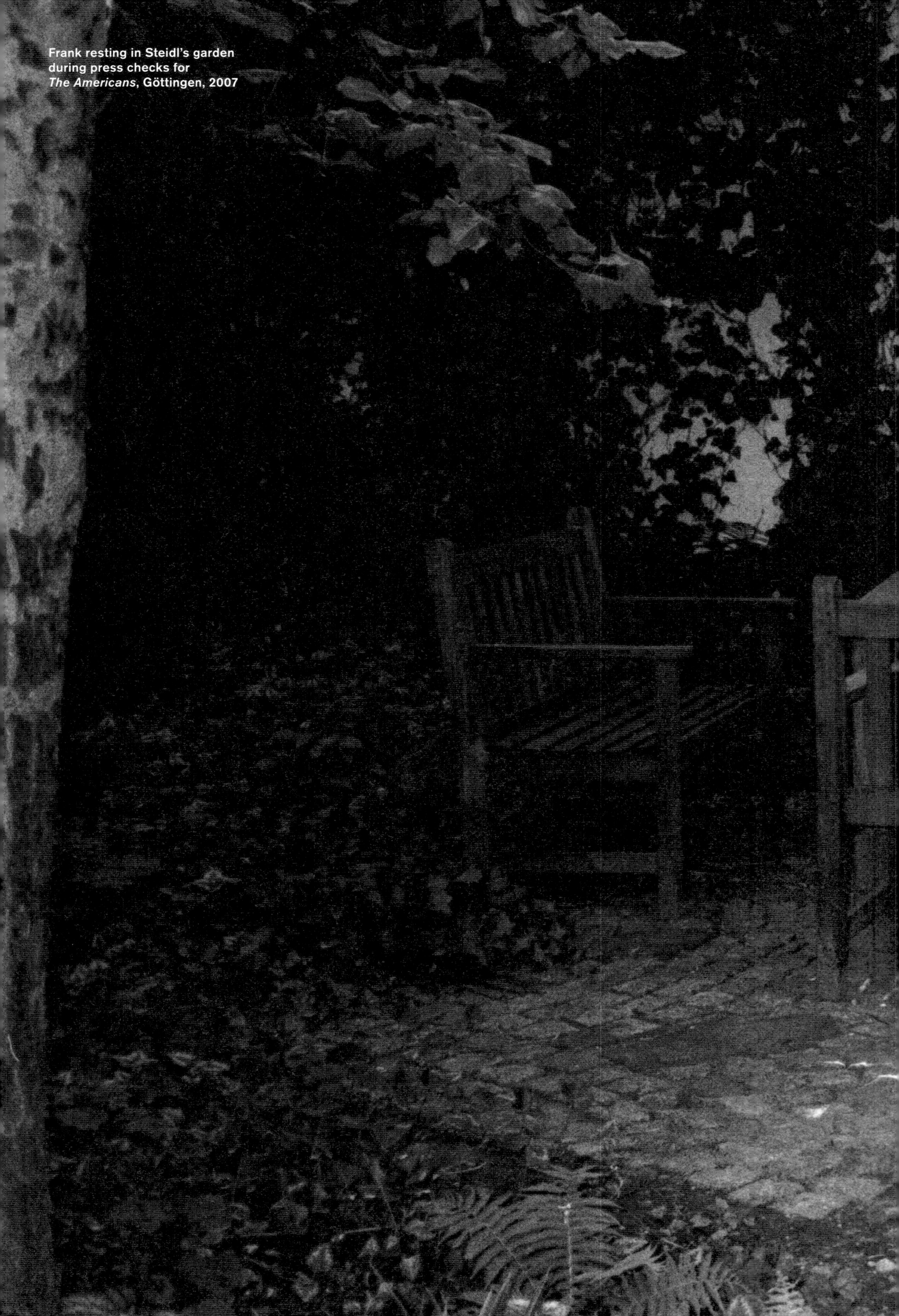

Frank resting in Steidl's garden
during press checks for
The Americans, Göttingen, 2007

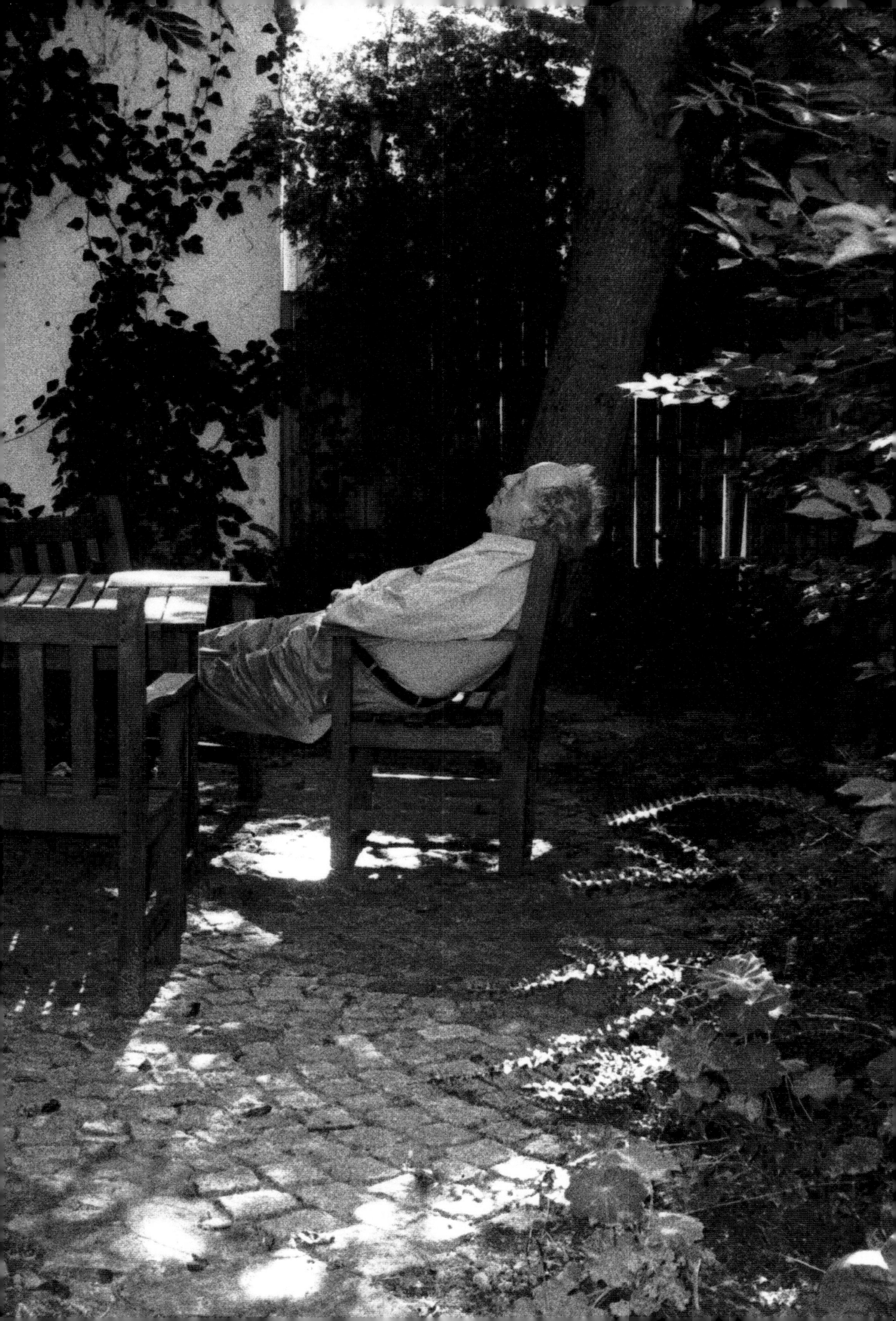